T0178232

Lecture Notes
in Business Information Processing

427

Series Editors

Wil van der Aalst ⓘ
RWTH Aachen University, Aachen, Germany
John Mylopoulos ⓘ
University of Trento, Trento, Italy
Michael Rosemann ⓘ
Queensland University of Technology, Brisbane, QLD, Australia
Michael J. Shaw
University of Illinois, Urbana-Champaign, IL, USA
Clemens Szyperski
Microsoft Research, Redmond, WA, USA

More information about this series at http://www.springer.com/series/7911

Artem Polyvyanyy · Moe Thandar Wynn ·
Amy Van Looy · Manfred Reichert (Eds.)

Business Process Management Forum

BPM Forum 2021
Rome, Italy, September 06–10, 2021
Proceedings

Springer

Editors
Artem Polyvyanyy ⓘ
The University of Melbourne
Carlton, VIC, Australia

Amy Van Looy ⓘ
EB24
Ghent University
Ghent, Belgium

Moe Thandar Wynn ⓘ
NICTA Queensland Res Lab
Queensland University of Technology
Brisbane, QLD, Australia

Manfred Reichert ⓘ
University of Ulm
Ulm, Germany

ISSN 1865-1348   ISSN 1865-1356 (electronic)
Lecture Notes in Business Information Processing
ISBN 978-3-030-85439-3   ISBN 978-3-030-85440-9 (eBook)
https://doi.org/10.1007/978-3-030-85440-9

This Springer imprint is published by the registered company Springer Nature Switzerland AG
The registered company address is: Gewerbestrasse 11, 6330 Cham, Switzerland

Preface

This volume covers all papers presented at the BPM Forum of the 19th International Conference on Business Process Management (BPM 2021) held during September 6–10, 2021, in Rome, Italy. Similar to previous years, the BPM Forum offers innovative research papers characterized by their high potential to stimulate interesting discussion and scientific debate, although without yet reaching the same rigor as those papers accepted for the main conference. In this sense, the BPM Forum papers characterize themselves by novel ideas about emergent BPM topics.

While last year's edition was fully online due to the worldwide COVID-19 pandemic, BPM 2021 was organized in a mixed setting, allowing for physical and online presence. In this pandemic context, the conference received a total of 123 submissions. All papers were first screened based on their fit to the conference call (in terms of topic and template use). During the review procedure, three to four Program Committee members evaluated each paper. One Senior Program Committee member was responsible for moderating the discussion and summarizing a meta-review, assuring a thorough quality check. Finally, the Program Committee accepted 23 papers for the main conference and 16 papers for the BPM Forum (the latter compiled in this volume).

In the wake of the COVID-19 pandemic, we are grateful for a warm welcome at the Sapienza Università di Roma, Italy. We thank the members of the Program Committees and Senior Program Committees of the three conference tracks (Foundations, Engineering, and Management). We also acknowledge our sponsors for their support in making this conference happen: Signavio, Celonis, DCR Solutions, P4I – Partner-s4Innovation, Springer, Sapienza Università di Roma, and the organizing agency Consulta Umbria. Finally, we also appreciate the use of EasyChair for streamlining an intensive reviewing period.

Finally, special thanks goes to Massimo Mecella (general chair of BPM 2021) and his Organizing Committee, including Simone Agostinelli, Dario Benvenuti, Eleonora Bernasconi, Francesca de Luzi, Lauren Stacey Ferro, Francesco Leotta, Andrea Marrella, Francesco Sapio, and Silvestro Veneruso. We applaud their team efforts for realizing our gatherings under safe conditions.

September 2021

Artem Polyvyanyy
Moe Thandar Wynn
Amy Van Looy
Manfred Reichert

Organization

The 19th International Conference on Business Process Management (BPM 2021) was organized by the research group on Data Management, Service-Oriented Computing, and Process Management of the Dipartimento di Ingegneria informatica automatica e gestionale Antonio Ruberti, Sapienza Università di Roma, Italy. The conference was conducted in a hybrid mode due to the ongoing travel restrictions in many countries imposed by the global COVID-19 pandemic. Therefore, the participants could choose to attend the event in Rome or connect and participate in the talks and discussions virtually via the Internet.

Steering Committee

Mathias Weske (Chair)	University of Potsdam, Germany
Boualem Benatallah	University of New South Wales, Australia
Jörg Desel	FernUniversität in Hagen, Germany
Marlon Dumas	Tartu Ülikool, Estonia
Jan Mendling	Humboldt University Berlin, Germany
Manfred Reichert	Ulm University, Germany
Hajo A. Reijers	Utrecht University, The Netherlands
Stefanie Rinderle-Ma	Technical University of Munich, Germany
Michael Rosemann	Queensland University of Technology, Australia
Shazia Sadiq	The University of Queensland, Australia
Wil van der Aalst	RWTH, Aachen University, Germany
Barbara Weber	University of St. Gallen, Switzerland

Executive Committee

General Chair

Massimo Mecella	Sapienza Università di Roma, Italy

Main Conference PC Chairs

Artem Polyvyanyy (Track Chair, Track I)	The University of Melbourne, Australia
Moe Thandar Wynn (Track Chair, Track II)	Queensland University of Technology, Australia
Amy Van Looy (Track Chair, Track III)	Ghent University, Belgium
Manfred Reichert (Consolidation Chair)	Ulm University, Germany

Workshop Chairs

Andrea Marrella   Sapienza Università di Roma, Italy
Barbara Weber   University of St. Gallen, Switzerland

Demonstrations and Resources Chairs

Francesco Leotta   Sapienza Università di Roma, Italy
Arik Senderovich   University of Toronto, Canada
Marcos Sepúlveda   Pontificia Universidad Católica de Chile, Chile

Tutorial and Panel Chairs

Claudio Di Ciccio   Sapienza Università di Roma, Italy
Avigdor Gal   Technion – Israel Institute of Technology, Israel
Shazia Sadiq   The University of Queensland, Australia

Publicity Chairs

Adriano Augusto   University of Melbourne, Australia
Chiara Di Francescomarino   Fondazione Bruno Kessler, Italy
Flavia Santoro   University of the State of Rio de Janeiro, Brazil

Doctoral Consortium Chairs

Estefania Serral Asensio   KU Leuven, Belgium
Remco Dijkman   Eindhoven University of Technology, The Netherlands
Fabrizio Maria Maggi   University of Bolzano, Italy

Industry Forum Chairs

Massimiliano de Leoni   University of Padua, Italy
Minseok Song   Pohang University of Science and Technology,
                                  South Korea
Maximilian Röglinger   University of Bayreuth, Germany

RPA Forum Chairs

José González Enríquez   University of Seville, Spain
Peter Fettke   German Research Center for Artificial Intelligence
                                  (DFKI) and Saarland University, Germany
Inge van de Weerd   Utrecht University, The Netherlands

Blockchain Forum Chairs

Søren Debois   IT University of Copenhagen, Denmark
Pierluigi Plebani   Politecnico di Milano, Italy
Ingo Weber   TU Berlin, Germany

Organizing Committee Chair

Massimo Mecella   Sapienza Università di Roma, Italy

Organizing Committee Members

Simone Agostinelli	Sapienza Università di Roma, Italy
Dario Benvenuti	Sapienza Università di Roma, Italy
Eleonora Bernasconi	Sapienza Università di Roma, Italy
Francesca de Luzi	Sapienza Università di Roma, Italy
Lauren Stacey Ferro	Sapienza Università di Roma, Italy
Francesco Sapio	Sapienza Università di Roma, Italy
Silvestro Veneruso	Sapienza Università di Roma, Italy

Organizing Agency

Consulta Umbria, Italy

Track I: Foundation

Senior Program Committee

Jörg Desel	FernUniversität in Hagen, Germany
Claudio Di Ciccio	Sapienza Università di Roma, Italy
Chiara Di Francescomarino	Fondazione Bruno Kessler, Italy
Dirk Fahland	Eindhoven University of Technology, The Netherlands
Luciano García Bañuelos	Tecnológico de Monterrey, Mexico
Thomas Hildebrandt	IT University of Copenhagen, Denmark
Fabrizio Maria Maggi	Free University of Bozen-Bolzano, Italy
Marco Montali	Free University of Bozen-Bolzano, Italy
Oscar Pastor Lopez	Universidad Politécnica de Valencia, Spain
Arthur ter Hofstede	Queensland University of Technology, Australia
Wil van der Aalst	RWTH, Aachen University, Germany
Jan Martijn van der Werf	Utrecht University, The Netherlands
Hagen Voelzer	IBM Research – Europe, Germany
Matthias Weidlich	Humboldt-Universität zu Berlin, Germany
Mathias Weske	University of Potsdam, Germany

Program Committee

Lars Ackermann	University of Bayreuth, Germany
Adriano Augusto	University of Melbourne, Australia
Ahmed Awad	Tartu Ülikool, Estonia
Diego Calvanese	Free University of Bozen-Bolzano, Italy
Johannes De Smedt	KU Leuven, Belgium
Søren Debois	IT University of Copenhagen, Denmark
Rik Eshuis	Eindhoven University of Technology, The Netherlands
Peter Fettke	DFKI and Saarland University, Germany
Hans-Georg Fill	University of Fribourg, Switzerland
Maria Teresa Gómez López	Universidad de Sevilla, Spain
Guido Governatori	Data61, Australia
Gianluigi Greco	Università della Calabria, Italy

Richard Hull	New York University, USA
Akhil Kumar	Penn State University, USA
Sander J. J. Leemans	Queensland University of Technology, Australia
Irina Lomazova	HSE University, Russia
Xixi Lu	Utrecht University, The Netherlands
Felix Mannhardt	Eindhoven University of Technology, The Netherlands
Andrea Marrella	Sapienza Università di Roma, Italy
Werner Nutt	Free University of Bozen-Bolzano, Italy
Chun Ouyang	Queensland University of Technology, Australia
Daniel Ritter	SAP, Germany
Andrey Rivkin	Free University of Bozen-Bolzano, Italy
Arik Senderovich	University of Toronto, Canada
Tijs Slaats	University of Copenhagen, Denmark
Farbod Taymouri	University of Melbourne, Australia
Ernest Teniente	Universitat Politècnica de Catalunya, Spain
Sebastiaan J. van Zelst	RWTH Aachen University, Germany
Eric Verbeek	Eindhoven University of Technology, The Netherlands
Karsten Wolf	University of Rostock, Germany
Francesca Zerbato	University of St. Gallen, Switzerland

Track II: Engineering

Senior Program Committee

Boualem Benatallah	University of New South Wales, Australia
Andrea Burattin	Technical University of Denmark, Denmark
Josep Carmona	Universitat Politècnica de Catalunya, Spain
Remco Dijkman	Eindhoven University of Technology, The Netherlands
Jochen De Weerdt	KU Leuven, Belgium
Marlon Dumas	Tartu Ülikool, Estonia
Avigdor Gal	Technion – Israel Institute of Technology, Israel
Chiara Ghidini	Fondazione Bruno Kessler, Italy
Jorge Munoz-Gama	Pontificia Universidad Católica de Chile, Chile
Luise Pufahl	Hasso-Plattner-Institut, Germany
Hajo A. Reijers	Utrecht University, The Netherlands
Stefanie Rinderle-Ma	Technical University of Munich, Germany
Shazia Sadiq	The University of Queensland, Australia
Pnina Soffer	University of Haifa, Israel
Boudewijn Van Dongen	Eindhoven University of Technology, The Netherlands
Barbara Weber	University of St. Gallen, Switzerland
Ingo Weber	Technische Universität Berlin, Germany

Program Committee

Marco Aiello	University of Stuttgart, Germany
Robert Andrews	Queensland University of Technology, Australia
Abel Armas-Cervantes	University of Melbourne, Australia

Cristina Cabanillas	Universidad de Sevilla, Spain
Fabio Casati	University of Trento, Italy
Massimiliano de Leoni	Università degli Studi di Padua, Italy
Joerg Evermann	Memorial University of Newfoundland, Canada
Walid Gaaloul	Télécom SudParis, France
Daniela Grigori	LAMSADE – Université Paris-Dauphine, France
Georg Grossmann	University of South Australia, Australia
Gert Janssenswilen	UHasselt – Universiteit van vandaag, Belgium
Mieke Jans	UHasselt – Universiteit van vandaag, Belgium
Anna Kalenkova	University of Melbourne, Australia
Dimka Karastoyanova	University of Groningen, The Netherlands
Agnes Koschmider	Christian-Albrechts-Universität zu Kiel, Germany
Henrik Leopold	Kühne Logistics University, Germany
Elisa Marengo	Free University of Bozen-Bolzano, Italy
Rabeb Mizouni	Khalifa University, United Arab Emirates
Helen Paik	University of New South Wales, Australia
Cesare Pautasso	University of Lugano, Switzerland
Pierluigi Plebani	Politecnico di Milano, Italy
Pascal Poizat	Université Paris Nanterre, France
Barbara Re	Università di Camerino, Italy
Manuel Resinas	Universidad de Sevilla, Spain
Renuka Sindhgatta	Queensland University of Technology, Australia
Marcos Sepúlveda	Pontificia Universidad Católica de Chile, Chile
Natalia Sidorova	Eindhoven University of Technology, The Netherlands
Minseok Song	POSTECH, South Korea
Seppe Vanden Broucke	KU Leuven, Belgium
Stefan Schönig	Universität Regensburg, Germany
Nick van Beest	Data61, Australia
Han van der Aa	Universität Mannheim, Germany
Nicola Zannone	Eindhoven University of Technology, The Netherlands

Track III: Management

Senior Program Committee

Wasana Bandara	Queensland University of Technology, Australia
Jörg Becker	University of Muenster (ERCIS), Germany
Daniel Beverungen	Paderborn University, Germany
Adela Del Río Ortega	Universidad de Sevilla, Spain
Paul Grefen	Eindhoven University of Technology, The Netherlands
Mojca Indihar Štemberger	University of Ljubljana, Slovenia
Marta Indulska	The University of Queensland, Australia
Peter Loos	Saarland University, Germany
Jan Mendling	Humboldt University Berlin, Germany
Juergen Moormann	Frankfurt School of Finance & Management, Germany
Maximilian Roeglinger	FIM Research Center, Germany

Michael Rosemann	Queensland University of Technology, Australia
Flavia Santoro	University of the State of Rio de Janeiro (UERJ), Brazil
Peter Trkman	University of Ljubljana, Slovenia
Jan vom Brocke	University of Liechtenstein, Liechtenstein

Program Committee

Tahir Ahmad	Ghent University, Belgium
Alessio Maria Braccini	Università degli Studi della Tuscia, Italy
Ann-Kristin Cordes	University of Münster, Germany
Dries Couckuyt	Ghent University, Belgium
Patrick Delfmann	University of Koblenz-Landau, Germany
Michael Fellmann	University of Rostock, Germany
Renata Gabryelczyk	University of Warsaw, Poland
Andreas Gadatsch	Hochschule Bonn-Rhein-Sieg, Germany
Thomas Grisold	University of Liechtenstein, Liechtenstein
Tomislav Hernaus	University of Zagreb, Croatia
Christian Janiesch	TU Dresden, Germany
Ralf Knackstedt	University of Hildesheim, Germany
Andrea Kő	Corvinus University of Budapest, Hungary
John Krogstie	Norwegian University of Science and Technology, Norway
Michael Leyer	University of Rostock, Germany
Alexander Mädche	Karlsruhe Institute of Technology, Germany
Paul Mathiesen	Queensland University of Technology, Australia
Martin Matzner	Friedrich-Alexander-Universität Erlangen-Nürnberg, Germany
Sven Overhage	University of Bamberg, Germany
Ralf Plattfaut	Fachhochschule Südwestfalen, Germany
Geert Poels	Ghent University, Belgium
Jens Poeppelbuss	Ruhr-Universität Bochum, Germany
Dennis Riehle	University of Muenster, Germany
Stefan Sackmann	University of Halle-Wittenberg, Germany
Alexander Schiller	University of Regensburg, Germany
Werner Schmidt	Technische Hochschule Ingolstadt Business School, Germany
Oktay Turetken	Eindhoven University of Technology, The Netherlands
Irene Vanderfeesten	Open University of the Netherlands, The Netherlands
Axel Winkelmann	University of Wuerzburg, Germany

Additional Reviewers

Ebaa Alnazer
Nour Assy
Vladimir Bashkin
Sebastian Bräuer
Adam Burke
Silvano Colombo Tosatto
Carl Corea
Sebastian Dunzer
Jasper Feine
Laura Genga
Ilche Georgievski
Ulrich Gnewuch
Marie Godefroid
Torsten Gollhardt
Lukas-Valentin Herm
Ambrose Hill
Felix Holz
Felix Härer
Georgi Kerpedzhiev
Krzysztof Kluza
Julian Koch

Ingo Kregel
Yulia Litvinova
Niels Martin
Alexey A. Mitsyuk
Sabine Nagel
Maximilian Raab
Henning Dirk Richter
Tim Rietz
Johannes Schneider
Thorsten Schoormann
Anja Seiffer
Brian Setz
Tobias Seyffarth
Syed Wajid Ali Shah
John Shepherd
Johannes Tenschert
Frank Vanhoenshoven
Julian Weidinger
Sven Weinzierl
Bastian Wurm
Sandra Zilker

Contents

Business Process Modeling

Interactive and Minimal Repair of Declarative Process Models 3
  Carl Corea, Sabine Nagel, Jan Mendling, and Patrick Delfmann

Augmenting Modelers with Semantic Autocompletion of Processes 20
  Maayan Goldstein and Cecilia González-Álvarez

DMN 1.0 Verification Capabilities: An Analysis of Current Tool Support . . . 37
  Carl-Christian Grohé, Carl Corea, and Patrick Delfmann

Consistency Checking of Goal Models and Case Management Schemas 54
  Rik Eshuis and Aditya Ghose

Process Analytics

Detection of Statistically Significant Differences Between Process Variants
Through Declarative Rules 73
  Alessio Cecconi, Adriano Augusto, and Claudio Di Ciccio

Silhouetting the Cost-Time Front: Multi-objective Resource Optimization
in Business Processes 92
  Orlenys López-Pintado, Marlon Dumas, Maksym Yerokhin,
  and Fabrizio Maria Maggi

Are We Doing Things Right? An Approach to Measure Process
Inefficiencies in the Control Flow 109
  Fareed Zandkarimi, Jonas Rennemeier, and Jana-Rebecca Rehse

Evaluating Compliance State Visualizations for Multiple Process Models
and Instances 126
  Manuel Gall and Stefanie Rinderle-Ma

Process Mining

Initial Insights into Exploratory Process Mining Practices 145
  Francesca Zerbato, Pnina Soffer, and Barbara Weber

Discovering Business Process Architectures from Event Logs 162
  Dorina Bano, Adriatik Nikaj, and Mathias Weske

Privacy-Preserving Continuous Event Data Publishing   178
    Majid Rafiei and Wil M. P. van der Aalst

Expectations vs. Experiences – Process Mining in Small and Medium Sized
Manufacturing Companies   195
    Florian Stertz, Juergen Mangler, Beate Scheibel,
    and Stefanie Rinderle-Ma

Classifying and Detecting Task Executions and Routines in Processes
Using Event Graphs   212
    Eva L. Klijn, Felix Mannhardt, and Dirk Fahland

Looking Beyond Activity Labels: Mining Context-Aware Resource Profiles
Using Activity Instance Archetypes   230
    Gerhardus van Hulzen, Niels Martin, and Benoît Depaire

Decision Support for Knowledge Intensive Processes Using RL
Based Recommendations   246
    Asjad Khan, Aditya Ghose, and Hoa Dam

Generating High Quality Samples of Process Cases in Internal Audit   263
    Yaguang Sun, Lyth Al-Khazrage, and Ömer Özümerzifon

Author Index   281

Business Process Modeling

Interactive and Minimal Repair of Declarative Process Models

Carl Corea[1]([✉]), Sabine Nagel[1], Jan Mendling[2], and Patrick Delfmann[1]

[1] University of Koblenz-Landau, Koblenz, Germany
{ccorea,snagel,delfmann}@uni-koblenz.de
[2] WU Vienna, Vienna, Austria
jan.mendling@wu.ac.at

Abstract. We present an approach for resolving inconsistencies in declarative process models while guaranteeing a minimal information loss (w.r.t. the number of deleted elements). To this aim, we show how smallest correction sets, i.e., the smallest sets of constraints that need to be deleted in order to resolve inconsistencies, can be computed via an application of Reiter's hitting set theorem. In this context, as deleting certain constraints might be highly sensitive or not plausible in a real-life sense, we extend our approach with functionalities for enabling a close human-in-the-loop interaction, such as prioritizing constraints, as well as metrics that offer modelers insights into the impact of deleting constraints. Furthermore, we implement our approach and show that our inconsistency resolution approach outperforms existing approaches in terms of runtime and information loss in experiments with real-life data sets.

Keywords: Declarative process models · Inconsistency resolution · Minimal correction sets · Hitting sets

1 Introduction

While declarative process models allow to specify flexible processes, the logic-based nature of declarative constraints leaves models prone to logical inconsistencies [3,5,12]. As a simple example, consider the declarative process model D_1 (we will formalize syntax and semantics later), defined via

$$D_1 = \{\text{INIT}(a), \text{RESPONSE}(a,b), \text{RESPONSE}(b,c), \text{NOTRESPONSE}(a,c)\},$$

with the intuitive meaning that 1) a process must start with a task a, 2) a task a must be eventually followed by a task b, which must 3) eventually be followed by a task c, and 4) a task a must never be followed by a task c. D_1 is inconsistent, as it demands contradictory reactions to the occurrence of task a. Therefore, the

---

Part of the research project "Handling Inconsistencies in Business Process Modeling", funded by the German Research Association (reference number: DE1983/9-1).

© Springer Nature Switzerland AG 2021
A. Polyvyanyy et al. (Eds.): BPM Forum 2021, LNBIP 427, pp. 3–19, 2021.
https://doi.org/10.1007/978-3-030-85440-9_1

shown model is unsatisfiable and the inconsistency must be resolved in order to use the model for its intended purpose of governing compliant company behavior. Mind that contradictions in models of real-life complexity are difficult to spot, since they often arise from combinations of several constraints. Here, modelers need to be supported at design-time in order to resolve such inconsistencies.

In response, recent works [3,4] have presented methods for inconsistency repair. While this is a clear benefit for companies, a current limitation is that those approaches cannot guarantee a minimal information loss, i.e., that only the smallest possible set of constraints is actually deleted. For example, as the approach in [4] is only an approximation algorithm, it can easily occur that twice as many constraints are deleted compared to the optimum. Here, new methods are needed to counteract this risk of unnecessary information loss (**R1**).

Furthermore, existing approaches are geared towards *automated* resolution. However, as deleting constraints might be highly sensitive, automated approaches might yield implausible results. For example, if a system computes that inconsistency can be resolved by deleting only one constraint, this result is of no use if that constraint is business-critical and must be retained. This calls for a close integration of human experts in determining suitable resolution strategies (**R2**).

To address the research problems raised above, the contribution of this work is consequently twofold:

- **(R1) Minimal Information Loss.** We show how *minimal correction sets* (MCS) can be computed via a reduction to a hitting set enumeration problem, i.e., an application of *Reiter's hitting set theorem* [16]. This allows to compute the cardinality-smallest set(s) of constraints that have to be deleted to restore consistency, i.e., inconsistency is resolved while guaranteeing the smallest possible information loss w.r.t. the number of deleted constraints.
- **(R2) Human-in-the-loop Integration.** We extend our computation approach with a human-in-the-loop perspective, allowing users to impact the computation of minimal correction sets, e.g., by prioritizing certain constraints. Also, to support modelers in understanding different resolution options, novel metrics are presented that help modelers understand the impact of their choices, e.g., the effectiveness of customized resolution strategies.

The remainder of this work is structured as follows. In Sect. 2, we provide preliminaries on declarative process models and discuss limitations of related works addressed in this paper. Section 3 presents our approach for computing MCS via hitting sets. Our approach is then implemented and evaluated in experiments with real-life data sets in Sect. 4. We conclude in Sect. 5.

2   Preliminaries and Related Works

In this section, we discuss preliminaries on declarative process models, the notion of inconsistency in declarative models, as well as related work.

2.1 Declarative Process Models

Declarative process models are constituted of a set of constraints, that confine the allowed behavior of company activities [14]. As opposed to traditional process models, this allows for a high degree of flexibility within these set bounds.

Definition 1 (Declarative Process Models). *A declarative process model is a tuple $M = (A, T, C)$, where A is a set of activities, T is a set of constraint templates, and C is the set of actual constraints, which instantiate the template elements in T with tasks in A. We denote $\mathfrak{M}$ as the universe of all such models.*

In this paper, we consider DECLARE [14], which is a declarative process modeling language and notation. DECLARE offers easy-to-use predefined templates, that can be parametrized with company activities in order to specify declarative constraints. For example, the DECLARE constraint RESPONSE(a, b) states that if a task a occurs, it must be eventually followed by a task b. An advantage of DECLARE is that the semantics of template types can be defined with temporal logic, allowing to exploit the amenities of temporal logic checking, while hiding complexity from the end user. We define the semantics of DECLARE constraints with the temporal logic LTL_p [13]. An LTL_p formula is given by the grammar

$$\varphi ::= a|(\neg\varphi)|(\varphi_1 \wedge \varphi_2)|(\bigcirc\varphi)|(\varphi_1 \mathbf{U}\varphi_2)|(\ominus\varphi)|(\varphi_1\mathbf{S}\varphi_2).$$

Each formula is built from atomic propositions $\in A$ (relative to a declarative process model), and is closed under the boolean connectives, the unary temporal operators $\bigcirc$ (next) and $\ominus$ (previous), and the binary temporal operators $\mathbf{U}$ (until) and $\mathbf{S}$ (since). For any such formula, the semantics is then defined relative to a trace t. Due to space limitations, we omit a presentation of the concrete semantics and refer the reader to [5]. Based on such LTL_p formulae, the semantics of individual DECLARE constraints can then be defined. A standard set of DECLARE templates and corresponding semantics can be found in [3].

2.2 On the Notion of Inconsistency in Declarative Process Models

Based on the LTL_p semantics, it can be verified whether a constraint c is satisfied by a trace t by checking if c evaluates to true over t [12]. Given a declarative model $\mathbf{M}$, let $\mathfrak{T}^{\mathbf{A}}$ denote the set of all possible sequences that can be constructed based on the activities $\mathbf{A} \in \mathbf{M}$. An evaluation of a declarative model M over a trace t is thus a function $\epsilon : \mathfrak{M} \times \mathfrak{T}^{\mathbf{A}} \to \{\top, \bot\}$, defined via

$$\epsilon(\mathbf{M}, t) = \begin{cases} \top \text{ if for all } c \in \mathbf{C} : c \text{ evaluates to true for } t \\ \bot \text{ otherwise} \end{cases}$$

We define the *language* $\mathcal{L}$ of a model $\mathbf{M}$ as all traces that satisfy $\mathbf{M}$, i.e.,

$$\mathcal{L}(\mathbf{M}) = \{t \in \mathfrak{T}^{\mathbf{A}} \mid \epsilon(\mathbf{M}, t) = \top\}.$$

Thus, an inconsistent declarative process model is a model where $\mathcal{L} = \emptyset$, i.e., it cannot accept any traces.

Consider the exemplary declarative process models M_1, M_2, defined via

$$M_1 = \{\text{INIT}(a), \text{RESPONSE}(a, b), \text{NOTRESPONSE}(a, b)\}$$
$$M_2 = \{\text{RESPONSE}(a, b), \text{NOTRESPONSE}(a, b)\}$$

In M_1, the constraint $\text{INIT}(a)$ confines that a trace must start with an event a. The remaining two constraints $\text{RESPONSE}(a,b)$ and $\text{NOTRESPONSE}(a,b)$ would also have to be satisfied in the same trace. As the latter two constraints are contradictory, there can exist no trace that satisfies M_1, i.e. $\mathcal{L}(M_1) = \emptyset$.

The notion of classical inconsistency was recently extended with the concept of *quasi-inconsistency* [5,6]. In the declarative model M_2 there exist two "contradictory" constraints, but there is no confinement regarding the occurrence of an activity a. In result, M_2 can accept an arbitrary amount of traces, i.e., any trace that does not contain the activity a. Thus, as $\mathcal{L}(M_2) \neq \emptyset$, M_2 is not classically inconsistent. Yet, the constraints in M_2 are highly problematic, as they will always be activated together, but yield contradictory conclusions. Following [5], M_2 is, therefore, *quasi*-inconsistent. For a formal definition, we first need some notation on reactive constraints and constraint activation.

Considering DECLARE constraints such as $\text{RESPONSE}(a, b)$, we see that such constraints describe a form of cause and reaction relation between the tasks a and b, i.e., given an activity a, the reaction should be b. Thus, following works such as [2], declarative constraints can be rewritten as so-called *reactive constraints*.

Definition 2 (Reactive Constraints [2]). *Given a declarative process model* $M = (A, T, C)$, *let* $\alpha \in A$ *be an activation and* φ *be an* LTL_p *formula over* A. *Then, a reactive constraint (RCon)* Ψ *is a pair* (α, φ), *denoted as* $\Psi = \alpha \Rightarrow \varphi$.

As an example, $\text{RESPONSE}(a, b)$ can be rewritten as $a \Rightarrow \Diamond b$. For a constraint c, we denote $A_a(c)$ and $A_r(c)$ as the respective activating and reacting activities. For a declarative process model, if the reaction of a constraint c is an activation to a constraint c', we also say that the $A_a(c)$ transitively activates c' [5].

Consequently, we define quasi-inconsistency and issues as follows.

Definition 3 (Quasi-Inconsistent Subset [5]). *For a constraint set* C, *a quasi-inconsistent subset is defined as a pair* (A, C), *s.t.* $C \subseteq C$, A *activates* C *and* $A \cup C \models \perp$.

To clarify, we consider constraints that will a) always be activated together, and b) yield an inconsistency, should they be activated.

Example 1. We recall M_2. Then, we have the quasi-inconsistent subset q, with

$$q = (\{a\}, \{\text{RESPONSE}(a, b), \text{NOTRESPONSE}(a, b)\})$$

For a model M, the set $\text{MIS}(M)$ is the set of minimal quasi-inconsistent subsets, i.e., subsets where removing any constraint resolves the issue.

In this section, we have introduced the concepts of inconsistency and quasi-inconsistency. We acknowledge that [12] also introduce the notion of conflicting sets, which are conflicting constraints that were activated by a given trace. However, in this work, we only consider the introduced forms of "inconsistencies", i.e., "inconsistencies" that arise independent of specific traces and need to be resolved at design-time. For the remainder of this paper, we will refer to both quasi-inconsistencies and "classical" inconsistencies as "issues", for readability. We also denote MIS as all minimal quasi-inconsistent subsets and all "classical" minimal inconsistent subsets[1] by a slight misuse of notation. Basically, we are interested in all (potential) inconsistencies, as these issues need to be resolved.

2.3 Related Works and Contributions

Consider the model M_3 in Fig. 1, which has six issues that need to be resolved. Here, several works have presented means for inconsistency resolution [3, 4, 12].

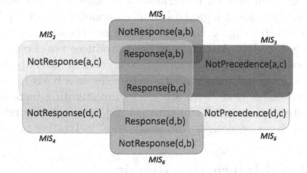

Fig. 1. Exemplary model M_3, containing six minimal issues (highlighted)

A central approach is to start by deleting constraints that have the highest number of overlaps, as this maximizes the number of minimal issues being resolved by deleting one constraint. Hence, approaches such as [4, 12] would delete the constraint RESPONSE(b, c), as it is part of the most overlapping sets (4). This resolves all issues but MIS_1 and MIS_6, which means two more constraints have to be deleted (i.e., three deletions in total). However, this is not the optimal solution, as inconsistency could be resolved by deleting only two constraints (RESPONSE(a, b), RESPONSE(d, b)) (these two constraints are part of less overlaps, still, it would be an optimal solution to start with deleting these constraints). This shows that while the existing solutions produce "minimal" solutions/repair sets (in terms of set inclusion), they do not always yield the *cardinality-smallest* solutions, i.e., they can run into local optima due to the

---

[1] Given a model $\mathbf{M}$ and a corresponding constraint set $\mathbf{C}$, a minimal inconsistent subset is defined as a set $m \subseteq \mathbf{C}$, s.t. $\mathcal{L}(m) = \emptyset$ and $\nexists m' \subseteq m$ with $\mathcal{L}(m') = \emptyset$.

approach designs as greedy algorithms. This can result in unnecessary information loss[2]. In this work, we present an approach to compute the cardinality-smallest set(s) of constraints that have to be deleted to restore consistency, i.e., our approach guarantees a minimal information loss w.r.t. the number of deleted constraints. This is achieved by means of so-called *hitting sets*. Please note that the mentioned existing approaches [3,4,12] do not use hitting sets to resolve inconsistencies (cf. above for the resulting limitations). Furthermore, existing approaches [3,4] are geared towards *automated* resolution. However, as deleting certain constraints might be highly sensitive, such automated approaches might yield implausible results in a real-life sense. Here, new results are needed that extend inconsistency resolution with a human-in-the-loop perspective. In this regard, we, therefore, present novel means, that allow the user to impact the computation of resolution strategies, while being supported with insights to understand the impact of different resolution options.

In general, our work is also related to to other works that use hitting sets for the diagnosis and repair of knowledge representation formalisms. This idea by Reiter [16] has been applied in various other logical formalisms, e.g., first-order logic [7], propositional logic [10] or non-monotonic logics [1]. Here, this work is the first to investigate Reiter's hitting set theorem in the context of declarative process models. Also, this works introduces novel concepts towards the "customization" of hitting set computation according to company needs, e.g., allowing users to define preference relations of rules as a basis for computation.

We also acknowledge that there are works investigating inconsistency resolution in declarative processes at run-time [11,12], which is beyond the scope of this report, as we focus on design-time analysis of declarative models.

3 Minimal and Interactive Repair

In this work, we present an approach to resolve inconsistencies (i.e., minimal issues) in declarative process models by deleting (the smallest possible set of) constraints. Importantly, as the plausibility of automatedly computed resolution operations has to be carefully considered, the approach is geared towards a semi-automated resolution, allowing humans to understand, evaluate and select suitable resolution strategies. Our approach overview is shown in Fig. 2. At first, all inconsistent subsets are detected. Then, viable repair operations are computed based on minimal correction sets, i.e., minimal hitting sets (cf. Sections 3.1, 3.2). Last, to select suitable repair operations, our approach provides metrics and further means to support modelers in evaluating possible solutions (cf. Section 3.3).

---

[2] The approach in [3] would behave analogously, except not by deleting constraints but iteratively building a new, maximally consistent model, which could also "drop" more constraints than necessary.

Fig. 2. Approach overview

3.1 Inconsistency Resolution Based on Minimal Correction Sets

For determining resolution strategies, experts need to identify which constraints should be removed from a model to resolve all minimal issues. To avoid unnecessary information loss, it is especially interesting to identify minimal sets of constraints that can be removed to resolve inconsistency. In the following, we refer to such sets as *minimal correction sets*, i.e., a set of constraints that – when deleted – resolves all minimal issues, and is minimal in terms of set-inclusion.

Definition 4 (Minimal Correction Sets). *Given a constraint set C, $C \subseteq \mathbf{C}$ is a minimal correction set of C, if $MIS(\mathbf{C} \backslash C) = \emptyset$, and $\forall C' \subset C : MIS(\mathbf{C} \backslash C') \neq \emptyset$. Let X be a constraint set or a declarative process model, we denote $MCS(X)$ as the set of minimal correction sets for the constraints in X.*

Such minimal correction sets can be computed by considering so-called hitting sets, following [16].

In set theory, a set H is called a *hitting set* of a set of sets $S = \{S_1, ..., S_n\}$ iff $H \cap S_i \neq \emptyset$ for every $i = 1, ..., n$.

Example 2. Consider the set of sets $S' = \{\{1,2,3\}, \{1,3,5\}, \{4,5,6\}\}$. Furthermore, consider the following exemplary sets $H_1 - H_3$, defined via

$$H_1 = \{1, 4\} \qquad H_2 = \{1, 2, 3, 4, 5, 6\} \qquad H_3 = \{1, 2, 3\}.$$

H_1 and H_2 are hitting sets w.r.t. S', as $H_{1/2} \cap S_i \neq \emptyset$ for all $i = 1..3$. However, we see that H_2 is not minimal, as we could remove several elements and H_2 would still be a hitting set. Also, we see that H_3 is not a hitting set for S', as it has no elements in common with the last inner set of S'.

To compute minimal correction sets, we consequently propose to consider minimal hitting sets, by adapting Reiter's hitting set theorem as follows:

Theorem 1 (Hitting Set-Based MCS (adapted from [16])). *Given a constraint set C, $C \subseteq \mathbf{C}$ is a minimal correction set of $\mathbf{C}$ iff C is a minimal hitting set w.r.t. $MIS(C)$.*

Example 3. Consider the following constraint set M_5, defined via

$$M_5 = \textsc{NotResponse}(a,b) \qquad \textsc{ChainResponse}(a,b) \qquad \textsc{Response}(a,b)$$
$$\textsc{NotResponse}(c,d) \qquad \textsc{ChainResponse}(c,d) \qquad \textsc{Response}(c,d)$$

Then we have:

$$MIS(M_5) = \{\mu_1, \mu_2, \mu_3, \mu_4\}$$
$$\mu_1 = \{\text{NOTRESPONSE}(a,b), \text{CHAINRESPONSE}(a,b)\}$$
$$\mu_2 = \{\text{NOTRESPONSE}(a,b), \text{RESPONSE}(a,b)\}$$
$$\mu_3 = \{\text{NOTRESPONSE}(c,d), \text{CHAINRESPONSE}(c,d)\}$$
$$\mu_4 = \{\text{NOTRESPONSE}(c,d), \text{RESPONSE}(c,d)\}$$

Consider the exemplary hitting sets $H_4 - H_6$, defined via

$$H_4 = \{\text{NOTRESPONSE}(a,b), \text{NOTRESPONSE}(c,d)\}$$
$$H_5 = \{\text{NOTRESPONSE}(c,d), \text{CHAINRESPONSE}(a,b), \text{RESPONSE}(a,b)\}$$
$$H_6 = \{\text{NOTRESPONSE}(a,b), \text{NOTRESPONSE}(c,d), \text{CHAINRESPONSE}(a,b)\}.$$

$H_4 - H_6$ are hitting sets for $MIS(M_5)$. However, H_6 is not minimal, as we could remove CHAINRESPONSE(a,b) and H_6 would still be a hitting set. Correspondingly, only H_4 and H_5 are minimal correction sets for M_5.

While minimality of hitting sets enforces that the hitting sets are not reducible, this does not mean "smallest" per se. In the scope of deleting only the smallest possible amount of constraints, it could, however, be interesting to consider the cardinality-smallest minimal correction sets.

Definition 5 (Smallest viable repair). *Given a declarative process model M and the set of minimal correction sets $MCS(M)$, the set of smallest minimal correction sets is defined as $MCS_{MIN}(M) = \{S \subseteq MCS(M) : |S| = min(MCS(M))\}$.*

Corollary 1. *The smallest possible number of constraints that have to be deleted from a declarative model M to resolve all minimal issues is $min(MCS(M))$.*

In turn, this allows to present users a list of all possible smallest viable repairs.

In this section, we have presented means to compute minimal correction sets based on hitting set enumeration. While this approach can be used to identify the cardinality-smallest sets of constraints for inconsistency resolution, there is still a major conceptual problem, namely that of plausibility: Even if algorithms can compute a (smallest) set of constraints that could be deleted to resolve the inconsistency, this does not mean that these solutions are plausible in a real-life sense. We therefore propose to extend inconsistency resolution with a human-in-the-loop perspective.

3.2   Human-in-the-Loop Features

To allow for a human-in-the-loop integration, repair operations should not be automatedly applied, but rather recommended to the user. Also, experts should be able to influence or constrain the actual computation of viable correction sets. Therefore, we raise the following two requirements for a human-in-the-loop integration in inconsistency resolution:

1. To compute a recommendation of repair operations, it should be possible to rank minimal corrections, e.g., by an arbitrary quality metric.
2. The computation of which constraints to delete should be relative to a user-definable configuration, e.g., by allowing to prohibit the deletion of certain constraints or provide superiority relations.

As motivated in Sect. 2.3, related work on inconsistency resolution in declarative process models cannot satisfy these requirements. We consequently address these issues in the following.

First, via Definition 5, correction sets can already be ranked by their size. Next to the correction set size, this can be generalized for arbitrary measures γ to allow for a general ranking of correction sets.

Definition 6 (γ-Repair Ranking). *Let a declarative process model M and the set of minimal correction sets $MCS(M)$. Then, considering a measure γ : $MCS(M) \rightarrow \mathbb{R}_{\geq 0}^{\infty}$ that assigns to a minimal correction set a non-negative numerical value, a γ-repair ranking over all $m \in MCS(M)$ is any ranking $\langle m_1, ..., m_n \rangle$ that satisfies $\gamma(m_1) \leq ... \leq \gamma(m_n)$.*

Thus, this ranking can sort all MCS relative to a measure γ. Importantly, the semantics of the ranking are defined such that the ranking sorts all minimal correction sets from "best" to "worst" option, relative to γ.

Continuing, it should be possible to confine the deletion of certain constraints in order to leverage the computation of plausible correction sets following requirement 2. Here, we consider whitelists, i.e., a whitelist $W \subseteq M$ is a list of constraints not to be deleted. Intuitively, a whitelist can "block" certain minimal correction sets, as these could include whitelisted constraints. Therefore, it is necessary to provide means to present users with the (next) best viable repair, while also considering the whitelist. To this aim, we adapt the notion of smallest viable repairs and extend this for arbitrary quality measures. This allows to determine the set of best possible γ-repairs relative to a whitelist.

Definition 7 (Best Viable γ-Repair). *Given a declarative process model M, a measure $\gamma : MCS(M) \rightarrow \mathbb{R}_{\geq 0}^{\infty}$ that assigns to a minimal correction set a non-negative numerical value, and a whitelist $W \subseteq M$, the best viable γ-repair w.r.t. W is defined as $MCS_{\gamma}^{W}(M) = \{S \subseteq MCS(M) \mid \forall s \in S : \nexists x \notin S \text{ s.t. } \gamma(x) < \gamma(s), \text{ and } s \notin W\}$.*

The best viable γ-repair thus finds the "best" minimal correction sets w.r.t. a measure γ, (e.g., the correction set size) while also considering the whitelist. Given a declarative process model M and a measure γ, we denote the set of best viable γ-repairs as BCS_{γ}.

Example 4. Consider the minimal correction sets $MCS_1 - MCS_4$:

$MCS_1 = \{\textbf{NOTRESPONSE(a,b)}, \text{NOTRESPONSE}(c,d)\}$

$MCS_2 = \{\textbf{NOTRESPONSE(a,b)}, \text{CHAINRESPONSE}(c,d), \{\text{RESPONSE}(c,d)\}.$

$MCS_3 = \{\text{CHAINRESPONSE}(a,b), \text{RESPONSE}(a,b), \text{CHAINRESPONSE}(c,d),$
$\qquad\quad \text{RESPONSE}(c,d)\}.$

$MCS_4 = \{\text{NOTRESPONSE}(c,d), \text{CHAINRESPONSE}(a,b), \text{RESPONSE}(a,b)\}$

Assume a whitelist $W = \{\textbf{NOTRESPONSE(a,b)}\}$, i.e., this constraint should not be deleted. This prohibits to select the correction sets MCS_1 and MCS_2, as deleting the corresponding constraints would violate the whitelist constraints. Considering again the correction set sizes, i.e., $\gamma(M) = |M|$, the best viable γ-repair BCS_γ would therefore be $\text{BCS}_\gamma = \{MCS_4\}$. Note that MCS_3 is not part of the best viable repair: While it satisfies the whitelist constraints, it does not satisfy the first condition that there should be no other remaining correction sets with lower γ value (here: set size).

Intuitively, a large whitelist might overly restrict the set of viable γ-repairs. Thus, next to entirely blocking certain constraints in a binary manner, modelers should rather also have the possibility of a more fine-grained configuration that allows for more flexibility. Therefore, we propose to allow users to weight constraints, and calculate the fitting correction sets accordingly.

Definition 8 (Weighted Declarative Process Model). *A weighted declarative process model is a tuple* $M = (A, T, C, w)$, *where* A *is a set of activities,* T *is a set of constraint templates,* C *is the set of actual constraints, which instantiate the template elements in* T *with tasks in* A, *and* $w : C \to \mathbb{R}_{\geq 0}^{\infty}$ *is a weighting function for constraints.*

A weighted declarative process model extends declarative models with definable constraint weights. In order to allow modeling superiority relations between constraints, arbitrary weights can be defined manually or derived automatically. This allows to compute weighted correction sets.

Definition 9 (Correction Set Weight). *Given a weighted declarative process model* $M = (A, T, C, w)$ *and the corresponding minimal correction sets* $\mathsf{MCS}(C)$, *the weight* $w(M)$ *of any* $M \in \mathsf{MCS}(C)$ *is defined as* $\sum_{c \in M} w(c)$.

As the correction set weight can essentially be used as an assessment function γ for correction sets, it is therefore possible to compute a repair ranking via Definition 6 using the correction set weights, i.e., a larger correction set weight indicates a higher "cost" to remove this correction set.

Example 5. We recall the correction sets $MCS_1 - MCS_4$ from Example 4. Furthermore, assume the expert has determined the following constraint weights:

$$\text{NOTRESPONSE}(a,b) = 3 \qquad \text{CHAINRESPONSE}(a,b) = 1$$
$$\text{RESPONSE}(a,b) = 1 \qquad \text{NOTRESPONSE}(c,d) = 3$$
$$\text{CHAINRESPONSE}(c,d) = 1 \qquad \text{RESPONSE}(c,d) = 1$$

In the example, the expert has prioritized two constraints. In turn, we have that

$$w(MCS_1) = 3 + 3 = 6 \qquad\qquad w(MCS_2) = 3 + 1 + 1 = 5$$
$$w(MCS_3) = 1 + 1 + 1 + 1 = 4 \qquad\qquad w(MCS_4) = 3 + 1 + 1 = 5.$$

We see that while MCS_1 is smaller than MCS_2-MCS_4 (and in general it would be favorable to select smaller correction sets), the "costs" of selecting MCS_1 are higher as this would mean to delete two highly prioritized constraints. This information can thus be used for considering the trade-off between selecting correction sets of smaller size or keeping constraints of higher priority.

3.3 Understanding Support

In the previous section, we introduced means to enable a close human-in-the-loop integration. While this allows users to provide a fine-grained configuration for correction set computation, it also places an increased pressure on the human to ultimately choose which correction sets to select. Given that there can easily be multiple best viable repairs, users must be supported in understanding the consequences of choosing between these correction sets, in order to determine suitable resolution strategies. We, therefore, propose a metric to assess the quality of a correction set selection, as well as means to understand the behavioral changes resulting from applying a certain correction set, explained as follows.

Assuming a modeler is comparing the sizes of different correction sets, a smaller correction set can in general be considered as better than a larger correction set. However, it might not be plausible to apply the smallest correction set, as a user might deem that the respective constraints must be kept. Thus, the user might be forced to select a larger correction set. However, if the next viable correction set is too large, a user might have to carefully consider whether keeping certain constraints is "worth" deleting a (much) higher number of other constraints. Especially when considering correction set measures other than the size, e.g., complex correction set weights, deciding and balancing such a decision is a difficult task for experts. Here, we propose to compute distance-based metrics to support users in understanding the trade-off between different choices.

For a declarative model $\mathbf{M}$, consider any quality measure $\gamma : \mathsf{MCS}(\mathbf{M}) \to \mathbb{R}^{\infty}_{\geq 0}$, where a higher value indicates a higher "cost" of removing the individual correction set. Then, the smallest possible cost is the minimum over all best viable γ-repairs $\mathsf{BCS}_\gamma(\mathbf{M})$, i.e., the smallest possible cost (w.r.t. γ) $\mathrm{MIN}_\gamma(\mathbf{M})$ $= min_{B \in \mathsf{BCS}_\gamma(\mathbf{M})} \gamma(B)$. This allows to compute an absolute distance metric for assessing arbitrary correction sets.

Definition 10 ((Distance-based) Additional Correction Set Costs from Baseline). *Given a declarative process model $\mathbf{M}$ and a correction set measure γ, the additional cost c_{add_γ} of any correction set M relative to the smallest possible cost is defined as $c_{add_\gamma}(\mathbf{M}, M) = \gamma(M) - \mathrm{MIN}_\gamma(\mathbf{M})$.*

This metric provides an assessment of correction sets for determining the additional costs relative to the smallest possible costs w.r.t. γ .

Example 6. We recall the correction set $MCS_1 - MCS_4$ from Example 4. Judging from a set size perspective, i.e., $\gamma(M) = |M|$, we have that $\gamma(MCS_1) = 2$, $\gamma(MCS_2) = \gamma(MCS_4) = 3$ and $\gamma(MCS_3) = 4$. Thus, the smallest possible costs MIN_γ are 2. Here, the additional costs of selecting MCS_2 or MCS_4 would be 1, and 2 for selecting MCS_3. If the additional costs from the baseline become too large, they might outweigh the costs of keeping certain constraints. The proposed distance-based metric can thus support users in making an informed decision as to whether the whitelist or rule weights should be altered.

While the distance-based additional cost metric can produce valuable insights, an ultimate selection of specific correction sets might not only depend on numeric factors such as the number of deleted constraints, but rather on the actual behavioral consequences following the deletion of a specific correction set. Here, experts need to be supported in understanding the behavioral consequences of the different available options. To this aim, we propose so-called fragment-based language profiles in order to present modelers the *exact difference in behavioral changes* for different resolution options.

To understand behavioral changes, given a declarative model **M**, one could theoretically compute the language of **M** and the language of any **M'** derived by deleting a set of constraints from **M**. Then, one could simply compare the languages of **M** and **M'** in order to identify all behavioral changes, i.e., differences in accepted traces. However, this is not feasible, as the languages can be infinitely large. Instead, we propose to consider only fragments of the possible languages, explained as follows.

Consider the constraint set **M** = {RESPONSE(a,b), NOTRESPONSE(a,b)}, which is quasi-inconsistent. Then, consider a correction set C = {RESPONSE(a,b)}, indicating that this constraint could be deleted to resolve the issue in **M**. The question then arises which behavioral changes would follow deleting this constraint, i.e., given a model **M'** = **M** \ C, what would be the difference $\mathcal{L}(M') - \mathcal{L}(M)$? Regardless of any actual or possible trace for **M**, in the example, any changes in language for **M'** only apply for any trace that contains a or b. For instance, a trace cde would behave identically for **M** and **M'**, whereas the trace a could not satisfy **M** but possibly satisfy **M'**. Therefore, only the permutations of the distinct events within the correction set constraints need to be considered. For example, for the above correction set C = {RESPONSE(a,b)}, the distinct events are a, b, so all possible event combinations, i.e., trace fragments, would be a, b, ab, ba. By evaluating these fragments against the original model **M** and a corresponding altered model **M'**, changes in the different language profiles following a deletion of the correction set relative to the original rule base can be identified, as shown in Fig. 3. By deleting the correction set C = {RESPONSE(a,b)}, the two trace fragments a and ba would become possible (which were not possible before). The expert can thus inspect whether this is deemed as appropriate behavior. For example, if the sequence ba should never occur in the company processes, the expert could see that the current correction set would result in unwanted behavior, and seek for a different solution.

Trace Fragments	M	M' = M\C
a	✗	✓
b	✓	✓
ab	✗	✗
ba	✗	✓

Fig. 3. Fragment-based visualization of behavioral changes

To compute the actual behavioral differences between the models, we encode the satisfiability of the individual trace fragments relative to a model as a so-called *language profile*. Let a finite list of trace fragments be $t = (t_1, ..., t_n)$. Then, for a model M, a language profile is a $1 \times n$ matrix

$$\lambda M^t = \begin{bmatrix} \lambda t_1 \\ \vdots \\ \lambda t_n \end{bmatrix}, \text{ with every } \lambda t_i = \begin{cases} 1, \text{ if } M \models t_i \\ 0 \text{ otherwise} \end{cases}$$

Definition 11 (Behavioral Change Profile). *Given a set of trace fragments t and two models M, M', the behavioral change profile is defined as $\lambda M^t - \lambda M'^t$, where an index 1 indicates a change in behavior, and an index 0 indicates an identical behavior of the two models for the corresponding trace fragment.*

Example 7. Consider the trace fragments and models M, M' shown in Fig. 3. Then, behavioral change profile $b = [1, 0, 0, 1]$ (transposed), indicating a behavior change for the trace fragments a and ba.

Considering behavioral change profiles provides important insights to modelers, as it enables experts to understand the changes in behavior between two models, e.g., to inspect whether deleting certain constraints could lead to unwanted or non-compliant process behavior.

A possible limitation of applying behavioral change profiles could be the amount of fragments that need to be considered. For correction sets and the number of contained events, the number of permutations/fragments that need to be computed could grow factorial. However, this is only a problem if the correction sets would contain a very high number of constraints. Based on the overall goal to mitigate unnecessary deletions of constraints, our approach intuitively favors smaller correction sets by design. To anticipate our empirical results from Sect. 4, we also found that correction sets were generally small for real-life data sets, i.e., 3–5 constraints, of which only the distinct events have to be considered. Also, only fragments that contain at least one activation over the constraints in the correction set need to be considered, as traces without an activation will not be affected by the deletion of the correction set. Therefore, the number of fragments can be further confined, e.g., in Fig. 3, the trace b would technically not need to be considered. Thus, the computation of behavioral change profiles is feasible for smaller correction sets, e.g., as in the analyzed real-life data sets (cf. Section 4). For settings with a large number of fragments, efficient algorithms should be investigated in future work.

4   Tool Support and Evaluation

We implemented our inconsistency repair approach as a proof-of-concept. The project can be viewed online[3]. Also, an online-demo is available[4]. Here, users can upload their declarative models, view the model as a 3d-graph, scan for any minimal issues and compute minimal correction sets directly in the browser. The computation of minimal issues is based on our previous work in [5].

At the core, our approach is strongly dependent on the performance of the hitting set enumeration. Fortunately, this computation task has gained recent momentum and powerful enumeration algorithms are available [8,15]. In our implementation, we integrated the PySat library[5] for computing hitting sets, which has been broadly studied and evaluated. However, these libraries have been mostly tested in more theoretical contexts, such as SAT solving.

To evaluate the plausibility of applying our proof-of-concept in a BPM setting, we conducted runtime experiments with real-life data-sets from the Business Process Intelligence (BPI) Challenge[6]. Here, we used data sets from the last four years, i.e., logs of a loan application process (BPI 17, 31.509 cases), a governmental funding process (BPI 18, 43.809 cases), a purchase order process (BPI 19, 251.734 cases), and a domestic travel expense refund process (BPI 20, 10.500 cases). From these logs, we mined DECLARE models using the declarative process discovery tool Minerful [3]. As mining parameters, we selected a support factor of 75%, as well as confidence and interest factors of 12.5%, following the experiment setup in [3]. Note that as shown in [5], these parameters allow for contradicting constraints to be added to the initial model, which is needed for our evaluation. In the future, it might be interesting to further examine the effects of mining parameters on the resulting inconsistencies and repeat the evaluation with different parameter configurations. We applied our proof-of-concept implementation to all models to compute the smallest viable repairs. As a baseline, we compared our approach to the approach in [4] (approximation algorithm) to test how many unnecessary deletions could be avoided by using an exact approach as proposed in this work[7]. The experiments were run on a machine with 3 GHz

---

[3] https://bit.ly/38kyxD0.

[4] https://bit.ly/38lSU2N.

[5] https://pysathq.github.io/docs/html/api/examples/hitman.html.

[6] https://icpmconference.org/2020/bpi-challenge/.

[7] We acknowledge that the approach in [3] could have also been considered as a baseline; however, that approach cannot resolve quasi-inconsistencies and is therefore not fully comparable. Also, as the approach in [3] is also an approximation algorithm, it can be expected to also not compute the smallest possible number of deletions for all cases, which is why we consider the selected baseline [4] as representative.

Intel Core i7 processor, 16 GB RAM (DDR3) under macOS. Table 1 shows the experiment results for the analyzed real-life data sets. As the model mined from the BPI19 log did not yield any minimal issues, it was omitted for readability.

Table 1. Overview of evaluation results for the analyzed real-life data sets

Log	Constraints	# of MIS	# of Deleted constraints			Runtime		
			Baseline [4]	This work	Δ	Baseline [4]	This work	Δ
BPI 17	305	28954	5	3	40% (2)	92243 ms	30782 ms	67%
BPI 18	70	25303	7	4	43% (3)	18093 ms	13733 ms	24%
BPI 20	357	747	7	5	29% (2)	1952 ms	795 ms	59%

For all declarative models, our algorithm was able to resolve all minimal issues by deleting less constraints compared to the baseline from [4]. More specifically, the information loss could be lowered by up to 43% (BPI 18). The runtime of our algorithm was also lower for all cases, with a time reduction of up to 67% (BPI 17). Thus, for the analyzed real-life data sets, our proposed approach was noticeably faster, and could reduce the number of deletions, i.e., resolve inconsistency with less information loss. Regarding the reduced number of deletions, this result is generalizable, as existing methods are prone to follow a non-optimal solution due to running into local optima (cf. Section 2.3). Thus, our approach guarantees to delete less or equal amounts of constraints for any model compared to [3, 4, 12]. Regarding runtime, we do not see a conceptual reason for the faster results, therefore, more experiments are needed in future works. The faster runtime could be attributed to the use of the PySat library, which might have faster inconsistent subset computation than [4].

5 Conclusion

In this paper, we have presented an approach for minimal and interactive inconsistency repair of declarative process models, where users can customize the computation of repair solutions and are supported in assessing different viable options with metrics and behavioral change analysis. Our evaluation indicates that our proposed approach can outperform existing means w.r.t. runtime and information loss. In this context, we see the following limitations of our work.

Our work implicitly uses the number of deleted constraints as an information loss measure. Here, other information loss measures have been investigated [9] and might be applicable for temporal logics. For example, instead of minimizing the *number* of deleted constraints, it could be beneficial to delete those constraints that have a low impact on the number of allowed traces. Note, however, that our approach already supports modelers towards this aim via behavioral change profile analysis of possible repairs.

Furthermore, our work only considers repair via deletion. While we argue that this can be plausible in the scope of inconsistency resolution, other change patterns such as weakening have also been proposed [9] and should be investigated in future work (e.g., relaxing a constraint CHAINRESPONSE to RESPONSE).

A central limitation of using the proposed approach based on hitting set diagnosis is that the constraints are viewed as abstract elements of a set. Here, it might be necessary to develop further means for distinguishing minimal inconsistent subsets in DECLARE based on the specific temporal constraints. In this way, it would be possible to further assess the severity of inconsistencies and to implement a more fine-grained prioritization of detected problems. In this context, it is also noteworthy that this work is limited to standard DECLARE templates with at most two parameters. Thus, it should be investigated how arbitrary constraints (e.g., using logical operators) must be handled, especially regarding their effect on behavioral changes.

In this work, the repair was geared towards inconsistencies. For future work, we aim at extending our approach to also consider other types of problematic structures in declarative models, such as hidden dependencies [17]. For any type of minimal structure, it can be expected that computing "minimal repair sets" via Reiter's hitting set theorem will be applicable. We aim to evaluate our proposed approach in experiments with human participants, especially in regard to the cognitive effects of the proposed metrics and behavioral change analysis. Also, we aim to implement and evaluate our proposed approach of behavioral change profile analysis.

References

1. Brewka, G., Thimm, M., Ulbricht, M.: Strong inconsistency. Artif. Intell. **267**, 78–117 (2019)
2. Cecconi, A., Di Ciccio, C., De Giacomo, G., Mendling, J.: Interestingness of traces in declarative process mining: the Janus LTLp$_f$ approach. In: Weske, M., Montali, M., Weber, I., vom Brocke, J. (eds.) BPM 2018. LNCS, vol. 11080, pp. 121–138. Springer, Cham (2018). https://doi.org/10.1007/978-3-319-98648-7_8
3. Di Ciccio, C., Maggi, F.M., Montali, M., Mendling, J.: Resolving inconsistencies and redundancies in declarative process models. Inf. Syst. **64**, 425–446 (2017)
4. Corea, C., Deisen, M., Delfmann, P.: Resolving inconsistencies in declarative process models based on culpability measurement. In: 2019 Proceedings der 14. International Tagung der WI, Siegen, Germany, pp. 139–153. AISeL (2019)
5. Corea, C., Delfmann, P.: Quasi-inconsistency in declarative process models. In: Hildebrandt, T., van Dongen, B.F., Röglinger, M., Mendling, J. (eds.) BPM 2019. LNBIP, vol. 360, pp. 20–35. Springer, Cham (2019). https://doi.org/10.1007/978-3-030-26643-1_2
6. Corea, C., Thimm, M.: On quasi-inconsistency and its complexity. AI **284**, 103276 (2020)
7. Felfernig, A., Friedrich, G., Jannach, D., Stumptner, M.: Consistency-based diagnosis of configuration knowledge bases. Art. Intell. **152**(2), 213–234 (2004)
8. Gainer-Dewar, A., Vera-Licona, P.: The minimal hitting set generation problem: Algorithms and computation. SIAM J. Discret. Math. **31**(1), 63–100 (2017)
9. Grant, J., Hunter, A.: Measuring consistency gain and information loss in stepwise inconsistency resolution. In: Liu, W. (ed.) ECSQARU 2011. LNCS (LNAI), vol. 6717, pp. 362–373. Springer, Heidelberg (2011). https://doi.org/10.1007/978-3-642-22152-1_31

10. Jabbour, S.: On inconsistency measuring and resolving. In: 2019 22nd European Conference on Artificial Intelligence, The Hague, Netherlands. Frontiers in Artificial Intelligence and Applications, vol. 285, pp. 1676–1677. IOS Press (2016)
11. López, M.T.G., Gasca, R.M., Rinderle-Ma, S.: Explaining the incorrect temporal events during business process monitoring by means of compliance rules and model-based diagnosis. In: 2013 17th IEEE International Enterprise Distributed Object Computing Conference Workshops, Vancouver, Canada, pp. 163–172. IEEE Computer Society (2013)
12. Maggi, F.M., Westergaard, M., Montali, M., van der Aalst, W.M.P.: Runtime verification of LTL-based declarative process models. In: Khurshid, S., Sen, K. (eds.) RV 2011. LNCS, vol. 7186, pp. 131–146. Springer, Heidelberg (2012). https://doi.org/10.1007/978-3-642-29860-8_11
13. Markey, N.: Past is for free: on the complexity of verifying linear temporal properties with past. Acta Informatica **40**(6), 431–458 (2004). https://doi.org/10.1007/s00236-003-0136-5
14. Pesic, M., Schonenberg, H., van der Aalst, W.M.P.: DECLARE: full support for loosely-structured processes. In: 2007 11th International Enterprise Distributed Object Computing Conference, Annapolis, USA, pp. 287–300. IEEE Computer Society (2007)
15. Pill, I.H., Quaritsch, T., Wotawa, F.: On the practical performance of minimal hitting set algorithms from a diagnostic perspective. Int. J. Progn. Health Manage. **7**(2), 1–15 (2016)
16. Reiter, R.: A theory of diagnosis from first principles. AI **32**(1), 57–95 (1987)
17. De Smedt, J., De Weerdt, J., Serral, E., Vanthienen, J.: Discovering hidden dependencies in constraint-based declarative process models for improving understandability. Inf. Syst. **74**, 40–52 (2018)

Augmenting Modelers with Semantic Autocompletion of Processes

Maayan Goldstein[1]([✉]) and Cecilia González-Álvarez[2]

[1] Nokia Bell Labs, Kfar Sava, Israel
maayan.goldstein@nokia-bell-labs.com
[2] Nokia Bell Labs, Antwerp, Belgium
cecilia.gonzalez_alvarez@nokia-bell-labs.com

Abstract. Business process modelers need to have expertise and knowledge of the domain that may not always be available to them. Therefore, they may benefit from tools that mine collections of existing processes and recommend element(s) to be added to a new process in design time. In this paper, we present a method for process autocompletion at design time, that is based on the semantic similarity of sub-processes. By converting sub-processes to textual paragraphs and encoding them as numerical vectors, we can find semantically similar ones, and thereafter recommend the next element. To achieve this, we leverage a state-of-the-art technique for encoding natural language as vectors. We evaluate our approach on open source and proprietary datasets and show that our technique is accurate for processes in various domains.

Keywords: Process model autocompletion · Semantic similarity · Sentence embeddings · Next-element recommendation

1 Introduction

Business processes are used across different domains and organizations. Commercial companies and the public sector alike have adopted process models as a means for visualizing and executing their business logic. As the volume of existing process models in an organization increases, it becomes evident that reuse and automation are paramount to enable faster design of high-quality models [11,12].

One way to enable automation is by suggesting what should come next in a model that is being constructed, as exemplified in Fig. 1. Using knowledge from previous experience to recommend the next steps in a process design saves the modeler much of the guesswork and time-consuming effort of reading documentation trying to determine what options are available.

Autocompletion systems have become popular in recent years as they boost productivity and improve quality. For instance, modern e-mail applications suggest how to automatically complete sentences for the user, saving time, improving grammar and style, and avoiding typos [8]. Software developers that are using tools for automatic completion of their code [31], benefit from richer

© Springer Nature Switzerland AG 2021
A. Polyvyanyy et al. (Eds.): BPM Forum 2021, LNBIP 427, pp. 20–36, 2021.
https://doi.org/10.1007/978-3-030-85440-9_2

Fig. 1. Autocompletion problem: the modeler expects recommendations of elements that follow the task with a bold outline (process excerpt from [1]).

development experience leading to fewer bugs and better code reuse. Our goal is to provide process modelers with a similar user experience.

There are two main driving forces for the accelerated development of auto-completion tools in the recent years: first, the growth in the amount of text and open source code available on the web, and second, recent advances in deep learning that benefit from large volumes of information. These two factors contribute to the widespread adoption of deep learning models that are highly accurate and easily transferable to various domains [13,23].

However, autocompletion of business process models has not experienced a breakthrough yet, as vast repositories of open-source models do not exist. As machine learning techniques that train recommendation systems from scratch require large amounts of data, they are inapplicable for process autocompletion.

Several past attempts to solve the autocompletion problem focused on syntactic information, such as the structure of process model graphs, and did not take into account the semantic meaning of the processes and their fragments [12, 15,24,39]. Other researchers investigated semantic-based approaches [5,20,21, 34,36,37]. However, semantic similarity between sub-processes determined with modern deep learning techniques has not been fully explored yet.

Our Contributions. In this paper, we propose to use semantic similarities among processes to enable the autocompletion of the next element(s) at design time. Our approach takes into account the limited availability of data in the field by leveraging pre-trained models for natural language processing (NLP). It also overcomes the obstacle of handling elements that bear similar meaning, but somewhat different textual description, by matching tasks with similar labels rather than exact matches only. Our solution transforms sequences of process elements into paragraphs of text and represents them as sentence embeddings, which are learned representations of text that capture semantic information as vectors of real numbers.

The computed embeddings of element sequences can be compared to each other via techniques that measure the distance between vectors. Thus, given a partially completed process, we can find processes in a repository of existing business processes that are semantically similar to it. Thereafter, we can recommend the most likely element to be added to the process, based on these similar processes.

We also present a framework for evaluation of next-element recommendation systems, filling the gap of previous works on autocompletion. We evaluate the effectiveness of our approach using metrics widely utilized in NLP and recommendation systems.

2   Semantic Autocompletion in a Nutshell

Semantic autocompletion aims at recommending process elements based on semantic similarity of the process being developed to other processes from a given repository.

Our autocompletion engine works following the procedure illustrated in Fig. 2. The unfinished process at the top is an excerpt from a process taken from the university admissions dataset [1] and represents the application procedure for master students in Frankfurt university.

The autocompletion engine may suggest the modeler that is developing this process which is the most likely next element to the last one added. In our example, the last element is the task "Rank students according to GPA and the test results", marked with a bold outline. To autocomplete the process, our algorithm first traverses all the sub-processes of a predefined length leading to that specific task. In the example, we consider sub-processes of length three, resulting in the two paths marked with a star and a diamond. Next, we convert each sub-process into a paragraph of text by concatenating the labels and type names of the elements in the sub-process.

Third, for each paragraph, we compute its vector embedding, such that an arbitrary length text is converted to a fixed length numerical vector. Then, each computed embedding of the target process is compared to the embeddings of all the sub-processes from an existing dataset of processes (exemplified at the bottom of the figure), via a similarity metric. Finally, if there are sub-processes in the input dataset that are semantically similar to the sub-process of interest, the top matching recommendations are shown to the user. These recommendations are the elements that appeared in the dataset for other universities right after the most similar paths (that is, were connected to those paths via a connector).

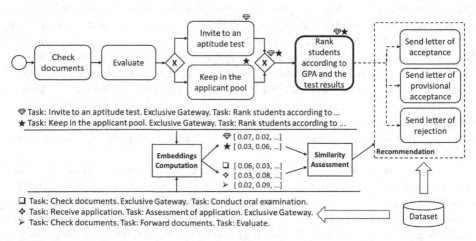

Fig. 2. Overview of our approach for the autocompletion of a partial process model. Based on the most semantically similar paths in the input dataset, up to 3 top recommendations are shown to the modeler.

3 Preliminaries

Finding similarities between processes is key to our autocompletion strategy, that is fully explained in Sect. 4. This section serves as a background on how we apply vector representations of text to our problem. We also provide formal definitions for concepts used throughout the rest of the paper.

3.1 Universal Sentence Encoder, Embeddings and Similarity

The way we convert paragraphs of text into vectors relies on a pre-trained deep learning model called the Universal Sentence Encoder (USE) [7]. USE encodes text as high-dimensional numerical vectors that can be used for text classification, semantic similarity assessment, clustering, and other tasks that involve natural language processing (NLP). Intuitively, embeddings are a mathematical representation of the semantics of the sentences.

The main advantage of embeddings is that sentences of an arbitrary length are transformed into vectors of real numbers of the same length. This enables comparison of pairs of sentences by means of computing a similarity score between vectors representing the sentences.

Let U be the USE model [7]. Given an input sentence p, which is a list of words in English, we define *sentence embedding* as follows:

Definition 1 (Sentence and paragraph embedding). *For an input sentence (or paragraph) p, the embedding of p is given by $\boldsymbol{p} = U(p)$.*

Where $U(p) \in \mathbb{R}^n$, and n is the length of the embedding vector. Note that a paragraph that contains multiple sentences will be also encoded as a vector of length n.

Once sentences are encoded as vectors, we can calculate how close those vectors are to each other, and use this information as a measure of how semantically similar the corresponding texts are. Cosine similarity is often used in NLP to compare embeddings, and is defined as follows:

Definition 2 (Cosine similarity). *Given embeddings $\boldsymbol{p}$ and $\boldsymbol{q}$ for two sentences p and q, the cosine similarity is computed as:*

$$\cos(\boldsymbol{p}, \boldsymbol{q}) = \frac{\boldsymbol{p} \cdot \boldsymbol{q}}{\|\boldsymbol{p}\| \|\boldsymbol{q}\|} = \frac{\sum_{i=1}^{n} p_i q_i}{\sqrt{\sum_{i=1}^{n} p_i^2} \sqrt{\sum_{i=1}^{n} q_i^2}} \tag{1}$$

We now define a similarity matrix between two sets of sentence embeddings $X = (\mathbf{x_1}, ..., \mathbf{x_r})$ and $Y = (\mathbf{y_1}, ..., \mathbf{y_m})$:

Definition 3 (Similarity matrix). $M(X, Y) = (cos(\mathbf{x_i}, \mathbf{y_j})), i = 1, ..., r; j = 1, ..., m$, *where* $\mathbf{x_1}, ..., \mathbf{x_r}, \mathbf{y_1}, ..., \mathbf{y_m}$ *are embedding vectors.*

3.2   Process Model

A process consists of a set of elements and connections between those elements, which can be described by a directed graph as follows:

Definition 4 (Process as a directed graph). *Let $G = \{V, E, s, t\}$ where V is a set of elements, E is the set of flows, $s \in V$ is the "start" event at which the process starts, and $t \in V$ is the "end" event at which the process terminates.*

Each node $v \in V$ can represent an event, a gateway used as a decision point, or a non-compound, high-level activity. Each node may have a label and always has a type, that is $v = (label, type)$, whereas, optionally, $label = NULL$.

While making a recommendation for node v, we first need to extract all sub-processes of predefined length that end in v. We then compare these sub-processes to sub-processes extracted from the input dataset to find the most similar ones. We refer to these sub-processes as "slices":

Definition 5 (Slice). *Given a process $G = \{V, E, s, t\}$ and a number $n \in \mathbb{N}$, we say that $S_n = \{V_s, E_s\}$ is a slice of G of length n, if $V_s \subseteq V$, $E_s \subseteq E$, $|V_s| = n$, and S_n is a path graph.*

Note that since S_n is a path graph [4], its nodes can be topologically ordered such that we can later process the labels and the types of the nodes as if they were sentences following one another. We treat each slice as a paragraph of text, comprised of n sentences.

3.3   Process Matching and Element Autocompletion

Our solution makes its recommendations based on the best matching slice found in its input dataset. That is, for the last node v in an incomplete process, it extracts all the slices leading to that node, and for each such slice looks for the most similar slice in the input dataset. The best match is defined as follows:

Definition 6 (Best match). *Given a slice p, the best match to p within the input dataset I is defined as $t = argmax_{q \in I}(cos(\mathbf{p}, \mathbf{q}))$, where $\mathbf{p}$ and $\mathbf{q}$ are the embeddings of slices p and q, respectively.*

Practically, an autocompletion tool offers several options for the user to choose from, therefore we are normally interested to look at the top k matches rather than at the best match only. In such a scenario we choose k matches with the highest similarity score to slices ending in v.

Once the top k matches are identified, our solution produces a list of recommendations for the next element. It does so by looking at the element that followed each one of the matches in the input dataset. Examples of slices and next elements extracted from the process in Fig. 2 are shown in Table 1. In some cases, we may have more than one element following the slice, as we show in the second row of the table.

Table 1. Sample slices of length $n = 3$ for the process in Fig. 2.

Slice: Start Event. Task: Check documents. Task: Evaluate.
Next: Exclusive Gateway
Slice: Task: Check documents. Task: Evaluate. Exclusive Gateway.
Next: [Task: Invite to an aptitude test.; Task: Keep in the applicant pool.]
Slice: Task: Evaluate. Exclusive Gateway. Task: Invite to an aptitude test.
Next: Exclusive Gateway
Slice: Exclusive Gateway. Task: Invite to an aptitude test. Exclusive Gateway.
Next: Task: Rank students according to GPA and the test results

Note that the same match t may occur within multiple processes. In such case, the modeler will receive recommendations based on all of the relevant processes. As an example, consider the following scenario: processes A and B in the input dataset contain the slice $x \rightarrow y \rightarrow z$. However, in A, this slice is connected to node a (that is, $x \rightarrow y \rightarrow z \rightarrow a \subseteq A$), while in B, it is connected to b (that is, $x \rightarrow y \rightarrow z \rightarrow b \subseteq B$). In such a case, if a new process C is being constructed, with $x \rightarrow y \rightarrow z \subseteq C$, then if the user asks for a recommendation on what should follow z, both a and b will be recommended. Formally, we define a recommendation as follows:

Definition 7 (Recommendation). *For a match $t \in I$, we say that the element r is a recommendation, if there is an edge from the last node of t to r in the corresponding process.*

4 Approach

Our solution recommends which elements should be added to a process model that is under construction based on an input dataset that is built from a repository of processes. This dataset contains the embeddings for all the slices of predefined length n extracted from those processes. The construction of the input dataset is done as follows: for each process, we traverse the graph representing the process in a depth-first order, starting from node s, to extract all the slices of length n (see Definition 5). We then compute the embedding vectors for the slices (see Definition 1). For each computed embedding we store additional information comprised of the slice itself, a reference to the process from which this slice was extracted, and the elements that followed the slice in the corresponding process, as in Table 1.

During the autocompletion phase, our solution follows the steps presented in Algorithm 1. It receives as one of its parameters the node v for which it needs to recommend the next element(s). It first determines what are the slices that lead to node v (that is, end in node v). This is done in routine *ExtractSlices* (line 2), which traverses the graph starting from node v backwards, based on the incoming edges. Note that we only attempt to make a recommendation if we have at least one such slice.

`26    M. Goldstein and C. González-Álvarez`

Next, our recommender computes the embedding for each extracted slice. All the embeddings are stored in matrix X (line 7). We then compute the similarity matrix between X and the input set embeddings stored in D (line 9).

Our algorithm proceeds in line 10, where we find the top k matches for the slices from S with *ExtractTopMatches* routine. This routine looks for the best match based on the highest similarity score, records the matching slice and corresponding next-element recommendations, and repeats until k recommendations are collected and presented to the end user. In case that we have the same recommendation for two different matches, we present it only once.

Algorithm 1. Pseudo-code for the autocompletion step. Given process G and element v, recommend what other element(s) should be added to G after v.

1: **function** RECOMMENDELEMENT(G, v, n, k, D) ▷ G - process (graph), v - node in G (element), $n \in \mathbb{N}$ - length, k - maximum number of top recommendations, D - input dataset embeddings

2: $\quad S \leftarrow ExtractSlices(G, v, n)$
    $\qquad\qquad\qquad\qquad$ ▷ Extract slices of length n that terminate in v (Definition 5)

3: $\quad X \leftarrow \emptyset$ $\qquad\qquad\qquad\qquad\qquad\qquad$ ▷ Embeddings for slices in S

4: $\quad R \leftarrow \emptyset$ $\qquad\qquad\qquad\qquad\qquad\qquad$ ▷ Recommended elements

5: $\quad$ **for** $p \in S$ **do**

6: $\quad\quad \mathbf{p} \leftarrow U(p)$ $\qquad\qquad\qquad\qquad$ ▷ Compute embedding (Definition 1)

7: $\quad\quad X \leftarrow X \cup \mathbf{p}$

8: $\quad$ **end for**

9: $\quad M \leftarrow M(X, D)$ $\qquad\qquad$ ▷ Compute similarity matrix (Definition 3)

10: $\quad T \leftarrow ExtractTopMatches(M, k)$ ▷ Extract k most similar entries in D to S

11: $\quad$ **for** $t \in T$ **do**

12: $\quad\quad r \leftarrow$ Get recommendations for t $\qquad\qquad\qquad$ ▷ (Definition 7)

13: $\quad\quad R \leftarrow R \cup r$

14: $\quad$ **end for**

15: $\quad$ **return** R

16: **end function**

---

5 Evaluation

5.1 Datasets

We evaluated our approach on four datasets of process models from different domains. These are summarized in Table 2. The first dataset (labeled `Airport`) comprises 24 processes capturing airport procedures [2]. The second dataset contains 40 processes available from the Integrated Adaptive Cyber Defense (`IACD`) initiative [16]. These processes are used for modeling security automation and orchestration workflows. In `IACD`, almost 85% of the elements are unique, that is, they appear only once in the entire dataset. The third dataset (labeled `Proprietary`) is a collection of proprietary processes used in a product for security orchestration. It resembles the `IACD` dataset and contains 18 models. Unlike

IACD, the processes in that dataset reuse almost one third of the elements among them. The last dataset (Universities) is used to model admission procedures for master students in German universities [1]. The dataset comprises 9 models, with 40% of the identically labeled elements occurring in at least two models.

Table 2. Characterization of the datasets used in the experiments. For each dataset, from left to right, we show its number of processes, the number of elements in each process, how many of the elements are unique and appear only once in the dataset, the number of slices extracted for a length of 3, the average number of elements per process, the percentage of elements that are used in more than one process, and the average number of slices per element.

Dataset	Processes	Elements	Unique	Slices	Elements/Process	Shared elements	Slices/Element
Airport	24	984	655	20241	41	33.5%	20.6
IACD	40	676	571	1191	16.9	15.5%	1.8
Proprietary	18	508	348	1713	28.2	31.5%	3.4
Universities	9	451	272	10759	50.1	40%	23.8

The efficiency of a recommendation system depends heavily on the data distributions of the input dataset and the process that is being developed. Simply put, if the processes are completely unrelated to each other, then it is very difficult to make meaningful suggestions. On the other hand, if the processes share semantic meaning, then our recommendation engine can leverage that and provide useful suggestions to the end-user.

The datasets used in the experiment have quite different characteristics. For example, in IACD only 15.5% of the elements are shared among the processes. Also, the processes in IACD are relatively small, as captured by the "Elements/Process" column, which means that, during the input dataset construction, we can extract only a small number of slices.

In contrast, all of the processes in the Universities dataset cover similar procedures, thus we expect a significant amount of reuse. Even elements with different labels often bear similar meanings, e.g., "Accept" task label is similar to "Send letter of acceptance". The processes here and in the Airport dataset are also larger than in the other two datasets, allowing our autocompletion engine to mine a more diverse input dataset to be used for its recommendations.

Validation Methodology. We use the leave-one-group-out cross-validation technique to evaluate the accuracy of our approach. Each process, in turn, is evaluated against the rest of the processes that serve as the input dataset to mine recommendations from. This gives us an opportunity to use all available process models as an input and as a validation dataset. For each cross-validation fold, we choose a different process model and generate sub-processes with an increasing number of elements, in order to simulate different stages of the model construction. For each sub-process, we also record the next element's type and label that should be recommended (the ground truth). At each evaluation step, we perform the autocompletion step of Algorithm 1 for each one of the sub-processes and obtain different accuracy metrics comparing the top recommendations against the ground truth. In Sect. 5.3 we present the averages of the accuracy metrics that we obtain from the cross-validation folds.

5.2 Metrics

In our evaluation we use two types of metrics; one type focuses on evaluating the precision and recall of the recommendations, and a second type assesses the quality of the predictions that are semantically similar to the ground truth.

Table 3. Cosine similarity, BLEU and METEOR values for sample recommendations and ground truth values from the Universities dataset [1].

Recommendation	Ground truth	Cosine	BLEU	METEOR
Send letter of acceptance	Send letter of provisional acceptance	0.82	0.80	0.91
Attach additional requirements	Collect additional required documents	0.58	0.35	0.60
Send interview invitation	Invite for talk	0.60	0	0.17
Check bachelor's degree	Wait for bachelor's certificate	0.62	0.25	0.16

For the first type, we use precision@k and recall@k [14]. Precision@k is the fraction of elements in the top k recommendations that match the ground truth, while recall@k is the coverage of the ground truth in the top k recommendations. Note that this type of metrics only captures cases where the labels of the elements recommended by our solution match the ground truth precisely. In our experiments we used $k = 3$.

For the second type, we focus on the metrics BLEU [27] and METEOR [23], that are frequently used to evaluate machine translation systems [25]. BLEU is the precision of n-grams of a machine translation's output compared to the ground truth reference. This metric is weighted by a brevity penalty to compensate for recall in overly short translations. METEOR is similar to BLEU but takes explicit ordering of words into account. During its matching computation it also considers translation variability via word inflection variations, synonym and paraphrasing. Additionally, we report the Cosine similarity of the predictions to the ground truth, computed based on Definition 2. This type of metrics captures both exact and similar matches between recommendations and the ground truth.

Table 3 shows values of Cosine similarity, BLEU and METEOR for some sample recommendations to gain intuition on these metrics. Note that higher scores of BLEU, METEOR, and Cosine are correlated with higher semantic similarity of sentences. BLEU and METEOR's range is $[0, 1]$, while Cosine similarity spans from -1 to 1. Values over 0.3 represent understandable to good translations [22] for both BLEU and METEOR; values over 0.4 represent high quality translations, and they exceed 0.5 for very-high quality translations. Values of 0.2 to 0.3 represent cases where one could see the gist of the translation, but it is not very clear.

5.3   Experiments

We first study the effect that the selected slice length has on the quality of the recommendations made by our autocompletion engine. We then compare our solution to a random algorithm that makes recommendations based on the statistical distribution of the elements in the input dataset.

At the beginning, we allowed the algorithms to make predictions based on all available elements in the processes. We learned quickly that the majority of the predictions (over 80%) were for ground truth of end events and gateways. Clearly, one may suggest an autocompletion engine that always suggests to use these two types of elements and get quite good precision and recall. However, this is not very useful for the model designer. We therefore also checked the quality of the suggestions when gateways and end events were excluded from recommendations and the ground truth (we refer to this case as Filtered).

Slice Length Study. We varied the length of the slice from $n = 1$ to $n = 5$ and collected the metrics for each dataset. Figure 3 shows the results of this experiment for the Filtered case. The graphs in the figure plot the slice lengths on the x-axis and metric scores on the y-axis for the five metrics discussed in Sect. 5.2. On average[1], the best results are for a slice length of $n = 3$, although the effect of the slice length on each dataset varies.

For Airport (Fig. 3a) and Universities (Fig. 3d) datasets, our autocompletion engine's accuracy increases and then decreases slightly as the slice gets longer, with the best results observed at $n = 3$. The IACD dataset (Fig. 3b) is the most stable of all the four datasets with respect to the effect of the slice length on the algorithm. For the Proprietary dataset (Fig. 3c) the accuracy improves until $n = 3$ and then remains stable.

For the case where all the elements are taken into consideration[2], slice length of $n = 2$ gives slightly better results than $n = 3$ for some datasets. We use slice of length $n = 3$ throughout the rest of the experiments to enable easy comparison. However, we observe that one may need to carry out a preliminary slice length study for each new domain/dataset to get the best recommendations. This can be done automatically during the input dataset construction process.

Comparison to a Random Algorithm. In this experiment we studied the efficiency of our solution (labeled Slicing) in comparison to an algorithm that autocompletes the process at random (labeled Random). We collected the occurrences of each element in the dataset, and randomly selected the top recommendations based on the statistical distribution of the elements. Thus, elements that occurred more frequently had a higher chance of being selected.

We set the slice length for our algorithm to $n = 3$ based on the previous experiment. The random algorithm's performance is agnostic to this choice, as it takes no slices into account. We executed the experiment with Random 30 times, and computed averages over all runs.

---

[1] Computed as average over all four datasets, but not shown due to space limitation.
[2] Not visualized due to space limitation.

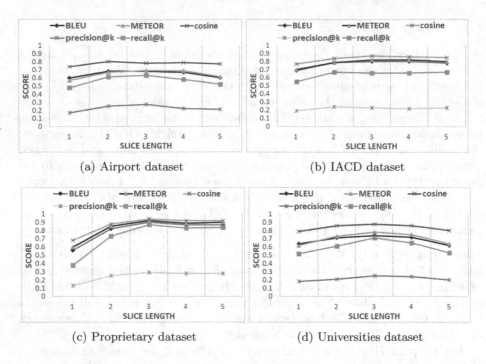

(a) Airport dataset

(b) IACD dataset

(c) Proprietary dataset

(d) Universities dataset

Fig. 3. Evaluation metrics for slice lengths of 1 to 5, $k = 3$, for `Filtered` case.

The results of this experiment are shown in Table 4 and Fig. 4. Table 4 gives the values of the metrics computed for our algorithm and for the random algorithm, for the two different configurations (including all the nodes, or filtering out gateways and end events). We use the $\pm$ notation to present the average and the standard deviation for each metric. Figure 4 shows the ratio between the averages of the metrics computed for the two algorithms for easier comparison.[3]

When all the elements are taken into account, our algorithm achieves scores over 0.56 for `BLEU` and `METEOR` metrics, which indicates a very good match between the ground truth and the recommendations [22]. `Cosine` similarity is also high, especially for the `Universities` dataset. Our algorithm performs much better than the random algorithm with respect to `BLEU`, `METEOR` and `Cosine` similarity. It also has a much higher precision and recall. Note that since at every step we recommend the top 3 elements, then a precision of 0.29 (for the `Universities` dataset, with all the elements, and for the `Proprietary` dataset, in the `Filtered` case) means that, in average, we suggest one element out of 3 correctly almost always. The random algorithm reaches up to 0.13 precision when all the elements are taken into account. There are many gateways and end elements in both the input and the validation datasets, so the random algorithm suggests them frequently, and, therefore, gets many accurate predictions.

---

[3] Some precision and recall values are rounded to 0 when only two decimal places are used. For such cases, we use higher precision values to compute the ratio.

Table 4. Evaluation metrics computed for `Slicing` and `Random`, for all the elements (top half) and for filtered out gateways and end events (bottom half).

All elements								
Dataset/	Airport		IACD		Proprietary		Universities	
Metric	Slicing	Random	Slicing	Random	Slicing	Random	Slicing	Random
BLEU	0.56 ± 0.27	0.37 ± 0.29	0.71 ± 0.33	0.29 ± 0.22	0.7 ± 0.29	0.37 ± 0.28	0.64 ± 0.24	0.44 ± 0.28
METEOR	0.63 ± 0.4	0.34 ± 0.38	0.75 ± 0.34	0.26 ± 0.26	0.81 ± 0.33	0.4 ± 0.37	0.77 ± 0.34	0.44 ± 0.39
Cosine	0.8 ± 0.31	0.6 ± 0.34	0.82 ± 0.27	0.43 ± 0.23	0.89 ± 0.24	0.63 ± 0.31	0.87 ± 0.26	0.64 ± 0.32
precision@3	0.21 ± 0.18	0.09 ± 0.15	0.22 ± 0.17	0.02 ± 0.08	0.28 ± 0.14	0.1 ± 0.15	0.29 ± 0.18	0.13 ± 0.16
recall@3	0.61 ± 0.49	0.27 ± 0.44	0.63 ± 0.48	0.06 ± 0.25	0.81 ± 0.33	0.3 ± 0.46	0.78 ± 0.34	0.4 ± 0.49
Filtered								
Dataset/	Airport		IACD		Proprietary		Universities	
Metric	Slicing	Random	Slicing	Random	Slicing	Random	Slicing	Random
BLEU	0.68 ± 0.32	0.3 ± 0.13	0.8 ± 0.28	0.32 ± 0.18	0.9 ± 0.24	0.21 ± 0.2	0.74 ± 0.28	0.35 ± 0.21
METEOR	0.69 ± 0.38	0.15 ± 0.14	0.82 ± 0.27	0.29 ± 0.22	0.92 ± 0.21	0.21 ± 0.23	0.78 ± 0.34	0.2 ± 0.21
Cosine	0.78 ± 0.27	0.4 ± 0.14	0.87 ± 0.21	0.44 ± 0.18	0.94 ± 0.16	0.39 ± 0.2	0.88 ± 0.21	0.47 ± 0.18
precision@3	0.27 ± 0.27	0 ± 0.04	0.23 ± 0.17	0.01 ± 0.06	0.29 ± 0.12	0.01 ± 0.06	0.25 ± 0.18	0.01 ± 0.06
recall@3	0.63 ± 0.48	0.01 ± 0.11	0.66 ± 0.47	0.03 ± 0.17	0.87 ± 0.34	0.03 ± 0.17	0.71 ± 0.45	0.03 ± 0.17

When we narrow down the analysis only to activity tasks, we learn that our algorithm outperforms the random algorithm for all the datasets, as witnessed by all the metrics. Its precision is up to 64x higher than that of the random algorithm, with the recall having up to 63x improvement.

5.4 Findings

We can distill the following key findings from our empirical evaluation:

- *Our autocompletion engine is applicable to various domains*: The recommendations obtained for the presented datasets are quite accurate as all the metrics attest to. Precision of 0.21 to 0.29 means that in average one out of three to five suggestions is correct. Since each recommendation contains three options, it means that most recommendations include one exact match to the ground truth. A recall of up to 0.87% indicates that we manage to cover the majority of the expected elements in our recommendations. Even if a suggestion is not an exact match to the ground truth, the high values of the BLEU, METEOR, and Cosine metrics indicate a significant similarity between them.
- *Slicing window length has a mild impact on the quality of autocompletion*: The results from our first experiment show that our recommendation engine can indeed get better predictions for some slice sizes. We therefore recommend tuning this parameter during the input dataset construction procedure for each new dataset. However, metrics measurement changes are not drastic enough to claim that this parameter has a significant impact on our algorithm.
- *Semantic similarity based evaluation metrics exhibit mostly high correlation among them*: The results from both the slice length study and the comparison of `Slicing` to `Random` show that the METEOR and BLEU metrics have a Pearson correlation of over 0.85, except when the `Random` algorithm is applied in the

`Filtered` case. We witnessed similar results for `METEOR` and `Cosine`, with a Pearson correlation of over 0.88. The semantic similarity based metrics had a low correlation to the metrics used to evaluate exact matches.

The main difficulty in selecting the right metrics is related to the fact that none of them are tuned specifically to the problem at hand. For example, measuring precision based on exact matches does not reveal the full potential of our algorithm, as predictions similar to the ground truth (e.g., "Accept" versus "Send letter of acceptance") are not considered as a match. A fruitful area of future research would be to study to what extent these metrics correlate with the feedback of subject matter experts on the quality of the recommendations.

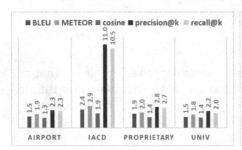 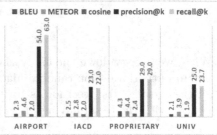

(a) Slicing/Random ratio, all elements   (b) Slicing/Random ratio, filtered

Fig. 4. Ratio between the values of the metrics measured for the `Slicing` versus the `Random` algorithm. `UNIV` stands for the `Universities` dataset.

5.5   Threats to Validity

Several threats to validity may affect this study. Due to lack of evaluation on open source datasets, we found it difficult to compare our results to those made by other researchers. We hope our work can serve as a baseline for such comparisons.

During the embeddings computation, we adopted a version of `USE` that was only trained on English sentences. This means that we can not apply it for models in other languages. In the future, we plan to investigate whether multi-language models or other encoders may improve our autocompletion solution.

Another threat is related to slice extraction, which takes only path graphs into account. Our approach inherently misses some information hidden in complex graph structures. Therefore, it may fail to detect matches between subprocesses that represent the same behavior but have a different structure. We could mitigate this threat with a pre-processing step that normalizes equivalent model patterns to a predefined standard [18].

6   Related Work

Similarity between process models has been a subject of interest for a while now [28, 32]. The main goal of this line of research is to determine if two processes are similar to each other, or implement a query to find a process, rather than recommending how to autocomplete a process.

One of the first attempts to combine structural and semantical information while assessing models similarity was accomplished with BPMN-Q [3]. BPMN-Q allows users to formulate structure-related process model queries and uses Word-Net [26] knowledge to make the search semantically aware. While some works also relied on WordNet for word-to-word semantic similarity [29], others [37] proposed domain-specific ontologies that represent processes to solve that task.

Later, the concept of a causal footprint, which is a collection of behavioral constraints imposed by a process model, was introduced in [33]. These constraints are converted into vectors and are compared via a similarity score.

Some researchers focused on detecting similarities between processes based on graph edit distances between them [10, 17], while others [30] combined techniques related to the structure of graphs with per-element similarity.

Process similarity techniques also enable process autocompletion. One such example is the tool FlowRecommender [39], that suggests next elements based on pattern matching for graphs. It was evaluated on a synthetic dataset and only focused on validating the structural accuracy of the prediction. As an improvement to this technique, the authors proposed to traverse the process graphs, and compare them via a string edit distance similarity metric [24]. The approach focused on finding isomorphic graphs when labels had to match precisely.

In a more recent work [34], the authors used bag-of-words to predict the top k most similar models from a repository to a process that is being modeled. They focused only on structural comparisons to detect differences between models [35]. Unfortunately, the authors did not evaluate their approach on any open dataset, making it difficult to compare their approach to ours.

Yu et al. used graph embeddings to search processes with a query that contained arbitrary text [38]. This work focused on a single node matching against the search query. Earlier, transfer learning enabled search and retrieval of processes from logs [19], where unique content-bearing workflow motifs were extracted from the set of processes. These motifs were treated as features and then each process was represented as a vector in this feature space. Based on this representation, similarity metrics can be computed between processes, and used in the future to improve our solution.

In an alternative method for encoding process models as vectors [9], De Koninck et al. developed representation learning architectures for embedding trace logs and models to enable comparison between them. The learned architecture focused on the structural properties of processes, rather than their semantics.

Finally, Burgueño et al. [6] proposed to use contextual information taken from process description to auto-generate the process. Indeed such documentation, when available, could be used to improve our autocompletion technique.

7 Conclusions and Future Work

In this paper, we presented a novel technique for design-time next-task recommendation in business process modeling that is based on semantic similarity of processes. Our solution supports business modelers by autocompleting the next element(s) during process construction. We used a state-of-the-art NLP technique that detects similarities between sentences and adopted it to the domain of business processes models. This allowed us to overcome the challenge of having little data to train a traditional machine learning recommender model.

Our evaluation shows that the suggestions made by our recommendation engine are accurate for datasets with different characteristics and from different domains. Moreover, our solution is suitable for applications in commercial products, as the evaluation on a proprietary dataset shows.

In the future, we plan to conduct a user study where process modelers will rate the predictions made by our tool. This will allow us to better assess the efficiency of our approach in practical settings and also learn which metrics are most suitable for the evaluation of other process recommendation systems.

Another interesting direction would be to investigate how the BPMN execution semantics could be taken into account. For instance, we could analyze execution traces of processes from the input dataset and encode the traces in addition to paths.

References

1. Antunes, G., Bakhshandeh, M., et al.: The process model matching contest 2015, GI-Edition. Lecture Notes in Informatics, Proceedings, vol. 248, pp. 127–155 (2015)
2. APROMORE: An advanced process model repository (2021). https://git.io/Jmgci
3. Awad, A., Polyvyanyy, A., Weske, M.: Semantic querying of business process models. In: 12th International IEEE Enterprise Distributed Object Computing Conference, pp. 85–94. IEEE (2008)
4. Bondy, J.A.: Graph Theory With Applications. Elsevier Science Ltd., New York (1976). GBR
5. Born, M., Brelage, C., Markovic, I., Pfeiffer, D., Weber, I.: Auto-completion for executable business process models. In: Ardagna, D., Mecella, M., Yang, J. (eds.) BPM 2008. LNBIP, vol. 17, pp. 510–515. Springer, Heidelberg (2009). https://doi.org/10.1007/978-3-642-00328-8_51
6. Burgueño, L., Clarisó, R., Li, S., Gérard, S., Cabot, J.: A NLP-based architecture for the autocompletion of partial domain models, November 2020
7. Cer, D., Yang, Y., yi Kong, S., Hua, N., Limtiaco, N., John, R.S., et al.: Universal sentence encoder (2018)
8. Cornea, R.C., Weininger, N.B.: Providing autocomplete suggestions (2014), US Patent 8,645,825
9. De Koninck, P., vanden Broucke, S., De Weerdt, J.: act2vec, trace2vec, log2vec, and model2vec: representation learning for business processes. In: Weske, M., Montali, M., Weber, I., vom Brocke, J. (eds.) BPM 2018. LNCS, vol. 11080, pp. 305–321. Springer, Cham (2018). https://doi.org/10.1007/978-3-319-98648-7_18

10. Dijkman, R., Dumas, M., García-Bañuelos, L.: Graph matching algorithms for business process model similarity search. In: Dayal, U., Eder, J., Koehler, J., Reijers, H.A. (eds.) BPM 2009. LNCS, vol. 5701, pp. 48–63. Springer, Heidelberg (2009). https://doi.org/10.1007/978-3-642-03848-8_5
11. Fellmann, M., Zarvic, N., Metzger, D., Koschmider, A.: Requirements catalog for business process modeling recommender systems. In: Wirtschaftsinformatik, pp. 393–407 (2015)
12. Fellmann, M., Zarvić, N., Thomas, O.: Business processes modeling recommender systems: User expectations and empirical evidence. Complex Syst. Inf. Model. Q. **14**, 64–79 (2018)
13. Floridi, L., Chiriatti, M.: GPT-3: its nature, scope, limits, and consequences. Mind. Mach. **30**(4), 681–694 (2020). https://doi.org/10.1007/s11023-020-09548-1
14. Hawking, D., Craswell, N., Bailey, P., Griffihs, K.: Measuring search engine quality. Inf. Retr. **4**(1), 33–59 (2001). https://doi.org/10.1023/A:1011468107287
15. Hornung, T., Koschmider, A., Oberweis, A.: Rule-based autocompletion of business process models. In: CAiSE Forum, vol. 247, pp. 222–232. Citeseer (2007)
16. IACD playbooks, workflows, and local instance examples (2021). https://www.iacdautomate.org/playbook-and-workflow-examples
17. Ivanov, S., Kalenkova, A.A., van der Aalst, W.M.: BPMNDiffViz: a tool for BPMN models comparison. In: BPM (Demos), pp. 35–39 (2015)
18. Kluza, K., Kaczor, K.: Overview of BPMN model equivalences: towards normalization of bpmn diagrams. In: 8th Workshop on Knowledge Engineering and Software Engineering (KESE2012), vol. 28, pp. 38–45 (2012)
19. Koohi-Var, T., Zahedi, M.: Cross-domain graph based similarity measurement of workflows. J. Big Data **5**(1), 1–16 (2018). https://doi.org/10.1186/s40537-018-0127-6
20. Koschmider, A., Hornung, T., Oberweis, A.: Recommendation-based editor for business process modeling. Data Knowl. Eng. **70**(6), 483–503 (2011)
21. Koschmider, A., Song, M., Reijers, H.A.: Social software for business process modeling. J. Inf. Technol. **25**(3), 308–322 (2010). https://doi.org/10.1057/jit.2009.21
22. Lavi, A.: Evaluating the output of machine translation systems. In: AMTA Tutorial (2010)
23. Lavie, A., Agarwal, A.: Meteor: an automatic metric for mt evaluation with high levels of correlation with human judgments. In: Proceedings of the Second Workshop on Statistical Machine Translation, pp. 228–231 (2007)
24. Li, Y., Cao, B., Xu, L., Yin, J., Deng, S., Yin, Y., Wu, Z.: An efficient recommendation method for improving business process modeling. IEEE Trans. Industr. Inf. **10**(1), 502–513 (2014)
25. Mathur, N., Wei, J., Freitag, M., Ma, Q., Bojar, O.: Results of the WMT20 metrics shared task. In: Fifth Conference on Machine Translation, pp. 688–725 (2020)
26. Miller, G.A.: Wordnet: a lexical database for English. Commun. ACM **38**(11), 39–41 (1995)
27. Papineni, K., Roukos, S., Ward, T., Zhu, W.J.: BLEU: a method for automatic evaluation of machine translation. In: Proceedings of the 40th annual meeting of the Association for Computational Linguistics, pp. 311–318 (2002)
28. Schoknecht, A., Thaler, T., Fettke, P., Oberweis, A., Laue, R.: Similarity of business process models-a state-of-the-art analysis. ACM Comput. Surv. **50**(4), 1–33 (2017)
29. Shahzad, K., Pervaz, I., Nawab, A.: Wordnet based semantic similarity measures for process model matching. In: BIR Workshops, pp. 33–44 (2018)
30. Starlinger, J., Brancotte, B., Cohen-Boulakia, S., Leser, U.: Similarity search for scientific workflows. Proc. VLDB Endow. **7**(12), 1143–1154 (2014)

31. Tab9: Ai smart compose for your code (2021). https://www.tabnine.com/
32. Thaler, T., Schoknecht, A., Fettke, P., Oberweis, A., Laue, R.: A comparative analysis of business process model similarity measures. In: Dumas, M., Fantinato, M. (eds.) BPM 2016. LNBIP, vol. 281, pp. 310–322. Springer, Cham (2017). https://doi.org/10.1007/978-3-319-58457-7_23
33. van Dongen, B., Dijkman, R., Mendling, J.: Measuring similarity between business process models. In: Seminal Contributions to Information Systems Engineering, pp. 405–419. Springer, Heidelberg (2013). https://doi.org/10.1007/978-3-642-36926-1_33
34. Wang, J., Gui, S., Cao, B.: A process recommendation method using bag-of-fragments. Int. J. Intell. IoT Comput. **1**(1), 32–42 (2019)
35. Wang, J., Lu, J., Cao, B., Fan, J., Tan, D.: KS-Diff: a key structure based difference detection method for process models. In: IEEE International Conference on Web Services (ICWS), pp. 408–412. IEEE (2019)
36. Wieloch, K., Filipowska, A., Kaczmarek, M.: Autocompletion for business process modelling. In: Abramowicz, W., Maciaszek, L., Węcel, K. (eds.) BIS 2011. LNBIP, vol. 97, pp. 30–40. Springer, Heidelberg (2011). https://doi.org/10.1007/978-3-642-25370-6_4
37. Yongsiriwit, K., Sellami, M., Gaaloul, W.: Semantic process fragments matching to assist the development of process variants. In: 2015 IEEE International Conference on Services Computing, pp. 712–719 (2015)
38. Yu, X., Wu, W., Liao, X.: Workflow recommendation based on graph embedding. In: 2020 IEEE World Congress on Services (SERVICES), pp. 89–94 (2020)
39. Zhang, J., Liu, Q., Xu, K.: Flowrecommender: a workflow recommendation technique for process provenance. In: Proceedings of the 8th Australasian Data Mining Conference (AusDM 2009). ACS Press (2009)

DMN 1.0 Verification Capabilities: An Analysis of Current Tool Support

Carl-Christian Grohé, Carl Corea$^{(\boxtimes)}$, and Patrick Delfmann

University of Koblenz-Landau, Koblenz, Germany
{ccgrohe,ccorea,delfmann}@uni-koblenz.de

Abstract. While the Decision Model and Notation standard (DMN) is evolving into an increasingly popular standard for modelling decision logic, a wealth of recent research unfortunately shows that DMN modelling is prone to various types of human modelling errors. As such errors may lead to incorrect decision-making or even compliance breaches, this raises a strong need for modelling tools to offer error verification capabilities, that can pin-point potential modelling errors and subsequently alert the user. Currently, it is however still unclear to which extent the state-of-the-art modelling tools can detect these errors. Such insights are however strongly needed to assess the current support for modellers in the quality assurance of DMN models, and to guide future research. In this report, we therefore conduct an in-depth DMN tool analysis in regard to DMN verification capabilities. Our results indicate that the current coverage of verification capabilities in industrial tools is alarmingly low, and there needs to be urgent work on extending existing approaches.

Keywords: BPMN tool analysis · Decision Model and Notation (DMN) · DMN verification · Modeling errors

1 Introduction

As a close counterpart to BPMN, the Decision Model and Notation standard (DMN)[1] is receiving increasing popularity for modelling company decision-logic. While the modelling of decision-logic can be conducted in an intuitive and graphical manner, a wealth of recent research indicates DMN modelling is prone to various types of human modelling errors, such as overlapping rules or missing rules in the decision-tables [1,9,18]. For example, BATOULIS AND WESKE [1] reported on a case study with a large insurance company, where those authors found that the analyzed rules contained overlaps. This raises a strong need for modelling tools to offer verification capabilities that can pin-point such errors and subsequently alert the user. However, as numerous possible DMN error types

This research is part of the research project "Handling Inconsistencies in Business Process Modeling", which is funded by the German Research Association (reference number: DE1983/9-1).

[1] https://www.omg.org/spec/DMN/About-DMN/.

A. Polyvyanyy et al. (Eds.): BPM Forum 2021, LNBIP 427, pp. 37–53, 2021.
https://doi.org/10.1007/978-3-030-85440-9_3

have been proposed in recent works, it is currently unclear to which extent current modelling tools can detect these errors. This information would however be essential to ensure that current tools are actually capable to sufficiently support modellers at design-time. In this report, we therefore conduct an in-depth tool analysis to investigate the current support of DMN error verification capabilities in state-of-the-art modelling tools. To this aim, we conduct a tool search to identify prominent DMN modelling tools, and subsequently assess these tools w.r.t. their respective DMN verification capabilities. Based on our tool analysis, we compare the capabilities of current tools and identify research gaps to guide the future development of modelling tools.

A further problem in regard to assessing DMN tools is that while various works have proposed different types of possible modelling errors that can occur in DMN, there is currently no comprehensive "catalogue" of all possible DMN error types. Again, such an overview would be needed to assess the capabilities offered by current tools, e.g. as a basis for a tool analysis. Therefore, we also propose a novel classification of DMN error types based on a literature synthesis.

The contributions of this work are as follows:

- **Classification of DMN error types.** We present a novel classification of DMN error types on the basis of a literature analysis (Sect. 2).
- **Tool Support.** We then identify state-of-the-art modelling tools and test to which extent these tools support the verification of the introduced error types (Sect. 4). Our test approach method is presented in Sect. 3.
- **Research Agenda.** Based on the tool analysis, we identify current research gaps and propose a research agenda to guide the future development of DMN/ BPMN modelling tools (Sect. 4.2).

2   Background

In this section, we provide the research background on the DMN standard, as well as error types that can occur in DMN decision models.

2.1   DMN 1.0 Standard

The Decision Model and Notation (DMN) is an OMG standard for modelling operational decision-logic. DMN decision models are constituted of two different levels, namely a *decision requirements level* (which specifies the general elements of the decision making and their relations), and a *decision logic level* (which specifies the actual decision logic via decision tables).

Figure 1 shows the decision requirements level of an exemplary decision model to determine the creditworthiness of customers in a loan application process. The depicted graph structure is also referred to as a *decision requirements diagram* (DRD). A central concept in DRDs is a *decision*. A DRD decision requires a certain *input* and yields a corresponding *output*. The respective inputs can be either specific values (represented via a *data input node*), or can be derived by antecedent (sub)decisions (that themselves are dependent on their inputs and pass their output as a "new" input to following decisions). For example, in Fig. 1, the top-level decision for credithworthyness (1) has two inputs. The first input is a direct data input node for the customer age (2). The second input is information on whether the customer id was found on a blacklist, which is derived from a subdecision (3), the decision of which is then passed to the top-level decision (4).

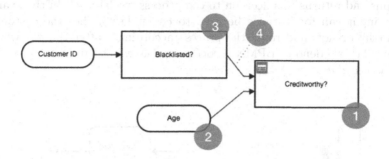

Fig. 1. Decision requirements level for an exemplary decision model.

For every (sub)decision, the concrete decision logic can be encoded by means of decision tables. For example, Fig. 2 shows the decision logic corresponding to the top-level decision (*Creditworthy?*) from Fig. 1. The decision table is subdivided into inputs (1) and outputs (2). Corresponding to the DRD, the decision table has two inputs, i.e., whether the customer was found in a blacklist and the customer age. Here, input and output columns have a predefined datatype, e.g. integer or boolean (3). The two rules in the shown decision table can be understood such that a customer who was not found on a blacklist and is at least 21 years of age is considered as credithworthy, and a customer who was blacklisted is not seen as credithworthy, regardless of age (4). For data types such as integers or dates, a wide variety of comparison operators such as $[<, >, \leq, \geq]$ or ranges can be used to specify the exact premise. On a further note, it is also possible to define a list of predefined values, i.e., a list of values that can be used to populate individual cells.

Creditworthy?	Hit Policy:	Unique		
When		And		Then
Blacklisted?	1	Age	2	Out 2
boolean		integer 3		boolean
1 false		>= 21		true
2 true	4	-		false
+	-		-	

Fig. 2. Exemplary decision table corresponding to the DRD in Fig. 1.

DMN models can be integrated with BPMN models, with the goal that the decision logic is abstracted from the process models. To this aim, *business rule tasks* can be annotated with an underlying decision model. For example, Fig. 3 shows an exemplary BPMN process model. As can be seen, the task before the XOR-gateway is a business rule task (1), which in the example is meant to be annotated with the decision model introduced above. During process execution, the case-dependent facts (e.g., a customer loan application) are passed to the decision model at run-time (2). Then, the decision model computes a corresponding output and returns this decision to the process model level. In the example, the user input can for instance be used to conclude whether the customer is creditworthy or not, and route the process accordingly after the gateway (3). Following [11], we denote (BPMN) process models which are linked to decision models as *decision-aware process models*.

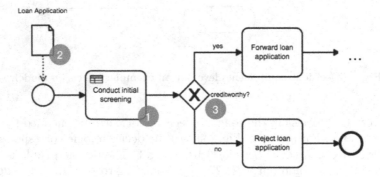

Fig. 3. Exemplary decision-aware process model.

While DMN provides a rich standard on how to *represent* decisions, the actual contents of the decision models are still the responsibility of human modellers. In this context, human modelling errors are widely acknowledged as a core problem for organizations [9]. Intuitively, many different forms of errors can occur on all the introduced levels (DRD-level, decision logic level, decision-aware process model level), or even in-between these levels. For example, numerous works such as [1,5,18] have discussed potential modelling errors in decision tables, e.g. *overlapping* rules or *missing* rules. For instance, in the exemplary decision table from Fig. 2, a rule is missing for the case that the customer was not blacklisted but is younger than 21. In such a case, no decision-making would be possible. Furthermore, changes to any of the introduced artifacts, e.g. DRD or decision tables, can induce inconsistencies between the different levels of the decision model. For example, assume a modeller deletes a decision input on the decision requirements level. This input must also be deleted in the corresponding decision table, as there is otherwise a mismatch between these two levels. This aspect is especially relevant for the synchronization of process models and decision models. For instance, if an input is deleted from the process model (e.g., the loan application in the above example), this input must also be deleted from the decision model, as otherwise the decision might not be executable at run-time.

To conquer the problem of modelling errors in decision models, verifying the correctness of decision models has been a core focus in practice and academia. Essentially, this relates to developing means for ensuring error-freeness within the decision models (resp. the decision-aware process models) [9]. However, as there can be many different types of errors (cf. the above discussion), this is far from being an easy task. In the following, we present a discussion of current DMN verification techniques.

2.2   DMN Verification Capabilities

In the context of verifying the correctness of decision models, various works have investigated different aspects regarding the verification of certain error types, cf. e.g. [7,9] for an overview. The ability to verify (the presence of) certain error types is also referred to as a *verification capability*. While the existing works can be seen as beneficial in regard to supporting modellers, a core problem with research in this regard is the lack of a standardized classification of DMN error types/verification capabilities. That is, there exists no standard definition or overview of existing verification capabilities. This is however highly problematic from both an academic as well as practical standpoint, as it impedes to ensure that an approach or a tool offers (all) important verification capabilities. In this work, we will not claim to provide a "gold-standard" classification of DMN verification capabilities, yet, we present a novel classification which merges existing classifications, as a basis for our tool analysis. In a previous work[13], we have identified two classifications of concrete error types, namely [18, 20]. Furthermore, in own work by the authors of this paper[13][2], a classification of concrete error types is presented. In the following, we therefore develop a more comprehensive classification by unifying the error types presented in those works. The resulting classification framework is provided in Fig. 4.

Regarding error types in DMN decision models, we can identify three categories in which errors can occur:

- **Decision logic level errors.** Errors on the level of decision tables, e.g., overlapping rules.
- **Decision requirements level errors.** Errors on the level of the decision requirements diagram, e.g., unwanted circularity of the DRD graph, or mismatches between the DRD graph and the underlying decision tables.
- **Decision-aware process model level errors.** Errors with the integration between the DMN model and the BPMN model, e.g., mismatches between specified data inputs.

An early classification of decision table anomalies is proposed by Vanthienen et al. [20], as shown in Fig. 4. This work distinguishes intra-table anomalies and

---

[2] https://cloud.uni-koblenz-landau.de/s/SYGKdX3fs7CwNH7.

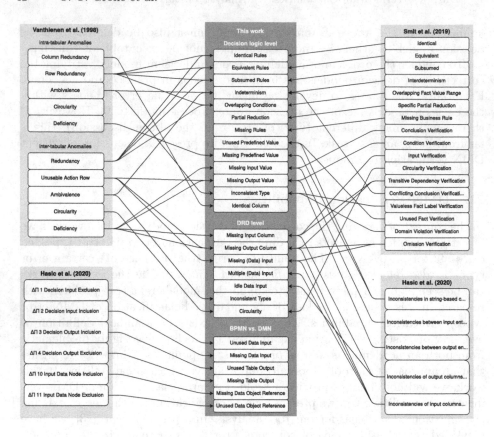

Fig. 4. Classification of error types, based on the classifications in [13,18,20].

inter-table anomalies, the former relating to errors within a single table, and the latter referring to issues arising from the relationship between multiple tables.

In [18], Smit et al. present a classification based on qualitative research with industrial partners. They conducted expert interviews to derive error types which were seen as relevant from a practitioner's viewpoint. The classification by Smit et al. [18] presents novel error types, such as missing rules. Also, it decomposes some errors presented by Vanthienen et al. [20] into more fine-grained error types, as expert opinions deemed it appropriate to view such errors at a different level of granularity. For instance, where Vanthienen et al. [20] identifies an error type of *redundant rows*, Smit et al. [18] distinguishes the concept of redundant rows into the subconcepts of *complete redundancy* (identical rules), *redundancy due to subsumption* and *semantic redundancy*.

Finally, in our own previous work [13], we identified further inconsistency types which can arise in decision models (resp. decision-aware process models) during the application of changes to the decision model.

Analysing the classifications discovered from literature, it can be seen that the existing classifications share many commonalities, e.g., identical error types, or more fine-grained versions of certain error types from other classifications. Subsequently, we synthesised a novel classification, merging all error types from the considered classifications into a unified view, shown in Fig. 4. Our proposed classification presents a comprehensive overview of 26 DMN error types discussed in academia, grouped into the three levels of the decision logic level, the decision requirements level, and the decision-aware process model level. Due to space limitations, we omit a discussion of the 26 individual verification capabilities and refer the reader to the supplementary document for detailed information[3].

In this section, we have presented a base classification of error types in DMN models. Regardless of the error type, recent evidence from the field suggests that DMN modelling is prone to human modelling errors in general [1,18]. Therefore, current state-of-the-art modelling tools should support the introduced verification capabilities in Fig. 4, in order to support modellers by pin-pointing modelers as a basis for re-modelling and improving decision models. In the following, we therefore assess the current tool support of DMN verification capabilities.

3   Research Methodology

The research aim of this work is to analyze to which extent current state-of-the-art modelling tools are capable to detect different DMN error types. Consequently, we performed a tool analysis based on the method of black-box-testing [16]. In this section, we present our research methodology, including the tool search, tool selection criteria and the concrete test approach.

3.1   Tool Search

Following the suggestions on tool search in [19], concrete DMN tools were researched via a keyword-based search online and a search in seminal software databases for the BPM sector. As suggested in [21], we applied quick-searches via Google as a starting point for our research. Here, we were able to identify seven pertinent software databases and catalogues, namely http://openrules.com, http://dmn-tck.io, https://bpmtips.com/, https://methodandstyle.com, http://sourceforge.net?q=dmn, https://www.openhub.net/ and https://bpm-confere nce.org. Using concept-mapping techniques based on the initial quick-searches, we derived the keywords of *"DMN Tool"*, *"DMN Model(l)er"*, *"DMN database"*, *"DMN Tool database"*, *"BPMN Tools DMN support"* and *"DMN Checker"*. These keywords were thus applied in a free Google search as well as the identified software databases. For the free google search, the first 15 search pages were considered as a design-choice. In result, our search returned a total of 33 potential tools. The full list of all 33 identified tools, including sources, can be found online[4].

We then assessed the identified tools for their suitability to be included in this study. To this aim, we defined the following inclusion criteria for tool selection:

---

[3] https://cloud.uni-koblenz-landau.de/s/yRbQWTiBtE9ZBFq.
[4] https://bit.ly/3omxoQB.

- **DMN Support.** The application must support the DMN standard as defined by the OMG specification. This is a relevant criterion to ensure that the analyzed tools can be used to verify DMN models, as some tools use other standards (that are however not compatible with DMN models).
- **Availability.** The application must be open-source or offer a free trial version. This was a necessary requirement as it was not feasible to attain commercial licenses due to funding constraints. Also, this requirement ensures that the analyzed tools can be directly used by practitioners, e.g. especially for small or medium sized companies, should they fit company needs.
- **Graphical Interface.** The application must offer a graphical interface for DMN modelling. This is required as it cannot be assumed that typical modellers are capable of running complex command line tools.
- **Support of DMN semantics.** The application must have an underlying data-model of DMN decision models, i.e., not only have a graphical/image-based representation of the decision model.

Following our selection criteria, a total of 14 DMN tools were included for our evaluation, namely *BPMN.io, Camunda, Cardanit, DMN Check, Fico, Flowable, Kogito, Open Rules, Pega, Red Hat, Signavio, Trisotech, Yaoqiang, MID Innovator.* We refer the reader to the supplementary online document[5], were the sources for the identified tools can be found, and the violation of selection criteria is specified for the excluded tools. In the following, we present our test approach for the selected DMN tools.

3.2   Test Approach

To test to which extent the selected tools are able to detect the introduced error types, we applied a black-box-testing approach, analyzing each tool individually. For all tools, the same test protocol was applied, which was subdivided into the phases of *preparation, evaluation* and *documentation*, as shown in Fig. 5.

Fig. 5. Applied test approach.

For every tool, the test was started by analyzing the official documentation of the tools. The main aim of this preparation was to gain an understanding of how the tools are to be installed and used. Subsequently, all tools were installed.

---

[5] https://bit.ly/3omxoQB.

Following the preparation phase, the main tool evaluation phase was conducted. Here, for all the 26 error types shown in Fig. 4, we modelled a respective instance of such error type incrementally. For example, for the verification capability "identical rules verification (single table)", we modelled a DMN table containing two identical rules, cf. e.g. Fig. 6.

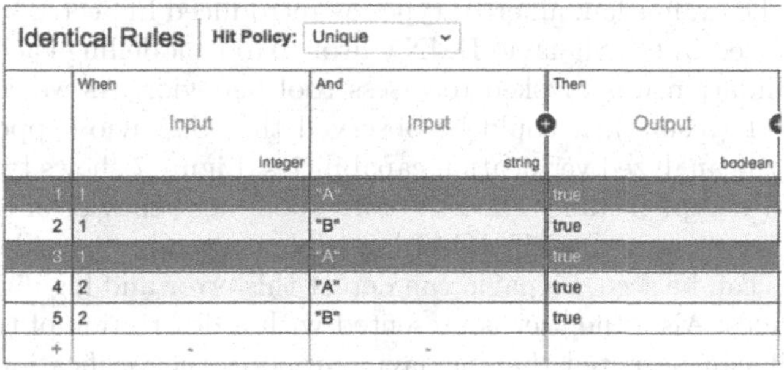
Identical Rules Hit Policy: Unique

	When Input integer	And Input string	Then Output boolean
1	1	"A"	true
2	1	"B"	true
3	1	"A"	true
4	2	"A"	true
5	2	"B"	true
+	-	-	

Fig. 6. Decision table containing identical rules (highlighted).

While we had originally planned to model *one* decision model containing all error types in advance and import this model into every tool, we realized that many tools did not offer an import functionality, or the import was prone to errors due to different XML encodings. Therefore, we manually modelled a new decision model for every tool. The result was then a "large" decision model containing an example for all 26 considered error type. The "large" decision model containing all error types can be downloaded online[6].

After each individual error type instance was modelled, the decision model was validated to test whether the tool could detect this error. In this context, the specific procedure how the validation was invoked depended on the individual tool. For example, many tools such as Signavio offer a separate button to invoke a validation of the model, whereas other tools such as Yaoquang BPMN editor implement a real-time verification that validates the model after every change by the user automatically. Furthermore, some tools such as Signavio offer the possibility to execute the decision models, e.g. using simulation-based approaches. In case such a feature was available, it was also applied in order to ensure that run-time verification features of the tools were also considered for testing.

Finally, given that a tool was able to identify a specific error type (regardless of how the validation was invoked), this verification capability was documented. Also, we documented the specific error message and general form in which the error was displayed to the user. For example, while some tools offered a simple error message, other tools offered more sophisticated insights into the errors, e.g. an assessment of the severity of the respective error.

[6] https://cloud.uni-koblenz-landau.de/s/jNGiom73ezKH64X.

3.3   Test Example: Signavio

To conclude this section, we illustrate an exemplary test process for Signavio. At first, the official documentation[7] was reviewed in order to gain an understanding of the Signavio modelling environment. For this tool, installation refers to the registration of a new account and setting up the browser-based environment. A test license could be attained for academic purposes.

Then, for the evaluation, all error types as introduced in Sect. 2.2 were incrementally modelled in the Signavio DMN editor. After modelling each individual error type, validation was invoked to assess tool behavior. As we will also discuss in Sect. 4.1 (results), it could be observed that Signavio supported some, but not all of the analyzed verification capabilities. Figure 7 shows two examples of modelled error type instances and the corresponding behavior of the Signavio tool. Figure 7(a) shows a modelled decision table containing two identical *rules* (i.e., rows). As can be seen, Signavio can detect this error and highlights the two problematic rules. Also, the user is presented with a description of the occurred error. Thus, it can be noted that Signavio supports the verification capability *identical rules vericiation*. Figure 7(b) depicts a modelled decision table containing two identical columns. As can be seen in the screenshot, Signavio does not detect any form of error in this case. Thus, it can be observed that Signavio does not support modellers in detecting this error type, i.e., Signavio does not support the verification capability *identical column verification*.

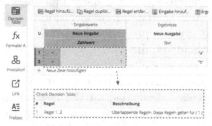 

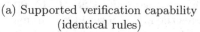

| (a) Supported verification capability (identical rules) | (b) Unsupported verification capability (identical columns) |

Fig. 7. Examples for supported/unsupported verification capabilities in Signavio.

Following our test approach method, all considered error types were modelled, and the Signavio tool was tested accordingly. The observations whether Signavio could detect an error, respectively the specific user feedback, were then documented. As we will show in the following section, our test approach method therefore allowed us to fully classify tool behavior in regard to the support of the considered verification capabilities.

---

[7] https://documentation.signavio.com/.

4   Tool Behavior Analysis

In this section, we discuss the overall verification capability support in state-of-the-art approaches based on our conducted test approach and distill a corresponding research agenda based on an identification of research gaps.

4.1   Result Summary

Our experiments assessed to which extent the 14 selected modelling tools allowed to detect the 26 different DMN error types introduced in Sect. 2.2. Table 1 shows our overall test results. For every tool, the supported verification capabilities are denoted with an "x", respectively "o" in case of partial support. We define a tool to support a verification capability if it provides means to identify or prevent the respective error type, i.e., regardless of the procedure of validation. This was an important design-choice, as the mechanisms how the tools handled modelling errors differed strongly for some cases. For example, some tools provide real-time modelling support that prevent users from persisting an erroneous model. While this is not a form of "on-demand" validation, the tool still supports modellers in detecting and preventing the specific error, thus, this is denoted as a support of a verification capability. Partial support can be reached if the tool only detects a (sub)part of the error as defined in Sect. 2.2. Importantly, none of the tools supported multi-table decision logic verification capabilities. Therefore, these capabilities are ommitted in Table 1 for readability.

Table 1. Overview of DMN verification capabilities supported by the analyzed tools. (x = full support, o = partial support.)

Tool	Decision Logic Capabilities													DRD level							BPMN/DMN					
	Identical Rules	Equivalent Rules	Subsumed Rules	Indeterminism	Overlapping Conditions	Partial Reduction	Missing Rules	Unused Predefined Value	Missing Predefined Value	Missing Input Value	Missing Output Value	Inconsistent Type	Identical Columns	Missing Input Column	Missing Output Column	Missing (Data) Input	Multiple (Data) Input	Idle Data Input	Inconsistent Types	Circularity	Unused Data Input	Missing Data Input	Unused Table Output	Missing Table Output	Missing Data Object Reference	Unused Data Object Reference
Bpmn.io																										
Camunda																										
Cardanit																										
DMN Check	X	X	X				X																			
Fico		X			X	X						X	o	X	X				X							
Flowable										X									X							
Kogito																										
Open Rules																										
Pega																										
Red Hat																										
Signavio	X	X	X	X	X	X	X	X				o	X	X	o	X	X		X							
Trisotech	X	X	X	X	X	X	X	X						X	X	X	X									
Yaoqiang																										
MID Innovator																										

From all 14 evaluated tools, only 5 support any verification capabilities, namely *DMN-Check, Fico, Flowable, Signavio* and *Trisotech*. This was quite a surprising result, as it shows that popular tools such as BPMN.io do not offer any means to support end-users during DMN modelling. The tools with the best capability support were Signavio, with 15 of 26 supported capabilities (57.7%), respectively Trisotech, with 11 of 26 supported capabilities (42.3%). The other three mentioned tools offer a much smaller degree of support - as mentioned all other tools offer no support at all. Considering only the five tools that supported at least one verification capability, the average coverage over all verification capabilities was 30,8% - considering all tools, the average coverage was only 10.9%.

Even for the tool that offered the highest degree of coverage (Signavio), only roughly 60% of possible error types could be detected. This strongly suggests the need for novel verification capabilities in current tools. Importantly, it is noticeable that there is no support at all for multi-table decision logic verification, and no support for DMN vs BPMN verification. This can be seen as highly problematic, as literature strongly suggests that modellers need to be supported in handling such issues [2,7][8]. Furthermore, there are certain error types on the decision logic- and decision requirements level that are not supported by any tool. This means that even if one would combine different tools, it is currently not possible to detect all error types as introduced in Sect. 2.2 with the analyzed tools. On a side note, Signavio is the only tool which is strictly better than all other tools, i.e., there exist no tool T such that T supports a verification capabiliy c and Signavio does not. This could be used as a metric for determining suitable tools, however, we acknowledge that tool selection is much more complex and strongly beyond the scope of this report.

4.2   Discussion of Tool Support and Research Agenda

The current support of verification capabilities in the assessed industrial tools seems alarmingly low. Many of the analyzed tools do not offer any means to aid modellers in detecting modelling errors. The lack of verification capabilities in industrial tools places a heavy burden on the human modellers. Following recent research [1,18], this burden can be considered as unfeasible in practice. In turn, in can be expected that the resulting DMN models will contain modelling errors. This however can have severe consequences for companies. For example, various works such as [8,9,12] show how a flawed decision logic can lead to inconsistent or erroneous decision making. This means that compliant process execution cannot be ensured. In case of compliance breaches due to flawed decision-making, this may even lead to sensitive financial fines for companies [12]. This emphasizes the need to extend the support for DMN verification capabilities in the analyzed industrial tools.

---

[8] Note also that as none of the tools support multi-table decision logic verification capabilities, this was entirely omitted from the above Table 1, thus, the actual coverage of verification capabilities is arguably lower.

Fortunately, research on developing specific verification capabilities has gained momentum in recent years and has brought forward a series of recent approaches. Such results could be integrated into industrial modelling tools, or used by companies to additionally validate decision models. However, as there was/is a lack of a general error classification, it is currently also unclear to which extent these *academic* works support DMN verification capabilities. In an own previous work [7], an initial survey of scientific works on DMN verification was conducted to identify relevant approaches that have been published in BPM community. In this report, we extend this survey by analyzing to which extent those academic works support the proposed verification capabilities. Table 2 shows an aggregated overview of DMN verification capabilities supported by the analyzed *industrial* tools identifed in Sect. 3(top), as well as the *scientific* approaches identified in [7]. For readability, the overview of industrial tools was simplified to only contain those approaches that support at least one capability.

Table 2. Simplified results of the tool analysis from Table 1, extended with an analysis of DMN verification capabilities supported by existing approaches in literature (adapated from [7]). (x = Full support, o = partial support. * = Authors of this work.)

Tool/Approach		Identical Rules	Equivalent Rules	Subsumed Rules	Indeterminism	Overlapping Conditions	Partial Reduction	Missing Rules	Unused Predefined Value	Missing Predefined Value	Missing Input value	Missing Output value	Inconsistent Type	Identical Columns	Missing Input Column	Missing Output Column	Missing (Data) Input	Multiple (Data) Input	Idle Data Input	Inconsistent Types	Circularity	Unused Data Input	Missing Data Input	Unused Table Output	Missing Table Output	Missing Data Object Reference	Unused Data Object Reference
		Decision logic level													DRD level							BPMN/DMN					
DMN Check		X		X	X								X														
Fico			X			X	X						X	o	X	X				X							
Flowable								X												X							
Signavio		X		X	X	X	X	X	X	X	o		X		X	o	X	X		X							
Trisotech		X		X	X	X	X	X	X						X	X	X	X									
Calvanese et al. (2016)	[4]	X	o	X		X		X					X														
Batoulis et al. (2017)	[2]	X		X	o	X	o	X					X													X	X
Calvanese et al. (2017)	[6]	X	o	X	o	X	o	X					X														
Ochoa et al. (2017)	[17]										X	X															
Batoulis et al. (2018)	[3]	X		X		X		o																			
Calvanese et al. (2018)	[6]	X	o	X	o	X	o	X					X														
Corea et al. (2018)*	[8]	X				X	X																				
de Leoni et al. (2018)	[14]										X	X			X	X				X						X	X
Corea et al. (2019)*	[7]	X	X	X	X	X	X	X	X	X	X	X	X	X													
Felli et al. (2019)	[11]										X	X			X	X				X						X	X
Hasic et al. (2019)*	[13]	X	X	X	X	X	X	X	X	X	X	X	X		X	X	X	X	X	X							

As can be seen, there is excellent support of decision logic level verification capabilities in academia. These results could therefore be integrated into industrial tools. Interestingly, the support for DRD level verification seems to be higher in industrial tools than in academic approaches. In general, it seems that modelling errors on a DRD level have not been sufficiently addressed in academia, while the support by industrial tools indicates that tool vendors deem such errors as important. This is an excellent example of how practice can yield valuable insights to guide research. It seems plausible that more qualitative research is necessary to further identify the actual requirements of DMN modelling tools, cf. e.g. [18] for a recent work in this direction. Finally, the BPMN vs DMN perspective is in general still pending further development. There are many error types in this level that currently cannot be detected by any means.

To summarize, the field of DMN verification seems to have gained positive momentum, and it seems the further development of verification techniques is much needed from a practitioners viewpoint. Yet, there is still much research that needs to be conducted as a basis for allowing for a closer integration of research and industry. We therefore propose the following research agenda:

- **A general classification of DMN error types.** A current problem for research on DMN verification is the lack of a generally accepted classification of DMN error types. As long as there is no definitive overview of possible errors in DMN modelling, it will remain impossible to warrant that tools offer a suitable amount of support in identifying important errors that could occur during modelling. This factor therefore remains a current threat to compliant process execution, and should therefore be addressed in future works.
- **Semantics of DMN error types.** In our analysis, we noticed that many approaches use completely different terminology for identical error types. Likewise, many approaches merge various error types of other works into one, which can be confusing to modelers. For example, the Signavio tool refers to various error type of our proposed classification (e.g. identical rules, subsumed rules, overlapping conditions,...) simply as "overlapping rules". Here, a shared terminological understanding could help to eliminate ambiguities and offer experts a more fine-grained feedback on modelling errors. As natural language descriptions of specific error types are also highly ambiguous, a definition of the semantics of DMN error types is urgently needed. A first work in this area is e.g. [4], however, there needs to be more work in this direction.
- **Novel means for supporting modellers.** At first, the unsupported verification capabilities should be implemented in industrial tools. Here, there have been various approaches from academia, which could be used as a basis for implementation. However, there are some error types which have not been addressed at all, thus, there is more work needed on concrete means for DMN verification. In general, it seems there is a sufficient support on the decision logic level, however, we can observe a lack of research on verification capabilities geared towards the decision requirements level, or the BPMN/DMN level. Also, next to a "simple" detection of certain errors in the decision mod-

els, we noticed that some tools offered more sophisticated feedback to the
user, e.g. a prioritization of identified problems. Especially in larger settings,
such additional means could provide valuable insights to guide modellers in
error resolution. Future works could therefore focus on novel means for the
prioritization or quantification of occurring errors.

- **Research on feedback presentation.** In our analysis, we noticed that
  many approaches have entirely different strategies on how to display error
  messages. In this context, recent works such as [10, 15] however indicate that
  small tweaks in the visualization of error feedback, e.g., the position on the
  screen, can have different cognitive effects on understanding, e.g. understanding accuracy or the mental effort needed to process the information. Here,
  future works should investigate the cognitive effects of different visualization
  techniques and develop guidelines for displaying user feedback in order to
  guide tool development.

5 Conclusion

In this work, we presented an analysis of the current tool support for DMN
verification capabilities. Here, we identified and tested a selection of industrial
tools, and also analyzed the support by recent academic works. Our results
show that the overall support of DMN error verification in industrial tools is
alarmingly low. Here, efforts should urgently be directed towards extending such
tools in order to support modellers, ultimately also counteracting compliance
breaches due to erroneous decision models. Even for the tool with the highest
degree of support (Signavio), only 60% of the introduced error types can be
detected, which emphasizes the need for future research. To this aim, we have
proposed a research agenda, identifying opportunities for future research.

We acknowledge that some tools could not be selected for our experiments
due to funding constraints. Therefore, experiments should be repeated (if possible) analyzing those tools which require a fee for access. However, due to the
applied tool search method [16, 19], we are confident that we have identified
prominent tools, e.g. *Signavio, Pega* or *bpmn.io*, and have captured the general
gist of the state-of-the-art in DMN verification.

References

1. Batoulis, K., Nesterenko, A., Repitsch, G., Weske, M.: Decision management in
   the insurance industry: standards and tools. In: Proceedings of the BPM 2017
   Industry Track, Barcelona, Spain, 2017. CEUR Workshop Proceedings, vol. 1985,
   pp. 52–63. CEUR-WS.org (2017)
2. Batoulis, K., Weske, M.: A tool for checking soundness of decision-aware business
   processes. In: Proceedings of the BPM Demo Track, Barcelona, Spain, 2017. CEUR
   Workshop Proceedings, vol. 1950. CEUR-WS.org (2017)
3. Batoulis, K., Weske, M.: Disambiguation of DMN decision tables. In: Abramowicz,
   W., Paschke, A. (eds.) BIS 2018. LNBIP, vol. 320, pp. 236–249. Springer, Cham
   (2018). https://doi.org/10.1007/978-3-319-93931-5_17

4. Calvanese, D., Dumas, M., Laurson, Ü., Maggi, F.M., Montali, M., Teinemaa, I.: Semantics and analysis of DMN decision tables. In: La Rosa, M., Loos, P., Pastor, O. (eds.) BPM 2016. LNCS, vol. 9850, pp. 217–233. Springer, Cham (2016). https://doi.org/10.1007/978-3-319-45348-4_13
5. Calvanese, D., Dumas, M., Laurson, Ü., Maggi, F.M., Montali, M., Teinemaa, I.: Semantics, analysis and simplification of DMN decision tables. Inf. Syst. **78**, 112–125 (2018)
6. Calvanese, D., Dumas, M., Maggi, F.M., Montali, M.: Semantic DMN: formalizing decision models with domain knowledge. In: Costantini, S., Franconi, E., Van Woensel, W., Kontchakov, R., Sadri, F., Roman, D. (eds.) RuleML+RR 2017. LNCS, vol. 10364, pp. 70–86. Springer, Cham (2017). https://doi.org/10.1007/978-3-319-61252-2_6
7. Corea, C., Blatt, J., Delfmann, P.: A tool for decision logic verification in DMN decision tables. In: Proceedings of BPM 2019 Demo Track, Vienna, Austria, 2019. CEUR Workshop Proceedings, vol. 2420, pp. 169–173. CEUR-WS.org (2019)
8. Corea, C., Delfmann, P.: A tool to monitor consistent decision-making in business process execution. In: Proceedings of BPM 2018 Demo Track, Sydney, Australia, 2018. CEUR Workshop Proceedings, vol. 2196, pp. 76–80. CEUR-WS.org (2018)
9. Corea, C., Delfmann, P.: A taxonomy for business rule organizing approaches in regard to business process compliance. J. Conceptual Model. **15**, 1–28 (2020)
10. Dani, V., Thom, H., Freitas, C.: Visual feedback about problems in business process models: systematic literature review, survey, case studies and recommendations. Universidade Federal do Rio Grande do Sul, Technical report (2019)
11. Felli, P., de Leoni, M., Montali, M.: Soundness verification of decision-aware process models with variable-to-variable conditions. In: 2019 19th International Conference on Application of Concurrency to System Design (ACSD), pp. 82–91. IEEE (2019)
12. Hashmi, M., Governatori, G., Lam, H., Wynn, M.T.: Are we done with business process compliance: state of the art and challenges ahead. Knowl. Inf. Syst. **57**(1), 79–133 (2018)
13. Hasic, F., Corea, C., Blatt, J., Delfmann, P., Serral, E.: Decision model change patterns for dynamic system evolution. Knowl. Inf. Syst. **62**, 3665–3696 (2020). https://doi.org/10.1007/s10115-020-01469-w
14. de Leoni, M., Felli, P., Montali, M.: A holistic approach for soundness verification of decision-aware process models. In: Trujillo, J.C., Davis, K.C., Du, X., Li, Z., Ling, T.W., Li, G., Lee, M.L. (eds.) ER 2018. LNCS, vol. 11157, pp. 219–235. Springer, Cham (2018). https://doi.org/10.1007/978-3-030-00847-5_17
15. Nagel, S., Corea, C., Delfmann, P.: Cognitive effects of visualization techniques for inconsistency metrics on monitoring data-intensive processes. Inf. Syst. Manage., 1–16 (2020)
16. Nidhra, S., Dondeti, J.: Black box and white box testing techniques. Int. J. Embed. Syst. Appl. (IJESA) **2**(2), 29–50 (2012)
17. Ochoa, L., González-Rojas, O.: Analysis and re-configuration of decision logic in adaptive and data-intensive processes (short paper). In: Panetto, H., et al. (eds.) OTM 2017. LNCS, vol. 10573, pp. 306–313. Springer, Cham (2017). https://doi.org/10.1007/978-3-319-69462-7_20
18. Smit, K., Versendaal, J., Zoet, M.: Verification capabilities for business rules management in the Dutch governmental context. In: Proceedings of the 21st Pacific Conference on Information Systems, PACIS 2017, Langkawi, Malaysia, 2017, pp. 201–212. AISel (2017)

19. Snoeck, M., Moreno-Montes de Oca, I., Haegemans, T., Scheldeman, B., Hoste, T.: Testing a selection of BPMN tools for their support of modelling guidelines. In: Ralyté, J., España, S., Pastor, Ó. (eds.) PoEM 2015. LNBIP, vol. 235, pp. 111–125. Springer, Cham (2015). https://doi.org/10.1007/978-3-319-25897-3_8
20. Vanthienen, J., Mues, C., Wets, G., Delaere, K.: A tool-supported approach to inter-tabular verification. Exp. Syst. Appl. **15**, 277–285 (1998)
21. Vom Brocke, J., Simons, A., Riemer, K., Niehaves, B., Plattfaut, R., Cleven, A.: Standing on the shoulders of giants: challenges and recommendations of literature search in information systems research. Commun. Assoc. Inf. Syst. **37**(1), 9 (2015)

Consistency Checking of Goal Models and Case Management Schemas

Rik Eshuis[1(✉)] and Aditya Ghose[2]

[1] Eindhoven University of Technology, Eindhoven, The Netherlands
h.eshuis@tue.nl
[2] University of Wollongong, Wollongong, Australia
aditya.ghose@uow.edu.au

Abstract. Case management is an approach for handling business processes that are knowledge-intensive. The knowledge work performed on case management schemas is driven by operational goals. Typically, organizational goals and their interdependencies are specified in goal models. A goal model defines how higher-level goals are achieved by lower-level goals. While goals have been related to classical activity-centric process models, the relation between declarative data-centric case management schemas and goal models has not yet been explored. This paper presents a structural approach to check consistency of a goal model and a declarative case management schema. The approach is supported by a tool and evaluated in a case study.

1 Introduction

Case management offers a data-centric, goal-oriented approach for managing business processes [1,29]. The work performed for a case is specified in a case management schema and focuses on the functional goals to be achieved and the business steps that need to be taken to acquire information and take decisions to reach the goals. Case management schemas are very suitable to support knowledge-intensive processes [7,22], since such processes are goal-oriented and typically are driven by data that knowledge workers need to make decisions on. Moreover, knowledge-intensive processes require flexibility due to uncertainty about the case being processed [30]. Case management schemas often use a declarative rather than a procedural style to provide such flexibility [8].

The declarative nature of case management schemas limits the understanding of their meaning for stakeholders. Rules attached to case management schemas constrain the allowed behavior. But rules have complex interdependencies, making it difficult to understand the full picture for an end user who has to execute the process or a process owner who wants to understand the process [12].

Goal models have been proposed in the area of requirements engineering as a means to understand and structure stakeholder intent [18]. Goal models specify objectives that a system needs to achieve and hierarchically structure them.

A. Polyvyanyy et al. (Eds.): BPM Forum 2021, LNBIP 427, pp. 54–70, 2021.
https://doi.org/10.1007/978-3-030-85440-9_4

However, goal models cannot be executed. Instead, goals are—often implicitly—realized by other models that provide a more fine-grained specification of behavior, such as class diagrams and sequence diagrams for software engineering [18] or process models for BPM. In the field of BPM, the relation between goal models and activity-centric process models has been explored [14,17,25] but goal models and declarative case management schemas have not been similarly analyzed. However, the goals implicitly specified by a declarative case management schema may not match the intended goals specified in a goal model.

This paper develops *a structural approach to check consistency of a goal model with a declarative case management schema.* The input is a user-defined correspondence function between a declarative case management schema and a goal model that maps milestones, i.e., operational objectives in a case management schema, to goals. The approach checks whether the goal interdependencies that are implied by goal-related milestones in a case management schema are consistent with the goal model. We introduce the notion of consistency degree to express the extent to which the relevant goal relations in the goal model are implied by the case management schema. As case management notation we use a simplified version of the Case Management Model and Notation (CMMN) [3].

The remainder of this paper is organized as follows. Section 2 gives a motivating example for the approach by presenting a goal model and a related case management schema. Section 3 defines goal models and case management schema. Section 4 defines consistency for case management schemas corresponding to goal models; the definition relies on rules that derive goal interdependencies from a case management schema. Section 5 introduces a tool implementation and evaluates the approach on a case study. We discuss related work in Sect. 6 and end the paper with conclusions in Sect. 7.

2   Motivating Example

To motivate the approach, we consider a leasing process that is inspired by the processes from IBM Global Financing (IGF) [4,9]. Figure 1 shows a fragment of a goal model for IGF. The boxes represent goals. The model uses goal decomposition to specify how the high-level goal Deal Refined is achieved: a deal is refined if its terms have been drafted, credit checked, and the price determined.

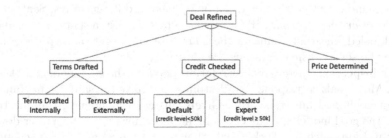

Fig. 1. Goal model of IGF business process. Arcs denote AND decomposition.

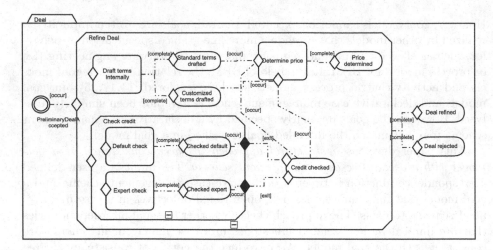

Fig. 2. Case management schema fragment of IGF business process that corresponds to the goal model in Fig. 1

Drafting terms can be outsourced [9]. Depending on the credit level, credit is checked either in the default way or using an expert. Both AND decomposition (lines connected by arcs) and XOR decomposition are used. XOR decomposition typically indicates different variants for a system design, i.e., variants of a process [24].

Figure 2 shows a declarative case management (CM) schema in CMMN notation that corresponds to the goal model. The schema contains stages (rectangles), in which work is performed, and milestones (ovals), which are business objectives. Stages and milestones are governed by business rules, called sentries, which

Table 1. Conditions of sentries in Fig. 2

Stage/milestone	Condition
Default check	**if** amount $< 50k$
Expert check	**if** amount $\geq 50k$
Standard terms drafted	**if** contract $=$ *"standard"*
Customized terms drafted	**if** contract $=$ *"customized"*
Deal refined	**if** accept $= true$
Deal rejected	**if** accept $= false$

define when stages are opened and milestones are achieved (white diamonds) and when stages get closed (black diamonds). Different opening sentries for the same stage indicate that the stage can be opened in different ways. Sentries have the form **on** $event_1, .., event_n$ **if** $condition$. The events in a sentry are visualized with a labeled line that connects the source of the event, as expressed in the label, to the sentry. The conditions are shown in Table 1.

Upon inspection, there is a clear relation between the goal model and the CM schema. Most goals correspond to milestones that have the same name, but there are other goals and milestones too. Given this correspondence, the question is whether the goal model and the CM schema are consistent. This paper develops a structural approach for checking whether a goal model and a CM schema are consistent, given a correspondence function between goals and milestones.

3   Preliminaries

3.1   Goal Models

Different goal modeling approaches exist, such as KAOS [18] and i*[32]. The goal models we present next use basic concepts that appear in all goal modeling languages. In general, there are behavioral goals and soft goals [18,32]. In this paper, we only focus on behavioral goals. Next, there are different types of behavioral goals: **achieve** and **cease**, **maintain** and **avoid** [18]. We focus in this paper on achieve goals, since these have a natural counterpart in business processes, which also aim at achieving organizational goals. We will include the other goal types in our study in future work.

Basics. A goal can be decomposed into subgoals. A decomposed goal is called the *parent* of each subgoal. We use both AND and XOR decomposition. An AND goal is achieved if all its subgoals are achieved while an XOR goal is achieved if exactly one of its subgoals is achieved. A subgoal can be annotated with a boolean condition, which expresses the condition under which the subgoal achieves the parent goal. Given two subgoals of the same parent goal, their two conditions are *conflicting* if their conjunction is false, so there is no assignment of values such that both conditions are satisfied simultaneously. For instance, the conditions of subgoals Checked Default and Checked Expert in Fig. 1 are conflicting, since no assignment for amount satisfies both **if** amount$<50k$ and **if** amount$\geq50k$.

   Goal models that use decomposition arrange goals in a hierarchy, where lower-level goals contribute to realizing higher-level goals. Leaf goals are realized by performing tasks. We assume as in KAOS [18] that goal models are structured in a tree, so there is a unique root node that is an ancestor of all other goals. For instance, in Fig. 1 the root node is the AND goal Deal Refined.

Relations. We next introduce binary relations on goals in a goal model. These goal relations will be used in the sequel in defining consistency between goal models and CM schemas.

- A goal g_1 *supports* another goal g_2, written $g_1 \rightarrow g_2$, if achieving g_1 contributes to achieving g_2. In that case g_2 is a parent or ancestor of g_1.
- A goal g_1 *complements* another goal g_2, written $g_1 \& g_2$, if they can be achieved simultaneously and g_1 does not support g_2 and vice versa. It means that there is an AND goal g_3 such that g_1 and g_2 support two distinct child goals of g_3 that have non-conflicting conditions.
- A goal g_1 *excludes* another goal g_2, written $g_1 \nmid g_2$, if g_1 and g_2 cannot be achieved simultaneously. This occurs if there is a goal g_3 such that g_1 and g_2 are equal to or support two distinct child goals of g_3, and either g_3 is an XOR goal or g_3 is an AND goal and the two child goals of g_3 have conflicting conditions.

   For the goal model in Fig. 1, for instance Credit Checked $\rightarrow$ DealRefined, Checked Default $\nmid$ Checked Expert and Credit Checked & Terms Drafted.

The three goal relations are irreflexive. The supports ($\rightarrow$) relation is asymmetric and transitive, while the complements (&) and excludes ($\not{\xi}$) relations are symmetric and intransitive. For instance, the goal model in Fig. 1 has Credit Checked&Price Determined and Price Determined&Checked Default, but Credit Checked $\not{\xi}$ Checked Default. Since the goals are arranged in a tree, each pair of distinct goals in the tree is related via one of the three relations.

3.2   Case Management Schemas

The definition of case management schemas below follows closely the CMMN standard [3], with a few exceptions that are discussed afterwards.

Basics. A case management (CM) schema consists of an information and a behavior model. The information model is expressed by data attributes. The behavior model consists of several elements. First, *milestones*, which are business objectives achieved while a case is being executed. Second, *tasks*, which are atomic activities in which work is performed. Third, *stages*, which are hierarchical, non-atomic pieces of work, similar to a subprocess in a imperative process notation. Fourth, *event listeners* that wait for external events to arrive from the environment and that trigger subsequent behavior. A stage may contain other stages, tasks, milestones or event listeners. In each CM schema, there is a unique top level stage that contains all other behavior model elements.

Each behavioral element can be active or inactive. CMMN allows more refined life cycle states for behavioral elements, such as enabled, suspended, etc., but to simplify the presentation we do not consider these here. Behavioral elements have rules that govern whether the elements become active (entry rule) or inactive (exit rule).

A rule is called a *sentry* in CMMN. A sentry has the form **on** $e_1, e_2, .., e_n$ **if** c, where each e_i is an event and c a condition, a boolean expression that can reference data attributes. Allowed events are external events and internal events such as exiting a stage S (event S_{exit}), completing a task T (event $T_{complete}$), and achieving a milestone m (event $m_{achieve}$).

To simplify the presentation, we have omitted a few CMMN modeling elements which do not impact the results of this paper. For instance, CMMN schemas allow discretionary stages and tasks, which are not planned in advance but whose execution is determined at run time by the user. Next, CMMN allows repeated behavior and autocompletion of stages. These can be incorporated without any major changes. Finally, CMMN distinguishes between the definition and the use of elements; for example, a sentry defines a rule while an entry or exit criterion is a use of a sentry. Here, we do not make this distinction.

Relations. Next we define two relations based on the structure of CM schemas. The relations are used in Sect. 4 to define consistency constraints. First, an event e *triggers* a sentry φ if e occurs in the **on** part of φ. For instance, in Fig. 2 event Default check$_{complete}$ triggers the entry sentry of milestone Checked default. Next, a stage S (a task T) owns a milestone m, written $owns(S, m)$ ($owns(T, m)$) if m has an entry sentry whose trigger event is the completion event of S (or T).

For GSM schemas [15], which informed the design of CMMN, a semantic constraint has been defined that also applies to CM schemas:

If a stage or task owns distinct milestones m_1 and m_2, then at most one of the two milestones evaluates to true.

The constraint expresses that milestones owned by the same stage are alternative business objectives. We use the constraint in the next section in defining one of the consistency relations between goal models and CM schemas.

4 Consistency

We first analyze the relation between goal models and declarative CM schemas. Next, we define rules that derive goal relation from a declarative CM schema that corresponds to a goal model. Then we explain how additional goal relations can be inferred in addition. Next, we define consistency between a declarative CM schema and a corresponding goal model. Related, we define the notion of consistency degree, which expresses to which extent the relevant goal relations in the goal model are derived and inferred. We illustrate the consistency definitions and the rules on the example introduced in Sect. 2 and end with discussion.

4.1 Relating Goal Models and Declarative Case Management Schemas

Each milestone represents a business objective that needs to be achieved. It is therefore natural to relate milestones in declarative CM schemas to **achieve** goals in a goal model. For instance, the goals in the goal model in Fig. 1 are similar to the milestones with the same names in the CM schema in Fig. 2. Stages have no counterpart in goal models, since they correspond to activities that are required to achieve milestones.

However, not all milestones are **achieve** goals. For Fig. 2, milestone Deal rejected is not a goal that needs to be achieved, but indicates that the process deviates from the "happy flow". Conversely, goal models can have other types of goals besides achieving, such as **maintain** or **avoid** goals [18]. However, these goal types have no counterpart in declarative CM schemas.

In the derivation rules for goal relations, defined below, we assume a correspondence function on goal models and declarative CM schemas that maps milestones to goals.

Definition 1 (Correspondence function). *Let GM be a goal model with a set G of goals, and $\mathcal{C}$ a CM schema with $\mathcal{M}$ a set of milestones. A correspondence function $\alpha : \mathcal{M} \rightarrow \mathcal{G}$ is a partial function that maps milestones to goals.*

The definition allows that a goal corresponds to multiple milestones. In that case, the milestones collectively realize the goal. Also, a goal can relate to no milestone, if the scope of the CM schema covers only part of the goal model. For instance, the CM schema in Fig. 2 does not contain a milestone Term Drafted Externally but is consistent with the goal model, even though it does not realize the entire goal model.

The definition excludes that a single milestone relates to multiple goals, so that a milestone realizes multiple goals. We plan as future work to extend the definition to cover such situations.

4.2 Deriving Goal Relations from Case Management Schemas

We define rules for deriving goal relations from a declarative CM schema that corresponds to a goal model. Given an interdependence in the CM schema between milestones corresponding to goals, each rule derives a relation between the corresponding goals that must hold in the goal model. The different rules are based on the different ways that distinct milestones in declarative CM schemas can be structurally related.

For the definitions below, let GM be a goal model, C a declarative CM schema and α a correspondence function relating C and GM. Let m_1, m_2 be distinct milestones in C and let $g_1 = \alpha(m_1)$ and $g_2 = \alpha(m_2)$ be their corresponding goals in GM. We require that g_1 and g_2 are distinct; if g_1 equals g_2 then no goal relation is inferred, since all goal relations are irreflexive (cf. Sect. 3.1). Next, we write milestone m triggers sentry φ as a shorthand for $m_{achieve}$ triggers φ. If m triggers φ, then if φ evaluates to true, it implies that m has been achieved. Consequently, if two milestone m_1 and m_2 both trigger φ, then both must have been achieved if φ evaluates to true.

Milestone Triggering Entry Sentry of Other Milestone. A milestone m_1 can trigger an entry sentry of another milestone m_2. For example, the milestone Checked default triggers the entry sentry of milestone Credit checked. In that case, achieving m_1 helps to achieve m_2, so goal g_1 supports g_2.

Definition 2 (Milestone-sentry rule). *If there is a sentry φ_1 such that m_1 triggers φ and φ is an entry sentry of m_2, then $g_1 \rightarrow g_2$.*

Two Milestones Triggering Same Sentry. Two milestones m_1 and m_2 can trigger the same entry sentry of a stage or milestone. For instance, milestones Terms drafted internally and Credit checked both trigger the entry criterion of stage Determine price. When evaluating the entry criterion, both milestones must have been achieved. Therefore, the goals g_1 and g_2 must complement each other.

Definition 3 (Sentry rule). *If there is an entry sentry φ_1 such that m_1 and m_2 both trigger φ, then $g_1 \& g_2$.*

Milestone Contained in Stage that Owns Other Milestone. A milestone m_1 can be contained in a stage that owns another milestone m_2. For instance, milestone Checked default is contained in stage Check credit that owns milestone Credit checked. Achieving m_1 helps to complete the stage and this way achieve m_2. Therefore g_1 supports g_2.

Definition 4 (Hierarchy rule). *If there is a stage S such that S contains m_1 and S owns m_2, then $g_1 \twoheadrightarrow g_2$.*

Milestone Triggering Entry Sentry of Stage or Task That Owns Another Milestone. Milestone m_1 can trigger an opening sentry of a stage or task that owns another milestone m_2. For instance, milestone Terms drafted internally triggers the entry sentry of task Determine price that owns milestone Price determined. If m_1 triggers the sentry, then when m_2 is achieved, m_1 is achieved too. Therefore g_1 and g_2 complement each other.

Definition 5 (Stage/task-milestone rule). *If there is a stage S or task T that owns m_2, and there is a sentry φ such that m_1 triggers φ and φ is an entry sentry of S or T, then $g_1 \& g_2$.*

Milestones Owned by the Same Stage. If m_1 and m_2 are owned by the same stage or task, then the goals g_1 and g_2 exclude each other, similar to the constraint on such milestones imposed by GSM Schemas. For example, milestones Standard terms drafted and Customized terms drafted are owned by the same task. If they belong to different goals, then these goals exclude each other.

Definition 6 (Stage/task-output rule). *If there is a stage S or task T that owns both m_1 and m_2, then $g_1 \, \xi \, g_2$.*

4.3 Inferring Goal Relations

We next explain how to infer additional goal relations from a given set of goal relations, for instance obtained by applying the goal derivation rules of Sect. 4.2 to a CM schema. Note that for goal models, these inference rules are superfluous, since each pair of goals is already related via one of the three relations.

As we explained in Sect. 3.1, relation $\twoheadrightarrow$ is transitive and relations $\&$ and ξ are symmetric. Therefore, if $g_1 \& g_2$, then $g_2 \& g_1$; if $g_1 \, \xi \, g_2$, then $g_2 \, \xi \, g_1$; and if $g_1 \twoheadrightarrow g_2$ and $g_2 \twoheadrightarrow g_3$, then $g_1 \twoheadrightarrow g_3$. We also use two additional inference rules for goal relations: if $g_1 \twoheadrightarrow g_2$ and $g_2 \& g_3$ then $g_1 \& g_3$; and if $g_1 \twoheadrightarrow g_2$ and $g_2 \, \xi \, g_3$ then $g_1 \, \xi \, g_3$. The correctness of these inference rules follows immediately from the definition of goal models and the goal relations in Sect. 3.1.

Given a set R of goal relations, we denote by $Infer(R)$ the set of goal relations that are inferred from R by applying the inference rules.

4.4 Consistency Checking

Based on the previous definitions, we now define a consistency check between a goal model and a declarative CM schema related by a correspondence function α. We first define two sets of goal relations. The first set is induced by the goal model, based on the goal relations defined in Sect. 3.1. The second set is derived from the CM schema, based on the goal derivation rules in Sect. 4.2.

Definition 7 (Goal relations). *Let GM be a goal model, C a CM schema and α a correspondence function relating C and GM. Denote by GR(GM)) the goal relations induced by the goal model GM. Denote by GR(C) the goal relations computed by applying the goal derivation rules of Sect. 4.2 to C.*

We next define consistency between a goal model and a declarative CM schema that are related by a correspondence function α. We also define the consistency degree, which expresses to which extent the relevant goal relations in the goal model are derived and inferred from the CM schema. A goal relation is relevant if the related goals are in the range of α.

Definition 8 (Consistency, Consistency degree). *Let GM be a goal model, C a CM schema and α a correspondence function. Then GM and C are consistent according to α if $GR(C) \cup Infer(GR(C)) \subseteq GR(GM)$ and their consistency degree is $\frac{|GR(C) \cup Infer(GR(C))|}{|GR(GM) \cap (range(\alpha) \times range(\alpha))|}$.*

We illustrate this definition and the goal derivation rules by applying them to the goal model and CM schema introduced in Sect. 2. We use a correspondence function α that maps milestones to goals with the same label. For instance, goal and milestone Deal refined are related. Also, α maps both the milestone Standard terms drafted and the milestone Customized terms drafted to goal Terms Drafted Internally. Thus, the correspondence function α covers 6 goals and 7 milestones.

The goal and the CM schema are consistent according to α. Applying the consistency constraints to the CM schema in Fig. 2 yields the 9 goal relations in the lefthand side of Table 2. From these 9 derived goal relations, 12 additional goal relations are inferred (cf. Sect. 3.1), shown in the righthand side of Table 2. Note that even though the milestones Standard terms drafted and Customized terms drafted are owned by the same stage, Definition 6 does not apply since both milestones link to the same goal Terms Drafted Internally.

The 6 goals covered by the correspondence function α have 23 relations according to the goal model: 4 leaf goals with distinct 5 goal relations each, and intermediate goal Credit checked with 3 additional goal relations. 21 of these goal relations are derived from the CM schema. The two missing goal relations are the exclusive relations between Checked default and Checked expert. Thus, the consistency degree is $21/23 = 0.91$.

4.5 Discussion

Semantic Consistency. The approach defines consistency using structural rules in Sect. 4.2. It is logical to also look at semantic consistency, that is, to infer the consistency of a goal model with the executions of a declarative CM schema, given a correspondence function. However, the executions of a CM schema do not have enough information to compute semantic consistency.

For instance, consider the CM schema in Fig. 3 with $\alpha = \{(m1, g1), (m2, g2), (m3, g3)\}$. The sole complete execution trace of C1 is a sequence of states. Only looking at achieved milestones in each state, in one state of this sequence only

Table 2. Goal relations for CM schema in Fig. 2

Derived goal relations (Definitions 2–6)	Inferred goal relations
Terms drafted internally → Deal refined	Terms drafted internally & Checked default
Terms drafted internally & Credit checked	Terms drafted internally & Checked expert
Terms drafted internally & Price determined	Checked default → Deal refined
Credit checked → Deal refined	Checked default & Terms drafted internally
Credit checked & Terms drafted internally	Checked default & Price determined
Credit checked & Price determined	Checked expert → Deal refined
Checked default → Credit checked	Checked expert & Terms drafted internally
Checked expert → Credit checked	Checked expert & Price determined
Price determined → Deal refined	Price determined & Terms drafted internally
	Price determined & Credit checked
	Price determined & Checked default
	Price determined & Checked expert

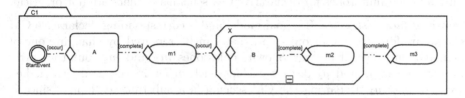

Fig. 3. CM schemas to illustrate issues semantic consistency

m1 has been achieved, which is followed eventually by a state in which both m1 and m2 have been achieved, and in the final state m1, m2 and m3 have been achieved. Now consider the CM schema C1' obtained from C1 by removing compound stage X but keeping B and m2, such that B succeeds m1 and m2 precedes m3. Only looking at achieved milestones, C1' has the same execution trace as C1. However, the goal relations implied by the rules in Sect. 4.2 for both CM schemas are different. The rules result for C1 in a goal relation g2 → g3, but for C1' in a goal relation g2&g3. The corresponding goal models are different: in the first one g2 is a subgoal of g3, in the second one g2 and g3 are both subgoals of an AND goal. In sum, different CM schemas relating to different goal models can yield the same execution traces. Therefore, execution traces are not rich enough to check consistency with a goal model.

Completeness. As the example shows, not all goal relations from the goal model are detected with the approach, so the approach is not complete. We were unable to define a simple structural constraint that results in milestones Checked default and Checked expert in Fig. 2 being exclusive. In this case, we could apply semantic reasoning over the execution traces and then derive that milestones Checked default and Checked expert are never achieved in the same execution trace, therefore the goals Checked default and Checked expert are exclusive. However, we explained above that execution traces in general are not rich enough to infer goal relations. Defining a complete approach using only semantic reasoning on execution traces is therefore not feasible. We believe that defining a complete approach, so identifying all possible goal relations, requires a combination of structural and semantic reasoning. We plan to study this in future work.

Deriving Constraints from Goal Models. The consistency between goal models and declarative CM schemas has been checked by deriving goal relations from the CM schemas by analyzing possible relations between distinct milestones. Checking consistency by deriving constraints for milestones from the goal model is not very useful, since a declarative CM schema can realize the same goal model in different ways. This is exemplified by different goal derivation rules that result in the same goal relations: the rules for Milestone-sentry (Definition 2) and Hierarchy (Definition 4) result in a supports $\rightarrow$ relation while the rules for Sentry (Definition 3) and Stage/task-milestone (Definition 5) result in a complements $\&$ relation. Consequently, relations $\&$ and $\rightarrow$ can be realized in different ways in declarative CM schemas. Checking consistency by deriving from the goal model constraints on milestones for declarative CM schemas is therefore not practical.

Repairing Inconsistencies. If a goal model and a corresponding declarative CM schema are found to be inconsistent, they can be repaired by changing one of them. For instance, if a stage S owns milestones m_1 and m_2, but the corresponding goals g_1 and g_2 do not exclude each other in the goal model, i.e., $g_1 \& g_2$ or $g_1 \rightarrow g_2$. Repairing the CM schema is a substantive change, since it would require that m_1 or m_2 is detached from S. Changing the goal model by for instance restricting the conditions of g_1 and g_2 seems more feasible. As another example, if a milestone-sentry consistency constraint is violated, then there is a milestone m_1 in the entry sentry of milestone m_2. If $g_1 \nleftrightarrow g_2$, then the relations in the goal model can be changed to ensure $g_1 \rightarrow g_2$. However, this is a major change. Changing the CM schema such that both milestones m_1 and m_2 are owned by the same stage seems more feasible. These two examples suggest that the consistency constraint that was violated is a major factor in deciding what model to change when repairing an inconsistency. We plan to study this in future work.

5   Evaluation

We evaluated feasibility by developing a prototype tool that implements the goal derivation and inference rules and next applying the approach and the tool to a real-world example. The prototype tool has been implemented in Java. Input to the tool are a CMMN model, in XML format, and a text file denoting the correspondence function, expressed as a list of pairs of goals and milestones. Both the tool and the used input files described in this section are publicly available.[1]

The tool first derives relations between the goals according to Definitions 2–6 by analyzing the structure of the CMMN model. Next, the tool infers additional goal relations from the derived goal relations. It outputs both the derived goal

---

[1] See https://github.com/heshuis/CMMNgoalanalyzer.

relations and the inferred goal relations. The tool also checks if all the goal relations are internally consistent, so each ordered pair of goals is related at most once, for instance if $g_1 \rightarrow g_2$ then neither $g_1 \& g_2$ nor $g_1 g_2$.

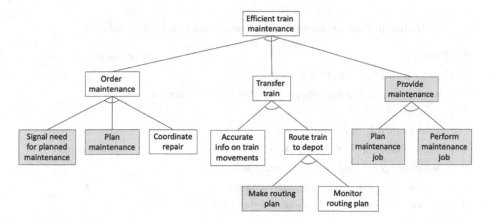

Fig. 4. Goal model of Maintenance Order process. Arcs denote AND decomposition. Gray shaded goals are in the correspondence function.

We applied the tool on a real-world example: the maintenance logistics process at Dutch Railways [27]. The process ensures that train units requiring maintenance arrive in time, via what is called a train path, at the maintenance location. Disruptions in the train schedule affect this transfer process. The process has been modeled before using agent-oriented modeling [16] and using Guard-Stage-Milestone (GSM) schemas [27].

The goal model, shown in Fig. 4, was derived by analysing the textual description of an agent-based perspective on the maintenance process [16]. The goal model contains 13 goals, of which 5 are hierarchical. Next, a CMMN model was created for Maintenance Order, the key artifact in the maintenance logistics process, based on an earlier developed GSM schema [27]. Since GSM and CMMN use similar constructs, the translation is straightforward. The CMMN model contains 20 milestones; due to space limitations it is not shown here.

We checked the consistency of the goal model and the CMMN model in three steps. First, we established a correspondence function between the goals and the milestones, based on the comparison between the agent-based model and the GSM schema [27]. Second, we applied the tool to the CMMN model and the correspondence function to derive and infer the goal relations. Finally, we checked for each derived and inferred goal relation whether it is consistent with the goal model.

This consistency check was performed in two iterations. In the first iteration, we used a CMMN model and a correspondence function that covered 5 milestones and 5 goals in a one-to-one mapping (shown in gray in Fig. 4). There was no milestone counterpart for goal **Provide maintenance**, even though all its subgoals were in the mapping. For the second iteration, we added this counterpart in the CMMN model by inserting a milestone for goal Provide maintenance and a stage that owns this milestone; the stage contains the milestones for goals Plan maintenance job and Perform maintenance job.

Table 3. Goal relations for the maintenance order CM schema

Goal relation	Iteration 1	Iteration 2
Derived goal relations (Definitions 2–6)		
Signal need for planned maintenance & Plan maintenance	x	x
Plan maintenance & Provide maintenance		x
Plan maintenance & Make routing plan	x	x
Plan maintenance & Plan maintenance job	x	(inferred)
Plan maintenance job & Perform maintenance job	x	x
Plan maintenance job –▸ Provide maintenance		x
Perform maintenance job –▸ Provide maintenance		x
Inferred goal relations		
Plan maintenance & Signal need for planned maintenance	x	x
Plan maintenance & Perform maintenance job		x
Plan maintenance & Plan maintenance job	(derived)	x
Make routing plan & Plan maintenance	x	x
Provide maintenance & Plan maintenance		x
Plan maintenance job & Plan maintenance	x	x
Perform maintenance job & Plan maintenance		x
Perform maintenance job & Plan maintenance job	x	x

Table 3 show the goal relations derived and inferred in both iterations. In the first iteration 8 goal relations were found, in the second iteration the same 8 plus 6 additional goal relations were derived. Goal relation Plan maintenance&Plan maintenance job was derived in the first iteration and inferred in the second iteration. Each goal relation that was found is consistent with the goal model in Fig. 4. Even though the CMMN model has several stages owning multiple milestones, there is no exclusive relation between goals, since for each such stage at most one milestone has a corresponding goal.

Not all goal relations from the goal model can be derived and inferred. For instance, the goal model specifies Signal need for planned maintenance & Provide maintenance, but this goal relation cannot be derived from the CMMN model or inferred from the other goal relations (since relation & is not transitive). The goal model specifies 20 goal relations for the 5 goals covered in iteration 1; the approach computes 8 relations, so the consistency degree is $8/20 = 40\%$. For iteration 2, the goal model specifies 28 goal relations for the 6 covered goals; the approach computes 14 relations, so the consistency degree is $14/28 = 50\%$. Thus, a small increase in size of the correspondence function can significantly improve the consistency degree.

The evaluation shows how the approach can help to check the consistency of a goal model and CM schema. Inferring goal relations is essential to get a good consistency degree. Still, a lot of goal relations could not be found; we plan to relax the inference rules to improve this. The evaluation also shows that the approach can help to further structure a CM schema for improved alignment.

6 Related Work

Several approaches have been defined that link goal modeling and process modeling, for instance to improve business processes [19,23] or to model business processes in a more flexible way [21,26,28]. We now focus on the three specific clusters of related work in the area of goal modeling and process modeling. None of the works discussed next focuses on declarative CM schemas.

First, there are approaches that check consistency of goal models and activity-centric process models expressed in BPMN [2,10,17,20]. Koliadis et al. [17] define a methodology that checks satisfaction of a BPMN process model against a KAOS goal model. Activities in the analyzed process models are extended with effect annotations. Accumulated effects along an execution path are checked against the KAOS goals. Gröner et al. [10] define an approach based on description logic for checking the consistency of different goal ordering relations and the main workflow patterns that can occur in procedural process models. Nagel et al. [20] translate different goal-ordering constraints into temporal logic formulas, which are verified against the behavior of the process models with a model checker. Akhigbe et al. [2] define OCL constraints that relate goal views to process views in User Requirements Notation (URN) models. All these approaches are heavy weight since they use a separate semantic domain for checking consistency, like description logic or temporal logic, whereas we define a lightweight approach by structurally relating goal models and CM schemas, without introducing a separate semantic domain.

Second, several approaches study the alignment of goal models and process models. Guizzardi et al. [11] propose a method that aids business analysts in aligning goal models expressed in Tropos with process models expressed in BPMN. The method identifies non-aligned goals and activities and supports analyzing the level of satisfaction of goals. We study declarative CM schemas, which differ considerably from BPMN. Cortes-Cornax et al. [5] define an approach that characterizes so-called intentional BPMN process fragments that realize KAOS goals. This way, goal-based analysis can be used to re-engineer processes. Our approach relates goals to certain constructs (milestones) in CM schemas, which are much less structured than BPMN models.

Third, some approaches transform goal models into process models. Horita et al. [14] define a pattern-based approach that translates KAOS goal models into BPMN process models. Ponsard and Darimont [25] refine and extend this work into a goal-oriented approach for analyzing and redesigning BPMN models. The reverse direction is analyzed by Vara et al. [31], who define mapping rules from process models to goal models. These works are based on procedural process models, which differ a lot from declarative CM schemas.

In the area of case management, there is work that checks structural consistency of CM schemas [6] or that proposes goal-oriented way of modeling procedural CM schemas [13], but no work that checks the consistency of a goal model and a declarative CM schema.

The main contribution of this paper is a structural approach for checking the consistency of goal models and CM schemas. The approach relies on a correspondence function that maps milestones to goals and is defined based on structural relations in the goal models and CM schemas.

7   Conclusion

We have presented a structural approach to check consistency of a goal model and a declarative case management schema. The approach checks whether the goal interdependencies implied by the declarative case management schema are consistent with the goal model. We have implemented the approach in a prototype tool and applied it to a real-world example, where the approach helped to show consistency and to improve the case management schema.

For further work, we plan to improve the inference rules of the approach and to apply the approach in more case studies. We will also study how to fix inconsistencies between a goal model and a declarative case management schema.

References

1. van der Aalst, W.M.P., Weske, M., Grünbauer, D.: Case handling: a new paradigm for business process support. Data Knowl. Eng. **53**(2), 129–162 (2005)
2. Akhigbe, O., Amyot, D., Anda, A.A., Lessard, L., Xiao, D.: Consistency analysis for user requirements notation models. In: Proceedings of the iStar 2016, pp. 43–48. CEUR-WS.org (2016)
3. BizAgi and others: Case Management Model and Notation (CMMN), v1.1 (December 2016). OMG Document Number formal/16-12-01, Object Management Group
4. Chao, T., et al.: Artifact-based transformation of IBM global financing. In: Dayal, U., Eder, J., Koehler, J., Reijers, H.A. (eds.) BPM 2009. LNCS, vol. 5701, pp. 261–277. Springer, Heidelberg (2009). https://doi.org/10.1007/978-3-642-03848-8_18
5. Cortes-Cornax, M., Matei, A., Dupuy-Chessa, S., Rieu, D., Mandran, N., Letier, E.: Using intentional fragments to bridge the gap between organizational and intentional levels. Inf. Softw. Technol. **58**, 1–19 (2015)
6. Czepa, C., et al.: Supporting structural consistency checking in adaptive case management. In: Debruyne, C., et al. (eds.) OTM 2015. LNCS, vol. 9415, pp. 311–319. Springer, Cham (2015). https://doi.org/10.1007/978-3-319-26148-5_19
7. Di Ciccio, C., Marrella, A., Russo, A.: Knowledge-intensive processes: characteristics, requirements and analysis of contemporary approaches. J. Data Seman. **4**(1), 29–57 (2015)

8. Eshuis, R., Debois, S., Slaats, T., Hildebrandt, T.: Deriving consistent GSM schemas from DCR graphs. In: Sheng, Q.Z., Stroulia, E., Tata, S., Bhiri, S. (eds.) ICSOC 2016. LNCS, vol. 9936, pp. 467–482. Springer, Cham (2016). https://doi.org/10.1007/978-3-319-46295-0_29

9. Eshuis, R., Hull, R., Sun, Y., Vaculín, R.: Splitting GSM schemas: a framework for outsourcing of declarative artifact systems. Inf. Syst. **46**, 157–187 (2014)

10. Gröner, G., Asadi, M., Mohabbati, B., Gašević, D., Silva Parreiras, F., Bošković, M.: Validation of user intentions in process models. In: Ralyté, J., Franch, X., Brinkkemper, S., Wrycza, S. (eds.) CAiSE 2012. LNCS, vol. 7328, pp. 366–381. Springer, Heidelberg (2012). https://doi.org/10.1007/978-3-642-31095-9_24

11. Guizzardi, R., Reis, A.N.: A method to align goals and business processes. In: Johannesson, P., Lee, M.L., Liddle, S.W., Opdahl, A.L., López, Ó.P. (eds.) ER 2015. LNCS, vol. 9381, pp. 79–93. Springer, Cham (2015). https://doi.org/10.1007/978-3-319-25264-3_6

12. Haisjackl, C., et al.: Making sense of declarative process models: common strategies and typical pitfalls. In: Nurcan, S., et al. (eds.) BPMDS/EMMSAD -2013. LNBIP, vol. 147, pp. 2–17. Springer, Heidelberg (2013). https://doi.org/10.1007/978-3-642-38484-4_2

13. Hewelt, M., Pufahl, L., Mandal, S., Wolff, F., Weske, M.: Toward a methodology for case modeling. Softw. Syst. Model. **19**(6), 1367–1393 (2020)

14. Horita, H., Honda, K., Sei, Y., Nakagawa, H., Tahara, Y., Ohsuga, A.: Transformation approach from KAOS goal models to BPMN models using refinement patterns. In: Proceedings of the SAC 2014, pp. 1023–1024 (2014)

15. Hull, R., et al.: Introducing the guard-stage-milestone approach for specifying business entity lifecycles. In: Proceedings of the WS-FM, pp. 1–24 (2010)

16. Jiang, J., Huisman, B., Dignum, V.: Agent-based multi-organizational interaction design: a case study of the Dutch railway system. In: Proceedings of the IAT 2012, pp. 196–203. IEEE Computer Society (2012)

17. Koliadis, G., Ghose, A.: Relating business process models to goal-oriented requirements models in KAOS. In: Proceedings of the PKAW 2006, pp. 25–39 (2006)

18. van Lamsweerde, A.: Requirements Engineering - From System Goals to UML Models to Software Specifications. Wiley (2009)

19. Lohrmann, M., Reichert, M.: Effective application of process improvement patterns to business processes. Softw. Syst. Model. **15**(2), 353–375 (2016)

20. Nagel, B., Gerth, C., Engels, G., Post, J.: Ensuring consistency among business goals and business process models. In: Proceedings of the EDOC 2013, pp. 17–26. IEEE Computer Society (2013)

21. Nurcan, S., Etien, A., Kaabi, R.S., Zoukar, I., Rolland, C.: A strategy driven business process modelling approach. Bus. Process. Manag. J. **11**(6), 628–649 (2005)

22. Pillaerds, J., Eshuis, R.: Assessing suitability of adaptive case management. In: Proceedings of the ECIS 2017, p. 37 (2017)

23. Poels, G., Decreus, K., Roelens, B., Snoeck, M.: Investigating goal-oriented requirements engineering for business processes. J. Database Manag. **24**(2), 35–71 (2013)

24. Ponnalagu, K., Ghose, A., Narendra, N.C., Dam, H.K.: Goal-aligned categorization of instance variants in knowledge-intensive processes. In: Motahari-Nezhad, H.R., Recker, J., Weidlich, M. (eds.) BPM 2015. LNCS, vol. 9253, pp. 350–364. Springer, Cham (2015). https://doi.org/10.1007/978-3-319-23063-4_24

25. Ponsard, C., Darimont, R.: Towards goal-oriented analysis and redesign of BPMN models. In: Proceedings of the MODELSWARD 2019, pp. 527–533 (2019)

26. Rolland, C., Prakash, N., Benjamen, A.: A multi-model view of process modelling. Requir. Eng. **4**(4), 169–187 (1999)

27. Smit, E., Eshuis, R.: Modeling rolling stock maintenance logistics at Dutch railways with declarative business artifacts. In: Di Francescomarino, C., Dijkman, R., Zdun, U. (eds.) BPM 2019. LNBIP, vol. 362, pp. 375–387. Springer, Cham (2019). https://doi.org/10.1007/978-3-030-37453-2_31

28. Soffer, P., Wand, Y.: Goal-driven multi-process analysis. J. Assoc. Inf. Syst. **8**(3), 9 (2007)

29. Swenson, K.D.: Mastering the Unpredictable: How Adaptive Case Management will Revolutionize the Way that Knowledge Workers Get Things Done. Meghan-Kiffer, FL (2010)

30. Vaculín, R., Hull, R., Heath, T., Cochran, C., Nigam, A., Sukaviriya, P.: Declarative business artifact centric modeling of decision and knowledge intensive business processes. In: Proceedings of the EDOC 2011, pp. 151–160 (2011)

31. de la Vara, J.L., Sánchez, J., Pastor, O.: On the use of goal models and business process models for elicitation of system requirements. In: Nurcan, S., et al. (eds.) BPMDS/EMMSAD -2013. LNBIP, vol. 147, pp. 168–183. Springer, Heidelberg (2013). https://doi.org/10.1007/978-3-642-38484-4_13

32. Yu, E., Giorgini, P., Maiden, N., Mylopoulos, J. (eds.): Social Modeling for Requirements Engineering. MIT Press (2010)

Process Analytics

Detection of Statistically Significant Differences Between Process Variants Through Declarative Rules

Alessio Cecconi[1]([✉]) [ID], Adriano Augusto[2] [ID], and Claudio Di Ciccio[3] [ID]

[1] Vienna University of Economics and Business, Vienna, Austria
cecconi@ai.wu.ac.at
[2] The University of Melbourne, Melbourne, Australia
a.augusto@unimelb.edu.au
[3] Sapienza University of Rome, Rome, Italy
claudio.diciccio@uniroma1.it

Abstract. Services and products are often offered via the execution of processes that vary according to the context, requirements, or customisation needs. The analysis of such process variants can highlight differences in the service outcome or quality, leading to process adjustments and improvement. Research in the area of process mining has provided several methods for process variants analysis. However, very few of those account for a statistical significance analysis of their output. Moreover, those techniques detect differences at the level of process traces, single activities, or performance. In this paper, we aim at describing the distinctive behavioural characteristics between variants expressed in the form of declarative process rules. The contribution to the research area is two-pronged: the use of declarative rules for the explanation of the process variants and the statistical significance analysis of the outcome. We assess the proposed method by comparing its results to the most recent process variants analysis methods. Our results demonstrate not only that declarative rules reveal differences at an unprecedented level of expressiveness, but also that our method outperforms the state of the art in terms of execution time.

1 Introduction

The execution of a business process varies according to the context in which it operates. The exhibited behaviour changes to adapt to diverse requirements, geographical locations, availability or preferences of the actors involved, and other environmental factors. The alternative enactments lead to the diversification of specialised processes that stem from a general model. Considering some real-world examples, the hospital treatment of sepsis cases follows a different clinical pathway according to their age; the credit collection of road traffic fines typically undergoes an additional appeal to the prefecture when the fine is high.

Recent trends in business process management have led to a proliferation of studies that tackle the automated analysis of process variants [19]. After

© Springer Nature Switzerland AG 2021
A. Polyvyanyy et al. (Eds.): BPM Forum 2021, LNBIP 427, pp. 73–91, 2021.
https://doi.org/10.1007/978-3-030-85440-9_5

Table 1. Description and notation of considered DECLARE constraints

Constraint	Verbal explanation
PARTICIPATION(a)	a occurs at least *once*
ATMOSTONE(a)	a occurs at most *once*
RESPONDEDEXISTENCE(a, b)	If a occurs, then b occurs as well
RESPONSE(a, b)	If a occurs, then b occurs after a
ALTERNATERESPONSE(a, b)	Each time a occurs, then b occurs afterwards, and no other a recurs in between
CHAINRESPONSE(a, b)	Each time a occurs, then b occurs immediately afterwards
PRECEDENCE(a, b)	b occurs only if preceded by a
ALTERNATEPRECEDENCE(a, b)	Each time b occurs, it is preceded by a and no other b recurs in between
CHAINPRECEDENCE(a, b)	Each time b occurs, then a occurs immediately beforehand
COEXISTENCE(a, b)	If b occurs, then a occurs, and vice versa
SUCCESSION(a, b)	a occurs if and only if it is followed by b
ALTERNATESUCCESSION(a, b)	a and b if and only if the latter follows the former, and they alternate each other
CHAINSUCCESSION(a, b)	a and b occur if and only if the latter immediately follows the former

the initial manual, ad-hoc endeavours on single case studies, the focus has shifted towards the data-driven detection of their behavioural differences from the respective event logs [3,4,10,18]. To date, however, the explanatory power of the existing techniques is limited: the results are (i) exposed as whole graphical models (e.g., directly-follows graphs) leaving the identification of the differences to the visual inspection of the analyst, or (ii) expressed as variations within the limited scope of subsequent event pairs (e.g., behavioural profiles).

To overcome this limitation, we propose an approach that infers and describe the differences between variants in terms of behavioural rules. Our declarative approach aims to (i) single out the distinct behavioural characteristics leading to the variations observed in the trace, while (ii) having a global scope as rules are exerted on the whole process runs. In our pursuit of explainability, we employ and adapt state-of-the-art techniques to guarantee the statistical significance of the inferred differentiating rules and expose the top-ranked distinctive characteristics in the form of natural language. We name our approach Declarative Rules Variant Analysis (DRVA).

In the following, Sect. 2 illustrates existing work in the areas upon which our approach is based. Section 3 describes in details our technique. Section 4 illustrates the results of our tool running on real-world event logs and compares them with state-of-the-art techniques. Finally, Sect. 5 concludes this paper and provides remarks for future research avenues.

2   Background and Related Work

In this section, we provide a brief overview of the use of declarative languages within the process mining area. We discuss the most recent studies on process variants analysis, and we introduce the statistical significance test that we adapted to our context.

2.1 Declarative Process Specification and Mining

A declarative specification represents the behaviour of a process by means of reactive constraints [5], i.e., temporal rules that specify the conditions under which activities can or cannot be executed. For the purposes of this paper, we focus on DECLARE, one of the most well-established declarative process modelling languages to date [12]. DECLARE provides a standard repertoire of templates, namely linear temporal-logic rules parameterised over tasks, here abstracted as symbols of a finite non-empty alphabet Σ. Table 1 illustrates the templates we use in the context of this paper. Declarative rules are typically expressed in an if-then fashion, whereby the "if" part is named *activator* and the "then" part is the *target*. For example, RESPONSE(a, b) requires that if a is executed (activator), then b must be eventually carried out (the target). PRECEDENCE(b, a) imposes that a cannot be executed if b has not occurred earlier in the process instance. RESPONDEDEXISTENCE(a, b) relaxes the condition exerted by RESPONSE(a, b) and PRECEDENCE(b, a) by requiring that if a is executed, then b has to occur in the same trace, regardless of whether it happens before or after a. RESPONSE(a, b) and PRECEDENCE(b, a) thus *entail* RESPONDEDEXISTENCE(a, b) and we say that RESPONDEDEXISTENCE *subsumes* RESPONSE and PRECEDENCE [7]. Subsumption is a partial order on the templates of DECLARE inducing the partial order of entailment on the rules that instantiate those templates. A *declarative specification* $M \ni r$ is a set of rules r that conjunctively define the behaviour of a process. We shall denote the universe of declarative rules as $\mathfrak{R} \supseteq M \ni r$.

The formal semantics of DECLARE rules are rooted in Linear Temporal Logic on Finite Traces (LTL$_f$). A trace $t \in \Sigma^*$ is a finite string of *events*. An event log (or *log* for short) is a multi-set of traces $L : \Sigma^* \to \mathbb{N}$ (in which equivalent elements can occur multiple times). We indicate the universe of event logs as $\mathfrak{L} \ni L$. We shall denote as $|t|$ the length of a trace t, as $|L|$ the cardinality of the event log, and as $|\hat{t}|$ the length of the longest trace in the log. Declarative process discovery tools can assess to what degree constraints hold true in a given event log. To that end, diverse measures $m : \mathfrak{R} \times \mathfrak{L} \to \mathbb{R}$ have been introduced to map a rule $r \in \mathfrak{R}$ and an event log $L \in \mathfrak{L}$ to a real number [5]. Among them, we consider *Support* and *Confidence* here. Their values range from 0 to 1. Support is computed as the fraction of events in which both activator (e.g., the occurrence of a for RESPONSE(a, b)) and target (e.g., the occurrence of b eventually afterwards in the trace) hold true. Confidence is the fraction of the events in which the rule holds true over the events in which the activator is satisfied. With a slight abuse of notation, we shall indicate the measure of r on a single trace t with $m(r, t)$.

2.2 Process Variants Analysis

The latest literature review on process variants analysis [19] identified more than thirty studies addressing the research problem, clearly showing a growing interest in the topic. Much of the early research work was centred on case studies, providing examples of variant analysis applications that highlighted its potential capabilities. Among the earliest studies, Poelmans et al. [14] combined process mining and data mining techniques to differentiate and analyse the healthcare pathways of patients affected by breast cancer and their response to therapies. Another of the most impactful studies is the one regarding a large Australian insurance company [17], in which Suriadi et al. describe a methodology to pinpoint the weaknesses in the processing of insurance claims that had slow turnaround time. Until recently, the vast majority of variant analysis studies focused on the detection of control flow differences of two or more process variants, with the frequent underlying goal to relate such differences to the outcome of the process variant. Also, proposed methods for variant analysis did not put much attention to the statistical significance of the detected differences, with the risk to catch random differences. Only recently proposed methods for variant analysis [4,10,18] account for statistical significance.

Bolt et al. [4] pioneered the introduction of statistical significance in variant analysis, designing a framework to compare process variants in the form of annotated transition systems through the application of statistical tests. Also, the framework allows the analysis of the decision points in different variants and how the underlying decision-making rules differ. The annotations on the transition systems can capture frequencies and elapsed time between the transitions, however, the framework was designed to be extended, with the option to capture new annotations.

Nguyen et al. [10] propose a variant analysis method based on the statistical comparison of *perspective graphs*. A perspective graph is an artifact that captures an attribute of an event log (e.g. activity, resource, etc.), and the relations between the observed attribute values. The two perspective graphs (one per process variant) are then statistically compared and a *differential perspective graph* is generated. The latter is analysed to determine the differences between the variants. By varying the attribute to generate the perspective graphs, the method allows for the analysis of different process perspectives.

Lastly, Taymouri et al. [18] propose a variant analysis method to separate statistically-significant different traces from common traces between the two input process variant logs. Each trace is encoded as a vector, then an SVM is used to classify the traces (assigning them to one of the two logs). A set of trace features (i.e. directly-follows relations) that can statistically discriminate the traces between the two logs is identified, and the logs are filtered by retaining only the traces containing those features. Finally, the two filtered logs are mapped into directly-follows graphs, called mutual-fingerprints, which rely on color-coding to show differences.

Of all the past studies, none is capable of analysing process variants to detect differences in the form of declarative rules [19], which is instead the focus of this paper. However, given that declarative rules can be difficult to interpret, and that variant analysis is of high interest for the practitioners audience, we follow the example of van Beest et al. [3] and provide a natural language translation of the detected differences [1].

2.3 Statistical Significance

It is likely that the data at hand captures only a portion of the whole data population, and it can include outliers. Process execution data is no exception. In fact, an event log usually contains only a part of the allowed process behaviour, on one hand, and infrequent behaviour, on the other hand [2]. To draw reliable observations from data samples, statistics provides several methods to assess the likelihood that an observation holds for the whole data population. These methods, known as *statistical significance tests*, estimate the probability that what is observed happened by chance. Traditionally, if such probability is low (below 0.05), the observation is assumed to hold for the whole data population.

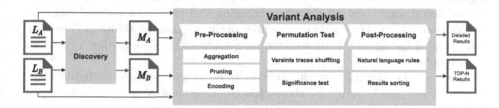

Fig. 1. Schema of our variant analysis approach based on declarative rules.

Of the many available methods to assess the statistical significance of the discovered declarative rules (which are similar to association rules) [9], we deem the *permutation test* [13] as the one that best fits for our purpose and context. The permutation test (also known as randomization test) is a non-parametric test originally designed to estimate the probability that two numerical series belong to the same population or not. In other words, it provides an answer to the question: "Are the two series statistically different?" The permutation test is carried out as follows. First, the difference of the averages of the two series is calculated (the *delta average*). Then, the elements of the two series are pooled and two new series are drawn at random to compute the delta average again. This step is repeated for all the possible permutations. The likelihood that the two original series are statistically different is assessed as one minus the percentage of delta average that is greater or equal to the original delta average. The original permutation test is computationally heavy because it requires a computation on all the possible permutations of the original series. However, successive studies have proposed approximated [8] and efficient [21] methods to reduce the computational effort and construct permutation tests for any settings [20], from pure maths [13] to medicine [11]. In the following, we show how we adapt the permutation test to address the problem of variant analysis.

3   Approach

In this section, we present in details our variant analysis technique based on declarative process specifications: Declarative Rules Variant Analysis (DRVA).

The core idea is to discover the declarative process specifications describing the behaviour of the input variants' event logs and to check, by running a permutation test, whether the difference between the two specifications are statistically significant. To assess the significance, intuitively, we verify whether the differences stemming from the variants' event logs are not due to rules that occur by chance.

Figure 1 presents the overview of the approach. Specifically, the variant analysis is divided into four phases: (1) A discovery phase, to mine the declarative specifications of the variants' behaviour; (2) A pre-processing phase, to prune redundant or irrelevant rules and encode the information for faster computation; (3) A statistical validation phase, in which the permutations and related significance test take place; and (4) A final post-processing phase, to sort the results according to a given relevance criterion and produce a natural language description of the output. In the remainder of this section, we thoroughly explain each step of the approach (illustrated as pseudo-code in Algorithm 1) and its implementation.

Some of the examples in this section refer to the publicly available SEPSIS event log (see Table 2), which records the treatment of patients with sepsis symptoms in a Dutch hospital. The two variants are generated as one containing

---

Algorithm 1: Computing the set of rules that differ in a statistically significant way. The computational cost of the steps is specified on the right-hand side.

Input: Log variants L_A and L_B, specifications M_A and M_B, a function m, parameters m_{min}, $m_{diff\text{-}min}$, α, π

Result: R, a set of rules exhibiting a statistically significant difference between the variants.

/* Pre-processing   */
1 $M_\cup \longleftarrow M_A \cup M_B$;   // Cost: $\mathcal{O}(|M_A| + |M_B|)$
2 $E_{diff}, E_A, E_B \longleftarrow \{\}$;   // Cost: $\mathcal{O}(1)$
3 **foreach** $r \in M_\cup$ **do**   // Block cost: $\mathcal{O}(|M_\cup| \times |\hat{t}| \times (|L_A| + |L_B|))$
4      $E_A \longleftarrow E_A \cup \{(r, m(r, L_A))\}$;   // Cost: $\mathcal{O}(|e_A| + |L_A|)$
5      $E_B \longleftarrow E_B \cup \{(r, m(r, L_B))\}$;   // Cost: $\mathcal{O}(|e_B| + |L_B|)$
6      $E_{diff} \longleftarrow E_{diff} \cup \{(r, |m(r, L_A) - m(r, L_B)|)\}$;   // Cost: $\mathcal{O}(1)$
7 **foreach** $r \in M_\cup$ **do**   // Block cost: $\mathcal{O}(|M_\cup|)$
8   **if** $(E_{diff}(r) < m_{diff\text{-}min}) \vee (E_A(r) < m_{min}) \vee (E_B(r) < m_{min})$ **then**   // Cost: $\mathcal{O}(1)$
9   Remove r from $M_\cup$ and its measurements from E_A, E_B, E_{diff} ;   // Cost: $\mathcal{O}(1)$
10 $M_\cup, E_A, E_B, E_{diff} \longleftarrow$ hierarchicalSimplification($M_\cup, E_A, E_B$) ; // Cost: $\mathcal{O}(|M_\cup| \times |h|)$
11 $L_A^m, L_B^m \longleftarrow$ encodeLog($L_A, L_B, M_\cup$) ;   // Cost: $\mathcal{O}(|M_\cup| \times (|L_A| + |L_B|))$
/* Permutation Test   */
12 $C \longleftarrow$ Initialize map such that for all $r \in M_\cup : C(r) = 1$;   // Cost: $\mathcal{O}(|M_\cup|)$
13 **for** $i \leftarrow 1$ **to** π **do**   // Block cost: $\mathcal{O}(|\pi| \times |M_\cup| \times (|L_A| + |L_B|))$
14      $L_{A_i}^m, L_{B_i}^m \longleftarrow$ shuffleLog(L_A^m, L_B^m) ;   // Cost: $\mathcal{O}(|L_A| + |L_B|)$
15   **foreach** $r \in M_\cup$ **do**   // Block cost: $\mathcal{O}(|M_\cup| \times (|L_A| + |L_B|))$
16   **if** $|m(r, L_{A_i}^m) - m(r, L_{B_i}^m)| \geq E_{diff}(r)$ **then**   // Cost: $\mathcal{O}(|L_A| + |L_B|)$
17              $C(r) \longleftarrow C(r) + 1$ // Cost: $\mathcal{O}(1)$
18 $R \longleftarrow \{\}$;   // Cost: $\mathcal{O}(1)$
19 **foreach** $r \in M_\cup$ **do**   // Block cost: $\mathcal{O}(|M_\cup|)$
20   p-value$(r) \longleftarrow \frac{C(r)}{\pi}$;   // Cost: $\mathcal{O}(1)$
21   **if** $p\text{-}value(r) \leq \alpha$ **then** $R \longleftarrow R \cup \{r\}$;   // Cost: $\mathcal{O}(1)$
22 **return** R

traces regarding only elderly patients above the age of 70 (L_A) and the other containing young ones below 35 (L_B).

3.1 Declarative Specifications Discovery

In order to compare the variants through a declarative lens, it is necessary to derive the declarative specifications of their behavior. Specifically, given the input variants event logs L_A and L_B, we want to retrieve the respective declarative specifications M_A and M_B. This can be done by executing existing declarative process discovery techniques [16].

We remark that the criteria used for the discovery influence the subsequent steps of the analysis. For example, discovering only specifications that are highly compliant to the event logs makes the variant analysis consider the most regular and stable behaviour of the processes. Looser specifications encompass also less frequent behaviours.

The discovery step is executed when only the event logs are given as input. Alternatively, our technique can receive as input the declarative specifications already discovered from the two logs, in such a case, the discovery step is skipped and our technique performs only the variant analysis with the input specifications. Hand-crafted or filtered input declarative specifications can be useful when it is desired to test the statistical significance of the differences between two variants according to specific rules. For example, if the analyst is interested only in the behavioural difference involving tasks ER Triage and LacticAcid, she can provide as input two specifications containing only rules involving these tasks (e.g., RESPONSE(ER Triage, LacticAcid), PRECEDENCE(ER Triage, IV Liquid), SUCCESSION(LacticAcid, Admission NC), and so on) together with the variants' logs.

3.2 Pre-processing

The variants analysis takes the variants' events logs L_A and L_B as input, together with the respective declarative process specifications M_A and M_B. As the permutation test is a computationally heavy task, it is desirable to keep only the essential information. Thus, to efficiently perform the statistical test, the data must be ① aggregated, to have a common view between the variants, ② cleaned via pruning, to remove redundant or irrelevant information, and ③ encoded, to improve performance.

① **Aggregation.** The declarative specifications M_A and M_B are merged into a unique specification $M_\cup = M_A \cup M_B$. To check their differences, all the rules in M_A must be checked in L_B and vice versa, thus the union of M_A and M_B allows us to consider all and only the distinct rules in both the logs.

The interestingness of each rule $r \in M_\cup$ is measured in each variant log L_A and L_B. We resort to the measurement framework for declarative specifications proposed in [5]. Among the various measures available, we consider Confidence as the best option because it measures the degree of satisfaction of a rule in a log independently from the rule frequency. The comparison of the most suitable measures (or combinations thereof) goes beyond the scope of the paper and paves the path for future work. In our example, $m(\text{RESPONSE}(\text{ER Triage}, \text{LacticAcid}), L_A) = 0.83$ and $m(\text{RESPONSE}(\text{ER Triage}, \text{LacticAcid}), L_B) = 0.53$, which means that 83% of the occurrences of ER Triage in L_A are eventually followed by LacticAcid. In L_B, the measure drops to 53% for that rule.

Finally, we retain these reference measurements of $M_\cup$ in each variant denoting them as functional relations E_A and E_B. Formally, we define $E_A : M_\cup \to \mathbb{R}$ as $E_A = \{(r, m(r, L_A)) : r \in M_\cup\}$ and $E_B : M_\cup \to \mathbb{R}$ as $E_B = \{(r, m(r, L_B)) : r \in M_\cup\}$. We compute also the reference absolute difference between the variants' measurements E_{diff}. Formally, we define $E_{\text{diff}} : M_\cup \to \mathbb{R}$ as $E_{\text{diff}} = \{(r, |m(r, L_A) - m(r, L_B)|) : r \in M_\cup\}$, where $|x|$ is the absolute value of x. For example, $E_A(\text{RESPONSE}(\text{ER Triage}, \text{LacticAcid})) = 0.83$, $E_B(\text{RESPONSE}(\text{ER Triage}, \text{LacticAcid})) = 0.53$, and their absolute difference is $E_{\text{diff}}(\text{RESPONSE}(\text{ER Triage}, \text{LacticAcid})) = 0.30$.

② **Pruning.** Not all the rules contained in $M_\cup$ are valuable for the statistical test. Specifically, we consider as ignorable those rules that do not meet one of the following criteria.

Minimum Difference: If a rule difference between the variants is considered too small by an analyst to be of interest, it can be discarded. For example, rule $r = \text{PRECEDENCE}(\text{ER Registration}, \text{CRP})$ is such that $E_{\text{diff}}(r) = 0.01$ as $E_A(r) = 0.98$ and $E_B(r) = 0.99$. The significance of such a difference is debatable: the difference appears to be negligible although the consideration is subjective and depending on the context of the analysis. Therefore, we allow the user to customise a threshold to this end: $m_{\text{diff-min}}$. According to this criterion, we remove all the rules $r \in M_\cup$ such that $E_{\text{diff}}(r) < m_{\text{diff-min}}$ from $M_\cup$ and all their measurements from E_A, E_B, and E_{diff}.

Minimum Interestingness: If, according to an analyst, a rule is not interesting enough in either of the variants to be considered, it can be discarded. For example, rule $r = \text{RESPONSE}(\text{ER Triage}, \text{Release A})$ is such that $E_{\text{diff}}(r) = 0.23$ yet the rule itself is not frequently satisfied in either of the variants as $E_A(r) = 0.41$ and $E_B(r) = 0.64$. Whether this is desirable or not depends on the context of the analysis. Therefore, we define the m_{min} threshold to let the user set the desired minimum value that the rule's measure should be assigned within the variants' logs. In this step, we remove all the rules $r' \in M_\cup$ such that $m(r', L_A) < m_{\text{min}}$ and $m(r', L_B) < m_{\text{min}}$ from $M_\cup$ and all their measurements from E_A, E_B, and E_{diff}.

No Redundancy: If two rules are such that one is logically implied by the other, we do not gather additional information by retaining both in the set of rules under consideration. DECLARE patterns are hierarchically interdependent, as the satisfaction of a rule implies the satisfaction of all the entailed rules. We can exploit the hierarchical relation of the DECLARE templates to prune the redundant rules as in [6]. However, we adapt the original pruning technique by inverting the preference: We keep the most generic rule rather than the strictest one if measurements are the same in at least one of the variants' event logs. We explain the rationale at the core of our design choice with an example from the Sepsis event log.

Figure 2 depicts the partial order that stems from the subsumption relation among DECLARE templates [6] having ALTERNATESUCCESSION(ER Sepsis Triage, IV Antibiotics) as its least element, and RESPONDEDEXISTENCE (ER Sepsis Triage, IV Antibiotics) and RESPONDEDEXISTENCE(IV Antibiotics, ER Sepsis Triage) as its maximal elements. For the sake of space, we shall indicate ER Sepsis Triage and IV Antibiotics with t and v, respectively. ALT.SUCCESSION(t, v) is the strictest rule in the set, as all the other rules can be derived from it. As the associated Confidence is higher in L_A (0.82) than in L_B (0.49) we can claim the following: "In L_A, v follows t and t precedes v with no other t or v occurring in between, more likely than in L_B". Looking at the measurements on L_A and L_B we see that there is no difference between its values and the ones of ALT.RESPONSE(t, v) or SUCCESSION(t, v), and it entails both. Recursively following the subsumption relation, we notice that the same measurements are associated to one of the maximal elements of the induced partial order: RESPONDEDEXISTENCE(t, v). The other maximal element, instead, is such that the associated Confidence is equal to 1.00 in L_A and L_B. This characteristic reverberates along the chain of entailment down to ALT.PRECEDENCE(t, v). With this example, we observe that the least restrictive rules point out more precisely where the cause of the differences between variants lies – in this case, the occurrence of v required by t is at the core of the distinct behaviours. The co-occurrence, order of execution, and lack of internal recurrence are characteristics that ALT.PRECEDENCE(t, v) exhibits although they are evidenced by both variants.

According to this criterion, we thus prune redundant rules only if the measurement between entailing and entailed rules are equivalent in at least one variant. Otherwise, we keep both. Formally, denoting with ⊨ the entailment relation, we remove the following subset of rules from $M_\cup$ and all their measurements from E_A, E_B, and E_{diff}: $\{r \in M_\cup : r \vDash r', r' \in M_\cup \setminus \{r\}$ and $m(r, L_A) = m(r', L_A)$ or $m(r, L_B) = m(r', L_B)\}$.

We remark that the first two criteria (minimum difference and minimum interestingness) are generically applicable to declarative rules and measures thereof, whereas the third one (no redundancy) is tailored for templates á-la-DECLARE and measures such as Confidence, as it requires a subsumption hierarchy of the repertoire of templates and the monotone non-decrease of the measure within the subsumption hierarchy (i.e., if $r \vDash r'$, then $m(r, L) \leqslant m(r', L)$) as shown in [6].

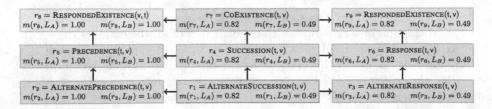

Fig. 2. Example of hierarchical simplification where the less restrictive rule is preferred over the more restrictive one, given equivalent measurements.

③ **Encoding.** The measures of a trace in a log are based on the measurements of the rule in each trace of the log itself [5]. Such trace measurement is independent from the log in which the trace resides, thus moving the trace from one log to another would not change it. We take advantage of this aspect to save computation steps: for each trace t in L_A and L_B, we cache the trace measurement $m(r, t)$ of every rule $r \in M_\cup$ in multi-sets L_A^m and L_B^m, i.e., $L_A^m = \{m(r, t) : t \in L_A, r \in M_\cup\}$ and $L_B^m = \{m(r, t) : t \in L_B, r \in M_\cup\}$. This step allows us to encode the traces into feature vectors that can be used within the permutation test, as discussed in the next section. For example, given a trace t and a specification $M_\cup = \{\text{RESP.}(\mathsf{a}, \mathsf{b}), \text{PREC.}(\mathsf{c}, \mathsf{d})\}$, the encoded trace is $t^m = \{(\text{RESP.}(\mathsf{a}, \mathsf{b}), m(\text{RESP.}(\mathsf{a}, \mathsf{b}), t)), (\text{PREC.}(\mathsf{c}, \mathsf{d}), m(\text{PREC.}(\mathsf{c}, \mathsf{d}), t))\}$. With a slight abuse of notation, we shall denote with $m(r, L^m)$ the measure of a rule r on log L after the encoding of all traces $t \in L$ in L^m.

To sum up, at the end of the pre-processing phase we have a unique declarative specification ($M_\cup$) with the measurements in the variants (E_A, E_B, and E_{diff}), and the evaluation of each rule in every trace cached for later reuse (L_A^m and L_B^m).

3.3   Permutation Test

In this phase, we check whether the differences between the declarative rule measurements in the variants are statistically significant. In other words, taken each $r \in M_\cup$, we calculate the likelihood that the absolute difference of its measurements between the variants, $E_{\text{diff}}(r)$, was due to a random factor. If the null hypothesis "$E_{\text{diff}}(r)$ occurred by chance" can be refuted, then the difference is significant. To that extent, we employ an adaptation of the permutation test we introduced in Sect. 2.3. We reshuffle traces between L_A and L_B and observe if the difference in the measures holds as in the original variants' logs. If so, it is likely that its difference was due to chance (i.e., the null hypothesis is confirmed). The rationale of this test is the following: if a difference can be detected by randomly shuffling the variants' traces, this difference has no real discriminative power between the variants.

The acceptance or refutation of the null hypothesis is done in the following two steps (we continue the numbering from the previous section): ④ The reshuffling, in which the data are rearranged and the measures of the rules under the

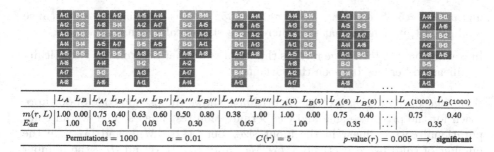

$|L_A\ L_B|$	$|L_{A'}\ L_{B'}|$	$|L_{A''}\ L_{B''}|$	$|L_{A'''}\ L_{B'''}|$	$|L_{A''''}\ L_{B''''}|$	$|L_{A(5)}\ L_{B(5)}|$	$|L_{A(6)}\ L_{B(6)}|$	$\cdots$	$|L_{A(1000)}\ L_{B(1000)}|$
$m(r,L)$ 1.00 0.00	0.75 0.40	0.63 0.60	0.50 0.80	0.38 1.00	1.00 0.00	0.75 0.40	$\ldots$	0.75 0.40
E_{diff} 1.00	0.35	0.03	0.30	0.63	1.00	0.35	$\ldots$	0.35
Permutations $= 1000$		$\alpha = 0.01$		$C(r) = 5$		$p\text{-value}(r) = 0.005 \implies$ **significant**		

Fig. 3. Visual example of the permutation test. The traces of the original logs L_A and L_B are coloured in dark gray and light grey, respectively.

null hypothesis are computed; ⑤ The significance test, in which only the rules that exhibit a statistically significant difference between variants are retained. Notably, thanks to the encoding of the logs presented in Sect. 3.2, the trace evaluations of every rule are readily available to compute the measures across the new set of traces. Thus, we can shuffle the evaluations on the traces rather than the traces themselves. Next, we elaborate on these operations.

④ **Reshuffling.** Figure 3 presents a graphical example of the reshuffling. At each iteration, the traces are randomly rearranged between the variants' logs, thereby generating altered logs on which the rule is measured. Specifically, at each iteration i: *(i)* The multi-set of all encoded traces in $L_A^m \cup L_B^m$ is shuffled into two new logs $L_{A_i}^m$ and $L_{B_i}^m$, such that $|L_A^m| = |L_{A_i}^m|$ and $|L_B^m| = |L_{B_i}^m|$ (permutation step); *(ii)* For each $r \in M_\cup$ the measures $m(r, L_{A_i}^m)$ and $m(r, L_{B_i}^m)$ are computed; *(iii)* Finally, for each rule $r \in M_\cup$ the difference of its measurements is compared to the reference difference of the rule $E_{\text{diff}}(r)$. The number of iterations is set as a user parameter π: according to [8], a suitable value for π is 1000. We denote with $C : M_\cup \to \mathbb{N}$ the function mapping a rule $r \in M_\cup$ to the number of iterations in which its difference is greater than or equal to the reference difference, i.e., $C(r) = \sum_{i=1}^{\pi} [\![|m(r, L_{A_i}^m) - m(r, L_{B_i}^m)| \geq E_{\text{diff}}(r)]\!]$ where $[\![\cdot]\!]$ is the indicator function mapping to 1 or 0 if the argument holds true or false, respectively.

⑤ **Significance Test.** At the end of the permutations step, the counter $C(r)$ tells us for each rule how frequently a difference greater or equal the reference one is observed. The likelihood to observe the rules difference under the assumption of the null hypothesis is the p-value of the test: $p\text{-value}(r) = \frac{C(r)}{\pi}$. The significance level α of the test is the p-value threshold below which the null hypothesis should be discarded. It is common to set $\alpha = 0.01$ when the permutation test consists of 1000 iterations [8]. A rule $r \in M_\cup$ has a statistically significant difference between the variants L_A and L_B if and only if $p\text{-value}(r) \leq \alpha$. Figure 3 illustrates an example of such a significance test where a difference of at least $E_{\text{diff}}(r)$ occurred for only 5 permutations out of the 1000 performed, e.g., in permutation $i = 5$. Therefore, p-value$(r) = 0.005$. As it is less than the significance level of 0.01, it suggest that the difference is statistically significant.

In conclusion, the technique returns the set of rules that determine a statistically significant difference between the variants.

About the Computational Cost. Algorithm 1 shows the pseudo-code of our approach for the pre-processing and the permutation test phases. The overall computational cost is linear in the input size. Let $|M_A|$, $|M_B|$, and $|M_\cup|$ be the number of rules in, respectively, M_A, M_B, and $M_\cup$, $|L_A|$ and $|L_B|$ the number of traces in L_A and L_B, $|\hat{t}|$ the maximum length of a trace in $L_A \cup L_B$, h the maximum hierarchical level of a rule in $M_\cup$, and π the number of iterations in the permutation test. Summing the costs of each step of Algorithm 1 (on the right side of every line), the overall computation cost of the approach is: $\mathcal{O}(|M_\cup| \times |\hat{t}| \times (|L_A| + |L_B|)) + \mathcal{O}(|M_\cup| \times \pi \times (|L_A| + |L_B|))$.

The overall performance is driven by the cost of the evaluation of the rules on the traces (the encoding phase) and by the permutation tests. We keep the two addenda separated to highlight their contribution. Depending on whether $|\hat{t}|$ is greater or less than π, the first or the second addendum prevails. We remark that the cost of computing the measures in the pre-processing (Lines 4 and 5) stems from the computational cost of the measurement framework [5], while the cost of re-computing the measures during the permutations (Lines 16) subtracts the trace evaluation time to that cost due to the encoding presented in Sect. 3.2. For as far as the hierarchical simplification (Lines 10), a DECLARE rule from the standard templates set may have at most $h = 11$ (the CHAINSUCCESSION template).

3.4   Post-processing

Once the rules with a statistically significant difference between the variants have been identified, we show them to the final user. All the relevant details are reported, namely the rule r, its p-value, its original measurements in the variants logs $m(r, L_A)$ and $m(r, L_B)$, and their absolute difference $E_{\text{diff}}(r)$. Furthermore, in order to enhance the clarity of the outcome, we perform the following additional steps: *(i)* providing a natural-language description of the output, and *(ii)* sorting the results according to a priority criterion.

⑥ **Natural Language.** We report the rules along with a natural language description explaining their behaviour in a concise manner. Indeed, the comprehension of temporal logic formulae is out of the reach for a general audience, and even the DECLARE rules taken by their own are not immediately grasped by non-knowledgeable users [1]. For example, RESPONSE(ER Triage, LacticAcid) is more readable than its LTLp$_f$ formulation, provided that the user has a prior knowledge of DECLARE. To explain differences between variants, we thus provide a description as follows: "In variant A, it is 30% more likely than in variant B that if ER Triage occurs, LacticAcid will occur afterwards".

⑦ **Sorting.** We give higher priority to those rules whose measure differs the most between variants. To ease the discoverability of prominent results, we sort the rules in descending order according to their measurement difference between the variants, $E_{\text{diff}}(r)$, and, in the case of equal difference, the highest measurement in L_A or L_B. For the sake of readability, the user can specify how many of the ranked rules should be initially displayed by means of a dedicated parameter, N.

3.5   Implementation and Remarks

We have implemented our approach, Declarative Rules Variant Analysis (DRVA), as a Java command-line tool.[1] Our tool returns two files: *(i)* a textual file containing the top-N statistically significant differences between the input logs reported in natural language, and *(ii)* one tabular file (CSV format) containing all the statistically-significant differences captured as declarative rules (and in natural language) with the entire quantitative information from the analysis. As input, it takes two event logs (L_A and L_B, in XES, MXML, or CSV formats), two declarative specifications (M_A and M_B, in JSON or XML formats) and the following list of user-defined parameters to tune the algorithm: *(i)* m, the measure to use for the comparison of the variants among those that are supported by the measurement framework described in [5] (the default is Confidence, as explained in Sect. 3.2); *(ii)* m_{min}, the minimum measure threshold that a rule should exceed in at least one variant (0.00 by default); *(iii)* $m_{\text{diff-min}}$, the minimum difference threshold that a rule should exceed between the variants (0.01 by default); *(iv)* π, the number of iterations to perform during the permutation test, set to 1000 by default as explained in Sect. 3.3; *(v)* α, the significance level, namely the maximum p-value to deem a rule as statistically relevant to discriminate the variant (0.01 by default); *(vi)* N, the number of top rules to display in the textual output (see Sect. 3.4), set to 10 by default.

Our tool can be put in pipeline to a declarative discovery algorithm which mines the declarative specifications out of the variants' logs. In the experiment presented in following Sect. 4, we pass the output of the MINERful discovery algorithm [7] to DRVA.

4   Evaluation

Given that no previous work addressed the problem of variant analysis via declarative rules [19], in this section, we provide a qualitative comparison with the latest process variants analysis approach that discovers statistically-significant differences [18], which already demonstrated its advantages [18] with respect to other baselines [4,10]. Henceforth, we will refer to the approach of Taymouri et al. [18] as MFVA (Mutual Fingerprints Variant Analysis). Furthermore, we also consider the work of van Beest et al. [3] as a baseline for comparison

---

[1] Available at: https://github.com/Oneiroe/Janus.

given that its output is in natural language statements – henceforth referred to as PESVA (Prime Event Structure Variant Analysis). However, we note that PESVA does not take into account the statistical significance of the detected differences and it is not based on declarative rules either. Instead, PESVA outputs two type of statements: *(i)* frequency-based statements, which highlight differences in branching probabilities of the process decision points; and *(ii)* behaviour-based statements, which highlight differences in directly-follow, and concurrent relations, as well as optional tasks.

Dataset and Setup. We reproduce the experimental setup proposed in [18]. The evaluation dataset consists of four publicly available event logs. Each of the logs can be divided into two variants (based on process-instance attribute values). The descriptive statistics characterizing the four logs are shown in Table 2. The original logs (not partitioned by the variants) can be downloaded from the 4TU Research Data Centre.[2] The process variant logs can be downloaded from our online repository together with the full set of results of this evaluation which, due to space limits, we could not report in this section.[3] In the following, we focus our discussion on the most interesting results.

Table 2. Descriptive statistics of the evaluation dataset [18]

Log		Traces		Events		Trace length		
Name and DOI	Variant	Total	Distinct	Total	Distinct	Min	Avg	Max
BPIC13	Company = A_2	553	25.5%	4,221	3	2	8	53
(https://doi.org/10.4121/uuid: a7ce5c55-03a7-4583-b855-98b86e1a2b07)	Company = C	4,417	13.8%	29,122	4	1	7	50
BPIC15	Municipality = 1	1,199	97.6%	36,705	146	2	33	62
(https://doi.org/10.4121/uuid: 915d2bfb-7e84-49ad-a286-dc35f063a460)	Municipality = 2	831	99.6%	32,017	134	1	39	96
RTFMP	Fine Amount ≥ 50	21,243	0.7%	91,499	11	2	4	20
(https://doi.org/10.4121/uuid: 270fd440-1057-4fb9-89a9-b699b47990f5)	Fine Amount < 50	129,127	0.1%	469,971	11	2	4	11
SEPSIS	Patient Age ≥ 70	678	85.7%	10,243	16	3	15	185
(https://doi.org/10.4121/uuid: 915d2bfb-7e84-49ad-a286-dc35f063a460)	Patient Age ≤ 35	76	67.1%	701	12	3	9	52

In our evaluation, we give each pair of log variants as an input to DRVA, MFVA, and PESVA. While DRVA and PESVA produce natural language statements, MFVA returns graphs named *mutual fingerprints*.Since the different outputs do not allow for a straightforward comparison, we first analyse the results of DRVA and MFVA with the goal to highlight the commonalities and differences in their output, then we compare our output with that of PESVA. We

---

[2] https://data.4tu.nl/search?categories=13503.
[3] https://github.com/Oneiroe/DeclarativeRulesVariantAnalysis-static.

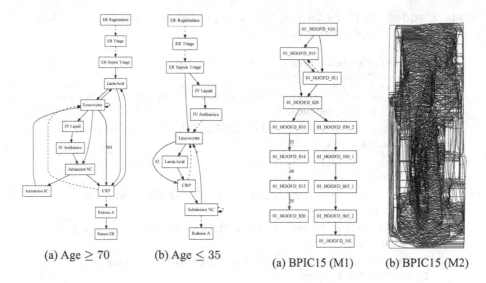

(a) Age ≥ 70   (b) Age ≤ 35

(a) BPIC15 (M1)   (b) BPIC15 (M2)

Fig. 4. SEPSIS logs, MFVA output [18]   **Fig. 5.** BPIC15 logs, MFVA output [18]

remark that the three tools provide alternative perspectives of the process variants differences. Therefore, they should not be seen as mutually exclusive tools, but rather complementary.

After the qualitative comparison, we also conduct a performance comparison of the three tools, reporting their execution times. All the experiments were run on an Intel Core i7-8565U@1.80 GHz with 32 GB RAM equipped with Windows 10 Pro (64-bit), with a timeout of 3 h per variant analysis. The input parameters we used for our DRVA are the default ones explained in Sect. 3.5. The declarative process models are discovered through MINERful [7] with a Support threshold

Table 3. SEPSIS logs – DRVA output (our approach)

	Statistically significant differences (*Variant A*: Age ≥ 70; *Variant B*: Age ≤ 35)
1	In *Variant A*, it is 37.4% more likely than in *Variant B* that Admission NC occurs in a process instance
2	In *Variant A*, it is 37.4% more likely than in *Variant B* that if ER Registration occurs, Admission NC will occur afterwards without any other occurrence of ER Registration in between
3	In *Variant A*, it is 37.4% more likely than in *Variant B* that if ER Sepsis Triage occurs, also Admission NC occurs
4	In *Variant A*, it is 37.4% more likely than in *Variant B* that if ER Triage occurs, also Admission NC occurs
5	In *Variant A*, it is 33.9% more likely than in *Variant B* that IV Antibiotics occurs in a process instance
6	In *Variant A*, it is 33.9% more likely than in *Variant B* that if ER Registration occurs, also IV Antibiotics occurs
7	In *Variant A*, it is 33.9% more likely than in *Variant B* that if ER Sepsis Triage occurs, IV Antibiotics will occur afterwards without any other occurrence of ER Sepsis Triage in between
8	In *Variant A*, it is 33.9% more likely than in *Variant B* that if ER Triage occurs, also IV Antibiotics occurs
9	In *Variant A*, it is 31.2% more likely than in *Variant B* that IV Liquid occurs in a process instance
10	In *Variant A*, it is 31.2% more likely than in *Variant B* that if ER Registration occurs, also IV Liquid occurs
11	In *Variant A*, it is 31.2% more likely than in *Variant B* that if ER Sepsis Triage occurs, also IV Liquid occurs
12	In *Variant A*, it is 31.2% more likely than in *Variant B* that if ER Triage occurs, also IV Liquid occurs

Table 4. BPIC15 logs – DRVA output (our approach). The list reports the first 10 top-ranked behavioural differences.

	Statistically significant differences (*Variant A*: Municipality = 1; *Variant B*: Municipality = 2)
1	It happens only in *Variant A* that 01_HOOFD_456 may occur at most once in a process instance
2	It happens only in *Variant A* that 01_HOOFD_492_1 may occur at most once in a process instance
3	It happens only in *Variant A* that 01_HOOFD_492_2 may occur at most once in a process instance
4	It happens only in *Variant A* that if 01_HOOFD_456 occurs, also 01_HOOFD_010 occurs
5	It happens only in *Variant A* that if 01_HOOFD_456 occurs, also 01_HOOFD_015 occurs
6	It happens only in in *Variant B* that if 16_LGSD_010 occurs, also 01_HOOFD_490_2 occurs
7	It happens only in *Variant B* that if 16_LGSD_010 occurs, also 01_HOOFD_495 occurs
8	It happens only in in *Variant B* that if 16_LGSD_010 occurs, also 02_DRZ_010 occurs
9	It happens only in in *Variant B* that if 16_LGSD_010 occurs, also 04_BPT_005 occurs
10	It happens only in in *Variant B* that if 16_LGSD_010 occurs, also 09_AH_I_010 occurs

of 0.5 and a Confidence threshold of 0.0, so as to keep the specifications loose enough to capture rare behaviour too. Markedly, the execution times reported for DRVA include the discovery times.

Results and Discussion. Figure 4 shows the output of MFVA given the variants of the SEPSIS log as an input. In the figure, dashed arcs and red arcs capture a statistically significant difference. The former evidence a change in the processing-time between the traces of the two variants, while the latter capture a difference in frequency (annotated on the arcs). Table 3 shows the output of DRVA given the same logs. We can notice that the difference ranked first in the table (PARTICIPATION(Admission NC) is more likely to occur if the age of the treated patient is over 70) makes explicit a difference that could not be directly inferred by visually comparing Fig. 4(a) with Fig. 4(b), although the alternative paths may suggest a behavioural change. The same holds for the fifth and ninth evidence. We observe that the other statements are related to the three we mentioned (also highlighted in Table 3). A further simplification step to enhance the ranking according to the discriminative power of the statements is an intriguing problem that paves the path for future endeavours building upon this work.

When the behaviour becomes less rigid and more flexible, the variants tend to have a higher percentage of distinct traces, like in the BPIC15 logs. In such cases, the output of MFVA becomes too simplistic (see Fig. 5(a)) or so complex to the extent of being even barely interpretable (see Fig. 5(b)). This result is, in general, typical of approaches based on graphs depicting processes imperatively [4, 10, 18]. In fact, the more flexible the behaviour recorded in the log, the larger the output graph (unless filtering is applied). On the other hand, our approach shows the differences as a list of declarative statements, focusing on the differences rather than on the overall picture (see Table 3 and 4). This is a benefit shared with PESVA, which also outputs natural language statements. However, PESVA suffers from scalability issues (PESVA timed out after running for three hours on BPIC15) and the differences identified by PESVA are limited in scope, which may hamper explanatory power and understandability. On the SEPSIS variants, e.g., PESVA indicates that "Task IV Liquid(4) can be skipped in model 2, whereas in model 1 it is always executed". Such a natural language formulation may be difficult to be interpreted, at times, in fact, task IV Liquid(4) does not refer to any execution of IV Liquid, but to the IV Liquid event that occurs as the fourth one. Our statements, instead, are broader in scope because they are not extrapolated by prime event structures but by declarative rules, therefore they refer to rules exerted on the whole process run rather than on the single occurrence of events. Also, we remind that the differences captured by PESVA are not guaranteed to be statistically significant.

In terms of execution time, DRVA outperforms MFVA and PESVA when analysing the BPIC13, BPIC15, and SEPSIS logs: considering the best execution times between those of MFVA and PESVA, the runs required 81.8 s, 4901.3 s, and 5.1 s, respectively. DRVA required instead 4.9 s, 326.7 s, and 4.6 s, respectively. For the analysis of the RTFMP log, instead, our technique required 38.1 s, thus outperforming MFVA (1152.9 s) but not PESVA (21.7 s). Nevertheless, we underline that our approach appears to be more scalable than the MFVA and PESVA: to process the BPIC15 log, indeed, the former took more than an hour and a half, whereas the latter timed out at three hours.

5 Conclusion

In this paper, we proposed a novel method to perform variant analysis and discover statistically-significant differences in the form of declarative rules expressed in natural language. We compared our method with state-of-the-art methods noticing that DRVA provides a different level of expressiveness, easier output interpretation, and faster execution time. Future research endeavours include the extension of our method to encompass the full spectrum of LTLp$_f$ formulae [5] and hybrid models [16] as the rule language in place of standard DECLARE, as well as multi-perspective specifications beyond the sole control-flow structure [15]. Also, we aim at further simplifying the output via redundancy-reduction techniques such as those in [6], to be adapted in order to improve the distinction of variants rather than reducing the rules of a single specifications.

Other interesting avenues are the identification of statistically significant performance rules as opposed to behavioural rules, and the enhancement of the statistical soundness of the results addressing the multiple testing problem through p-value correction techniques [9].

Acknowledgments. The work of C. Di Ciccio was partially funded by the Italian MIUR under grant "Dipartimenti di eccellenza 2018–2022" of the Department of Computer Science at Sapienza and by the Sapienza research project "SPECTRA".

References

1. van der Aa, H., Balder, K.J., Maggi, F.M., Nolte, A.: Say it in your own words: Defining declarative process models using speech recognition. In: BPM Forum, pp. 51–67 (2020)
2. Aalst, W.: Data science in action. In: Process Mining, pp. 3–23. Springer, Heidelberg (2016). https://doi.org/10.1007/978-3-662-49851-4_1
3. van Beest, N.R., Dumas, M., García-Bañuelos, L., La Rosa, M.: Log delta analysis: interpretable differencing of business process event logs. In: BPM, pp. 386–405 (2016)
4. Bolt, A., de Leoni, M., van der Aalst, W.M.: Process variant comparison: using event logs to detect differences in behavior and business rules. Inf. Syst. **74**, 53–66 (2018)
5. Cecconi, A., De Giacomo, G., Di Ciccio, C., Maggi, F.M., Mendling, J.: A temporal logic-based measurement framework for process mining. In: ICPM, pp. 113–120 (2020)
6. Di Ciccio, C., Maggi, F.M., Montali, M., Mendling, J.: Resolving inconsistencies and redundancies in declarative process models. Inf. Syst. **64**, 425–446 (2017)
7. Di Ciccio, C., Mecella, M.: On the discovery of declarative control flows for artful processes. ACM Trans. Manag. Inf. Syst. **5**(4), 24:1–24:37 (2015)
8. Edgington, E.S.: Approximate randomization tests. J. Psychol. **72**(2), 143–149 (1969)
9. Hämäläinen, W., Webb, G.I.: A tutorial on statistically sound pattern discovery. Data Mining Knowl. Disc. **33**(2), 325–377 (2019)
10. Nguyen, H., Dumas, M., La Rosa, M., ter Hofstede, A.H.: Multi-perspective comparison of business process variants based on event logs. In: ER, pp. 449–459 (2018)
11. Nichols, T.E., Holmes, A.P.: Nonparametric permutation tests for functional neuroimaging: a primer with examples. Human Brain Mapping **15**(1), 1–25 (2002)
12. Pesic, M., Bosnacki, D., van der Aalst, W.M.: Enacting declarative languages using LTL: avoiding errors and improving performance. In: SPIN, pp. 146–161 (2010)
13. Pitman, E.J.: Significance tests which may be applied to samples from any populations. Suppl. J. Roy. Stat. Soc. **4**(1), 119–130 (1937)
14. Poelmans, J., Dedene, G., Verheyden, G., Van der Mussele, H., Viaene, S., Peters, E.: Combining business process and data discovery techniques for analyzing and improving integrated care pathways. In: ICDM, pp. 505–517 (2010)
15. Schönig, S., Di Ciccio, C., Maggi, F.M., Mendling, J.: Discovery of multi-perspective declarative process models. In: ICSOC, pp. 87–103 (2016)
16. Slaats, T.: Declarative and hybrid process discovery: Recent advances and open challenges. J. Data Semant. **9**(1), 3–20 (2020)

17. Suriadi, S., Wynn, M.T., Ouyang, C., ter Hofstede, A.H., van Dijk, N.J.: Understanding process behaviours in a large insurance company in Australia: a case study. In: CAiSE, pp. 449–464 (2013)
18. Taymouri, F., La Rosa, M., Carmona, J.: Business process variant analysis based on mutual fingerprints of event logs. In: CAiSE, pp. 299–318 (2020)
19. Taymouri, F., La Rosa, M., Dumas, M., Maggi, F.M.: Business process variant analysis: survey and classification. Knowl.-Based Syst. **211**, 106557 (2021)
20. Welch, W.J.: Construction of permutation tests. J. Am. Stat. Assoc. **85**(411), 693–698 (1990)
21. Wu, J., He, Z., Gu, F., Liu, X., Zhou, J., Yang, C.: Computing exact permutation p-values for association rules. Inf. Sci. **346**, 146–162 (2016)

Silhouetting the Cost-Time Front: Multi-objective Resource Optimization in Business Processes

Orlenys López-Pintado[1], Marlon Dumas[1(✉)], Maksym Yerokhin[1], and Fabrizio Maria Maggi[2]

[1] University of Tartu, Tartu, Estonia
{orlenys.lopez.pintado,marlon.dumas,maksym.yerokhin}@ut.ee
[2] Free University of Bozen-Bolzano, Bolzano, Italy
maggi@inf.unibz.it

Abstract. The allocation of resources in a business process determines the trade-off between cycle time and resource cost. A higher resource utilization leads to lower cost and higher cycle time, while a lower resource utilization leads to higher cost and lower waiting time. In this setting, this paper presents a multi-objective optimization approach to compute a set of Pareto-optimal resource allocations for a given process concerning cost and cycle time. The approach heuristically searches through the space of possible resource allocations using a simulation model to evaluate each allocation. Given the high number of possible allocations, it is imperative to prune the search space. Accordingly, the approach incorporates a method that selectively perturbs a resource utilization to derive new candidates that are likely to Pareto-dominate the already explored ones. The perturbation method relies on two indicators: resource utilization and resource impact, the latter being the contribution of a resource to the cost or cycle time of the process. Additionally, the approach incorporates a ranking method to accelerate convergence by guiding the search towards the resource allocations closer to the current Pareto front. The perturbation and ranking methods are embedded into two search metaheuristics, namely hill-climbing and tabu-search. Experiments show that the proposed approach explores fewer resource allocations to compute Pareto fronts comparable to those produced by a well-known genetic algorithm for multi-objective optimization, namely NSGA-II.

Keywords: Business process optimization · Resource allocation · Multi-objective optimization · Process simulation

1 Introduction

A business process brings together several activities performed by participants (a.k.a. resources) that are typically divided into groups (a.k.a. resource pools) according to their areas of responsibility. Each resource pool has a capacity,

A. Polyvyanyy et al. (Eds.): BPM Forum 2021, LNBIP 427, pp. 92–108, 2021.
https://doi.org/10.1007/978-3-030-85440-9_6

determined by the number of resources in the pool. For example, in a loan application handling process, there may be a resource pool grouping multiple clerks responsible for all activities related to collecting and validating data, a Credit Officer pool responsible for preparing initial loan decisions, and a Senior Credit Officer pool for validating these decisions and handling exceptional cases.

The problem of resource allocation is that of determining how much capacity (i.e., how many resources) to allocate to each resource pool so as to minimize or maximize one or more performance measures. In this respect, for a given workload, the more there are resources in a pool, the less busy these resources are (low resource utilization). Conversely, the less there are resources in a pool, the busier the resources are (high resource utilization). Higher resource utilization leads to lower cost per instance (as resources are used to their full extent) and high waiting times (due to resource contention). Conversely, lower resource utilization leads to higher cost per instance and to lower waiting times [10]. Managers need to balance these two ends of the spectrum, aiming for a resource allocation that minimizes both the costs and the waiting times. Typically, no single solution exists that minimizes time and cost simultaneously. Instead, there is a set of (incomparable) optimal solutions (a.k.a. Pareto front) so that no objective, e.g., time and cost, can be improved without scarifying any other.

This paper presents an approach to compute a set of Pareto-optimal resource allocations for a business process. The approach iteratively explores the space of possible resource allocations and uses the simulation model to assess the cost and cycle time of each explored allocation.[1] The search space is traversed using hill-climbing and tabu-search meta-heuristics. In each iteration, we estimate the resource utilization and the overall resource performance (i.e., their impact on the cost-time space), and we use these indicators to guide a perturbation method that selects a subset of neighbors that are likely to Pareto-dominate solutions in the current Pareto front, instead of exploring the entire neighborhood of each allocation. The search strategy employs a ranking method to prioritize new candidate allocations. Additionally, to cater for the fact that the output of a simulation model is subject to stochastic variations, we propose a notion of Pareto-dominance based on the median absolute deviation of the simulation outputs. These mechanisms lead to two enhanced variants of hill-climbing plus an enhanced variant of tabu-search. The paper reports an experimental evaluation to assess the convergence, spread, and distribution of the discovered Pareto fronts and the number of explored resource allocations, relative to a well-known genetic algorithm for multi-objective optimization (NSGA-II) [8].

The rest of the paper is structured as follows. Section 2 discusses related works. Section 3 introduces key concepts and meta-heuristics for multi-objective optimization and concepts related to process simulation. Section 4 describes the perturbation and ranking methods and the enhanced hill-climbing and

---

[1] In the experiments, we use simulation models discovered from execution data, but the approach can take as input a manually designed simulation model or any stochastic model capable of estimating costs and cycle times for different resource allocations.

tabu-search variants. Then, Sect. 5 discusses the implementation and evaluation, while Sect. 6 concludes the paper.

2 Related Work

Several previous studies have addressed the problem of resource allocation in business processes. However, the bulk of these studies addressed resource allocation as a single-objective optimization problem, i.e., either by optimizing one performance measure or combining several into a linear function [13,16,19,23].

In [19], the authors proposed an evolutionary algorithm for finding the optimal resource allocation of a business process. The framework's input is a Colored Petri Net, including all the parameters necessary for simulation, such as arrival rate, processing times for each task, and branching probabilities for each decision point. The paper optimizes the resource allocation regarding cycle time and cost, combined into a single performance measure through a linear function. Similar approaches using genetic algorithms and simulation models on single objective-problems were presented in [9,14]. In the present paper, instead of combining the time and the cost, we compute an entire Pareto front, which allows the user to explore the available trade-offs between cycle time and resource cost.

The work presented in [16] addresses the optimization problem as an exploration of the space of possible resource allocations. The approach considers the resource utilization to define three strategies to discover the optimal resource allocation while performing a reduced search of the solution candidates. The authors addressed the resource allocation as a single-objective optimization problem, i.e., minimizing the number of resources constrained by a specified maximum waiting time. This paper adopts a different approach that considers resource utilization in a multi-objective optimization setting to discover not a single optimal but a set of optimal solutions.

In [11], the authors analyze the relationship between resource allocation and various performance measures, including time. The authors use a grid-search approach, i.e., an exhaustive exploration of all possible resource allocations given a minimum and a maximum number of resources per pool. This approach can be applied to explore the resource allocation space when the number of pools is small. However, it does not scale up to larger search spaces.

The problem of design-time resource allocation tackled in the present paper is related to the problem of runtime scheduling and runtime assignment of resources to work items in a business process. The latter problems have been tackled in various previous studies. For example, [18] and [22] consider the problem of deciding how to schedule the work items generated by each execution of a business process, taking into account that resources have availability constraints (i.e., they are available at some times but not at others). Meanwhile, [12] tackles the problem of deciding which specific resource should be assigned to a given work item, given the characteristics of each resource. The contribution of the present paper and those of the above papers are complementary. After selecting a given resource allocation using the techniques proposed in this paper, it is perfectly possible to optimize the runtime scheduling and assignment of resources to work items using the techniques developed in the above papers.

The problem of resource allocation has also been studied outside the field of business process optimization. For example, in [6], the authors present an algorithm to discover Pareto fronts relying on ant colony optimization, assessing several performance measures for a given resource allocation. From this latter study, we share the idea of formulating the resource allocation as a multi-objective problem but adapted to the meta-heuristics hill-climbing and tabu-search.

3 Overview of Multi-objective Optimization and Business Process Simulation

3.1 Pareto Fronts and Meta-heuristic Optimization Algorithms

In an n-dimensional space, a solution B is Pareto dominated by another solution A, if A is better than B for at least one objective, and A is at least as good as B for the remaining objectives [2], e.g., $B = (2, 5, 10)$ and $C = (3, 8, 12)$ are Pareto dominated by $A = (1, 5, 10)$, under minimization constraints. The set of solutions that are not dominated by any other are called Pareto optimal. The set of non-dominated points are called the Pareto set, and the evaluation of the objective functions on those points constitutes the Pareto front [2]. For example, in the two-dimensional space cost-time associated with the execution of a business process, the Pareto set contains the resource pools whose respective cost-space evaluations constitute a Pareto front, i.e., the pairs cost-time are Pareto-optimal. However, the problem of resource allocation is a well-known NP-complete problem. Thus, as no efficient solution exists (i.e., exploring the entire solution space is not possible in practical scenarios), some meta-heuristic algorithms can be used to approximate the Pareto fronts.

Among many other classifications, existing meta-heuristic optimization algorithms can be broadly classified into single-solution-based and population-based. Single-solution algorithms keep one solution and search for better solutions at each step through a perturbation function. Population-based algorithms keep a population of solutions and build a new population at each step by perturbing and combining solutions in the existing population. Indeed, single-solution approaches are more efficient (i.e., they explore a lower number of solutions), but population-based techniques lead to more optimal solutions at the cost of exploring a higher number of solution candidates [4]. This paper focuses on enhancing two of the most well-known single-solution-based meta-heuristics, named hill-climbing and tabu-search. Besides, we use one population-based approach, the genetic algorithm NSGA-II, as a baseline in our experiments.

Hill-climbing is an optimization technique that performs a local search around a given point. At each iteration, the algorithm selects the best possible point to move in the current point neighborhood. Therefore, the algorithm improves the current solution on each iteration unless the entire neighborhood does not contain better solutions. Classic applications of this algorithm assume a single objective [4] (e.g., time, cost, or a linear combination of both). However, in [20], the authors describe a modification of hill-climbing for multi-objective optimization (i.e., to compute a Pareto front). To that end, not a single solution but a Pareto front is stored. Thus, the new solution candidates are generated by taking each point in the current front and generating its neighborhood. The greedy nature of hill-climbing allows it to converge fast, but it may stop at a local optimum.

The tabu-search algorithm is an extension of hill-climbing that avoids the limitation of getting stuck in a local optimum. Unlike hill-climbing, tabu-search stores the current best point, but it also accepts inferior solutions if no improvement is found from the current best solution's neighborhood. Thus, it accepts Pareto-dominated solutions temporarily to visit new parts of the search space, aiming to converge to the global optimum in subsequent iterations. The implementation includes a so-called tabu list, so solutions already visited or restricted by any other rules are marked as *tabu*, thus not revisited (i.e., at least in a short-term period) [4]. Although classical variants of the tabu-search algorithm assume a single-objective, like hill-climbing, it can be extended to a multi-objective space by considering a Pareto front instead of a single solution [20].

NSGA-II, the acronym of Non-dominated Sorting Genetic Algorithm, is a well-known genetic algorithm designed explicitly for multi-objective optimization [8]. The algorithm's idea is to keep a population of points, some of which are in the Pareto front, and others are not but well placed along with one of the dimensions. At each iteration, the algorithm generates off-springs by sampling from the neighborhood of the points in the current population. The best new solutions are added to the population, and a subset of the existing solutions (which are not Pareto optimal) are removed. To determine which solutions to add or remove, the algorithm measures how far the solutions in the current population are separated from each other.

3.2   Resource Pools, Event Logs and Business Process Simulation

A resource allocation is a sequence of resource pools $R = \{r_1, ..., r_n\}$, each responsible for a subset of activities in a process. The functions $rCount : R \rightarrow \mathbb{N}+$ and $rCost : R \rightarrow \mathbb{R}+$ retrieve, respectively, the number of resources and cost (per time unit) of using one resource in a pool r_i.

An event is a tuple $e = \ <\lambda, r, \gamma_s, \gamma_c>$, where λ is the label of one activity in a business process (i.e., e is an instance of the activity λ), $r \in R$ is the resource who performed λ, and γ_s, γ_c are, respectively, the time-stamps corresponding to the beginning and end of the event. A trace (a.k.a. process case) is a non-empty sequence of events $t = \ <e_1, e_2, ..., e_n>$, and an event log $eLog = \ <t_1, t_2, ..., t_m>$ is a non-empty sequence of traces corresponding to the execution of a process.

A simulation model consists of a process model M, e.g., written in the Business Process Model and Notation (BPMN) notation, a set of resource pools R, and a function $activityResource : A \rightarrow R$ that maps each activity $a \in A$ in the process model to a resource $r \in R$. Simulation models also include the mean inter-arrival time of cases and probability distributions for arrival cases, activities' processing times, and gateways' branching [5]. Simulation models can be executed using simulation engines like BIMP [1], which produces a set of possible execution traces used to perform quantitative analysis of business processes. Henceforth, we will use the notation $rpLog$ referring to event logs obtained from real executions of business process and the notation $smLog$ to point out simulated event logs. In our approach, we consider the following functions computed from an event log $eLog$:

- $eventDuration(e =< \lambda, r, \gamma_s, \gamma_c >, eLog)$ represents the time-span, $\gamma_c - \gamma_s$, between the beginning and end of event e, (a.k.a. processing time), plus the time-span from the moment activity λ is enabled until the starting of the corresponding event (a.k.a. waiting time),
- $traceDuration(t, eLog)$ and $procDuration(eLog)$ retrieve the time-span between the beginning and end of trace t and the entire process, respectively,
- $cTime(R, eLog)$, i.e., cycle time, computes the average $traceDuration$ of all the traces $t \in eLog$, involving the resource pools in R,
- $aCost(R, eLog) = procDuration(eLog) * \sum_{r \in R}[rCost(r) * rCount(r)]$ corresponds to the cumulative costs of all the resources during the process execution. These costs consider not only the resources which performed each event $e \in eLog$ but all the resources allocated to the resource pools, which must be available at any time of the execution,
- $resourceUtilization(r, eLog)$ divides the time in which resources in pool r were busy by $procDuration(eLog)$, i.e., the percentage of time in which the resources are busy.

4   Computing the Pareto-Optimal Resource Allocations

4.1   Initial Resource Allocation and Process Simulation

To discover the simulation model from an event log $rpLog$ provided as input, we use the tool named Simod [5]. It produces a process model in BPMN extended with the probability distributions of each element/branch. Besides, it provides the initial resource allocation R_0 and the mapping function $activityResource$. The incoming iterations produce only new resource allocations $R_1, R_2, ..., R_n$, i.e., the control-flow of the BPMN model, and the mapping $activityResource$ remain unaltered. Henceforth, we will describe the steps of our approach based on the corresponding resource allocation (a.k.a. solution candidate) R_i.

For each resource allocation R_i, the evaluation of the objective functions $cTime$ and $aCost$ requires to simulate the process, i.e., to assess the impact of the current allocation on the execution. Due to the simulations' stochastic nature, running a single simulation per allocation may lead to inaccurate evaluations. Thus, we run a number $smCount \geq 10$ of simulations, keeping the results from the simulated log $smLog$ with median values of the function $cTime$. Also, we calculate the absolute median deviation (MAD) for both objective functions, i.e.,

$MAD = median(\{|F_M - f_1|, ..., |F_M - f_n|\})$, where $F_M = median(\{f_1, ..., f_n\})$
with $f_i = f(R, smLog_i), \forall 1 \le i \le n = smCount$, and $f \in \{aCost, cTime\}$.

The MAD serves to introduce a more strict Pareto dominance relation, considering the simulation results' variability. In the classical Pareto dominance relation, a resource allocation R_i dominates R_j ($R_i < R_j$) if R_i has a lower cycle time and cost than R_j, i.e., $f(R_i) \le f(R_j), f \in \{cTime, aCost\}$. In a more strict dominance relation, R_i strongly dominates R_j ($R_i << R_j$) if $f(R_i) \le f(R_j)$ and $|f(R_i) - f(R_j)| > min(MAD(f(R_i)), MAD(f(R_j))), f \in \{aCost, cTime\}$. Thus, the cycle time and cost of R_i should be lower than R_j by a difference of at least the minimum MAD between the two objective functions. In other words, although R_i may dominate R_j, they are still close to discard R_j as a Pareto optimal solution due to the simulations' variance.

4.2   Perturbation Method: Generating Solution Candidates

Like any hill-climbing and tabu-search approaches, our proposal constructs the Pareto front incrementally. At each iteration, instead of exploring the entire neighborhood of the Pareto front like in traditional approaches[2], we heuristically select which resources might have a higher impact on the process execution. Specifically, we introduce a perturbation that relies on two criteria to decide which resource pool to improve, i.e., resource utilization and resource impact.

We hypothesize that a high resource utilization may increase the cycle times, i.e., the resources are too busy, which might harm their overall performance. Thus, increasing the number of resources might lead to reducing the overall cycle time. Conversely, low resource utilization may affect the execution costs, i.e., there are some lazy resources with low efficiency, which might not be necessary. Thus, decreasing the number of resources may lead to a decrease in the execution costs without increasing the cycle times. Therefore, at each iteration, we select the pools with higher/lower resource utilization and accordingly add, remove or exchange resources to/from/between them.

Another issue to solve on the perturbation based on the resource utilization is the number of resources to add or remove. Adding/removing one resource leads to a shorter evolution step. Thus, it may increase the chances of finding a new allocation improving the current one, but it may require a high number of iterations to converge to the optimal. Conversely, adding/removing a higher number of resources to reach some desire utilization ratio may converge faster to the optimal allocation. Specifically, we use inverse proportion to estimate the amount of resources to add or remove by the formula:

$$amount = (resourceUtilization(r, smLog) * rCount(r)/dRu) - rCount(r) + 1$$

where dRu is a desired value for the resource utilization. In this paper, the perturbation function adds/removes the corresponding $amount$ to/from the resource

---

[2] The neighborhood of a Pareto front might consist of 2^{mn} solutions (i.e., straightforwardly adding/removing one to/from each pool), where m and n are the size of the Pareto front and the number of resource pools, respectively. The latest makes the searching space too wide, especially when the number of resources is high.

Algorithm 1. Construction of the Pareto front

```
 1: function APROXIMATEPARETOFRONT(rpLog)
 2:     (SM, R₀) ← DISCOVERSMODEL(rpLog)
 3:     smLog₀ ← SIMULATEPROCESS(SM, R₀)
 4:     PFront ← {< R₀, aCost(R₀, smLog₀), cTime(R₀, smLog₀) >}
 5:     PriorityQ ← ∅
 6:     ENQUEUE(PriorityQ, R₀, dist(R₀, PFront))
 7:     while Q not empty do
 8:         if STOPPINGCRITERIAMET then
 9:             return PFront
10:         SCandidates ← FINDCANDIDATES(POP(PriorityQ))
11:         for each Rᵢ ∈ SCandidates do
12:             smLogᵢ ← SIMULATEPROCESS(SM, Rᵢ)
13:             if ISNONDOMINATED(Rᵢ, smLogᵢ, PFront) then
14:                 UPDATEPARETOFRONT(PFront, Rᵢ, smLogᵢ)
15:                 ENQUEUE(PriorityQ, Rᵢ, dist(Rᵢ, PFront))
16:             else if IsTabuSearch then
17:                 ENQUEUE(PriorityQ, Rᵢ, dist(Rᵢ, PFront))
18:     return PFront
```

---

pools with higher/lower utilization to reach an ideal utilization, e.g., between 0.7–0.8 as Gartner analysts suggest, or any values set by the process analysts goals. The perturbation method also exchanges the minimum *amount* between the pools with higher and lower utilization. However, although the calculated *amount* introduces a higher step accelerating the convergence, it may also skip solution paths in the middle. Thus, the perturbation method uses both values unitary and the calculated *amount* to generate the next solution candidates.

To tackle other issues, i.e., not related to resource utilization, which may be harming the process performance, we use a heuristic considering the resources' impact. To that end, for each resource pool r, we calculate the aggregated costs and cycle times of the activities assigned to r, i.e., from the mapping function *activityResource*. Thus, the perturbation function will update the resource pools not improved from the previous heuristic regarding utilization, whose aggregated times and costs are above the average. Specifically, it increases the number of resources on pools showing higher cycle times since adding more resources may reduce the workload, thus decreasing the waiting times. Conversely, it reduces the number of resources on pools with higher costs since fewer resources performing the same activities more efficiently would reduce costs.

4.3 Ranking Method: Hill-Climbing and Tabu-Search Variants

Algorithm 1 sketches our proposal, which takes an event log as input. The steps in lines 2–3 discover the simulation model, the initial resource allocation R_0, and runs the first simulation, as described in Sect. 4.1. The initial Pareto front *Front* contains the initial resource allocation discovered from the event log and the values *aCost* and *cTime* retrieved from the initial simulation.

A key difference of our approach with traditional variants of hill-climbing and tabu-search consists of sorting the solution candidates (i.e., resource allocations) based on their Euclidean distance to a Pareto front *PFront*:

$$dist(R_i, PFront) = \min_{p \in PFront} \| f(R_i) - f(p) \|_2 : f \in \{aCost, cTime\}.$$

Thus, the algorithm stores the solution candidates in a priority queue, which is initialized in lines 5–6.

At each iteration, the algorithm does not explore the neighborhood of each allocation in the current Pareto front. Instead, it uses the heuristics described in Sect. 4.2 to alter the solution candidate with the shortest Euclidean distance from the Pareto front (line 10). Next, it simulates the process for each allocation $R_i \in$ *SCandidates* retrieved by the perturbation method. Then, lines 11–17 verify, after evaluating the objective functions $aCost$ and $cTime$, if the allocation R_i is dominated (or not) by any allocation in the current Pareto front. Accordingly, a solution candidate is added to the Pareto front and the priority queue depending on the meta-heuristic search strategy as follows:

- **HC-STRICT**, or hill-climbing strict, considers the classical Pareto dominance relation. The resource allocation R_i is added to the Pareto front if it is Pareto-optimal, i.e., if the pair cost-time from R_i is not dominated by any of the pairs cost-time in $PFront$. Similarly, R_i is only added to the priority queue if it is Pareto-optimal. Also, each resource allocation dominated by R_i is discarded. Note that after updating $PFront$, the distance $dist$ to $PFront$ must be updated for each element in the priority queue.
- **HC-FLEX**, or hill-climbing flexible, considers a more strict Pareto dominance relation defined by the MAD, which produces a larger Pareto front. Thus, we relax the Pareto front definition to include classically dominated elements, i.e., those separated by at most the median absolute deviation for both objective functions $aCost$ and $cTime$. The steps to update the $PFront$ and the priority queue are the same as for $HC - STRICT$, but constructing a relaxed Pareto front.
- **TS-STRICT**, or tabu-search strict, uses the classical Pareto dominance relation. However, unlike hill-climbing, tabu-search also adds to the priority queue all the discarded, i.e., not Pareto-optimal resource allocations. So, when no Pareto-optimal allocation exists in the queue, the tabu-search will generate the subsequent solution candidates from the non-optimal resource allocation with the shortest distance to the current Pareto front.

The algorithm stops (lines 7–8) if any of the following conditions hold: (1) the queue is empty, (2) after exploring a specified maximum number of allocations, i.e., those generated by the perturbation function, (3) after producing a maximum number of consecutive Pareto non-optimal allocations. Then, $PFront$ is returned as approximation of the optimal resource allocation.

5   Evaluation

In multi-objective optimization, measuring the quality of a Pareto front approximation retrieved by an algorithm is not trivial. According to [2], a good approximation must minimize the distance to the actual Pareto front (a.k.a. convergence). Besides, a good Pareto front should consist of a highly diversified set of points, which are also well distributed across the front (a.k.a. spread and distribution). Accordingly, we designed an evaluation to answer the following question: **Q1** How good are the Pareto fronts discovered by our proposal with respect to convergence, spread, and distribution? Secondly, as one of the goals of this paper is reducing the searching space through heuristics, our evaluation also answers the question: **Q2** How many solutions (objective function evaluations) do the algorithms need to explore to retrieve the Pareto front?

5.1   Implementation and Experimental Setup

To assess our proposal, we implemented the full approach presented in this paper in Python 3.8. Also, we adapted the resource allocation problem to the tool Pymoo [3], which implements the genetic algorithm NSGA-II. The source code and the instructions to execute the three variants, i.e., HC-STRICT, HC-FLEX, and TS-STRICT, and the NSGA-II algorithm, can be accessed from https:// github.com/orlenyslp/bpm-r-opt.

In our experiments, we run the four algorithms HC-STRICT, HC-FLEX, TS-STRICT, and NSGA-II, taking the NSGA-II as a baseline to be compared with the results obtained by our approach. In the case of our approach, we set the maximum number of solutions to explore (i.e., function evaluations) to 10 000 and at most 800 (8%) consecutive Pareto non-optimal allocations. As for the NSGA-II, we configured the input with the default values recommended in [3], with a population size of 40 and a maximum of 250 generations (i.e., at most 10 000 function evaluations). For all the algorithms, we run 15 simulations per allocation (using the BIMP engine [1]) to calculate the values of $aCost$ and $cTime$. Also, to avoid giving any unfair advantages to an algorithm due to the simulations' stochastic nature, we memorized in files the simulation results. So, we can assert that if two algorithms explore the same resource allocation, they will get the same values of $aCost$ and $cTime$. Additionally, the memorization reduces the number of simulations, thus the execution times, when multiple algorithms explore common areas in the solution space.

As a starting point, we used simulation models derived from event logs using the Simod simulation discovery tool [5]. We derived simulation models from one synthetic event log and seven real-life ones. The synthetic log (namely *purchasing-example*) is part of the academic material of the Fluxicon Disco tool[3]. The first real-life log (*production*) is a log of a manufacturing process[4]. The second one (*consulta-data-mining*) is an anonymized log of an academic recognition process executed at a Colombian University, available in the Simod tool distribution. The third real-life log is a subset of the BPIC2012 log[5] – a log of a loan application process from a Dutch financial institution. We focused on the subset of this log consisting of activities that have both start and end timestamps. Similarly, we used the equivalent subset of the BPIC2017[6], which is an updated

---

[3] https://fluxicon.com/academic/material/.
[4] https://doi.org/10.4121/uuid:68726926-5ac5-4fab-b873-ee76ea412399.
[5] https://doi.org/10.4121/uuid:3926db30-f712-4394-aebc-75976070e91f.
[6] https://doi.org/10.4121/uuid:5f3067df-f10b-45da-b98b-86ae4c7a310b.

version of the BPIC2012 log (extracted in 2017 instead of 2012). We extracted the subsets of the BPIC2012 and BPIC2017 logs by following the recommendations provided by the winning teams of the BPIC 2017 challenge.[7]

Table 1. Characteristics of the business processes used in the experimentation.

	Production	Purchasing Example	Consulta Data-mining	Insurance	Call-centre	bpi-12	bpi-17-filt	bpi-17
Real traces	225	608	954	1182	3885	8616	8941	30 276
Simulation traces	550	1500	4000	4000	8000	18 000	18 000	24 000
Activities	23	23	18	11	8	8	9	9
Number of pools	7	6	4	2	3	4	2	3
Total resources	54	47	337	125	66	68	116	141
Simulation time	0.48	0.50	0.49	0.52	0.75	0.67	0.69	0.88

Table 1 gives descriptive statistics of the processes used in the experiments, such as the number of traces in the event log, the number of activities, resource pools, and the sum of the resources across the pools discovered by Simod. The row simulation time shows the average execution times (in seconds) obtained by running one simulation of the corresponding process using the BIMP engine. The number of traces produced per simulation (number of simulated traces) was set to at least two times the number of real traces to minimize stochastic variations.

Since data about salaries/costs of the resources involved in the process execution is missing in the event logs, we assigned each resource with the unitary cost for the experiments. Thus, the total resource pool cost is determined by the number of resources multiplied by the duration of the process execution, i.e., from the beginning of the first trace to the end of the last one.

5.2 Metrics and Experimental Results

As the actual Pareto front is unknown, we follow the approach presented in [7] which creates a reference Pareto front $PRef$ to compare the results retrieved by many solvers. Specifically, $PRef$ is the set containing the non-dominated (i.e., Pareto-optimal) solutions from the entire search space explored by all the runs of the four algorithms discussed in this paper. Henceforth, we will call $PRef$ the reference Pareto front (joint from many algorithms) and $PAprox$ the approximated (by one algorithm) Pareto front. Then, to answer the experimental question **Q1**, we used four metrics:

- Hyperarea [21] (HA) measures convergence and distribution. So far, it is considered the most relevant and widely used measure to compare algorithms in the evolutionary community [2]. Hyperarea is the area in the objective space dominated by a Pareto front delimited by a point $(c, t) \in \mathbb{R}^2$, which we set as the maximum cost and time among all the solutions explored. If $PRef$

---

[7] https://www.win.tue.nl/bpi/doku.php?id=2017:challenge.

Table 2. Results of the performance metrics.

		Insurance	bpi-17-filt	bpi-17	Call-centre	bpi-12	Consulta	Purchasing	Production
Hyperarea	HC-Strict	0.999715	0.999993	0.999388	0.979741	0.999999	0.939581	0.999966	0.984928
	HC-Flex	0.999878	0.999993	0.999702	0.979741	1.0	0.970996	0.999993	0.999878
	TS-Strict	0.999997	1.0	0.999989	0.999997	1.0	0.95116	0.999999	0.999878
	NSGA-II	1.0	1.0	0.999776	0.975051	1.0	0.999964	0.999995	0.991984
Hausdorff	HC-Strict	792 368.4	21 283.4	767 578.4	333 931.8	67 756.9	114 721.2	12 093.5	60 122.4
	HC-Flex	747 515.1	17 290.5	24 078.9	333 931.8	88 807.0	188 411.5	10 503.3	6102.8
	TS-Strict	1 307 871.7	0.0	23 275.6	25 645.6	55 421.4	209 925.0	12 411.9	6102.8
	NSGA-II	0.0	9033.2	42 653.2	426 892.2	105 021.1	11 404.6	93 709.6	775 721.6
Delta(Δ)	HC-Strict	1.247804	1.311345	1.314798	1.075864	1.128014	1.200819	1.471674	0.918048
	HC-Flex	1.119086	1.27965	0.856219	1.075864	1.181983	0.887497	1.454444	0.585820
	TS-Strict	1.117958	1.206904	0.876539	1.069856	1.197563	0.905387	1.496234	0.585820
	NSGA-II	1.458937	1.244832	0.753908	1.166828	0.995971	1.223205	1.326563	1.102538
Purity	HC-Strict	0.888889	0.90625	0.833333	0.333333	0.692308	0.777778	0.695652	0.466667
	HC-Flex	0.615385	0.911765	0.842105	0.333333	0.75	1.0	0.666667	0.923077
	TS-Strict	1.0	1.0	1.0	0.973684	0.666667	1.0	0.954545	0.923077
	NSGA-II	1.0	1.0	1.0	0.0625	1.0	1.0	0.848485	0.722222

is available, the hyperarea ratio is a real number, between 0 and 1, given by $HA(PAprox)/HA(PRef)$. A higher hyperarea ratio means a better $PAprox$, being 1 the maximum possible ratio indicating that $PAprox$ dominates the same solution space as $PRef$.

– Averaged Hausdorff distance [17] measures convergence using the distances between $PAprox$ and $PRef$. Specifically, it gets the greatest distance from each point in one set to the closest point in the other set, i.e., given by $max(min\|p_i, PRef\|_2, min\|p_j, PAprox\|_2)$, $\forall p_i \in PAprox, p_j \in PRef$. A lower Hausdorff distance means a better $PAprox$.

– Delta(Δ) [7,8] measures spread and distribution. It is given by the formula:

$$\Delta = \frac{d_0 + d_n + \sum_{i=1}^{n-1} |d_i - d'|}{d_0 + d_n + (n-1)d'}$$

where $d_i, 0 \leq i \leq n = |PAprox|$ is the Euclidean distance between consecutive solutions, with d_0 and d_n being the Euclidean distances between the extreme solutions in $PRef$ and the extreme solutions in $PAprox$. Besides, d' is the average of those distances. A lower value of Δ means a better $PAprox$.

– Purity [7] is a cardinality measure used to compare Pareto fronts constructed by different algorithms. It is given by $|PAprox \cap PRef|/|PAprox|$. Thus, it measures the ratio of solutions in $PAprox$ included in $PRef$. A higher purity means a better $PAprox$ in terms of percentage of non-dominated solutions, being 1 the maximum value possible.

Table 2 shows the results of the performance metrics achieved by the four algorithms, highlighting the best score for each metric on each of the event logs.

The experiments show that, in most of the logs, the tabu-search TS-STRICT scored the best results in each of the four metrics assessed, followed by the genetic algorithm NSGA-II. As expected, the algorithm hill-climbing HC-STRICT exposes the lowest performance among all the solvers, with its flexible variant HC-FLEX, i.e., considering the MAD deviation, improving its results. However, both variants of hill-climbing also constitute good initial approximations of the Pareto front. They exhibit performances that are close in terms of the metric evaluations to the NSGA-II and TS-STRICT. In all the cases, the algorithms scored hyperarea ratios superior to 0.93 (being 1.0 the max possible), meaning that they dominate at least 93% of the solution space dominated by the reference Pareto front. Also, the Hausdorff distances and Δ spread do not evidence a bad performance of any algorithm compared to the others. For example, although HC-STRICT never obtains the best measurement, it achieves better scores than the NSGA-II algorithm in 50% of the logs in both metrics. Finally, the purity rates show that both variants of hill-climbing add fewer points to $PRef$ compared to TS-STRICT and NSGA-II. These results were expected as hill-climbing uses a more local searching strategy. Thus, it explores a reduced number of allocations but still discovers Pareto fronts with sound values of convergence, spread, and distribution according to the Hyperarea, Hausdorff, and Δ metrics.

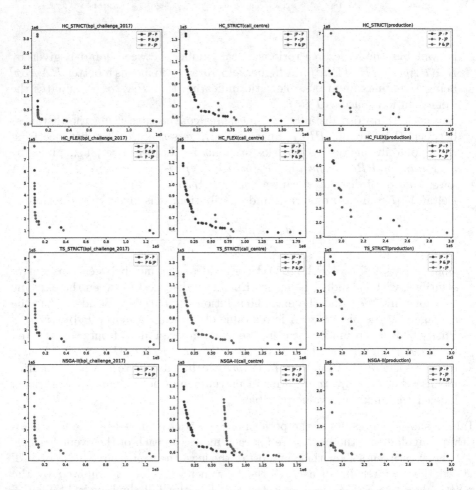

Fig. 1. Approximated Pareto Fronts from logs *bpi-17*, *call-centre* and *production*. The times in *cTime* (y-axis) and *procDuration* to compute *aCost* (x-axis) are in seconds.

Figure 1 compares the Pareto fronts $PAprox$ discovered by each algorithm from the event logs *bpi-17, call-centre* and *production* with the reference Pareto front $PRef$.[8] The points $(aCost, cTime)$ in blue are in $PRef$ but not in $PAprox$, the ones in green are in $PRef$ and $PAprox$, while the ones in red are the points in $PAprox$ but not in $PRef$. The figure illustrates how the approximations obtained by TS-STRICT and NSGA-II share more solutions with $PRef$, while the solutions discovered by the hill-climbing variants span local regions of $PRef$. Across all the experiments, the event log *call-centre* (in the middle) led to the most disperse results. In this case, TS-STRICT found 37 of the 38 non-dominated points in $PRef$, while NSGA-II, HC-STRICT, and HC-FLEX found different sets containing only 2 of the points in $PRef$. However, those points excluded from $PRef$ were still close, dominating a high solution space region as the hyper-area ratio shows.

To answer the research question **Q2**, we use data profiles [15] to assess how well each algorithm performed in terms of number of evaluations of the objective function (that require the calculation of $aCost$ and $cTime$). Specifically, we plot the cumulative percentage of non-dominated solutions added in $PAprox$ after a given number of function evaluations.

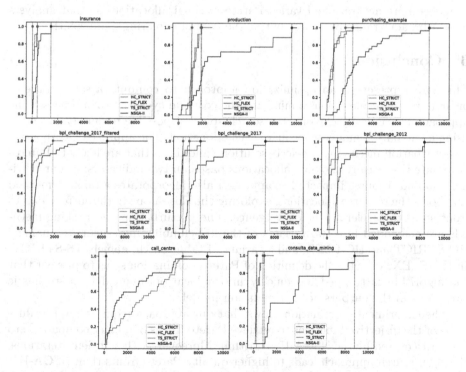

Fig. 2. Pareto front growing ratio (y-axis) in terms of function evaluations (x-axis).

---

[8] The Pareto fronts from the remaining event logs, and the full results obtained in the experiments, can be accessed from the code repository.

Figure 2 illustrates the cumulative growing ratio of the Pareto fronts $PAprox$, i.e., between 0 (no points) and 1 (all the points in $PAprox$), progressing with the number of function evaluations. The figure sketches with the dotted lines at which function evaluation each algorithm added the last point in $PAprox$. As expected, hill-climbing achieves the best performance, carrying out a significantly lower number of function evaluations than the other solvers. The algorithm NSGA-II shows the worst performance, followed by TS-STRICT. Unlike the variants proposed in this paper that explore each resource allocation only once, the NSGA-II algorithm may explore a resource allocation several times, thus requiring multiple calculations of $aCost$ and $cTime$. Regarding the different resource allocations explored, on average, the HC-STRICT traversed 361 allocations, HC-FLEX 1468, TS-STRICT 2982, and NSGA-II 4641.

The experimental evaluation evidenced that HC-STRICT, followed by HC-FLEX, requires fewer function evaluations to construct a Pareto front with acceptable accuracy. However, they also discover fewer non-dominated solutions than TS-STRICT, which exhibits Pareto fronts with higher accuracy. Accordingly, we can conclude that the hill-climbing variants provide a proper initial approximation of the Pareto fronts so that the business analysts obtain a solution in shorter computational times. In contrast, the TS-STRICT (like NSGA-II) provides more accurate and varied Pareto optimal allocations so that analysts have a broader range of choices but at the cost of exploring more solutions.

6 Conclusion

This paper presented an optimization approach to compute a set of Pareto-optimal resource allocations minimizing the cost and cycle time of a process. The approach heuristically explores the search space of possible resource allocations using a simulation model to evaluate each allocation. The approach incorporates a perturbation method that selects solution candidates that are likely to Pareto-dominate the already explored allocations based on two indicators: resource utilization and resource impact. The approach also incorporates a ranking method that sorts the resource allocations, exploring the closest one to the current Pareto front so as to accelerate the convergence. The perturbation and ranking methods are embedded into two variants of the hill-climbing meta-heuristic, namely HC-STRICT and HC-FLEX, and a variant of tabu-search, namely TS-STRICT. In HC-FLEX, we relax the definition of Pareto-domination so as to prevent that the algorithm is trapped too quickly into a local optimum due to stochastic variations in the outputs of the simulation model.

The experimental evaluation shows that our approach requires fewer evaluations of the objective functions to retrieve Pareto fronts of quality comparable to those discovered by the NSGA-II algorithm. Moreover, with sufficient iterations, the tabu-search approach leads to higher-quality Pareto fronts than NSGA-II.

A limitation of the current approach is that the exploration of the search space is done in a sequential manner. An avenue for future work is to speed up the approach by parallelizing the generation of solution candidates and their evaluation via simulation. Secondly, our proposal focuses on optimizing the number of resources per pool, assuming that all resources in a pool have identical characteristics. Another future work direction is to extend the approach to models with differentiated resources (e.g., different resources have different performance) as well as resources shared across pools or processes.

Acknowledgment. Work funded by European Research Council (PIX project).

References

1. Abel, M.: Lightning Fast Business Process Model Simulator. Master's thesis, University of Tartu (2011)
2. Audet, C., Bigeon, J., Cartier, D., Le Digabel, S., Salomon, L.: Performance indicators in multiobjective optimization. Eur. J. Oper. Res. **292**(2), 397–422 (2021)
3. Blank, J., Deb, K.: Pymoo: multi-objective optimization in python. IEEE Access **8**, 89497–89509 (2020)
4. Boussaïd, I., Lepagnot, J., Siarry, P.: A survey on optimization metaheuristics. Inf. Sci. **237**, 82–117 (2013)
5. Camargo, M., Dumas, M., González, O.: Automated discovery of business process simulation models from event logs. Decis. Support Syst. **134**, 113284 (2020)
6. Chaharsooghi, S.K., Kermani, A.H.M.: An effective ant colony optimization algorithm (ACO) for multi-objective resource allocation problem (MORAP). Appl. Math. Comput. **200**(1), 167–177 (2008)
7. Custódio, A.L., Madeira, J.F.A., Vaz, A.I.F., Vicente, L.N.: Direct multisearch for multiobjective optimization. SIAM J. Optim. **21**(3), 1109–1140 (2011)
8. Deb, K., Agrawal, S., Pratap, A., Meyarivan, T.: A fast and elitist multiobjective genetic algorithm: NSGA-II. IEEE Trans. Evol. Comput. **6**(2), 182–197 (2002)
9. Djedović, A., Žunić, E., Avdagić, Z., Karabegović, A.: Optimization of business processes by automatic reallocation of resources using the genetic algorithm. In: IEEE BIHTEL 2016 Proceedings, pp. 1–7 (2016)
10. Dumas, M., La Rosa, M., Mendling, J., Reijers, H.A.: Fundamentals of Business Process Management, 2nd edn. Springer, Heidelberg (2018). https://doi.org/10.1007/978-3-662-56509-4
11. Durán, F., Rocha, C., Salaün, G.: Analysis of resource allocation of BPMN processes. In: ICSOC 2019 Proceedings, pp. 452–457 (2019)
12. Huang, Z., van der Aalst, W.M.P., Lu, X., Duan, H.: Reinforcement learning based resource allocation in business process management. Data Knowl. Eng. **70**(1), 127–145 (2011)
13. Huang, Z., Lu, X., Duan, H.: A task operation model for resource allocation optimization in business process management. IEEE Trans. Syst. Man Cybern. Part A **42**(5), 1256–1270 (2012)
14. Lee, H., Kim, S.S.: Integration of process planning and scheduling using simulation based genetic algorithms. Int. J. Adv. Manuf. Technol. **18**(8), 586–590 (2001)
15. Moré, J.J., Wild, S.M.: Benchmarking derivative-free optimization algorithms. SIAM J. Optim. **20**(1), 172–191 (2009)
16. Peters, S.P.F.: Analysis and Optimization of Resources in Business Processes. PhD dissertation, Technische Universiteit Eindhoven (2021)
17. Schütze, O., Esquivel, X., Lara, A., Coello, C.A.C.: Using the averaged hausdorff distance as a performance measure in evolutionary multiobjective optimization. IEEE Trans. Evol. Comput. **16**(4), 504–522 (2012)

18. Senkul, P., Toroslu, I.H.: An architecture for workflow scheduling under resource allocation constraints. Inf. Syst. **30**(5), 399–422 (2005)
19. Si, Y., Chan, V., Dumas, M., Zhang, D.: A Petri nets based generic genetic algorithm framework for resource optimization in business processes. Simul. Model. Pract. Theory **86**, 72–101 (2018)
20. Weise, T.: Global optimization algorithms-theory and application. Self-Published Thomas Weise (2009)
21. Wu, J., Azarm, S.: Metrics for quality assessment of a multiobjective design optimization solution set. J. Mech. Des. **123**(1), 18–25 (2001)
22. Xu, J., Liu, C., Zhao, X., Yongchareon, S., Ding, Z.: Resource management for business process scheduling in the presence of availability constraints. ACM Trans. Manag. Inf. Syst. **7**(3), 9:1–9:26 (2016)
23. Yu, Y., Pan, M., Li, X., Jiang, H.: Tabu search heuristics for workflow resource allocation simulation optimization. Concurr. Comput. Pract. Exp. **23**(16), 2020–2033 (2011)

Are We Doing Things Right? An Approach to Measure Process Inefficiencies in the Control Flow

Fareed Zandkarimi[(✉)] [iD], Jonas Rennemeier, and Jana-Rebecca Rehse[(✉)] [iD]

University of Mannheim, Mannheim, Germany
{zandkarimi,rehse}@uni-mannheim.de

Abstract. A major dimension for assessing organizational performance is efficiency, i.e., the amount of output obtained from a given input. Organizational efficiency is closely connected to business process efficiency. Inefficiently executed processes may consume a lot of resources and still not achieve their internal goals. Because "you cannot improve what you cannot measure", process mining tools try to quantify process inefficiency with rather basic indicators, which provide only limited information. This paper introduces an approach that measures process inefficiencies in the control flow, taking factors like an activity's intended position in the trace and the allowed number of repetitions into account. Our evaluation results show that the process performance indicators that our approach defines capture aspects of process inefficiency that have not been taken into account in the baseline indicator that is currently provided in process mining tools.

Keywords: Process mining · Operational performance · Process performance · Process performance indicator · Business process inefficiency

1 Introduction

Operational efficiency, i.e., the amount of output obtained from a given input, is one of the major dimensions for assessing organizational performance [5]. The efficiency of an organization is closely connected to the efficiency of its business processes [18]. Inefficiently executed processes may consume a lot of time, cost, and personnel resources and still not achieve their internal goals. This is particularly problematic for support processes, like HR or purchasing, whose goal is to enable the execution of the organization's value-creating core processes.

For successful business process management (BPM), measuring process inefficiency is the first step towards improvement [27]. Inefficiencies in process execution like rework or change activities, loops, or cancellations can be observed in the event log that captures the execution of the respective process in an IT system. Companies like Uber [10, p. 60] and Siemens [24, p. 76] have been trying to harmonize their processes and reduce rework and loops to achieve higher

ⓒ Springer Nature Switzerland AG 2021
A. Polyvyanyy et al. (Eds.): BPM Forum 2021, LNBIP 427, pp. 109–125, 2021.
https://doi.org/10.1007/978-3-030-85440-9_7

efficiency levels. The identification of efficient processes also is a challenge for robotic process automation (RPA) because automating inefficient processes will amplify the inefficiency [20, p. 43]. However, there is no explicit indicator for process inefficiency in the process mining literature [27].

Process mining vendors appear to have recognized an industrial need for measuring process inefficiencies [1], but the indicators that they provide tend to be very basic and therefore do not provide a lot of value. For example, in Celonis, a case is labelled as inefficient if it contains an inefficient activity (e.g., change price) [2]. Process inefficiency is then defined as the ratio of inefficient cases in an event log. This indicator misrepresents process inefficiency with regard to the above understanding of efficiency as a relation of input and output, because it does not consider cases that include more than one inefficient activity.

In this paper, we present a novel approach for measuring process inefficiencies (AMPI). It is based on the idea that a process inefficiency is caused by either the type of activity (e.g., a deletion), its location (the activity is executed at the wrong position in the trace), or its frequency (the activity is executed more often than intended). Our approach defines a set of performance indicators, which measure the inefficiency of individual traces independent from the overall event log. It is defined on the trace level, hence allowing for a comparison between cases, and relies only on the control flow, hence requiring only a partial order within the trace. Therefore, we report on related work in Sect. 2. The process of developing AMPI is described in Sect. 3 and evaluated in Sect. 4. Section 5 discusses contributions and limitations, before the paper is concluded in Sect. 6.

2   Related Work

Our research takes a process-centric view on organizational performance, an important construct in strategic management. Researchers have defined countless measures for assessing an organization's performance in so-called performance measurement models (PMMs) [27]. Organizational PMMs [4,15] cover all aspects of the business, whereas business process PMMs [16,19] focus on individual business processes, which makes them particularly relevant for BPM [27].

Business processes are accepted as a significant construct in all of the mentioned PMMs. The Balanced Scorecard offers four main perspectives to managers (customers, internal processes, innovation, improvement activities). To define and measure the internal process perspective, companies must consider different variables for their business processes, e.g., project closeout cycle, project performance effectiveness index, and rework [14]. Similarly, the 4-level pyramid model by Cross and Lynch [4] contains "the vision" on the top and "operational measures" (including quality, delivery, process time, and cost) on the bottom.

Process performance measurement systems (PPMSs) play a major role in improving business processes for any process-oriented organization [16]. Dumas et al. describe time, cost, quality, and flexibility as the main dimensions of a PPMS [9, p. 253]. Because those dimensions are multi-faceted and rather abstract, various performance indicators are suggested to quantify the goals associated with each dimension. Such indicators for general organizational performance are called key performance indicators (KPIs). Process performance indicators (PPIs) are the process-related version of KPIs [23]. They should satisfy the SMART (specific, measurable, achievable, relevant, time-bounded) criteria for KPIs [25] and also be expressive, understandable, traceable, and automatically measurable [21]. The PPINOT metamodel allows for an unambiguous and complete definition and implementation of PPIs [21] and is enhanced by a graphical notation for defining and visualizing PPIs with business process models [22].

Process inefficiency, which is defined as the performance gap in comparison to a best practice, can either be design-related or intrinsic, i.e., related to process execution [3]. Design-related inefficiencies are highly domain-specific and have to be addressed during the design stage of the business process life cycle [9, p. 261]. However, even an efficiently designed process needs to account for the necessary flexibility in execution [13], so the mere conformance of an execution is not an indicator for its organizational performance [26]. For example, a process-executing IT system must allow for the termination of an incomplete process instance (e.g., on cancellation) or give employees the opportunity to correct or update wrong or outdated data. Nevertheless, those activities should be avoided to reduce intrinsic inefficiencies and improve the process's performance.

A recent review on PPIs did not find any explicit indicator for process inefficiency in the process mining literature [27]. However, there are a few studies that have dealt with measuring process inefficiencies. Dohmen and Moormann apply a three-stage approach to discover the association of intrinsic process execution characteristics and their efficiency score [6]. This case study measures the inefficiency of banking transactions by comparing them to the best-practice transactions. This means that the measure cannot be assessed for individual cases, but always depends on the most efficient transaction in the log. Also, the proposed method is domain-specific and limited to the financial sector. Van Den Ingh et al. describe an approach to measure process performance based on process mining [26]. Their approach evaluates variants of a P2P process based on control flow and context, but control flow inefficiency is assessed with very basic indicators, e.g., percentage of activities that was executed more than once. Höhenberger et al. applied automated model query approaches to collect weakness (process model) patterns [12]. Using their discovered patterns, they were able to find weaknesses in new process models from different context. This approach emphasizes the detection of patterns as the first step to discover and solve underlying root causes.

3   AMPI: An Approach for Measuring Process Inefficiency

3.1   Objectives

In the following, we describe AMPI, which, once applied to a specific process in a concrete context, results in a set of inefficiency PPIs. AMPI targets the following types of inefficiencies.

Non Value-Adding Activities. Activities can add value to the process by providing value to the customer (e.g., the receipt of goods in a P2P process) or to the business (e.g., the approval of a payment) [9, p. 186]. If activities do not fall within those two categories, they can be seen as inefficient. This includes activities like hand-offs or cancellations, but also so-called rework activities, like price changes (e.g., [10, p. 84]), which revoke the outcome of a previously executed activity.

Loops. Loops indicate a repetition of activities, which is perceived as inefficient because the same work has to be done twice. This is not the case for all activities. In a P2P process, for example, more than one occurrence of "release purchase requisition item" per case would be inefficient [10, p. 82], but a case can have multiple goods receipts. For unintended loops, the magnitude of the inefficiency is determined by number of iterations (the more executions, the more inefficient) and their length. Research has provided evidence for a "bullwhip effect" at a process level, meaning that occurring mistakes or problems should be addressed and handled as soon as possible, because otherwise, its consequences become more damaging [17]. If, for example the price of a purchase order item is changed twice in a row, it is less inefficient than if the second change happens after the invoice is confirmed.

Wrong Start and End Activities. Start and end activities of a process are particularly relevant, because they provide the basic information for initiating or concluding a case. If start activities are wrongly positioned, the other activities will lack information and therefore be incomplete. If end activities are wrongly positioned, follow-up activities cannot be executed efficiently. A purchase order item, for example, should not be created at the end of a P2P process, because it provides the informational basis for the entire case.

3.2   Outline

These examples show that for an insightful measure of process inefficiency, it is not sufficient to count the ratio of inefficient activities. Instead, AMPI takes the following steps to calculate the ratio of inefficient behavior in a trace.

1. Defining Activity Clusters: The basis of any inefficiency lies in the nature of the activities. We define a generic framework for classifying activities by their intended frequency (0, 1, multiple) and location (start, core, end). This results in nine activity clusters, which form the basis of AMPI.
2. Identifying Drivers of Inefficient Behavior: Some inefficiencies are revealed or exacerbated by certain conditions in the control flow, like repetitions of the same activity. We call those conditions "drivers" of inefficient behavior. They are defined and computed for each occurrence of an activity in a trace.
3. Calculating Cluster-based Inefficiencies: We calculate the (absolute) inefficiency per cluster by aggregating the relevant drivers of inefficiency for all activities in the cluster and all occurrences of that activity.
4. Computing the Trace-level Inefficiency: To compute the trace-level inefficiency, we normalize the cluster-based inefficiencies and then take the average across all clusters.

In the following, we say that $A = \bigcup_{j=1}^{m} a_j$ is the *universe of activities*. An *occurrence* or *event* $e(a)$ denotes the execution of an activity a within a process and can be denoted as a, if the context is clear. A *case* denotes one execution of a process, which has at least two attributes (an ID and a trace). A *trace* t is a finite sequence of occurrences $e_1, ..., e_n$, where each $t[k] = e_k$ denotes an occurrence of an activity $a \in A$ at the kth position of t, and $|t| = n$ denotes the *length* of the trace. $A^t = \bigcup_{e(a) \in t} a$ is the set of distinct activities for t. The *frequency* of any distinct activity $a^t \in A^t$ is defined as the number of occurrences, written $|a^t|$. Occurrences of a in t are denoted as a_i^t, where a_1^t indicates the first occurrence of a in t and a_l^t, $1 \leq l \leq |t|$ indicates the last occurrence of a in t. $[a_i^t]$ denotes the *location* of an occurrence in a trace, i.e., the index k, for which $e_k = a_i^t$.

3.3   Assigning Activities to Clusters

The first dimension of process inefficiency is the intended frequency of activities, which has three categories. The red category contains undesired activities, which do not add any value and should therefore not occur at all. The green category contains desired activities, which can be executed multiple times. Activities that should explicitly occur only once per trace fall into the yellow category.

The second dimension of process inefficiency is an activity's intended location in the trace. Therefore, we partition the trace into three sections. The start section and the end section contain the first and last activities of a trace, respectively. The core of the trace comprises all remaining activities in between the start and end. This separation recognizes the crucial role that start and end activities play in the trace, but leaves enough flexibility for process execution.

Combining the two dimensions with three categories each results in nine distinct activity clusters, as listed in Table 1. Readers should note that the same activity will usually be part of multiple clusters. The activity clusters are based on theoretical considerations and therefore independent from the analyzed process itself. To apply it to a concrete process, we need e.g., a process analyst or a domain expert to assign process activities to clusters.

3.4   Identifying Drivers of Inefficient Behavior

The clusters impose an intended behavior on their activities. Inefficiencies occur if activities do not adhere to this behavior. To identify these inefficiencies, we need to inspect the control flow context in which activities occur. This context reveals some inefficiencies, e.g., repetitions of yellow activities, and exacerbates others, e.g., loops. Below, we discuss four drivers of inefficient behavior in the control flow. Each driver is defined for an activity or an occurrence of an activity. Because AMPI should allow for the comparison of individual traces, the drivers are normalized to the trace length. When computing the overall trace inefficiency, we can then sum up the normalized drivers and obtain a normalized inefficiency value. This normalization at driver level is necessary, because the normalization basis depends on the nature of the cluster. Therefore, the following equations are only valid for their respective cluster and its assigned activities.

Table 1. Activity clusters defined by intended activity frequency and location

		Location		
		Start	Core	End
Frequency	0	Cluster S0	Cluster C0	Cluster E0
	1	Cluster S1	Cluster C1	Cluster E1
	Multiple	Cluster S2	Cluster C2	Cluster E2

Repetition. The intended activity frequency determines whether the repetition of an activity adds additional value to the process. Any additional occurrence above what is intended by the respective cluster is regarded as inefficient. For most clusters, those occurrences can just be counted when computing the overall trace inefficiency, but for clusters S1 or E1, which cover singular start or end activities, exceeding the intended frequency is particularly damaging. We account for such violations by individually factoring in their repetitions. Moreover, we also count for the variation of inefficient activities within one case, i.e., "multiple occurrences of one inefficient activity" is better (less inefficient) than "multiple occurrence of multiple inefficient activities". The rationale behind this decision lays in the nature of organizations where involving different actions usually requires extra communication and handover costs. However, performing the same action in the same company most likely costs relatively less overhead.

$$r_{S1}(a_i^t) = r_{E1}(a_i^t) = \frac{i-1}{\max(1, |t|-1)} \tag{1}$$

Location. The location of an activity is defined as its index in the trace. For each activity, the intended location can either be 0 (start activity), $|t| - 1$ (end activity), or any number in between (core activity). We assume inefficient behavior to be less severe early in the trace, so we differentiate between the first and all other occurrences. For C0 activities, an inefficiency of zero cannot be achieved if any C0 activity occurs at the core of the trace. For C1 activities, we assess their locations with help of two measures, l_{C1} and b_{C1}, to avoid twofold evaluation of activities where $l_{C1} = l_{S1}$. Whereas l_{C1} evaluates the location of C1 activities at the core, b_{C1} only assesses the start and end of the trace in terms of C1 activities. Location measures for clusters S0, E0, and C2 are not specified here, because the (absolute) location is the only relevant driver for these clusters.

$$l_{C0}(a_i^t) = \begin{cases} \frac{[a_i^t]}{\max(1,|t|-2)}, & \text{for } i = 1 \\ \frac{[a_i^t]-1}{\max(1,|t|-3)}, & \text{otherwise} \end{cases} \tag{2}$$

$$b_{C1}(a^t) = \begin{cases} 1, & \text{if } t[0] \text{ and } t[|t|-1] \in C1 \\ 0.5, & \text{if } t[0] \text{ or } t[|t|-1] \in C1 \\ 0, & \text{otherwise} \end{cases} \tag{3}$$

$$l_{S1}(a_i^t) = \frac{[a_i^t]}{\max(1,|t|-1)} \tag{4} \qquad l_{S2}(a_i^t) = \frac{1-i+[a_i^t]}{\max(1,|t|-i)} \tag{5}$$

$$l_{E1}(a_i^t) = 1 - \frac{[a_i^t]}{\max(1,|t|-1)} \tag{6} \qquad l_{E2}(a_i^t) = 1 - \frac{1-i+[a_i^t]}{\max(1,|t|-i)} \tag{7}$$

Distance. Not all repetitions of red or yellow activities are equally inefficient. To assess the impact of a repeated activity on the trace, we measure the distance between activities, defined as the absolute difference between their locations. We recall our assumption that repetitions are less inefficient if they are close together and ensure that we always compute the distance of a repetition to the first occurrence of the activity. As yellow activities should only occur once at most, any distance of a repeated activity is treated inefficient. In contrast, the optimal distance for green activities highly depends on the number of repeated activities. Note that $d_{C1} = d_{E1} = d_{S1}$, and $d_{E2} = d_{S2}$.

$$d_{C0}(a_i^t) = \frac{[a_i^t]-[a_1^t]-1}{\max(1,|t|-3)} \tag{8} \qquad d_{S1}(a_i^t) = \frac{[a_i^t]-[a_1^t]}{\max(1,|t|-1)} \tag{9}$$

$$d_{S2}(a_i^t) = \frac{1-i+[a_i^t]-[a_1^t]}{\max(1,|t|-i)} \tag{10}$$

Distinct Activities. In some situations, the previous measures are not suffi-cient to accurately assess process inefficiency. Consider a trace with a C0 activity at the core. The existence of a second distinct C0 activity at the core impacts the level of inefficiency to another degree than an additional C0-activity of the same type. This must be considered by an additional driver. For this purpose, we define the distinct activities per cluster as the number of distinct activities in a trace that are assigned to the same cluster.

$$da_{C0}(a^t) = \frac{|A^t| - 1}{\max(1, |t| - 3)} \tag{11}$$

$$da_{S2}(a^t) = da_{E2}(a^t) = \frac{|A^t| - 1}{\max(1, |t| - 1)} \tag{12}$$

3.5   Calculating Cluster-Based Inefficiencies

The drivers of inefficiency are defined on activities or occurrences and can be used to compute the (absolute) inefficiency level of the individual clusters (with regard to one trace). Because the idea behind the start and end dimensions are very similar, the computation and the formulas of the inefficiency levels of clus-ters S2, S1, and S0 are in line with those of E2, E1, and E0. For this purpose, we analyze the clusters with the same intended frequency together. Related activi-ties then only differ in their intended location.

Activities from S2 may occur multiple times at the start of a trace, so their occurrences do not represent inefficient behavior if they directly follow each other. Hence, repetitions do not impact the inefficiency, but location, distance, and distinct activities must be considered. The optimal location and distance of these activities depend on their number of occurrences. The second occurrence should, e.g., occur at location 1 with a distance of 1 to the first occurrence. The reverse holds true for activities assigned to cluster E2. In contrast, activities from S1 or E1 may occur only once in a trace, so repetitions play a crucial role. Their optimal location is at the start or end of the trace, so it is independent from other activities. The distance between the occurrences is considered, too.

$$\text{absolute inefficiency}_{S2}(t) = \sum_{a^t \in A^t} \sum_{i=1}^{|a^t|} l_{S2}(a_i^t) \times (1 + d_{S2}(a_i^t) + da_{S2}(a^t)) \tag{13}$$

$$\text{absolute inefficiency}_{E2}(t) = \sum_{a^t \in A^t} \sum_{i=1}^{|a^t|} l_{E2}(a_i^t) \times (1 + d_{E2}(a_i^t) + da_{E2}(a^t)) \tag{14}$$

$$\text{absolute inefficiency}_{S1}(t) = \sum_{a^t \in A^t} \sum_{i=1}^{|a^t|} l_{S1}(a_i^t) \times (1 + d_{S1}(a_i^t) + r_{S1}(a_i^t)) \tag{15}$$

$$\text{absolute inefficiency}_{E1}(t) = \sum_{a^t \in A^t} \sum_{i=1}^{|a^t|} l_{E1}(a_i^t) \times (1 + d_{E1}(a_i^t) + r_{E1}(a_i^t)) \tag{16}$$

The absolute inefficiency of S0 and E0 is determined in a different way. Here, most drivers do not have to be assessed because assigned activities should simply never occur. This behavior can be depicted by a binary location variable. In case of cluster S0, this variable is equal to one if the start of a trace is occupied by an assigned activity. The same applies to cluster E0 for the end of a trace.

$$\text{absolute inefficiency}_{S0}(t) = \begin{cases} 1, & \text{if } t[0] \in S0 \\ 0, & \text{otherwise} \end{cases} \tag{17}$$

$$\text{absolute inefficiency}_{E0}(t) = \begin{cases} 1, & \text{if } t[|t| - 1] \in E0 \\ 0, & \text{otherwise} \end{cases} \tag{18}$$

The core of a trace contains all activities that occur between the start and end. The activities assigned to clusters C2, C1, and C0 differ in their intended frequency. For the activities in C2, no restrictions are imposed, given that they occur in the core. So, the inefficiency level of cluster C2 is only determined by the location. If those activities are located at the start and end of the trace, the inefficiency level is equal to one. If either the start or the end is occupied by a C2 activity, the level is equal to 0.5 and only if both locations are free of C2 activities, no inefficiency in terms of cluster C2 is present.

The start and end of a trace must also be analyzed for cluster C1. Here, this is done by the bounds measure b_{C1}. In contrast to C2, additional drivers must be considered if a specific C1 activity occurs more than once. In case of repetitions, we assume the level of inefficiency to be moderate if the activities follow each other early in the trace. Based on this assumption, location and distance are relevant for the computation of the inefficiency of cluster C1.

For the analysis of cluster C0, we limit our view on the core of the trace. As those activities should not be executed, any occurrence increases the inefficiency. If a C0 activity occurs nevertheless, it should happen early in the trace, such that it has less impact on the trace overall. This is reflected by the location and distance measures. It follows that in case of repetitions, the optimal distance should be minimized. The more distinct C0 activities there are at the core of the trace, the more activities violate their intended behavior. Consequently, the number of distinct C0 activities increases the inefficiency level of cluster C0.

$$\text{absolute inefficiency}_{C2}(t) = \begin{cases} 1, & \text{if } t[0] \text{ and } t[|t| - 1] \in C2 \\ 0.5, & \text{if } t[0] \text{ or } t[|t| - 1] \in C2 \\ 0, & \text{otherwise} \end{cases} \tag{19}$$

$$\text{absolute inefficiency}_{C1}(t) = \sum_{a^t \in A^t} \left(b_{C1}(a^t) + \sum_{i=2}^{|a^t|} (d_{C1}(a_i^t) + l_{C1}(a_i^t)) \right) \tag{20}$$

$$\text{absolute inefficiency}_{C0}(t) = \sum_{a^t \in A^t} \sum_{i=1}^{|a^t|} (1 + da_{C0}(a^t)) \times (d_{C0}(a_i^t) + l_{C0}(a_i^t)) \tag{21}$$

3.6   Computing the Trace-Level Inefficiency

Once we have the (absolute) inefficiency values for the clusters, we compute the trace-level inefficiency as follows:

1. Per trace and cluster, we create an artificial worst trace of same length, which contains as much inefficient behavior (in terms of this cluster) as possible. This trace is an auxiliary construct and may not necessarily appear in the event log. It serves as a boundary for 100% inefficiency, such that we can express trace-level inefficiency as a normalized value between 0 and 1.
2. To compute the normalized inefficiency level of a cluster, we compute the absolute inefficiency value of the artificial worst trace (with regard to the respective cluster) according to our definitions above. We obtain the inefficiency level of our trace in question by dividing its absolute inefficiency values by those of the artificial worst trace.
3. The inefficiency of the trace is computed as the average inefficiency level of all clusters. If one cluster is not assigned any activities, this cluster is not considered in the calculation. Partial PPIs (e.g., for only one activity category) are computed as the average between the respective clusters.

4   Evaluation

4.1   Outline and Reproducibility

AMPI is evaluated in an experimental analysis by applying it in two different domains and implementing the resulting PPIs.[1] This demonstrates its applicability and generalization in two different contexts. To avoid representational bias, we did not apply any filter (e.g., for unfinished cases) to the logs.

Purchasing Process (BPI 2019). This event log describes a P2P process with 1.5 million events in 251,734 purchase order items (cases) [7]. Depending on the purchased item, those cases follow four separate flows of activities, which we call item categories 1 to 4. As the optimal control flow and therefore the cluster assignments differ among these categories, we partition the log into four sublogs and assess the inefficiency of each sublog individually.

Administrative Process (BPI 2020). The second log describes a travel reimbursement process, which distinguishes between domestic and international trips [8]. To account for the different process variants, the data is split into five sublogs: requests for payment (6,886 cases), domestic declarations (10,500 cases), prepaid travel cost (2,099 cases), international declarations (6,449 cases), and travel permits (7,065 cases). Again, we assess each sub log individually.

---

[1] The implementation and the full lists of activity assignments can be found at https://github.com/JonasRennemeier/Inefficiency_Index_2021.

Table 2. Inefficiency levels computed by AMPI for BPI 2019

Item category	Inefficient cases	PPI: start			PPI: core			PPI: end			PPI: all		
		Min	Max	Avg	Min	Max	Avg	Min	Max	Avg	Min	Max	Avg
1	0.66	0.0	0.17	0.0	0.0	0.50	0.09	0.0	0.60	0.05	0.0	0.28	0.05
2	0.39	0.0	0.56	0.01	0.0	0.50	0.02	0.0	0.59	0.03	0.0	0.43	0.02
3	1.00	0.0	0.60	0.17	0.0	0.33	0.09	0.0	0.59	0.28	0.1	0.43	0.18
4	0.31	0.0	0.17	0.01	0.0	0.50	0.03	0.0	0.83	0.06	0.0	0.38	0.03
Total	0.41	0.0	0.60	0.01	0.0	0.50	0.02	0.0	0.83	0.04	0.0	0.43	0.03

In the following, we show the separate inefficiency indicators for the start, core, and end categories of each log, defined as the arithmetic mean between the respective clusters. We also show the overall log inefficiency, defined as the arithmetic mean of the three. This separation should provide a more detailed insights into the sensitivity of AMPI.

4.2 Inefficiencies in a P2P Process: BPI 2019

Activity Assignment. Because this process contains four different variants, we need four different assignments of activities to clusters. Based on the process description, we assume that *Record goods receipt* and *Record subsequent invoice* may occur multiple times for item category 1 (C2). *Record goods receipt* is also assigned to S0 to account for maverick buying. *Create purchase requisition item* is a start activity that may not occur anywhere else in the trace (S1, C0, E0). *Clear invoice* is the intended end activity (E2). These assignments are applied to all other item categories, but have to be adapted to account for the intended process flow. For example, for item category 2, invoices have to be blocked until goods receipt, so *Remove payment block* is assigned to C1.

Inefficiency Assessment. Table 2 shows the results of computing the inefficiency of the BPI 2019 log. In total, 41% of cases contain some inefficient behavior. Item category 4 contains the least inefficient behavior and item category 2 also contains only 39% inefficient cases. In contrast, all cases from item category 3 are to some degree inefficient. Cases with the highest level of inefficiency often include an unusually high number of change activities, given their trace lengths. For example, the worst cases in terms of the inefficiency at the start begin with changing the approval three times before creating the PO item. The overall worst cases with an inefficiency of 0.83 at the end of the trace belong to item category 4. Such cases should end with the activity *Record goods receipt*, but often continue with change and deletion activities.

4.3 Inefficiencies in an Administrative Process: BPI 2020

Activity Assignment. This process also contains different flows of activities across the five separate logs. For example, employees require a permission to go

Table 3. Inefficiency levels computed by AMPI for BPI 2020

Log	Inefficient cases	PPI: start			PPI: core			PPI: end			PPI: all		
		Min	Max	Avg	Min	Max	Avg	Min	Max	Avg	Min	Max	Avg
Dom.	0.10	0.0	0.15	0.00	0.0	0.17	0.00	0.0	0.10	0.00	0.0	0.09	0.00
Int.	0.40	0.0	0.53	0.08	0.0	0.17	0.01	0.0	0.07	0.01	0.0	0.25	0.03
Perm.	0.60	0.0	0.54	0.05	0.0	0.22	0.03	0.0	0.50	0.00	0.0	0.24	0.03
Prep.	0.24	0.0	0.50	0.06	0.0	0.33	0.02	0.0	0.07	0.00	0.0	0.28	0.03
Req.	0.09	0.0	0.14	0.00	0.0	0.17	0.00	0.0	0.54	0.00	0.0	0.20	0.00

on an international trip, so *Permit submitted by employee* is assigned to cluster S1. For a domestic trip, employees can start the process by submitting a declaration instead. Any filing of a document (a permission, a declaration, etc.) can have a positive or negative outcome. For positive outcomes, the end activity is *Payment Handled* is assigned to cluster E1 for all logs. For negative outcomes, the university rejects the corresponding document and the employee needs to accept the rejection, so activities like *Declaration rejected by employee* or *Permit rejected by employee* are assigned to cluster E1.

Inefficiency Assessment. Table 3 reveals a substantial difference among the two types of trips. Whereas only 10% of domestic trips contain some inefficient behavior, we find 40% inefficient cases for international trips. On average, the inefficiency level is higher for international trips across all sections of a trace. Employees require a permission for those trips, but they often start the process without permission or by filing a declaration instead, which causes the high inefficiency level for the process start. On average, the end section of a trace exhibits a rather small level of inefficiency, because most cases have a positive outcome (employees get their costs reimbursed in 90.08% of cases). The trace core does not contain a high level of inefficiency either. This is due to the assignment of activities. Here, we allowed for repetitions of many activities, such that rejections are not necessarily considered inefficient.

4.4 Comparative Evaluation

In addition, we compare the results of AMPI to those of a baseline indicator (BI) that is currently used in a few process mining tools (e.g., Celonis, minit, disco, myInvenio). Like AMPI, BI evaluates only the control flow of a process. It is defined as a binary measure on case or activity level. A case is labeled as inefficient if it contains at least one inefficient activity (e.g., [10, p. 84]). Which activities are considered inefficient depends on the context of the process.

To compare the results of AMPI and BI for BPI 2019, we differentiate between the four item categories and plot the monthly start, core, end, and average inefficiencies, shown in Fig. 1. We see that BI most often calculates a higher inefficiency value than AMPI. BI also tends to decrease towards the end of the year, whereas AMPI indicates an increase across most sections. This increase

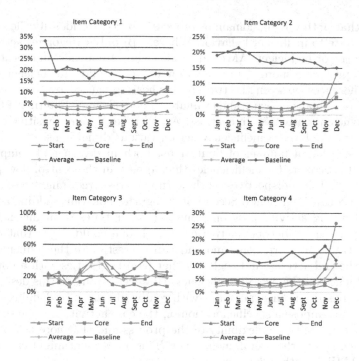

Fig. 1. Comparing AMPI and BI for BPI 2019

is particularly strong for the end category and can be explained by unfinished cases, which we did not filter out, to avoid representational bias towards AMPI. For a practical application of AMPI, we suggest using a sliding window approach to avoid a sharp cutoff of unfinished cases.

Because BI is a binary measure, whereas AMPI computes a value between 0 and 1, it is more reasonable to evaluate the differences over time instead of the differences between the values. For example, the inefficiency values for item categories 2 and 4 are rather stable according to AMPI, but varies significantly throughout the year according to BI. The differences between the two approaches also become apparent when analyzing cases of item category 3. Here, BI labels all cases as inefficient. We recall that AMPI also considers all cases of item category 3 to be inefficient, but the degree of inefficiency varies considerably.

5 Discussion

The comparisons between the inefficiency measures by AMPI and by BI illustrate the contributions of our approach. BI only considers the presence of (presumably) inefficient activities, instead of their order or frequency. Because AMPI considers more drivers of inefficient behavior, such as activity locations, it is able to find more inefficient cases than BI. Those advantages become more apparent, when comparing the different values over time. One commonality between AMPI and BI is that both rely on domain or process expertise to identify the activities that contribute to inefficient behavior. Whereas BI only categorizes activities as either efficient or inefficient, AMPI also takes their frequency and location into account to provide a more elaborated view on control-flow inefficiencies. All in all, the differences between the two approaches are caused by their respective nature. BI is a binary measure and evaluates the inefficiency in terms of the presence of inefficient activities. In contrast, AMPI takes a more sensitive approach and evaluates the level of inefficiency across various dimensions.

AMPI still has a number of limitations, both in design and computation. First, it only accounts for inefficiencies that appear in the control flow perspective, although other perspectives (such as time or resource) might have a larger impact on process inefficiency. Second, it recognizes non-value-adding activities, loops, and wrong activity positions, but not other types of inefficiencies such as interdependencies between activities. Third, one could argue that our separation of traces in start, core, and end can overestimate the influence of the start and the end activity and neglects other (core) activities with a potentially higher influence on the overall inefficiency. However, we made this design choice on purpose based on our experiences with real-world data. In defining the clusters, we do not impose a specific location on the core activities, because we have found that this limits the flexibility of the process and that core activities contribute much less to the overall inefficiency. This assessment might change when we apply AMPI to other domains.

The choice of clusters is another important limitation of AMPI. We assume that frequency and location are the two most relevant factors for inefficiency, but there might be others. Our selected categories are also chosen to cover non-value-adding activities, loops, and wrong activity positions, but could be further generalized to define, e.g., a specific intended frequency to each activity. Also, we weigh all activities within one cluster equally, although their actual impact may differ considerably. This could be addressed by defining an individual activity weight, which could be determined by experts or derived from the log itself.

AMPI cannot be calculated for traces with a length smaller than three, because the core of a trace cannot be empty. Also, AMPI only yields meaningful results for finished cases, because unfinished cases are always punished for a wrong end activity. For the overall inefficiency measure (the arithmetic mean between the start, core, and end inefficiency), one could argue that by weighing them all equally, we further increase the overemphasis on start and end activities.

Another limitation concerns our design choice to make AMPI independent of the other traces in the log. This allows us to compute inefficiency levels per trace and compare them across different lengths. However, it also requires the creation of an artificial worst trace as an auxiliary construct to define the "limits" of inefficiency that can hypothetically be achieved. It would be more realistic to use a real-life worst trace as comparison, but this would make the inefficiency of a single trace dependent on the other traces in the log.

The PPIs that follow from applying AMPI fulfill the KPI criteria of being specific (targeted towards process inefficiencies), measurable (shown in the evaluation), achievable (0% inefficiency is possible, although difficult), relevant (shown by the industrial need to measure inefficiency), and time-bounded (inefficiency is only measured for the time span of the event log). They also comply with the PPI requirements [21] in terms of traceability and automatic measurement. Their expressiveness and understandability depend on the application context and remain to be evaluated in more practical settings. Yet, these indices are significantly more complex (in terms of calculations, not structure) than common exemplary PPIs [21, 22] and cannot be linked to a few specific concepts (e.g., responsible, informed, scope) due to their context-independent design. Still, the resulting PPIs can be defined and utilized according to organization-specific policies and goals. So, despite this misalignment, AMPI can be framed under the PPINOT metamodel [21]. Below, we show a partial calculation of the inefficiency PPI for S2. PPINOT is designed as a generic tool to increase clarity of PPI definitions, so complex measures should be explained in natural language.

```
PPI{
    identifier: PPI_S2
    name: control-flow inefficiency cluster S2
    relatedTo: #process name
    goals:  reduce the level of control-flow inefficiency in the
            process with regards to cluster S2
    #sum over all distinct activities i of type S2
    target: simpleTarget.upperBound: 0.00 #desired value of 0.00
    scope: ProcessStateFilter.processState: finished
}
```

6   Conclusion

In this paper, we present our novel approach for measuring process inefficiency (AMPI). When applied to a specific process in a concrete context, AMPI yields a set of process performance indicators (PPIs) for measuring process inefficiency. AMPI accounts for several types of inefficient behavior (non-value-adding activities, loops, wrong activity positions) and allows for a comparison between cases. Compared to the baseline indicator for process inefficiency, which is currently used by a major process mining tool, AMPI provides a more sensitive and realistic way of quantifying inefficiencies in the control-flow of a process, which gives process analysts a better chance of finding improvement potentials.

Although AMPI is a significant improvement over the state of the art in measuring process inefficiencies, this problem is far from being solved. In future work, we want to address some of the limitations listed above and extend AMPI to go beyond control flow and include other factors like execution time. This might entail taking an even more domain-specific perspective to be able to identify different types of inefficiencies in processes. Our definition of inefficiency in this study does not reflect the absence or the disarrangement of desired activities. The required input for this study, assigning the clusters, is expected to be done manually, thus leaving space for human errors. This step can be automated in supplementary studies by means of more advanced techniques, e.g., semantic analysis, and deep learning techniques. Also, we want to follow up on a theoretical observation that we made during the evaluation. Our results suggest that the process inefficiency changes rather smoothly over time and does not show dramatic fluctuations. It appears to behave (or change) as an institutionalized habit. Hence, we could use AMPI as a basis to theorize about organizational routines and their reactions to endogenous and exogenous changes [11].

References

1. Aull, A.: 3 leading indicators of on-time delivery you shouldn't ignore (2020). https://www.celonis.com/blog/3-leading-indicators-of-otd
2. Badakhshan, P., Gosling, S., Geyer-Klingeberg, J., Nakladal, J., Schukat, J., Gsenger, J.: Process mining in the coatings and paints industry: the purchase order handling process. In: International Conference on Process Mining (ICPM) (2020)
3. Burger, A., Moormann, J.: Detecting intrinsic inefficiency on process level: benchmarking of transactions in banking. In: Ardagna, D., Mecella, M., Yang, J. (eds.) BPM 2008. LNBIP, vol. 17, pp. 146–157. Springer, Heidelberg (2009). https://doi.org/10.1007/978-3-642-00328-8_14
4. Cross, K., Lynch, R.: The "smart" way to define and sustain success. Natl. Prod. Rev. **8**(1), 23–33 (1988)
5. Davis, P., Peri, T.: Measuring organizational efficiency and effectiveness. J. Manag. Res. **2**(2), 87–97 (2002)
6. Dohmen, A., Moormann, J.: Identifying drivers of inefficiency in business processes: a DEA and data mining perspective. In: Bider, I., et al. (eds.) BPMDS/EMMSAD -2010. LNBIP, vol. 50, pp. 120–132. Springer, Heidelberg (2010). https://doi.org/10.1007/978-3-642-13051-9_11
7. van Dongen, B.: Dataset bpi challenge 2019 (2019). https://doi.org/10.4121/uuid:d06aff4b-79f0-45e6-8ec8-e19730c248f1
8. van Dongen, B.: Dataset bpi challenge 2020 (2020). https://doi.org/10.4121/uuid:ea03d361-a7cd-4f5e-83d8-5fbdf0362550
9. Dumas, M., La Rosa, M., Mendling, J., Reijers, H.: Fundamentals of Business Process Management, vol. 2. Springer, Heidelberg (2018). https://doi.org/10.1007/978-3-662-56509-4
10. El-Wafi, K.: Siemens: process mining for operational efficiency in Purchase2Pay. In: Process Mining in Action, pp. 75–96. Springer, Cham (2020). https://doi.org/10.1007/978-3-030-40172-6_12
11. Grisold, T., Wurm, B., Mendling, J., Vom Brocke, J.: Using process mining to support theorizing about change in organizations. In: Proceedings of the 53rd Hawaii International Conference on System Sciences (2020)
12. Höhenberger, S., Delfmann, P.: Supporting business process improvement through business process weakness pattern collections. Wirtschaftsinformatik **2015**, 378–392 (2015)
13. Hompes, B.F.A., Buijs, J.C.A.M., van der Aalst, W.M.P.: A generic framework for context-aware process performance analysis. In: Debruyne, C., et al. (eds.) OTM 2016. LNCS, vol. 10033, pp. 300–317. Springer, Cham (2016). https://doi.org/10.1007/978-3-319-48472-3_17
14. Kaplan, R., Norton, D.: Putting the balanced scorecard to work. In: The Economic Impact of Knowledge, vol. 27, no. 4, pp. 315–324 (1998)

15. Kaplan, R., Norton, D.: The Strategy-Focused Organization: How Balanced Score-card Companies Thrive in the New Business Environment. Harvard Business Press, Boston (2001)
16. Kueng, P.: Process performance measurement system: a tool to support process-based organizations. Total Qual. Manag. 11(1), 67–85 (2000)
17. Mahendrawathi, E., Arsad, N., Astuti, H.M., Kusumawardani, R.P., Utami, R.A.: Analysis of production planning in a global manufacturing company with process mining. J. Enterp. Inf. Manage. 31, 317–337 (2018)
18. Melville, N., Kraemer, K., Gurbaxani, V.: Information technology and organiza-tional performance: an integrative model of it business value. MIS Q. 28, 283–322 (2004)
19. Neely, A., et al.: Performance measurement system design: developing and testing a process-based approach. Int. J. Oper. Prod. Manag. 20(10), 1119–1145 (2000)
20. Reinkemeyer, L.: Process Mining in Action. Springer, Cham (2020). https://doi.org/10.1007/978-3-030-40172-6
21. del Río-Ortega, A., Resinas, M., Cabanillas, C., Ruiz-Cortés, A.: On the definition and design-time analysis of process performance indicators. Inf. Syst. 38(4), 470–490 (2013)
22. del Río-Ortega, A., Resinas, M., Durán, A., Bernárdez, B., Ruiz-Cortés, A., Toro, M.: Visual ppinot: a graphical notation for process performance indicators. Bus. Inf. Syst. Eng. 61(2), 137–161 (2019). https://doi.org/10.1007/s12599-017-0483-3
23. Rosenberg, A., Chase, G., Omar, R., Taylor, J., von Rosing, M.: Applying Real-World BPM in an SAP Environment. Galileo Press (2011)
24. Rowlson, M.: Uber: process mining to optimize customer experience and business performance. In: Process Mining in Action, pp. 59–63. Springer, Cham (2020). https://doi.org/10.1007/978-3-030-40172-6_10
25. Shahin, A., Mahbod, M.A.: Prioritization of key performance indicators: an inte-gration of analytical hierarchy process and goal setting. Int. J. Product. Perform. Manag. 56(3), 226–240 (2007)
26. Van Den Ingh, L., Eshuis, R., Gelper, S.: Assessing performance of mined business process variants. Enterp. Inf. Syst. 15, 676–693 (2020)
27. Van Looy, A., Shafagatova, A.: Business process performance measurement: a structured literature review of indicators, measures and metrics. Springerplus 5(1), 1–24 (2016). https://doi.org/10.1186/s40064-016-3498-1

Evaluating Compliance State Visualizations for Multiple Process Models and Instances

Manuel Gall[1,2]([✉]) and Stefanie Rinderle-Ma[3]

[1] Austrian Center of Digital Production, Vienna, Austria
[2] Faculty of Computer Science, University of Vienna, Vienna, Austria
manuel.gall@univie.ac.at
[3] Department of Informatics, Technical University of Munich, Garching, Germany
stefanie.rinderle-ma@tum.de

Abstract. Business process compliance refers to the formalization, enactment, verification, and monitoring of constraints for one or multiple process models and one or multiple process instances. Such complex compliance scenarios crave for visualization support that fosters traceability and understandability during design and runtime. It must be clear, for example, which processes and process instances are subject to which compliance constraint and, especially during runtime, which compliance state (e.g., satisfied or violated) is active. This paper analyzes existing visualization approaches for compliance-related information and demonstrates their usability and feasibility through a prototypical implementation and the application to a logistics scenario. The focus is on constraints that span across multiple processes and process instances. The preferred visualizations are then implemented in a real-world process scenario from the manufacturing domain and evaluated through in-depth interviews with three stakeholders. The interviews narrow down the results of the technical evaluation, indicating that *Color* is best suited for obtaining a quick overview and *Text* for in-detail analysis of compliance states.

Keywords: Business process compliance · Compliance visualization · Compliance traceability · In-depth interviews

1 Introduction

Business process compliance is expensive for companies, but the costs for non-compliance can be far higher [2]. Due to the COVID pandemic and digitalization needs companies gear up on compliance spendings, i.e., *"legal technology budgets will increase threefold by 2025"* [24]. Business process compliance means to formalize, enact, verify, and monitor compliance constraints stemming from, e.g., regulatory documents, in connection with process models and process instances [15]. Compliance scenarios can become complex due to the following reasons:

© Springer Nature Switzerland AG 2021
A. Polyvyanyy et al. (Eds.): BPM Forum 2021, LNBIP 427, pp. 126–142, 2021.
https://doi.org/10.1007/978-3-030-85440-9_8

1. Compliance scenarios may comprise a multitude of process models, process instances, and diverse constraints. [22], for example, describes a scenario for one organization in the higher education domain with 108 process models, 5831 activities, and 375 constraints. Compliance constraints can refer to none, a subset, or all process models and instances (we call a constraint *active* on a model or instance if it refers to it). Therefore *compliance traceability* is a desired goal, i.e., it has to be clear what belongs together.
2. Constraints may span multiple process models and instances, so called instance-spanning constraints (ISC), e.g., for bundling/unbundling of cargo [7]. Multiple ISC can be active on the same process instance. This might result in conflicting visualizations on a single activity.
3. Compliance states may have to be checked during design time and runtime [15]. Runtime checks include the distinction of life cycle states for process activities such as active or complete [18] and compliance constraints, i.e., pending, satisfied, and violated [18]. These states have to be visualized in a way that the states can be distinguished and thus support the understandability of the whole visualization.

Motivation (i)–(iii) shows overseeing and assessing the compliance states of all process models and instances for all constraints can become a cumbersome and arduous task for process analysts and compliance officers. Hence, with a focus on ISC (ii), this work tackles the following research questions:

RQ1 Which requirements need to be satisfied by an ISC visualization?
RQ2 How can ISC be visualized on running process instances?
RQ3 Which ISC visualization is best suited for assessing compliance states?

We will follow the design science research methodology [26] as follows: Requirements to be met by an ISC visualization are harvested from constraint management literature (cf. Sect. 2). Artifacts for ISC visualization are created based on literature from constraint visualization, information visualization, and graph visualization (cf. Sect. 3). Feasibility and coverage of all ISC visualizations are evaluated against the requirements based on a prototypical implementation (cf. Sect. 4). The findings are then further evaluated based on in-depth interviews with stakeholders in the context of a real-world scenario from manufacturing (cf. Sect. 5). Section 6 provides a conclusion.

2 Visualization Requirements

This section collects and groups visualization requirements for business process compliance. Grouping the requirements facilitates the comparison of existing approaches in this area. The grouping strategy is developed based on literature [8,9,20] and consists of the following four perspectives: process models, process instances, ISC, and ISC instances. The visualization requirements are collected from a selection of constraint management literature [12,13,16,18] and consider the constraint lifecycle states *pending*, *satisfied*, and *violated* [18]. The goal of collecting and grouping the visualization requirements is to identify how many of these requirements are satisfied by an existing visualization approach. Based on this assessment, recommendations for visualizing business process compliance scenarios can be derived. Visualization requirements are ($\mapsto$ **RQ1**):

- *Process Perspective*
  1. It should be possible to identify multiple active ISC in any state on one or multiple process models. [16,18]
- *Process Instance Perspective*
  2. For each activity it should be possible to identify the currently active constraint states. [13,16]
  3. For each activity it should be possible to identify the currently active ISC. [13,16]
  4. For each activity it should be possible to identify the active ISC and their constraint states. [13,16]
- *ISC Perspective*
  5. It should be possible to identify all ISC instance states based on the ISC visualization. [16]
  6. For each ISC instance it should be possible to identify on which activity they are currently active.[16]
- *ISC Instance Perspective*
  7. It should be possible to identify the process on which an ISC instance is active on. [16]
  8. It should be possible to identify the process instances on which an ISC instance is active on. [16]
  9. It should be possible to identify the activities on which an ISC instance is active on. [12,16]

Figure 1 (top) depicts a real-world manufacturing process model from EVVA Sicherheitstechnologie GmbH[1]. A pallet transports parts to the station, where an employee scans the product code. If the scan is successful, the product data is loaded. After loading, the employee is shown a step-by-step instruction on how to assemble the product. At the bottom, left of Fig. 1 two assembly lines are depicted with associated process instances. Assume an ISC requires that currently more than 2 instances are waiting for a pallet (depicted as ISC at bottom, middle). One ISC instance is created and active per assembly line (bottom, right). The colors of the ISC instances, i.e., yellow and red, reflect their compliance states, i.e., *pending* and *violated*. The corresponding ISC state is consequently visualized using both colors. For this example, we can say that *visualization requirement 5* is fulfilled.

3   Visualization Approaches

The goal for compliance visualization is to inform the user about the current state of each ISC on the process model and process instances of interest [18]. We define **ISC traceability** as the user's ability to identify an ISC in a specific

---
[1] www.evva.com.

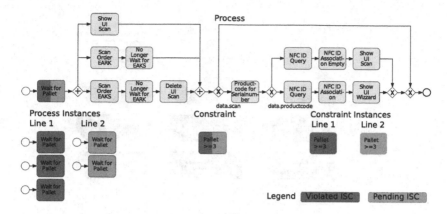

Fig. 1. Real-world manufacturing process: using color for ISC visualization.

state on multiple instances from multiple processes, i.e., the visualization can cover states of a single and multiple ISC at a time.

In order to answer **RQ2**, we collected approaches from constraint visualization [1, 4, 16–18, 25], information visualization [3, 19], and graph visualization [23]. The collected approaches focus on intra-instance constraint visualization and will be transferred to an ISC context for this work. Hence, we are confident that the eventually selected approach will be suitable for visualizing ISC as well as intra-instance constraints.

Figure 2 depicts the considered visualization approaches along three visualization tasks, i.e., visualizing *one constraint state*, *three constraint states*, and *three constraint states multiple ISC*. In detail, the first column shows one active constraint state, the second one –from left to right– constraint states *satisfied*, *pending*, and *violated*, and the third column multiple active ISC in all three constraint states.

In order to visualize multiple instances from multiple processes we use the 3D framework presented in [10]. Using a 3D setup allows us to use augmented reality (AR) and virtual reality (VR) capabilities in future development. Most of the approaches could be used in the same way in a 2D scenario. An exception are visualizations utilizing the additional axis, e.g., the *orientation* approach covers all three constraint states as rotating along the X, Y, and Z axis is possible. Using a 2D setting would not allow for three states to be covered by *orientation*. Assuming a 3D visualization, each of the cubes in the cells of Fig. 3 represents a process activity.

Some of the visualization approaches such as *size* do not allow to depict three constraint states on a single activity. Others such as *orientation* do not allow to depict multiple states of the same type. In such cases the associated cell is left empty. In the following, we discuss the different visualization approaches.

Symbols are represented near activities and ISC. By using the same symbol multiple times connections between perspectives, e.g., process instance and ISC instance can be drawn [16]. By utilizing a symbol's visual attributes, i.e., shape

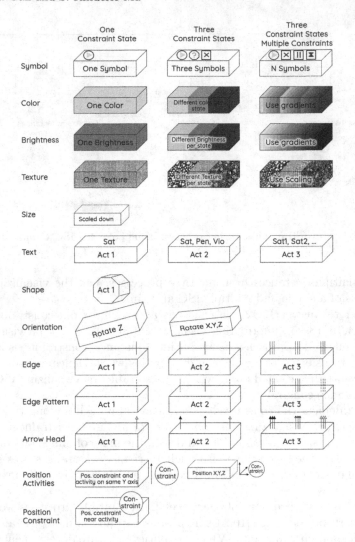

Fig. 2. Visualization approaches for constraint states on process activities.

and color additional information such as the constraint state can be encoded [25]. Multiple symbols close to an activity represent different ISC.

Color enables a range of applications. [1,4,16] use colors to express one of the constraint states for an activity. Colors can be used to further specify which ISC is currently active on a certain activity by using the same color [6,17]. To visualize multiple active ISC for a single activity color ranges [23] can be used. Using color ranges from, e.g., light green to dark green, allows to differentiate between multiple states.

Brightness [3] can be used in a similar way as *Color*. Multiple constraint states can be expressed by different brightness ranges.

Texture [3] represents the perceived surface of an object. Textures range from line drawings to colored images. To represent constraint states of an activity different textures can be used. Texture can encode information [11] by using color channel, tilling, smoothness, and many other attributes. Due to these different encodings a texture is suitable to represent different constraint states with ease.

Size: An activity and its associated ISC can be displayed using the same size. For discrimination to other activities, the size can be varied [19]. Specifically for visualizing constraint states, three groups can be defined, i.e., small for *pending*, medium for *verified*, and large for *violated*. Similar to the *Color Range*, each group can use a range for scaling, e.g., small uses a scaling of 30%–70%, medium 80%–120%, and large 130%–170%.

Text is mostly used to complement other visual styles such as *Colors* [18]. *Text* can be used without other visualizations [12,19] for constraint state representation. *Text* can be used to indicate if an ISC is currently active on an activity by writing the constraint state close to the activity or writing the name of the active ISC near the activity.

Shape: Activities [3] and the associated ISC can be set to the same unique shape to represent their association. Specific shapes such as triangular for state pending, can be used to express constraint states.

Orientation: By setting the same orientation [3] of activities and ISC, their association can be displayed. Different axis can be used to depict certain constraint states. For example, rotations on the X-Axis might equal to constraint state *satisfied*.

Edge: For each ISC, a directed edge [19] is created towards the activity. By placing the edge on fixed positions different constraint states can be encoded, e.g., front means *satisfied*, middle means *pending*, and back means *violated*.

Edge Pattern: For each edge it is possible to change the pattern [19] and to integrate information into the pattern. These patterns can be used for constraint state representation.

Arrow Head: For each edge it is possible to change the arrow head [19] and to integrate information into it. This works basically the same way as *Edge Pattern*.

Position [3] can be applied in two ways, i.e., *Position the Activities* or *Position the Constraint* [4,12,25]. *Positioning the Activities* moves the activity and ISC on the same axis position, for example, the same unique Y-Axis position. *Positioning the Constraint* positions the ISC instance near the activity bound by the ISC instance.

4   Implementation and Feasibility

The goal of the technical evaluation is to assess which visualization requirements from Sect. 2 are met by which visualization approaches (**RQ3**). For this, the visualization approaches –covered by a prototypical implementation– are applied to a set of four real-world ISC [21] in five logistics scenarios.

4.1   Evaluation Setup

According to [7], ISC can be classified along two properties, i.e., *context* and *modeling*. Context signifies if an ISC spans multiple processes or instances. Modeling refers to which process attributes such as time, data, and resource an ISC refers to. The possible combinations of context and modeling are reflected by the following four real-world ISC1 – ISC4 from the logistics domain (from [21]):

• Single context (one process, multiple instances), single modeling requirement (destination): *"For cargo distributed over several trucks, all cargo must arrive in the same destination."* (↦ **ISC1**)
• Single context (one process, multiple instances), multiple modeling requirements (date, customer): *"There should not exist more than 3 instances of post office delivery such that a specific input parameter (say date) is the same and the post office is also the same."* (↦ **ISC2**)
• Multiple context (multiple processes, multiple instances), single modeling requirement (time): *"The optimal case is all deliveries are on-time or 100% of on-time delivery. If the percentage of on-time delivery drops to 80%, it is considered as critical."* (↦ **ISC3**)
• Multiple context (multiple processes, multiple instances), multiple modeling requirements (priority, time): *"Prioritization and dynamic handling of cargo by cargo-vehicle interaction to ensure high priority cargo item precedence over low priority items."* (↦ **ISC4**)

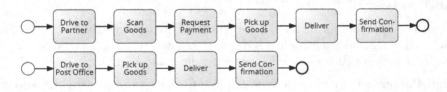

Fig. 3. Logistics process models: partner ordering and post office delivery.

Figure 3 depicts two artificial logistics process models *partner ordering* and *post office delivery*. Assume that the ISC1 – ISC4 are imposed on them and/or the process instances created based on the models.

Figure 4 gives an overview of the process models and instances (cf. Fig. 3) after completing the following scenarios. For constraint syntax we refer to [9].

• **Scenario1:** Partner(A) ships goods requiring two trucks (2 instances), both arriving at the same destination.
• **Scenario2:** Partner(B) ships goods requiring three trucks (3 instances). One of the trucks does not arrive at the desired location.
• **Scenario3:** A post office requires four deliveries (4 instances) within one day.
• **Scenario4:** Due to a massive traffic jam some deliveries (partner(A) instances 1 and 2, post office instances 2 and 3) are not on time.

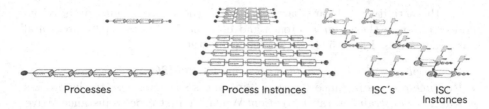

Fig. 4. Implementation overview from left to right: process models, process instances, ISC models, ISC instances

- **Scenario5:** Partner A and Post Office delivery share the same destination. Partner A's delivery has higher priority and therefore should arrive first.

ISC1 – ISC4 and **Scenario1 – Scenario5** are evaluated with the following constraint states. **ISC1** is executed two times, at first, for **Scenario 1** where the ISC state evaluates to satisfied. Secondly, for **Scenario2** where the ISC state evaluates to violated. **ISC2** is executed once and violated by **Scenario3**. **ISC3** is executed once and violated due to **Scenario4**. **ISC4** is executed once and violated by **Scenario5**.

4.2   Implementation

The visualization approaches collected in Sect. 3 are implemented in a prototype[2]. All scenarios are evaluated with all ISC active at the same time for two reasons. (a) In a real-world setting typically multiple processes and ISC are active. (b) We aim at a better understanding on how the visualization approaches handle multiple active ISC visually interfering with each other. We used the 3D process model visualization approach [10] created in Unity3D as foundation. For using the prototype, a tutorial was created. In this tutorial, one scenario (*Partner(B) ships goods*) is executed and an ISC is highlighted to gain insight on how the process execution is done. The tutorial allows to understand an ISC visualization approach based on a simple example corresponding to the previously introduced scenarios and ISC.

For a better comparison of the visualization approaches we chose to visualize them after all scenarios are completed. By using the next button it is possible to change between the visualization approaches.

Figure 5 depicts the *Color* visualization for **Scenario2** and **ISC1**. It illustrates an observation made during prototype development. All steps except for the first one depict two different approaches for process instance visualization. On the upper half of each step the process instances depict all process activities. On the bottom half of the steps the process instances only depict complete and running activities. For the sake of an easier understanding and to show that even such little visual decision can have a big impact on the understanding of an ISC visualization approach we opted to present both process instance visualizations.

---

[2] https://cviz.crowndefense.at/.

As the activity labels are barely readable, the focus is put on the visual representation of the *Color* approach and how the colors are represented in all four perspectives. Figure 5 shows the following steps.

- *Design phase:* Visualization of process model and ISC.
- *Runtime process instance creation:* 3 instances spawned next to the process.
- *Runtime constraint instance creation:* When the first process instance arrives at activity *Deliver*, a new ISC instance with state pending (yellow) is spawned.
- *Runtime constraint instance evaluation:* Little dots above the process instance visualization depict that two instances moved to the next activity. The state still remains in status pending as these instances arrived at the same destination.
- *Runtime constraint instance evaluation:* The goods for the remaining instance were delivered. These goods were delivered to a different destination and therefore violating the ISC and resulting in a change of color to red.

This example depicts a single scenario with one ISC. The prototype features multiple scenarios with multiple ISC.

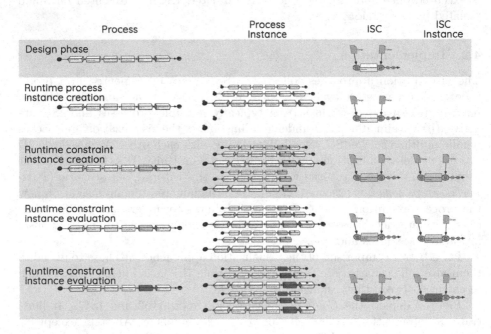

Fig. 5. Step by step example for ISC visualization with colors. Process instance activities are created during runtime. For labels see Fig. 3. (Color figure online)

4.3   Preselection

Table 1 gives an overview on the support for visualization requirements (columns 1–9) (cf. Sect. 2) per visualization approach (rows) (cf. Sect. 3). *Position* visualization approach yields the most surprising result for both, *Position Activity* and *Position Constraint*. Before the evaluation, we thought *Position* will be one of the top choices as it is used for intra-instance constraint visualization [12,25]. However, the biggest downside of *Position Constraint* is that it cannot reflect that ISC span multiple process instances without any modifications such as duplicating the ISC. The *Position Activity* approach yields better results compared to *Position Constraint*. The approach supports up to three ISC, if the ISC inherit different constraint states. We can position activities on the X,Y, and Z-Axis and use the same axis for the constraint states, e.g., the Y-Axis depicts a violated ISC. We would like to state that we are limited to 3 axes. Thus, if the constraint lifecycle would be extended, this approach cannot cope with the extensions. This limitation is the same for the *Orientation* approach. Currently, the *Orientation* approach rotates around all three axes. In case of a constraint lifecycle extension, some states could not be supported.

Table 1. ✓ full support, ■ support for 3 different constraint states, □ support for 1 constraint state, - not supported.

Visualization	1	2	3	4	5	6	7	8	9
Symbol	✓	✓	✓	✓	✓	✓	✓	✓	✓
Color	✓	✓	✓	✓	✓	✓	✓	✓	✓
Brightness	✓	✓	✓	✓	✓	✓	✓	✓	✓
Texture	✓	✓	✓	✓	✓	✓	✓	✓	✓
Size	□	□	□	□	□	□	✓	✓	✓
Text	✓	✓	✓	✓	✓	✓	✓	✓	✓
Shape	□	□	□	□	□	□	✓	✓	✓
Orientation	■	■	■	■	■	■	✓	✓	✓
Edge	✓	✓	✓	✓	✓	✓	✓	✓	✓
Edge Pattern	✓	✓	✓	✓	✓	✓	✓	✓	✓
Edge Head	✓	✓	✓	✓	✓	✓	✓	✓	✓
Position Activity	■	■	■	■	■	■	✓	✓	✓
Position Constraint	-	-	✓	-	-	-	-	□	-

Size and *Shape* only support one constraint state as using multiple sizes and shapes at the same time would change the semantics. For example, an activity is violated and satisfied at the same time. Then one state is represented by a large cube and the other by a small cube. If the mean is used the activity could be displayed with a medium sized cube. However, a medium sized cube could have different semantics. The same problem occurs for *Shape*. Different shapes could be merged, but the merging blurs the semantics.

4.4 Discussion of Selected Approaches

The evaluation has focused on a technical and quantitative point of view, so far, and has been used to narrow down the amount of visualization approaches for constraint visualization and ISC traceability.

Based on the results from Table 1, we keep the following approaches for discussion: *Symbol, Color, Brightness, Texture, Text, Edge, Edge Pattern*, and *Edge Head*. We narrow down this list by removing *Brightness* as *Brightness* can be expressed 1:1 by *Color*. From the three different edge approaches, we will keep the *Edge Pattern* approach as it subsumes *Edge*. We will also remove *Edge Head* as the visualization only shows the constraint state near the activity. *Edge Pattern* by contrast gives a more general overview while still being able to show the states near the activity. The remaining visualizations are *Symbol, Color, Texture, Text*, and *Edge Pattern*. *Color* and *Texture* are fairly similar. However, we will keep both for the discussion as one does not subsume the other.

We identified two usage scenarios: (i) getting a quick overview of all ISC (Requirements 5–9); (ii) looking into specific activities (Requirements 1–4). Based on our prototype we will give recommendations which approach to use for which scenario in the sequel.

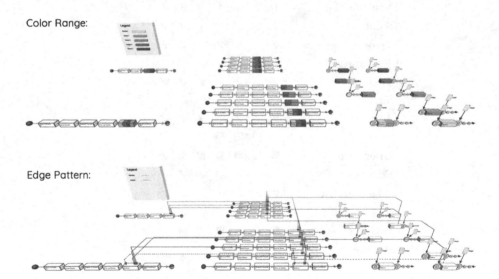

Fig. 6. Screenshot of prototype depicting all scenarios and ISC using *Color* on top and *Edge Pattern* on bottom.

Quick Overview: Our prototype shows for getting a quick overview *Symbol* and *Text* are not useful as they become too tiny to be identified on larger zoomed out graphs. *Edge Pattern* could provide potential insight into large graphs. However, ISC traceability is no longer supported as the visualization becomes cluttered with edges. Therefore, for getting a quick overview, we recommend *Color* and *Texture*. Figure 6 depicts the *Color* approach from the prototype. Even when zoomed out it is clear where the violations are located. ISC tracability is given as it is possible to see which ISC instance is connected to which activity. Figure 6 depicts the *Edge Pattern* approach on the bottom where an overview can be gained, e.g., how many activities are violated, but ISC traceability is nearly impossible.

In-Detail Analysis: *Edge Pattern* cannot be recommended for in-detail analysis as ISC traceability is not given. With a desktop environment it seems hard to follow a specific edge, especially when there are many edges on the screen. This could be different in AR/VR environments as the movement is more natural with head mounted displays. *Color* and *Texture* are well suited for getting an overview. However, for an in-detail analysis they perform in a mediocre way. For both approaches it is hard for the user to mentally align an ISC instance to a specific color or texture. On the left side of Fig. 7, for example, activities are shown, on the right side, all ISC instances.

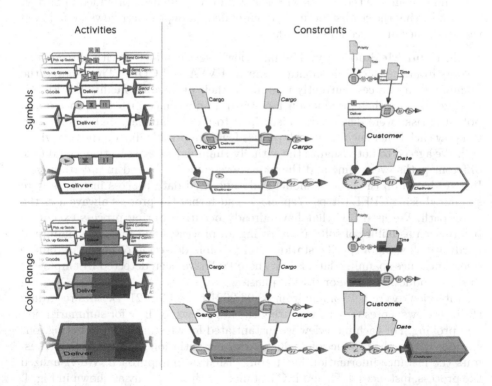

Fig. 7. Screenshot of prototype demonstrating in-detail analysis by depicting activities and ISC using *Symbol* and *Color* visualizations.

Based on the implementation, we can recommend *Text* and *Symbol* as both allow easier mental association of ISC and activity. We want to extend a bit more on these two visualization approaches as they have one critical advantage for in-detail analysis compared to the other approaches. The user can change the *Symbol* or *Text* for a more fitting representation utilizing better understanding and recognition of the ISC. All other approaches such as *Color* or *Edge Pattern* allow for similar changes, but their recognition would not be as good as *Symbol* or *Text*. For example a timed ISC (i.e., a ISC that refers to some temporal information of the process models and/or process instances) could use an hourglass symbol or be labeled with the text "timed". But what color or edge pattern could be chosen to represent a timed ISC?

As final recommendation we suggest the use of *Color* and *Texture* for getting an overview of constraint states and *Text* and *Symbol* for in-detail analysis of ISC.

5   In-Depth Interviews

The goal of the in-depth interviews is to identify new insights on ISC visualization and to compare the results with the technical evaluation provided in Sect. 4. For conducting the semi-structured, open-ended, in-depth interviews we followed the guidelines of Boyce and Neale [5].

Design and Methodology: The interviews were conducted with three stakeholders from the electronic montage unit at EVVA and CDP[3]. They shared the manufacturing process currently running in their production facility (cf. Fig. 1). During visits to their production facility and online meetings the process and potential risks were discussed. This helped to reduce language barriers and get to know each other such that both parties feel comfortable during the interviews [14]. We agreed to not visualize the actually running processes as they could take different paths every time and the interviews could be biased in a certain way. Instead based on the process model and annotated data process instances were simulated using CPEE (https://cpee.org/) such that the process always uses the same path. We used ISC that have already occurred during process execution before such as failure of software affecting all processes and instances, failure of hardware affecting a specific station, and possible detection of hardware failure due to instance spanning data. So far these ISC have been detected by employees during production phase or testing phase.

Interviews were held online from 02.03.2021 to 04.03.2021. Besides recording the interviews, notes were taken during the interviews to allow for summarization and probing. For each interview we instantiated four instances representing four stations within the production facility. After instantiation the used engine transmits the instance information live to our visualization approach. We visualized the process, instances, ISC, and ISC instances in the same way as shown in Fig. 4. Before the interviews started an overview of all representations was provided to

---

[3] https://acdp.at/.

the stakeholders. During the interviews, we followed the prepared questions outlined at https://bit.ly/3t7qxgE. However, questions could be shifted or omitted
depending on the respondent's answer to previous questions in order to, e.g.,
gain more details.

The recordings were transcribed and irrelevant phrases eliminated. The interviews were translated from German to English. Afterwards the transcripts were
sent to each of the stakeholders for confirmation. They all replied that the tran-
script is valid and represents the interview. In preparation for the discussion we
identified key topics, e.g., *Overall Best, Combination, Constraint States, Critical,
Worst Approach, Overview, In-Detail Analysis, Presentation,* and *AR/VR* and
applied color coding to verify that all information was captured[4].

Results and Discussion: Color is regarded as the *Overall Best* approach for
ISC visualization. *Color* by itself is suitable for visualizing *Constraint States* and
for visualizing traceability between processes/instances and ISC/ISC instances.
For all stakeholders it is important to find violated ISC rather quickly. They
suggest to use a *Combination* of different visualizations to allow for quick violation finding and traceability. The stakeholders were divided between different
approaches, e.g., *Shape, Rotation,* and *Scale* for visualizing that a violation happened. To add traceability they suggest the usage of either *Color* or *Symbol*.
This result is especially interesting as it differs from our technical evaluation.
Due to their limited expression we did not consider *Shape, Rotation,* and *Scale*
any further. To use those visualization approaches as indicator that something
happened is an interesting observation.

Textures are viewed *Critically* by the stakeholders. On the one side they
emphasize that *Textures* could convey more information compared to color. On
the other side they see problems with readability of text, the need for a legend
and a longer training period. The stakeholders rarely mentioned the approaches
Position Activities, Position Constraint, and *Brightness.*

Every stakeholder mentioned *Edge* as the *Worst Approach* as it clutters the
visualization, particularly for complex processes and instances. Traceability is
not given as in the following response: *"I went with the finger over the screen
and got nowhere."* This result is inline with the technical evaluation and we will
not consider edges for ISC representation.

For getting an *Overview* the stakeholders favor *Color.* For conducting an *In-
Detail Analysis* they are divided between *Symbols* and *Text. Text* was favored
because of the ability to express complicated information in a compact form:
"You can think up any text you want and display it without circumstances."
For *In-Detail Analysis, Text* is suitable to express information at different levels of granularity adapted to the user. These answers reflect the insight in the
technical evaluation that *Text* enables the representation of ISC and additional
information in a compact way.

The interview prototype presents processes, instances, ISC, and ISC instances
side by side. We asked the stakeholders if this *Presentation* meets their expectations. One stakeholder opted for separation of concerns, i.e., process/ISC on one

---

[4] Color coding available here https://bit.ly/3etUPX2.

side and instances on the other. Another stakeholder prefers the ISC instances as optional information. The third stakeholder stated that for some use cases a pure process and ISC visualization is sufficient, for other use cases all instances are necessary. Overall the stakeholders mentioned that the type of presentation depends on the role and use case. Based on these answers a flexible system that allows to hide and rearrange parts of the visualization is a good choice.

Stakeholders were divided on whether desktop, *AR*, or *VR* is preferred. One stakeholder was more skeptical in terms of *AR/VR* and is personally comfortable with desktop. However, the stakeholder can imagine that *AR/VR* brings advantages when visualizing process models and their ISC. The others prefer *AR/VR* over desktop and can imagine various applications, e.g., *AR* could be used on the shopfloor to display the process instances directly on the machines.

Limitations and Threats to Validity: We counter threats to validity with several measures. Firstly, the visualizations are based on various works from literature. Secondly, research bias is addressed as questions asked during the interview were defined in advance. Lastly, the stakeholders were not involved in the development/research in any kind. For the evaluation, we used process models from two domains, i.e., logistics and manufacturing. Since we have used ISC from each category of the ISC classification for the the logistics domain, we think that the presented results are transferable to other domains.

6   Conclusion and Outlook

This work evaluates compliance visualization approaches from literature with respect to complex process scenarios with instance-spanning constraints (ISC). The evaluation is based on literature, a technical evaluation, and in-depth interviews with stakeholders. In summary, for assessing compliance states, we recommend *Color* for *gaining a quick overview* and *Text* for *in-detail analysis*. Stakeholders favor a visual indicator showing that a rule is violated, i.e., *Size*, *Rotation*, and *Shape*. In future work we want to investigate the combination of multiple visualization approaches as suggested by the stakeholders. Further directions include the investigation of quantitative and qualitative requirements such as contradictions, subsumption, and root-cause.

Acknowledgments. This work has been partially supported and funded by the Austrian Research Promotion Agency (FFG) via the *"Austrian Competence Center for Digital Production"* (CDP) under the contract number 881843.

References

1. Awad, A., Weske, M.: Visualization of compliance violation in business process models. In: Business Process Management Workshops, pp. 182–193 (2009)
2. Becker, J., Delfmann, P., Dietrich, H., Steinhorst, M., Eggert, M.: Business process compliance checking - applying and evaluating a generic pattern matching approach for conceptual models in the financial sector. Inf. Syst. Front. **18**(2), 359–405 (2016)

3. Bertin, J.: Semiology of graphics; diagrams networks maps. Technical report (1983)
4. Böhmer, K., Rinderle-Ma, S.: Mining association rules for anomaly detection in dynamic process runtime behavior and explaining the root cause to users. Inf. Syst. **90**, 101438 (2020)
5. Boyce, C., Neale, P.: Conducting in-depth interviews: a guide for designing and conducting in-depth interviews for evaluation input (2006)
6. David, A., Larsen, K.G., Legay, A., Mikučionis, M., Poulsen, D.B.: Uppaal smc tutorial. Softw. Tools Technol. Transf. **17**(4), 397–415 (2015)
7. Fdhila, W., Gall, M., Rinderle-Ma, S., Mangler, J., Indiono, C.: Classification and formalization of instance-spanning constraints in process-driven applications. In: Business Process Management, pp. 348–364 (2016)
8. Gall, M., Rinderle-Ma, S.: Visual modeling of instance-spanning constraints in process-aware information systems. In: Advanced Information Systems Engineering, pp. 597–611 (2017)
9. Gall, M., Rinderle-Ma, S.: From instance spanning models to instance spanning rules. In: Enterprise, Business-Process and Information Systems Modeling, pp. 131–146 (2018)
10. Gall, M., Rinderle-Ma, S.: Assessing process attribute visualization and interaction approaches based on a controlled experiment. Int. J. Cooper. Inf. Syst. **29**(4), 2050007:1–2050007:33 (2020)
11. Gonçalves, L., Leta, F.: Macroscopic rock texture image classification using a hierarchical neuro-fuzzy class method. Math. Problems Eng. **2010** (2010)
12. Koetter, F., et al.: An universal approach for compliance management using compliance descriptors. In: Cloud Computing and Services Science, pp. 209–231 (2017)
13. Li, H., Yu-Shun, F.: Workflow model analysis based on time constraint petri nets. J. Softw. 15 (2004)
14. Louise Barriball, K., While, A.: Collecting data using a semi-structured interview: a discussion paper. J. Adv. Nurs. **19**(2), 328–335 (1994)
15. Ly, L.T., Maggi, F.M., Montali, M., Rinderle-Ma, S., van der Aalst, W.M.P.: Compliance monitoring in business processes: functionalities, application, and tool-support. Inf. Syst. **54**, 209–234 (2015)
16. Ly, L.T., Rinderle-Ma, S., Knuplesch, D., Dadam, P.: Monitoring business process compliance using compliance rule graphs. In: On the Move to Meaningful Internet Systems, pp. 82–99 (2011)
17. Maggi, F.M., Montali, M., van der Aalst, W.M.P.: An operational decision support framework for monitoring business constraints. In: Fundamental Approaches to Software Engineering, pp. 146–162 (2012)
18. Montali, M., Maggi, F., Chesani, F., Mello, P., Aalst, W.: Monitoring business constraints with the event calculus. ACM Trans. Intell. Syst. Technol. **5**, 1–30 (2013)
19. Moody, D.L.: The "physics" of notations: Toward a scientific basis for constructing visual notations in software engineering. IEEE Trans. Softw. Eng. **35**(6), 756–779 (2009)
20. Reichert, M., Bassil, S., Bobrik, R., Bauer, T.: The proviado access control model for business process monitoring components. Enterprise Modelling and Information Systems Architectures **5**(3), 64–88 (2010)
21. Rinderle-Ma, S., Gall, M., Fdhila, W., Mangler, J., Indiono, C.: Collecting examples for instance-spanning constraints. arXiv preprint arXiv:1603.01523 (2016)
22. Rinderle-Ma, S., Kabicher-Fuchs, S.: An indexing technique for compliance checking and maintenance in large process and rule repositories. Enterp. Model. Inf. Syst. Archit. Int. J. Concept. Model. **11**, 2:1–2:24 (2016)

23. Saraiya, P., Lee, P., North, C.: Visualization of graphs with associated timeseries data. In: IEEE Symposium on Information Visualization, pp. 225–232 (2005)
24. STAMFORD Conn.: Gartner predicts legal technology budgets will increase three-fold by 2025 (2021). https://gtnr.it/3qP2ySd
25. Vierhauser, M., Rabiser, R., Grünbacher, P., Egyed, A.: Developing a dsl-based approach for event-based monitoring of systems of systems: experiences and lessons learned (e). In: Automated Software Engineering, pp. 715–725 (2015)
26. Wieringa, R.J.: Design Science Methodology for Information Systems and Software Engineering. Springer, Heidelberg (2015). https://doi.org/10.1007/978-3-662-43839-8

Process Mining

Initial Insights into Exploratory Process Mining Practices

Francesca Zerbato[1(✉)], Pnina Soffer[2], and Barbara Weber[1]

[1] Institute of Computer Science, University of St. Gallen, St. Gallen, Switzerland
{francesca.zerbato,barbara.weber}@unisg.ch
[2] University of Haifa, Haifa, 3498838 Mount Carmel, Israel
spnina@is.haifa.ac.il

Abstract. Process mining enables organizations to streamline and automate their business processes. The initial phases of process mining
projects often include exploration activities aimed to familiarize with the
data and understand the process. Despite being a crucial step of many
analyses, exploration can be challenging and may demand targeted guidance and support. Still, little attention has been paid to understanding
how process analysts approach this exploratory phase. With this goal in
mind, in this paper, we report the results of an empirical study investigating exploration practices in process mining. Our study reveals that
analysts follow different behavior patterns when exploring event logs and
enact various strategies to understand the data and gain new insights.
The results remark the need for a deeper understanding of process mining
practices and inform future research directions to better support process
analysts and explain the cognitive processes underlying the analysis.

Keywords: Process mining · Empirical study · Data exploration

1 Introduction

Process mining enables the discovery, conformance checking, and enhancement
of business processes through the analysis of event logs recorded by information
systems supporting process execution [1]. Over the last decade, process mining
has gained remarkable momentum in academia and the industry, leading to a
wealth of techniques that empower organizations to streamline and automate
their business processes. However, so far, process mining research has privileged
the development of algorithms, approaches, and tools from a technical viewpoint,
paying less attention to learning how process analysts work in practice [13].

The work of analysts is often characterized by manual and knowledge-
intensive tasks [6,22]. In particular, in the initial phases of process mining
projects, analysts engage in different *exploration* activities [27], i.e., they dedi-
cate time to familiarize themselves with the data to develop an understanding
of the process [13], generate or refine questions, and discover new insights [7].

© Springer Nature Switzerland AG 2021
A. Polyvyanyy et al. (Eds.): BPM Forum 2021, LNBIP 427, pp. 145–161, 2021.
https://doi.org/10.1007/978-3-030-85440-9_9

Exploration is a crucial step of discovery-oriented applications across many data-science-related disciplines [11], including data analysis [2,10,14] and mining [16], and process mining [13,20,22]. For example, in data mining, the CRISP-DM methodology includes an "explore data" task within the "data understanding" phase, while the SEMMA and Two Crows models comprise an explicit "explore" step [16]. In process mining, exploration occurs mainly during event log inspection [22], in combination with process discovery [1,13], or whenever research questions lead to unexpected findings that need to be explained [7].

Recent interviews with data analysts [2,28] have shed light on exploration activities and related challenges that may benefit from guidance and tool support, such as choosing what to analyze or finding new insights. Given the affinity between data science and process mining, some of these findings may well apply to the latter area, raising the question of whether process analysts conduct similar activities or face similar challenges when exploring event logs and, if so, how they could be supported. However, so far, little attention has been paid to understanding how process analysts approach exploration in practice.

In this paper, we take a step in this direction and report the results of an empirical study designed to observe analysts as they engage in an exploratory process mining task. In this work, we specifically focus on "initial exploration", i.e., the phase in which analysts familiarize themselves with an event log before addressing specific analysis questions [28]. Mainly, we aim to understand (i) what activities analysts perform, (ii) what target artifacts they focus on, i.e., what are the objects of their analysis, and (iii) what are exploration goals and strategies. Accordingly, we formulate the following research questions.

(RQ1) *What are the patterns of behavior of the initial exploration?* With RQ1, we aim to discover patterns of behavior focusing on sequences of exploration activities performed on different target artifacts.

(RQ2) *What are the goals and strategies of the initial exploration? How do they relate to different patterns of behavior?* With RQ2, we aim to understand what exploration goals are and what strategies analysts implement to achieve them. Also, we look at the relationship between goals and patterns of behavior to investigate if different goals lead to different patterns of behavior.

To address RQ1 and RQ2, we analyze different kinds of *behavioral data*, namely the interactions with process mining software and target artifacts and subjective insights about exploration goals and strategies in the form of verbal data. Our study reveals that analysts follow different behavior patterns when exploring event logs and work with various goals in mind, enacting different strategies to familiarize themselves with the data and understand the process. Our findings contribute to an initial understanding of exploration in process mining and highlight activities that could benefit from practical guidance, e.g., choosing suitable analysis techniques based on event log characteristics. Starting from these preliminary results, we suggest avenues for future research investigating (exploratory) process mining practices to better meet the practical needs of process analysts through guidance and support and enhance our ability to explain empirical findings with the development of respective theories.

Our paper unfolds as follows. Section 2 reviews related work. Section 3 presents the method followed to design and conduct the empirical study. Section 4 reports the results of our analysis. Section 5 discusses the lessons learned and limitations of this study. Section 6 closes the paper and presents an agenda for future research.

2 Related Work

With this paper, we aim to advance the understanding of exploratory process mining practices by analyzing process analysts' behavior in the form of interaction and verbal data. Thus, our work is related to research on understanding exploration activities and goals in data science and, in particular, process mining.

Exploration has its roots in Exploratory Data Analysis (EDA), introduced by Tukey in the 1970s as the "foundation stone" of any analysis [27].

Nowadays, exploration is an essential step of many data-science-related endeavors [11], including data [16] and process mining methodologies [1,7]. For example, the L* lifecycle model [1] includes an activity "explore" in "Stage 2", the step aimed to create a control-flow model of the process under analysis. The PM^2 methodology [7] mentions "data-driven exploration" as a way to refine abstract questions since coming up with good questions at the start of a project is not easy. The authors also emphasize that exploration can generate unexpected findings and lead to concrete questions to investigate these findings further.

Related to our work are approaches investigating exploration activities in process mining. A few studies focused on supporting the exploration of process data, e.g., by easing the mapping of information among event data sources [26] or recommending interesting sets of process instances in event logs [22]. However, these approaches did not investigate how analysts approach exploration in practice. Klinkmüller et al. [13] examined process mining reports to understand the information needs of process analysts. The paper shed light on process mining practices in general, uncovering, for example, that analysts often combine familiarization with process discovery. Still, the study did not tap into the potential of user behavior analysis to unravel the dynamics of exploration processes.

So far, process mining research has paid little attention to understanding the behavior of analysts as they engage in process mining and, in particular, in exploration activities. Still, the analysis of interaction and verbal data has contributed to advancing user behavior understanding in neighboring areas, e.g., data science [2,10,14,28]. A growing body of literature has recently focused on understanding data exploration practices from different angles, uncovering typical analysis activities, goals, and related challenges. For example, the interview studies by Alspaugh et al. [2] and Wongsuphasawat et al. [28] revealed that analysts explore data for profiling and discovery goals but have to deal with fragmented tool spaces, repetitive tasks, and limited access to stakeholders. Liu et al. [14] interviewed data workers to understand cognitive, artifact, and execution alternatives of data sense-making processes, emphasizing the need to support the navigation and linking of alternatives across abstraction levels and tools.

Han et al. [10] used interaction and eye-tracking data to understand the behavior of data workers as they discover data quality issues, uncovering patterns of information usage and search strategies that can inform the design of data curation platforms. Besides providing insightful results, these studies uncover many new questions, remarking the need for more research to reveal the actual underlying practices of analysts [14] and enhance tool support [2,10,28].

To our knowledge, this is the first paper looking into the behavior of *process* analysts. Indeed, although some of the findings in [2,28] may apply to process mining, we advocate that it is not unlikely that the complex dynamics hidden in event logs would lead to unique exploration patterns, goals, and challenges.

3   Research Methodology

This section describes the planning and execution of our study and outlines the key aspects of the analysis conducted to address RQ1 and RQ2 (cf. Sect. 1).

Participants. For our study, we target academics and practitioners with varying levels of process mining experience and expertise. We recruited participants by reaching out to people in our professional networks. Participation was voluntary and based on the following requirements: (i) having analyzed at least one real-life event log over the past three years and (ii) having sufficient knowledge of Disco[1], the process mining tool chosen for our study.

Materials. The task was designed to observe participants as they use Disco to analyze the road traffic fine management event log [5], a real-life event log representing the process of managing fines by the Italian police. We chose Disco as it is a commercial, easy-to-use tool, often used for initial analyses [1]. Based on the details in [15], we prepared a document (referred to as "artifacts") with a description of the temporal constraints that need to be respected by the normative process, the activities and the attributes recorded in the event log, and a conceptual data model. The artifacts were intended as a source of domain knowledge and were at the participants' disposal for the whole session[2].

Procedure. We organized the task into an initial exploration, a guided exploration, and a semi-structured interview. We instructed participants to verbalize their thoughts in a think-aloud manner [8] as they performed the analysis. For the initial exploration, we gave participants up to 10 min to familiarize themselves with the event log. For the guided exploration, we provided participants with a guiding question aimed to replicate a high-level business goal and asked them to explore the event log at their own pace with this question in mind. Afterward, we assessed their understanding of the circumstances related to the guiding question with a comprehension test. Then, we repeated the procedure for a second guiding question. Finally, we interviewed participants to gain subjective insights into analysis strategies, goals, and challenges.

---

[1] Fluxicon Disco: https://fluxicon.com/disco/.
[2] Link to the material: https://drive.switch.ch/index.php/s/wevV2gXmoLBXrSY.

Table 1. Information about participants. I/A is a position in industry resp. academia, *
marks experience in process mining projects with customers for academics; PM EXPER-
TISE is a Likert scale with values "novice", "basic" "average", "good", "advanced";
PROCESS ANALYSIS refers to the past 3 years; #LOGS is the number logs analyzed in
the past 3 years; #TOOLS is the number of known process mining tools.

ID	GENDER	A/I	POSITION	PM EXPERTISE		PROCESS ANALYSIS		#TOOLS
				OVERALL	ANALYSIS	FREQUENCY	#LOGS	
P1	M	A	PhD student	Good	Good	Twice a year	>5	2
P2	M	A*	PhD student	Good	Good	Monthly	>5	5
P3	F	A	PhD student	Good	Good	Daily	>5	4
P4	M	I	Analyst	Advanced	Good	Twice a year	2–5	7
P5	M	A*	Post-doc	Average	Average	Monthly	2–5	2
P6	M	A*	Professor	Advanced	Good	Weekly	>5	3
P7	F	A*	Post-doc	Good	Good	Twice a year	2–5	5
P8	M	I	Programmer	Good	Average	Twice a year	2–5	5
P9	M	A	PhD student	Good	Good	Monthly	1	1
P10	F	A*	Professor	Good	Good	Twice a year	2–5	3
P11	F	A*	PhD student	Good	Good	Weekly	2–5	6
P12	F	A	PhD student	Average	Average	Monthly	>5	2

Execution. The data collection took place between July and September 2020 via
Zoom[3] meetings during which we recorded the participants' think-aloud audio
and their interaction with Disco and the artifacts, captured through screen sharing. Overall, 14 people participated in our study. Before the meetings, we provided instructions and administered a background questionnaire. During the
meetings, we ensured that Disco and the artifacts were visible on the shared
screen and reminded participants to speak.

Data Validation and Analysis. For each participant, we recorded around 2 h
of audios and videos. Two participants had difficulties using Disco, and thus,
we excluded them from the study. Table 1 lists some information about the 12
selected participants, who are employed by ten different academic institutions
or companies located in 5 different countries in Europe, Israel and Chile.

For the analysis, we followed a qualitative approach, focusing on the videos,
the think-aloud, and the interview parts referring to the initial exploration. Initially, we transcribed all the audio recordings. Then, building upon the principles
of grounded theory [4], we coded both the videos and transcripts iteratively, with
the support of the MAXQDA software[4]. First, one author coded all the data.
The other authors then checked the coded data independently, discussing dis-
agreements and iteratively revising the codes to ensure consistency.

To investigate behavior patterns (cf. RQ1), we analyzed the interaction traces
derived from the videos, i.e., the sequences of activities performed in Disco on
certain target artifacts. We defined a coding scheme by combining the function-

---

[3] Zoom: https://zoom.us.
[4] MAXQDA https://www.maxqda.com.

alities available in Disco, e.g., *inspect map*, typical data processing and analysis activities of the PM^2 methodology [7], e.g., *filtering*, activities happening outside Disco, e.g., *consult artifacts*, and the different aspects of the event log that can be analyzed, e.g., *paths*. Later, we augmented interaction traces with concurrent think-aloud and interviews to achieve triangulation and refine the coding. After several coding iterations, we obtained a hierarchy of 23 distinct codes for activities and 22 codes for target artifacts[5]. Then, we focused on identifying behavior patterns from the coded interaction traces. We started by selecting six high-level activities from the highest levels of our code hierarchy and exploiting different visualizations in MAXQDA to inspect and cluster similar sequences of coded segments qualitatively. After identifying potential candidate patterns, we backed up our qualitative insights with sequence alignments [12]. To this end, we sampled each participant's interaction trace into segments of 10-s length to keep track of the unfolding of activities over time. Then, for each segment, we took the code corresponding to the high-level activity performed for the largest amount of time in that segment and extended shorter sequences with segments of no interaction. As a result, we obtained twelve activity sequences of equal length on which we computed global pairwise trace alignments and used the obtained scores as a backup for our qualitative analysis.

To investigate exploration goals and strategies (cf. RQ2), we examined think-aloud and interview data. Initially, we fragmented the text using open and in-vivo coding [21]. Then, we refined and aggregated codes into categories using axial coding [4], obtaining a hierarchy of 21 codes related to goals and strategies. During axial coding, we relied on the videos to understand the participants' statements in the context of exploration activities. Indeed, since some participants were not always describing what activities they were doing while speaking about goals, strategies were not emerging clearly from the isolated analysis of verbal data. Finally, we used selective coding to find relationships among the inferred categories [21], ending up with three main categories.

4   Findings

In this section, we present the results of our analysis for RQ1 and RQ2.

4.1   Patterns of Behavior of the Initial Exploration (RQ1)

With RQ1, we focus on understanding what high-level activities analysts perform during the initial exploration, in which order, for how long, and on which target artifacts. The analysis of interaction traces and verbal utterances allowed us to identify three main patterns of behavior, henceforth BP$_1$–BP$_3$. In the following, we describe the main features of each behavior pattern, focusing on the two most representative participants, i.e., those showing the best pairwise alignment score (cf. Sect. 3). In parentheses, we show the number of participants for which a particular observation holds when not clear from the text. Also, we use (T) to label statements taken from the think-aloud transcripts and (I) for interviews.

---

[5] Link to coding scheme: https://drive.switch.ch/index.php/s/m6wud73z4ztL0ym.

BP₁: Artifacts as an initial focus, followed by attention to mainstream behavior and variants. This behavior pattern was observed in five participants, namely P3, P4, P7, P9, and P11. Figure 1(a) shows the sequences of codes (not normalized) derived from the interaction traces of P7 and P9 and the average time spent on specific high-level activities by all the participants in BP₁. All participants started by reading the artifacts containing information about the event log thoroughly. P7 claimed that the artifacts were useful to *"better understand what was happening in the process"*(I), while P9 said that *"it felt more important to understand this PDF file* [the artifacts] *than just to play around with the event log"*(I). Then, everyone inspected the process map in frequency view, i.e., the default view showing the control-flow model generated by Disco after loading the event log. All participants looked at the control-flow and the frequency of events, focusing on the most frequent paths. P7 used a variation filter to isolate the most frequent variants before inspecting the map. She then repeated the filtering and map inspection focusing on the least common ones. Performance metrics were used limitedly (2/5). Most participants (4/5) inspected the statistics after having explored the map, sometimes (3/5) going through the data attributes to know

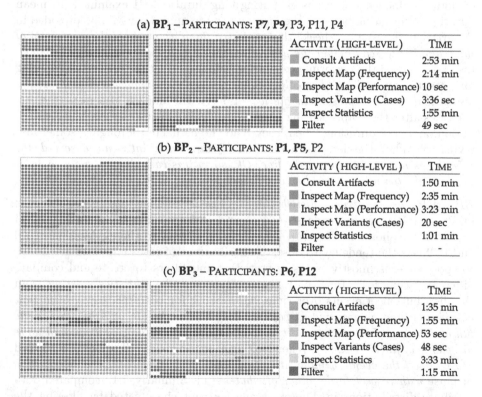

(a) BP₁ – PARTICIPANTS: P7, P9, P3, P11, P4

ACTIVITY (HIGH-LEVEL)	TIME
Consult Artifacts	2:53 min
Inspect Map (Frequency)	2:14 min
Inspect Map (Performance)	10 sec
Inspect Variants (Cases)	3:36 sec
Inspect Statistics	1:55 min
Filter	49 sec

(b) BP₂ – PARTICIPANTS: P1, P5, P2

ACTIVITY (HIGH-LEVEL)	TIME
Consult Artifacts	1:50 min
Inspect Map (Frequency)	2:35 min
Inspect Map (Performance)	3:23 min
Inspect Variants (Cases)	20 sec
Inspect Statistics	1:01 min
Filter	-

(c) BP₃ – PARTICIPANTS: P6, P12

ACTIVITY (HIGH-LEVEL)	TIME
Consult Artifacts	1:35 min
Inspect Map (Frequency)	1:55 min
Inspect Map (Performance)	53 sec
Inspect Variants (Cases)	48 sec
Inspect Statistics	3:33 min
Filter	1:15 min

Fig. 1. Summary of behavior patterns (a) BP₁, (b) BP₂, and (c) BP₃. For each pattern: (Left) Rendering of coded interaction traces for representative participants (in bold); (Right) Average time spent on high-level activities by all participants.

"what data we have there"–P7 (T) and learn typical values. Finally, most participants (4/5) inspected the variants, focusing on the control-flow of the most frequent ones. P7 and P3 also inspected specific cases to find examples of parallel and repeated tasks and look for attribute correlation. Towards the end, P9 used variation and attribute filters to isolate *"the happy cases for the police"*(T).

BP₂: Attention to the shape of the data, performance metrics, and bottlenecks.
This pattern was observed in P1, P2, and P5, with P1 and P5 being the most representative participants, as shown in Fig. 1(b). All participants started by focusing on the process map in frequency view, assuming activity labels to be self-explanatory. Indeed, artifacts were read at a later stage. All participants inspected the map at different levels of detail to check the structuredness or *"spaghetti-ness"* of the process, and two of them (2/3) focused on the most frequent paths. Participants focused on the shape of the data, as narrated by P2 *"The overall goal, I would say, is to get a feeling for the data [...] of how complex the data is"*(I) or P5 *"I was mostly driven by... by the dataset itself. I did some preliminary analysis from the structure, the time and the... attributes"*(I). Participants inspected the map in performance view at different stages of the exploration, focusing on paths exhibiting long duration. P1 examined the mean duration, alternating between the map and the temporal constraints provided in the artifacts to visually "check" them: *"I used them [the temporal constraints] at the beginning to see whether the process complies with these constraints"*–P1 (I). Instead, P5 used the performance metrics before reading the artifacts, searching for potential anomalies: *"I mostly focused on some anomalies and yeah, again, issues that could be present in the log"*–P5 (I). P2 and P5 also inspected the statistics after the map, focusing on the frequency of activities, variants' distribution, and case duration. Then, they read the artifacts thoroughly, sometimes trying to explain the detected anomalies: *"If the constraint is not observed, the offender is not obliged to pay the fine. Ok, so in this case, the anomaly could be that we take too much to send it, and he doesn't have to pay any longer"*–P5 (T).

BP₃: Attention to attribute distributions and patterns. This pattern was observed in P6 and P12, whose code sequences and average time spent on high-level activities are shown in Fig. 1(c). The common thread to the exploration of P6 and P12 was the tendency to observe distributions of cases and data attributes to spot patterns, mostly by using statistics and filters to create and compare different "scenarios". Both participants inspected the statistics starting from the distribution of events over time and looking for patterns, e.g., *"I am now checking if there is any evident pattern. Like this is the 6th of April, this is the 6th of January..."*–P6 (T) and *"it looks like that in the middle of the month there are plenty of fines"*–P12 (T). When looking at attribute distributions, P6 decided *"to filter all the events without an article and check if... how is the distribution of those with respect to the other attributes"*(T). Similarly, P12 compared data attribute distributions in different scenarios that she created by filtering the log based on the temporal constraints described in the artifacts. P6 said that attributes could help identify the causes underlying certain phenomena *"I would expect that if I can elicit the causes, I can do that from the attributes"*(I).

Comparing behavior patterns of the initial exploration. Fig. 2 sketches the behavior patterns that emerged from our analysis. While BP$_1$ and BP$_2$ capture opposite exploration approaches, BP$_3$ combines features of both of them.

Participants in BP$_1$ anchored their exploration to the domain knowledge embedded in the artifacts and explored the data in a top-down fashion through the lens of this knowledge, which helped them to guide their analysis, generate questions, and, sometimes, filter the data. P9 said *"I think most of my, um, knowledge came from just reading the artifacts [...] And I was thinking – Ok, why wouldn't you pay a fine? Ok, maybe I don't receive it by post or maybe I choose to ignore it..."* (I). They also spent a significant amount of time on process variants, looking into single cases better to understand the process and typical values of data attributes and their semantics.

In contrast, participants in BP$_2$ followed a bottom-up approach starting from the data. They focused on exploring the "problem space", looking at the shape of the log, observing the frequency of activities and variants, and collecting the *"hard numbers"*–P2 (T). They identified the most frequent path of the process as the "happy path" and read the artifacts towards the end of the exploration as a way to check their understanding of the process from the data. They also examined performance metrics to spot bottlenecks or outliers, e.g., *"Once I found something that could be interesting, for instance, one activity lasting a huge amount of time, then I dug deeper [...] to understand why this occurred"*–P5 (I).

Despite spending comparable amounts of time on the map in frequency view, participants in BP$_1$ and BP$_2$ used it at different levels of detail. Those in BP$_1$ used it mainly at the default level of abstraction to visualize the activities that they had read in the artifacts. Two of them changed the detail level to assess the structuredness of the process, but the majority preferred to do so by looking at the variants. Instead, those in BP$_2$ worked at a lower level of abstraction, increasing the number of displayed paths to focus on repetitions and deviations.

Participants in BP$_3$ distinguished themselves for finding patterns in event and attribute distributions using statistics and filters to create and compare scenarios. They used the artifacts to derive the domain knowledge needed for filtering and understanding data attribute semantics, similar to BP$_1$, but, espe-

Fig. 2. Comparing the representative participants of BP$_1$, BP$_2$ and BP$_3$. Spider charts are obtained by sampling activity sequences in segments of 30-sec length and selecting the activity performed for the largest amount of time in that segment.

cially at the beginning, they focused on the shape of the data, similar to BP_2. e.g., *"it was more about understanding the structure of data, the shape of the log, rather than the meaning of it"*–P6 (I). Also, they looked at data attributes focusing on aggregated data rather than on specific values within cases (cf. BP_1).

When examining target artifacts, some commonalities among behavior patterns emerged. Indeed, all participants focused on the control-flow, particularly on the structuredness of the process (9/12) and the mainstream behavior (11/12). The interest for such process characteristics across behavior patterns can be explained by looking into exploration goals and strategies (cf. Sect. 4.2).

4.2   Goals and Strategies of the Initial Exploration (RQ2)

With RQ2, we aim to understand the goals of the initial exploration and what strategies analysts follow to achieve them. Also, we look at the relationships between goals and the behavior patterns introduced in Sect. 4.1. Thus, here we refer to the ten participants whose behavior is captured by BP_1–BP_3.

Goals emerged from the analysis of the think-aloud and interview data. Similar to [2,28], participants remarked their intention to *"become familiar with the data and the process before determining any direction"*–P3 (I). Indeed, their main goals were to (i) learn the main log characteristics, (ii) conceptualize the process, and (iii) identify interesting things to explore in further analyses (cf. Table 2). However, participants enacted different strategies to pursue these goals.

Learn the main log characteristics. All participants aimed to collect basic information about the log, e.g., general statistics such as log size and time covered, activity frequency and naming, number and kind of available attributes, and process structuredness. Learning about the event log was helpful to *"get familiar with the process"*–P4 (I) or *"know what information is essentially available"*–P6 (I). Despite having the same goal in mind, participants pursued enacted different strategies to achieve it. Some participants focused on *"understanding the log"*–P7 (I) and *"getting the background"*–P7 (I) from the artifacts. Instead, others concentrated on data shape and complexity, focusing mainly on quantitative information about the log. Participants also emphasized checking how structured the process was to choose what kind of analysis to apply and estimate the effort required. A few participants mentioned the further goal of splitting the log to reduce its complexity, e.g., *"Why is it so complex? I would have looked into*

Table 2. Main goals of the initial exploration emerged from our analysis.

Exploration goal	Description
Learn main log characteristics	Learn what the log contains and gather descriptive statistics about the log and the process
Conceptualize the process	Form an idea of the process and its context
Identify interesting things	Identify aspects that are deemed interesting and worth more in-depth analyses

Table 3. Strategies followed to learn the main event log characteristics.

Goal: learn main log characteristics			
Strategy	Quote	BP	#
Understand available information from the artifacts	*"So like a little bit getting the background, so like, what are the tasks for what? And then also what are the attributes' meanings for all the things you provided and the artifacts were really helpful."*–P7 (I)	BP_1 BP_3	6
Assess data shape and complexity	*"I think this is part of any data science project, not especially for process mining, but to get a feeling of how complex the data is and I think the first start it to. . . to look at the process map and see how spaghetti-like the model is and, um ... then, also to get the hard numbers [...]"*–P2 (I)	BP_2 BP_3	4
Assess process structuredness	*"If the process would be extremely structured, I'd start guessing, for example, this is a xor-split [...] If it was extremely spaghetti, I would probably skip this inspection"*–P6 (I)	All	8

this and... potentially divided the log into sublogs"–P2 (I). Table 3 reports the described strategies, together with sample quotes, the behavior patterns (BP), and the number of participants (#) for which it was observed. Participants in BP_1 and one in BP_3 preferred to familiarize themselves with the semantics of activities and attributes over collecting quantitative data. Instead, most participants in BP_2 and one in BP_3 focused on the shape and complexity of the data. Most participants (8/10) across all behavior patterns assessed the structuredness of the process, looking at the map or the distribution of variants.

Conceptualize the Process. Conceptualizing the process entails going beyond direct observation, bringing together domain knowledge, prior experience, and common sense to form an idea of how the process looks. Table 4 lists the strategies aimed to pursue this goal, which was deemed important by all participants. Unsurprisingly, all participants used common sense to conceptualize the process. However, those in BP_2 relied on common sense to also interpret activity and attribute names. Some participants (6/10) combined common sense with domain knowledge derived from the artifacts and prior experience. For example, P7 relied on her previous experience in using temporal constraints to *"understand the payment culture"*. All participants in BP_1 and one in BP_3 used the domain knowledge in the artifacts to learn about the context of the process and identify, for example, the *"legal behavior"*–P9 (T). Participants in BP_3 conceptualized the process also by establishing connections among different observations, e.g., scenarios created with the help of filters. All participants identified the mainstream behavior of the process based on event frequency. Besides being *"the easiest thing to start with when you're exploring a log that you don't know"*–P11 (T), the mainstream behavior helped participants to discern exceptional behavior, which, in turn, was one of the most interesting aspects to explore.

Table 4. Strategies followed to conceptualize the process.

Goal: conceptualize the process			
Strategy	Quote	BP	#
Use common sense	*"I used common sense quite a lot [...] I had a vision of how the perfect process should look like"*–P2 (I)	All	10
Use domain knowledge and prior experience	*"These temporal constraints I know them from the medical field, it's always interesting to look at whether people follow this rule or don't follow this rule."*–P7 (I)	BP_1 BP_3	6
Compare and combine observations	*"I inspected how those [frequent variants] look from a control-flow point of view. So, in this way, I constructed a bit of a mental model of the process. And once I got this mental model of which are actually the most frequent paths, I went back to the map and looked at these pairwise relationships with this knowledge of how to put the local relationships [...] in the larger spectrum of... a complete trace"*–P6 (I)	BP_3	2
Identify mainstream behavior	*"We actually don't know what is exceptional [...] And that's why you focus on mainstream behavior first"*–P11 (I)	All	10

Identify Interesting Things. A common exploration goal was to identify interesting aspects worth being further analyzed. All participants identified as interesting "unexpected things that do not meet their assumptions" or "cases showing infrequent behavior", such as bottlenecks. To discover unexpected or exceptional and, thus, interesting things, participants followed the strategies described in Table 5. Some participants (6/10) relied on their knowledge of the mainstream behavior to build some "ground truth" and establish what was exceptional. Others (3/10) used the temporal constraints to anchor to the normative process and checked them "visually" from the process map or with filters. Two participants (2/10) focused explicitly on detecting anomalies by looking for outliers in the data and bottlenecks in the process. All participants in BP_1 and one in BP_3

Table 5. Strategies followed to identify interesting things.

Goal: identify interesting things			
Strategy	Quote	BP	#
Use mainstream behavior as ground truth	*"I think that path* [the most frequent] *is the more interesting one because it would tell me that this is the most likely correct path and that the others would be outliers"*–P9 (I)	BP_1 BP_3	6
Check temporal constraints	*"The constraints helped me to, uh, try to retrieve the cases that are not in line with the constraints. [...] Because when you look at the process, you want to see unusual stuff. So, it's easy to go to the temporal constraints"*–P12 (I)	All	3
Detect bottlenecks or anomalies	*"I mostly focused on some anomalies and yeah, again, issues that could be present in the log; that could indicate that the process could be improved"*–P5 (I).	BP_2	2

followed the first strategy. Three participants across all behavior patterns used the temporal constraints. Instead, anomaly detection was the main driver for those in BP_2.

5 Discussion and Limitations

The objective of this paper was to investigate exploration practices in process mining, with a focus on patterns of behavior (cf. RQ1) and goals and strategies (cf. RQ2) of the initial exploration. We discovered that process analysts approach exploration in different ways, e.g., working top-down after gathering knowledge from the artifacts, or bottom-up, starting from the data and using the artifacts to check their understanding of the log, similar to open-ended analyses [2].

Analysts examined data attributes from different angles, either focusing on distributions or looking into single cases to explain how the process evolves. We also learned that the initial exploration has the main goals to (i) learn the main log characteristics, which resembles what is called *profiling* in the data science literature [28], (ii) conceptualize the process, and (iii) find interesting things that are relevant to analyze deeper (e.g., as part of concrete research questions), which is similar to *discovery*, i.e., gaining new insights or making hypotheses [28].

While (i) is a goal of *"any data science project, not especially for process mining"*–P2 (I) and the same holds for (iii), the structure and behavior of the underlying process require analysts to engage in specific exploration strategies.

For example, many participants assessed the structuredness of the process to decide which kind of analysis to conduct. To this end, they relied on the visual inspection of the process map and the variants and prior experience, having different perceptions of whether the process was "lasagna" or "spaghetti". Although assessing process structuredness and, more in general, the structure and complexity of the data under investigation is typical of exploratory analyses [2, 28], it is a nontrivial task that could tip the balance towards choosing an analysis technique over another. For example, two participants said they would split a spaghetti log into sub-logs before starting the analysis. Still, selecting the "right" pre-processing or analysis technique based on event log characteristics can be challenging [24], and we hypothesize that, especially for novices, it may be difficult to choose among analysis approaches and tools. This is particularly so when dealing with alternatives [14] or combining artifacts and techniques not specific to process mining [13]. Recent reviews of process discovery [3] and variants analysis [25] methods could help to compare different approaches, as well as the metrics in [24] could help to gain control-flow insights. However, practical guidance to support analysts in assessing event log characteristics (e.g., structuredness, presence, and quality of resource data) and, based on them, evaluating the applicability of pre-processing and analysis techniques is still missing.

Another insight emerging from our analysis is the attention paid to exceptional behavior and, particularly, negative deviations [18]. All participants identified exceptional behavior as the most valuable aspect to analyze, especially when seeking improvement opportunities. Improvement was perceived differently: participants working top-down emphasized improvement opportunities for end-users (cf. BP_1), while those working bottom-up focused mainly on performance (cf. BP_2). Still, almost everyone tended to look for negative deviations, and only P9 focused on the "positive cases for the police" (T). The focus on negative deviations is in line with the observation that inductive BPM approaches, including process mining, often put a strong focus on "responding to pain points" [20], while the exploration of opportunities is less emphasized. However, research has shown that processes can be improved by learning from positive deviations [23] or experience gained through past executions [9]. We find the tendency to look at negative deviations at the start of the analysis somewhat surprising. Indeed, the interviews in [2, 28] did not mention interest for "negative" patterns, and the focus on deviations in the broader area of data science seems to be limited to spot outliers or data quality issues during profiling [28] or data curation tasks [10].

Overall, although some exploration goals overlap between data science and process mining, our analysis uncovered strategies that are not described in the data science literature, remarking the need for improving our understanding of process mining practices and develop targeted support for process analysts.

Limitations. Our study comes with some limitations. First, since we invited participants in our professional network, our sample was not drawn randomly from the overall process analysts population and is biased towards academics. Still, six academic participants were involved in process mining projects where the main goal was to analyze data for a customer (cf. Table 1) and, when interviewed, they provided insights into these experiences. Second, our study is subject to a limited number of participants. Still, twelve is considered an appropriate sample size for think-aloud studies [19], given the richness of the verbal data that we also augmented with interaction traces. Third, in this paper, we focused on exploratory process mining, i.e., the analysis phase aimed to familiarize with the data and refine abstract research questions. Thus, our findings cannot be generalized to other analysis phases, e.g., answering concrete questions. Finally, since all our subjects used Disco, we cannot claim that our findings can be generalized across tools. Indeed, Disco presents the map view after loading the event log and, thus, it would not be surprising if participants used the map at the beginning. Also, the functionality provided by the tool limits the analysis that our participants could perform and, as a consequence, the behavior we could observe in our data.

6   Conclusion and Outlook

In this paper, we have presented the findings of an empirical study investigating how process analysts approach exploration in practice, focusing on understanding common patterns of behavior, goals, and strategies of the initial exploration phase. Our findings revealed that analysts exhibit different behavior patterns when exploring an event log and work with different goals in mind, enacting various strategies to familiarize themselves with the data and the process. Besides providing novel insights into exploratory process mining practices, our findings can inform different directions for future research.

An obvious direction for future work is to improve the generalizability of our findings by conducting additional empirical studies to gain a comprehensive understanding of process mining across different analysis phases and tools. To this end, we will conduct quantitative and focused studies involving more practitioners and observing how analysts approach different analysis phases (e.g., familiarization, question answering) with one or more process mining tools. This will allow us to look into typical behavior patterns, goals, strategies, and challenges of process mining and, potentially, discern effective and non-effective behavior.

Gaining an in-depth understanding of (exploratory) process mining practices will provide empirical evidence for developing guidance and support for process analysts, for example, by enabling knowledge transfer from experienced analysts to novices. For instance, existing process mining methodologies could be complemented with practical recommendations, e.g., to choose analysis techniques based on event log characteristics or to foster the exploration of opportunity points [20], and tool support, e.g., to ease the comparison of "scenarios" (cf. BP$_3$) or process variants [25] along multiple process perspectives.

Another possible avenue for future research is the development of theories. In neighboring areas such as process modeling, cognitive theories have been used to explain empirical observations (e.g., [29]) and inform advancements, for example, to reduce the cognitive load when performing relevant tasks [17]. We suggest that the development of similarly relevant theories for explaining the cognitive processes involved in process mining, in general, and the exploratory phase, in particular, will contribute to advancement in this area.

Acknowledgment. This work is part of the Process Mining Support for End-users (ProMiSE) project, funded by the Swiss National Science Foundation (SNSF) under Grant No.: 200021_197032. We sincerely thank all our participants and Dr. Anne Rozinat, who provided us with Disco licenses.

References

1. van der Aalst, W.: Process Mining-Data Science in Action, 2 edn. Springer, Heidelberg (2016). https://doi.org/10.1007/978-3-662-49851-4
2. Alspaugh, S., Zokaei, N., Liu, A., Jin, C., Hearst, M.A.: Futzing and moseying: interviews with professional data analysts on exploration practices. IEEE Trans. Vis. Comput. Graph. **25**(1), 22–31 (2019)
3. Augusto, A., et al.: Automated discovery of process models from event logs: review and benchmark. IEEE Trans. Knowl. Data Eng. **31**(4), 686–705 (2019)
4. Corbin, J., Strauss, A.: Basics of Qualitative Research: Techniques and Procedures for Developing Grounded Theory. SAGE Publications (2014)
5. De Leoni, M., Mannhardt, F.: Road traffic fine management process. Eindhoven University of Technology (2015). Dataset
6. Diba, K., Batoulis, K., Weidlich, M., Weske, M.: Extraction, correlation, and abstraction of event data for process mining. Wiley Interdiscip. Rev. Data Min. Knowl. Discov. **10**(3), e1346 (2019)
7. van Eck, M.L., Lu, X., Leemans, S.J.J., van der Aalst, W.M.P.: PM^2: a process mining project methodology. In: Zdravkovic, J., Kirikova, M., Johannesson, P. (eds.) CAiSE 2015. LNCS, vol. 9097, pp. 297–313. Springer, Cham (2015). https://doi.org/10.1007/978-3-319-19069-3_19
8. Ericsson, K.A., Simon, H.A.: Protocol Analysis: Verbal Reports as Data. the MIT Press (1984)
9. Ghattas, J., Soffer, P., Peleg, M.: Improving business process decision making based on past experience. Decis. Support Syst. **59**, 93–107 (2014)
10. Han, L., Chen, T., Demartini, G., Indulska, M., Sadiq, S.W.: On understanding data worker interaction behaviors. In: International ACM SIGIR Conference on Research and Development in Information Retrieval, pp. 269–278. ACM (2020)
11. Idreos, S., Papaemmanouil, O., Chaudhuri, S.: Overview of data exploration techniques. In: Proceeding of the ACM SIGMOD International Conference on Management of Data, pp. 277–281. ACM (2015)
12. Jagadeesh Chandra Bose, R.P., van der Aalst, W.: Trace alignment in process mining: opportunities for process diagnostics. In: Hull, R., Mendling, J., Tai, S. (eds.) BPM 2010. LNCS, vol. 6336, pp. 227–242. Springer, Heidelberg (2010). https://doi.org/10.1007/978-3-642-15618-2_17
13. Klinkmüller, C., Müller, R., Weber, I.: Mining process mining practices: an exploratory characterization of information needs in process analytics. In: Hildebrandt, T., van Dongen, B.F., Röglinger, M., Mendling, J. (eds.) BPM 2019. LNCS, vol. 11675, pp. 322–337. Springer, Cham (2019). https://doi.org/10.1007/978-3-030-26619-6_21
14. Liu, J., Boukhelifa, N., Eagan, J.R.: Understanding the role of alternatives in data analysis practices. IEEE Trans. Vis. Comput. Graph. **26**(1), 66–76 (2019)
15. Mannhardt, F.: Multi-perspective process mining. Ph.D. thesis, Technische Universiteit Eindhoven (February 2018)
16. Mariscal, G., Marban, O., Fernandez, C.: A survey of data mining and knowledge discovery process models and methodologies. Knowl. Eng. Rev. **25**(2), 137 (2010)

17. Moody, D.: The "physics" of notations: toward a scientific basis for constructing visual notations in software engineering. IEEE Trans. Softw. Eng. **35**(6), 756–779 (2009)
18. Nguyen, H., Dumas, M., La Rosa, M., Maggi, F.M., Suriadi, S.: Mining business process deviance: a quest for accuracy. In: Meersman, R., et al. (eds.) OTM 2014. LNCS, vol. 8841, pp. 436–445. Springer, Heidelberg (2014). https://doi.org/10.1007/978-3-662-45563-0_25
19. Nielsen, J.: Estimating the number of subjects needed for a thinking aloud test. Int. J. Hum. Comput. Stud. **41**(3), 385–397 (1994)
20. Rosemann, M.: Explorative process design patterns. In: Fahland, D., Ghidini, C., Becker, J., Dumas, M. (eds.) BPM 2020. LNCS, vol. 12168, pp. 349–367. Springer, Cham (2020). https://doi.org/10.1007/978-3-030-58666-9_20
21. Saldaña, J.: The Coding Manual for Qualitative Researchers. Sage (2015)
22. Seeliger, A., Sánchez Guinea, A., Nolle, T., Mühlhäuser, M.: ProcessExplorer: intelligent process mining guidance. In: Hildebrandt, T., van Dongen, B.F., Röglinger, M., Mendling, J. (eds.) BPM 2019. LNCS, vol. 11675, pp. 216–231. Springer, Cham (2019). https://doi.org/10.1007/978-3-030-26619-6_15
23. Setiawan, M.A., Sadiq, S.: A methodology for improving business process performance through positive deviance. Int. J. Inf. Syst. Model. Des. **4**(2), 1–22 (2013)
24. Swennen, M., Janssenswillen, G., Jans, M., Depaire, B., Vanhoof, K.: Capturing process behavior with log-based process metrics. In: SIMPDA, pp. 141–144 (2015)
25. Taymouri, F., Rosa, M.L., Dumas, M., Maggi, F.M.: Business process variant analysis: survey and classification. Knowl. Based Syst. **211**, 106557 (2021)
26. Tsoury, A., Soffer, P., Reinhartz-Berger, I.: A conceptual framework for supporting deep exploration of business process behavior. In: Trujillo, J.C. (ed.) ER 2018. LNCS, vol. 11157, pp. 58–71. Springer, Cham (2018). https://doi.org/10.1007/978-3-030-00847-5_6
27. Tukey, J.W.: Exploratory Data Analysis, vol. 2. Reading, Mass (1977)
28. Wongsuphasawat, K., Liu, Y., Heer, J.: Goals, process, and challenges of exploratory data analysis: an interview study. arXiv:1911.00568 (2019)
29. Zugal, S., Soffer, P., Haisjackl, C., Pinggera, J., Reichert, M., Weber, B.: Investigating expressiveness and understandability of hierarchy in declarative business process models. Softw. Syst. Model. **14**(3), 1081–1103 (2015)

Discovering Business Process Architectures from Event Logs

Dorina Bano[✉], Adriatik Nikaj, and Mathias Weske

Hasso Plattner Institute, University of Potsdam, Potsdam, Germany
{dorina.bano,adriatik.nikaj,mathias.weske}@hpi.de

Abstract. Business process architectures are an important vehicle to organize business process models of an organization, since they provide a holistic view on the interrelationships between business process models. Current techniques to design business process architectures derive them directly from a repository of process models, neglecting processes execution information like event logs. In this paper, we propose an approach for automatically discovering a business process architecture from a set of event logs. The resulting architecture captures behavioral dependencies between two or more business process models, using information stored in event logs. We extended an existing business process architecture representation to accommodate such behavior. The application of the approach on two real-life event logs shows its effectiveness in discovering the intricate dependencies between business processes, based on data.

Keywords: Business process architecture · Process mining · Event log

1 Introduction

The business process management [1] lifecycle deals with the discovery, modeling, executing and analysis of business processes in a perpetual repetition in order to accommodate the ever-changing business requirements. An important artifact in this context is a process model repository, which often captures hundreds of models. With the increase in size and complexity of process model repositories it gets harder to manage them. The area of BPM addressing such a challenge is called Business Process Architecture (BPA) [2].

Typically, BPAs are designed using the relationships between process models in a given repository, i.e., BPA design is purely based on process models. In this paper we argue that these relationships might not be the ones that actually occur during business process executions and, hence, do not reflect their real-world relationships properly.

The approach presented in this paper is based on two types of process relations, trigger flow and information flow. Trigger flow represents situations when a process triggers the instantiation of another process. Information flow captures data exchange between processes. The resulting approach is able to discover

© Springer Nature Switzerland AG 2021
A. Polyvyanyy et al. (Eds.): BPM Forum 2021, LNBIP 427, pp. 162–177, 2021.
https://doi.org/10.1007/978-3-030-85440-9_10

complex process interdependencies that have occurred in process executions; we extend an existing BPA graphical representation to accommodate these relationships properly. The approach is applied on two real-life sets of event logs to prove its feasibility and effectiveness.

The remainder of this paper is organized as follows. Section 2 briefly discusses the basic notions needed to understand the rest of the paper. The main definitions relevant for the proposed approach are presented in Sect. 3, while Sect. 4 describes and illustrates our approach for discovering the BPA from a set of event logs. The extended graphical representation of the trigger and information flow behavior is presented in Sect. 5. Section 6 brief discusses the related work. Consecutively, Sect. 7 provides an evaluation of the approach before Sect. 8 concludes the paper.

2   Preliminaries

Each organization executes a set of business processes to deliver value to its customers. In process mining these processes can be discovered from so-called event logs, which represent traces of process execution in the form of ordered events. While the discovery of processes models from event logs is a thoroughly researched topic, the discovery of the relation between the event logs is overlooked. From a model perspective, the relationship between several business process models is studied in the area of Business Process Architectures (BPA). BPAs provide an abstract view of all business process models happening in one organization. Authors in [2] emphasize that different types of patterns are identified to express the relation between two different business processes. However, the following patterns are widely used throughout the literature:

- *decomposition* - a business process model is decomposed into other business process models each representing a sub process
- *specialization* - a business process model is a specialized version of another business process model
- *trigger flow* - an event of a business process models triggers the instantiation of another business process model
- *information flow* - an event of a processes model passes information to another event of a different process model.

In this paper we focus on discovering the trigger and information flow between two or more event logs/process models. To this end, Fig. 1 provides a simplified metamodel of BPA and event log repository to describe their relation at a conceptual level and to identify the addressed research gap. On the left-hand side, BPA is defined as a composition of *Process Models* and *Information or Trigger Flow Models* between them. The Process Model, in its simplest form, is a composition of the *Flow Node Models* and *Sequence Flow Models*. The *Flow Node Model*, which can be an *Activity or Event Model*, corresponds to some *Events* of an *Event Log*, on the right-hand side. An *Event Log*, one of the many in a company's *Event Log Repository*, is a collection of events that are grouped in

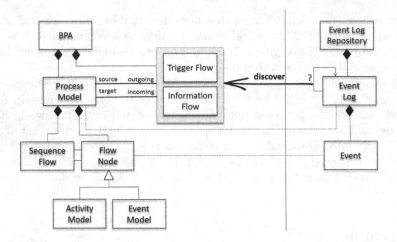

Fig. 1. The meta-model for describing the relation between the business process architecture and the event log

traces or cases. One *Event log* corresponds to exactly one *Process Model*. The aim of this paper is to discover the relationship between a set of event logs at a BPA level of abstraction.

To discover the trigger and information flow between at least two business process models it is necessary to identify respectively the *throwing* and *catching* event models. The throwing event model is considered as active because it sends a signal. It can be an *intermediate* or *end* event model. In contrast, the catching event model is considered as passive because it waits for the signal to arrive. It can be a *start* or *intermediate* event model.

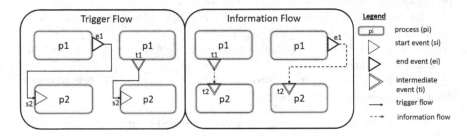

Fig. 2. Trigger and information flow patterns from [3]

To illustrate the BPA we use the graphical representation presented in [3] and depicted in Fig. 2. On the left-hand side of the figure, the throwing end event *e1* of process *p1* instantiates the process *p2* through the *catching start event s2*. The process can also be instantiated from an *intermediate event t1*. On the right-hand side, the information flow patterns represent the case where process *p2* receives information from an *intermediate* or *end* event of process *p1*.

3 Event Log Awareness

Given a set of event logs derived from a single organization, we show how to discover a business process architecture of that organization. The focus here is on the discovery of the trigger and information flow between processes. To realize that, we exhaustively investigate all unique pairs of event logs in the repository and draw the final BPA. Below we show how to analyze a pair of event logs in order to discover the trigger and information flow between them.

As a prerequisite, for a trigger or information flow to exist between two event logs, at least one event log has to be *aware* of the other. With awareness we mean here that a significant number (decided by the process mining expert) of cases of a given event log contain explicit information about the existence of cases pertaining to the other event log. In short, an event log is aware of another if a significant number of its cases are aware of the other. A case is aware of another case from a different event log if it contains specific information about it. Figure 3 depicts an example of case awareness. Formally we have:

Definition 1. *A cases C_i is aware of a case C_j, where C_i and C_j pertain to two different event logs E_i and E_j, if at least one event in case C_i contains information that refers to the case id of case C_j. Let's denote $Caw_{E_i,E_j} \subseteq E_i \times E_j$ the set of all ordered pairs of cases (C_i, C_j) where $C_i \in E_i$ is aware of $C_j \in E_j$.*

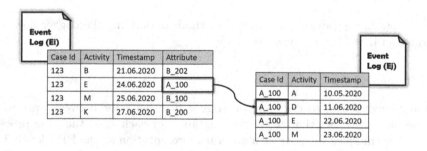

Fig. 3. Example of a case from event log E_i being aware of another case from event log E_j

Subsequently, we define the event log awareness:

Definition 2. *An event log E_i is aware of another event log E_j if its awareness is not less than a threshold τ, where $0\% \leq \tau \leq 100\%$ is specified by the process mining expert. The awareness of event log E_i for the event log E_j is defined as*
$$Aw_{E_i,E_j} = \frac{|Caw_{E_i,E_j}|}{|E_i|}.$$

As one may notice, the awareness is not symmetric, in that Caw_{E_i,E_j} may be different from Caw_{E_j,E_i}. Moreover, a case C_i from E_i can be aware of more than a single case from event log E_j as shown later in Sect. 7, where a case triggers two cases of the opposite log.

Given two event logs, we have to first check whether one of the event logs is aware of the other. If none of the event logs are aware then there cannot be a trigger or information flow to speak of. Otherwise, we have to analyze all the aware cases of the respective event logs. Specifically, we need to decide on a case basis whether there is a trigger or information flow. Only then we can discover the generalized trigger or information flow at the BPA model abstraction level. The discovery part is very crucial because the trigger or information flow might depend on a case to case basis. For example, in half of the cases the trigger or information flow source is a throwing *activity A* and in the other half is a throwing *activity B*. To capture this kind of behavior, we extend the BPA modeling language in Sect. 5.

Event logs usually do not contain explicit information whether certain events in them are catching or throwing. Therefore, we have to deduce this information via other means. Specifically, in order to detect whether there is an information or trigger flow between two events where at least one case is aware of the other (see Definition 1) we have to analyze:

1. the causality relationships between these events
2. and, in case of information flow, the information contained in these events, i.e., the event attributes.

4   Discovering the BPA

In this section, we provide the detailed methods of deriving the trigger flow and information flow from a pair of event logs.

4.1   Trigger Flow

As mentioned above, to discover the trigger flow behavior between two event logs we have to detect the trigger flow instance for each case, then use process discovery techniques to arrive at a general representation at the BPA level. The overall approach to discover the trigger flow between two event logs is described in Fig. 4.

For simplicity purposes, every pair of aware cases from the opposite event logs (from hereon referring to cases belonging to two different event logs respectively) are merged into one joined case where the new case id is the cross product of the original case ids. Each event is annotated accordingly in order to specify which event log it originates from. All the merged cases are put together in a joined event log E_{ij}.

For each pair of opposite cases, where one is aware of the other, we have to detect the source and the target of the trigger flow instance. The target of a

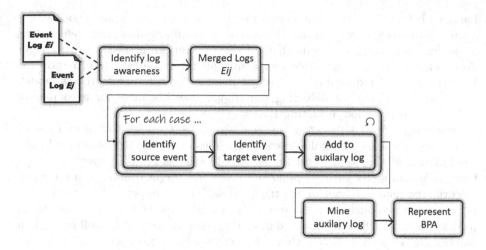

Fig. 4. The overall method for discovering the trigger flow patterns between two event logs

trigger flow is always a start event. On a case level, the target of the trigger flow instance must always be the first event of the case. Therefore, the only candidate for the target of the trigger flow instance between the two start events is the one that occurs second.

```
1  input: merged event log Eij
2  output: auxiliary event log (Eaux)
3  #i_event and j_event refer to events that originate
       respectively from Ei and Ej
4  for case in Eij{
5    start_event_i = first_i_event(case)
6    start_event_j = first_j_event(case)
7    if start_event_i.index < start_event_j.index{
8      target_event = start_event_j
9    }
10   else{
11     continue #jump to the next case
12   }
13   for event_index = target_event.index-1 to 0 step-1{
14     candidate_event = case.get_event_with_index(event_index)
15     if candidate_event is i_event{
16       source_event = candidate_event
17       add source_event to Eaux
18       add target_event to Eaux
19       break}}}
```

Listing 1.1. The algorithm for detecting the trigger flow instances between two event logs

Once the candidate target of the trigger flow instance is fixed, we have to detect its source, which is a throwing event from the opposite event log that happens before the target event. From all the possible events we choose as the source of the trigger flow instance the latest event among those that refer to the id of the target case. We argue that this is very important because the trigger flow source event is responsible for passing all the important information (at least the *case id*) required to start a new instance on the target process model. The exact algorithm for detecting the trigger flow instances for each pair of aware cases is provided in Listing 1.1.

If a trigger flow is detected between two cases, then its source and target events are added to an auxiliary event log. This event log has as a case id the combination of the source and target case id (the same as in event log E_{ij}). Once it is completed with all possible source and target events, it is mined to discover the final behavior of the trigger flow. This is important as the trigger flow between two business process models in a BPA might not always be static, in that the trigger flow might have more than one source and as well more than one target. We show in Sect. 7 that it is very important to capture this behavior on the BPA level to enable comprehensive analyses.

4.2   Information Flow

Similarly to the way we discover trigger flows between two event logs, we have to consider on a case basis about the existence of data flowing between events of opposite event logs. The method overview is presented in Fig. 5. An information flow instance between two aware cases assumes the existence of a throwing and a catching event from opposite cases that manifests a data flow, i.e., the information contained in the throwing event is passed to the catching event. In other words, we look for new information appearing in one event that stems from an event of the opposite event log.

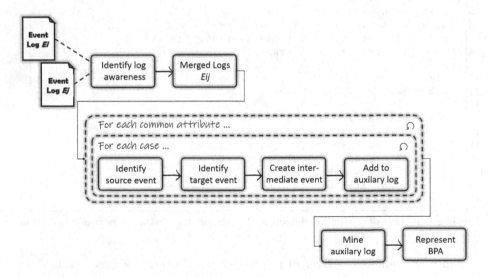

Fig. 5. The overall method for discovering the trigger flow patterns between two event logs

Differently from trigger flows where we consider only the *start events* of the processes, here we have to consider all the possible events with few exceptions, e.g., *start events* cannot be throwing and *end events* cannot be catching.

A joint event log E_{ij} is created in the same manner as described above for discovering the trigger flows. What is slightly different is that all the common attributes between two event logs have to be identified first. If two event logs share no common attributes other than the case id (which is a given since at least one event log is aware of the other), then there is no information flow to consider. It is worth pointing out that the attribute name may not be sufficient to check whether two attributes from different logs have the same domain and value ranges or, in short, refer to a common thing. That is why this step might require a process mining expert to create a mapping of attributes that are believed to represent the same thing.

Once the common attributes are identified, the search space for the data flowing from one event log to another is reduced just to these attributes. From this point on, we consider one attribute at a time for determining whether there is an information flow that concerns the attribute at hand.

```
1  input: merged event log Eij
2  output: auxiliary event log (Eaux)
3  #i_event and j_event refer to events that originate respectively from
        Ei and Ej
4  for case in Eij{
5      checked_event = first_i_event(case)
6      if checked_event == Null{
7              continue}#jump to the next case
8      last_found_index = -1
9      for event in case{
10       if event is i_event{
11         if event.attribute.value <> checked_event.attribute.value{
12           target_index = event.index
13           source_found = False
14           for s=last_found_index to target_index-1{
15             if event_with_index(s) is j_event and event_with_index(s).
                     attribute.value == event.attribute.value{
16               source_event = event_with_index(s)
17               target_event = event
18               source_found = True
19               last_found_index = s
20               break
21             }
22           }
23           if source_found{
24             intermediate_event = new event
25             intermediate_event.case = source_event.case
26             intermediate_event.name = source_event_name+target_event_name
                     +attribute.name intermediate_event.timestamp = mean_value
                     (source.event.timestamp, target.event.timestamp)
27             add source_event to Eaux
28             add intermediate_event to Eaux
29             add target_event to Eaux
30           }
31         }
32       checked_event=event}}}
```

Listing 1.2. Information flow algorithm

Considering a single common attribute between two event logs, we cycle through all the pairs of cases where one is aware of the other. For each pair of cases we consider only the events that access the attribute. Anytime a new attribute value appears in an event, i.e., the attribute value is not present in all preceding events from the same case, we look at the opposing case to determine whether this value appears in any of the events that happened prior to the original one. If yes, we take the latest event where that occurs as the source of the information flow instance and the event with the new value as its target.

The source and the target event of the information instance is added to an auxiliary event log similar to the one used for the trigger flow. However, here we add one more event (between source and target) that is labeled as the composition of the source and target label plus the attribute at hand. As a timestamp, it takes the median time of the original events. This step is added because a) there might exist more than one information flow between two cases related to the same attribute and b) information flows for different attributes need to be distinguishable from each other. This algorithm is described in Listing 1.2.

Once the auxiliary event log is completed we apply a process discovery technique to discover the behavior of the information flow. The output is a behavioral model, usually represented as Petri net, that captures the behavior of the information flow for one common attribute. This model is then translated into a BPA. If two or more information flows overlap, i.e., they have the same source and target, they can be represented as one information flow that represents the passing of composed information.

Since the behavior of the trigger and information flow is a new concept we extend the BPA representation from [3] with some new lightweight notions to capture exclusive or parallel patterns between trigger and information flows in the section below.

5   The Extension of the BPA's Graphical Representation

The state-of-the-art research on BPA does not suffice in capturing behavior of the trigger and information flow that we observed by analyzing a set of real-life event logs (see Sect. 7). In this section we address this gap by introducing an extension of the graphical representation of BPA (presented in Fig. 2).

For representing the complex behavior of the trigger and information flow we borrow the concept of gateways from BPMN 2.0 [4], specifically the *XOR* and *AND* gateway. Figure 6 shows how these gateways are used given a set of specific scenarios.

Figure 6a) represents the case when there exists more than one start event in an event log, i.e., traces do not always start with the same event instance. In contrast, Fig. 6b) represents the case where there is more than one event in the first event log that triggers the process instantiation of the second event log. The same can be observed for the information flow in Fig. 6c) and d).

Despite the gateways being represented in the space between the processes, they represent the behavior of either the source events (for join gateways) or

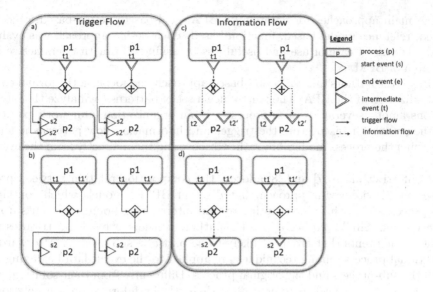

Fig. 6. Complex behaviour of trigger and information flow

target events (for split gateways) of the respective trigger/information flow. For example, the difference between the trigger flow's XOR and AND splits in Fig. 6a) consists in that, in the former, $s2$ and $s2'$ start events are in a exclusive relation between each other, while in the latter, they are in a parallel relation. Obviously, this information is found in the event log of process $p2$. This information is required in addition to the auxiliary logs to determine whether we use an XOR or AND gateway.

In Fig. 6 the orchestration of these gateways happens inside the processes. However there might be more complex cases where, for example, a process is triggered only after two or more processes have been executed or, after a process is executed, there is a decision on which following process to trigger. Such cases are not covered in this paper and require the analyzing of more than two processes at once across the process repository. The gateways in those cases would lay outside the processes similar to a process choreography setting where enforcing gateways becomes much more complicated [5].

Depending on the process discovery approach applied to the auxiliary event log a behavior model is obtained. The majority of algorithms output a Petri Net model. Known techniques, like in [6], can be used to derive the process gateways from a Petri Net model.

6   Related Work

Business process architecture is subject to extensive research work. One of the earliest publications from Dijkman et al. [2] gives an overview and classification of the main approaches for designing a BPA: goal-based, action-based, object-based, reference model based, function-based. Each design approach was evaluated in terms of ease of use and usefulness by asking 39 practitioners active in the area of BPM.

In [3], the authors take an action-based approach and focus on the formal conceptualization of the BPA. They introduce a set of patterns to analyze the interactions among several business processes in an organization. Our work extends on their work for discovering the trigger and information flow patterns not by analyzing the process models but rather discovering them directly from the event logs.

Conforti et al. in [7] and [8] address the composition relation between processes by providing an approach that discover BPMN models which contains sub-processes and their interrupting or non-interrupting boundary events from an event log. Similar to our approach, authors consider event log attributes to identify the events that are more likely to be part of a sub-process. Afterwards, traditional process mining techniques are applied to the event data belonging to both the sub-process and the original process. Differently from their solution, we consider a set of event logs to determine their trigger/information flow relations and represent them on a higher abstraction level like BPA.

In [9] Menijvar et al. propose an approach to support fast detection of clones in big business process repositories. Each process model within one repository is indexed in order to identify duplicate fragments and later can be refactored into shared sub-processes. Differently from our approach, the refactoring is made based only on the activity labels since the business process model is the only source of information.

Lu et al. [10] propose an approach to detect hierarchical process models from event logs. The discovered processes are represented as multi-level interleaved sub-processes. The authors consider activity trees, which are defined as the hierarchical relation between the process activities. The proposed approach can be fully automated or fully supervised by a process expert. Our approach can be fully automated given that the attributes labels are consistent across the event log repository.

In [11] Enegle et al. present the EDImine Framework, which is used for gaining business/economic insights from Electronic Data Interchange (EDI) messages happening between inter-organizational business processes. To use the EDI messages for inter-organizational process mining the authors explain how the EDI messages are correlated into the event log cases. The resulting event log is than made available to business process mining experts. Different from our work, the authors start from the electronic data exchanged between organizations to extract an event log.

7   Evaluation

To evaluate the effectiveness of our approach, we are using the real-life event logs provided in the scope of the BPI Challenge 2017 [12] and BPI Challenge 2020

[13]. To evaluate the feasibility of our algorithms (presented in Sect. 4) we implemented them in Python through the PM4PY framework [14]. The implemented algorithms are available on the GitHub repository[1].

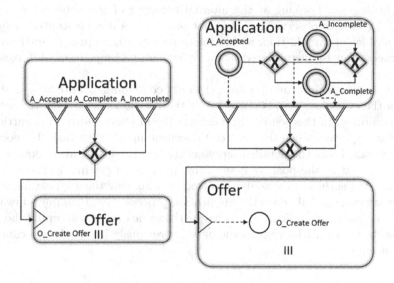

Fig. 7. The discovered trigger flows (simple and detailed representation) of the BPI Challenge 2017

The 2017 BPI challenge deals with loan applications. There are two event logs: 1) the *Application* event log is about customers' application for obtaining a bank credit; 2) the *Offer* event log is about credit offers proposed by the financial institute as a response to the customer's application. The *Application* event log contains 1.160.405 events and 31.509 cases, while the *Offer* event log contains 93.846 events and 42.995 cases. Both event logs contain events from January 2016 till February 2017. Before applying the BPA discovery approach, we first clean the *Application* log of any event that is also found in the *Offer* log. This is performed because we are only interested in discovering the BPA's trigger and information flow patterns instead of the composition or specialization patterns where common events are of the most importance.

Following our approach, we first check whether these event logs are aware of each other according to Definition 1. Indeed that is the case: The *ApplicationID* attribute of the *Offer* event log refers to the *CaseID* attribute of the *Application* event log in all cases, hence $Aw_{Offer,Application} = 1$.

After determining the awareness the event logs are joined into one event log, which is subject to the two algorithms presented in Sect. 4. The output auxiliary event log is mined based on the Inductive Visual Miner algorithm [15]. The resulting process architecture model is obtained and illustrated in Figs. 7 and 8.

---

[1] GitHub: https://github.com/DorinaBano/BPA_from_event_log.git.

We discovered that the application process has a 1-to-n trigger relation with the offer process in that each application process instance can trigger more than one offer process instance. Specifically, there are three intermediate events in the application process as sources of the trigger flow: *A_Accepted, A_Complete* and *A_Incomplete*. Looking at the internal behavior of the application process (see Fig. 7), we can observe that the offer process is always instantiated by the *A_Accepted* event. In addition, within the same application process instance, the offer process can be instantiated again by either *A_Complete* or *A_Incomplete* events.

With respect to information flow, the only common attribute that is shared between the event logs and is not static is the user associated with the activity being performed. In this sense, Fig. 8 depicts the implicit information carried by particular employees when they switch to performing different tasks between the two event logs. From the detailed representation of the information flow, we can understand that in the positive case of the application getting accepted: 1) the user who returns the offer was also involved in validating the application; and 2) the user who successfully ends the application processes (*A_Pending* is always at the end of a positive application process) is the same one who accepted the offer. Likewise, the person who cancels the offer is previously involved with canceling the application.

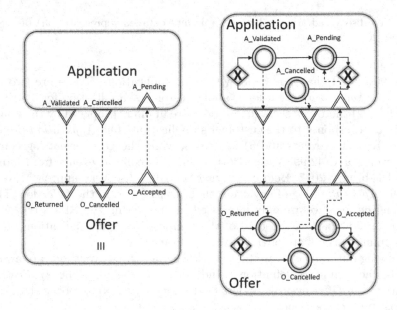

Fig. 8. The discovered information flows (simple and detailed representation) of the BPI Challenge 2017

BPI Challenge 2020 is concerned with five event logs and it contains information about travel expense claims from the Eindhoven University of Technology

(TU/e) located in the Netherlands. Two types of trips are distinguished in the provided event logs: 1) domestic trips - the employee applies for reimbursement after the trip has taken place and 2) international declaration trips - the permission has to be approved by the supervisor before the trip starts.

Three out of five provided event logs are aware of each other (based on Definition 2): 1) *PrePaidTravelCost* which contains 2,099 cases and 18,246 events; 2) *InternationalDeclaration* with 6,449 cases, 72151 events; 3) *Permit* which holds 7,065 cases, 86,581 events. The *Permit id* attribute of the *PrePaidTravelCost* event log refers to the *CaseID* attribute of the *Permit* event log. In addition, the *Permit id2* attribute of the *InternationalDeclaration* event log refers to the *CaseID* attribute of the *Permit* event log. This implies that *PrePaidTravelCost* and *InternationalDeclaration* are both aware of *Permit* event log. Again, we cleaned the duplicate events for each pair of event logs under consideration.

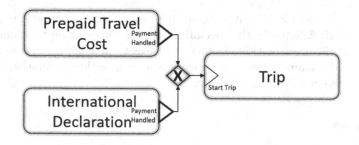

Fig. 9. The discovered trigger flows of the BPI Challenge 2020

The BPI Challenge 2020 does not contain an explicit information flow pattern as most of the attributes in the event logs are static, in that they do not change inside a case.

The resulting BPA with respect to the trigger flow for the aware event logs is illustrated in the Fig. 9. The start event *Start Trip* of the *Permit* log is triggered either by the *Payment Handled* event of the *PrePaidTravelCost* event log or by the same event of the *InternationalDeclaration* event log. This means that whenever the last event *Payment Handled* occurs in both event logs, the start event *Start Trip* of the *Permit* log is triggered. This can be explained by the fact that there are cases in the *Permit* event log where there are no payments being handled. For those cases, the payment is handled in the previous processes. After the payment is handled the trip can start.

Looking at the discovered BPAs from these real-life event logs, we can conclude that the new insights, coming from the BPA's trigger and information flow, cannot be obtained by individually analyzing the event logs or, even better, just analyzing the process models.

8   Conclusion

This paper provides an approach for discovering a business process architecture from a set of event logs that are extracted from the execution of processes within the same organization. The business process architecture provides a high level perspective on an enterprise's running processes and the relation between these processes. It aids in identifying and understanding the complex interdependencies and relationships between the processes.

Our approach focuses on two such interdependencies: the trigger flow and the information flow between two or more given processes. Together they provide useful insights on how the information is shared between processes and how the instantiation of a process depends on the execution of another process. The approach is not only able to identify such relations but also their complex behavior, for example, a single process that spawns multiple instances of another process. The feasibility and effectiveness of the approach are evaluated by being applied on two real-life event logs.

Future work includes the investigation of other types of relations between processes in a BPA, namely, the specialization and composition relations. These would require the investigation of exact same events that appear across multiple event logs to determine whether a process is a composition of another one or a detailed process of a more general one.

References

1. Weske, M.: Business Process Management - Concepts, Languages, Architectures, 3rd edn. Springer, Heidelberg (2019)
2. Dijkman, R., Vanderfeesten, I., Reijers, H.: The road to a business process architecture: an overview of approaches and their use. BETA Working Paper. Technische Universiteit Eindhoven (2011)
3. Eid-Sabbagh, R.-H., Dijkman, R., Weske, M.: Business process architecture: use and correctness. In: Barros, A., Gal, A., Kindler, E. (eds.) BPM 2012. LNCS, vol. 7481, pp. 65–81. Springer, Heidelberg (2012). https://doi.org/10.1007/978-3-642-32885-5_5
4. OMG: Business Process Model and Notation (BPMN), Version 2.0, January 2011
5. Nikaj, A., Batoulis, K., Weske, M.: REST-enabled decision making in business process choreographies. In: Sheng, Q.Z., Stroulia, E., Tata, S., Bhiri, S. (eds.) ICSOC 2016. LNCS, vol. 9936, pp. 547–554. Springer, Cham (2016). https://doi.org/10.1007/978-3-319-46295-0_34
6. Lohmann, N., Verbeek, E., Dijkman, R.: Petri net transformations for business processes – a survey. In: Jensen, K., van der Aalst, W.M.P. (eds.) Transactions on Petri Nets and Other Models of Concurrency II. LNCS, vol. 5460, pp. 46–63. Springer, Heidelberg (2009). https://doi.org/10.1007/978-3-642-00899-3_3
7. Conforti, R., Dumas, M., García-Bañuelos, L., La Rosa, M.: Beyond tasks and gateways: discovering BPMN models with subprocesses, boundary events and activity markers. In: Sadiq, S., Soffer, P., Völzer, H. (eds.) BPM 2014. LNCS, vol. 8659, pp. 101–117. Springer, Cham (2014). https://doi.org/10.1007/978-3-319-10172-9_7

8. Conforti, R., Dumas, M., García-Bañuelos, L., Rosa, M.: BPMN miner: automated discovery of BPMN process models with hierarchical structure. Inf. Syst. **56**, 284–303 (2016)

9. Menijvar, M.D., Garcia-Banuelos, L., Rosa, M.L., Uba, R.: Fast detection of exact clones in business process model repositories. Inf. Syst. **38**(4), 619–633 (2013)

10. Lu, X., Gal, A., Reijers, H.A.: Discovering hierarchical processes using flexible activity trees for event abstraction. In: van Dongen, B.F., Montali, M., Wynn, M.T. (eds.) pp. 145–152. IEEE (2020)

11. Engel, R., et al.: Analyzing inter-organizational business processes - process mining and business performance analysis using electronic data interchange messages. Inf. Syst. E Bus. Manag. **14**(3), 577–612 (2016)

12. van Dongen, B.: BPI Challenge 2017 (2017). https://doi.org/10.4121/uuid: 3926db30-f712-4394-aebc-75976070e91f

13. van Dongen, B.: BPI Challenge 2020. https://doi.org/10.4121/uuid:52fb97d4-4588-43c9-9d04-3604d4613b5 (2020)

14. Berti, A., van Zelst, S.J., van der Aalst, W.: Process mining for Python (PM4Py): bridging the gap between process- and data science. Presented at the (2019)

15. Leemans, S.J.J., Fahland, D., van der Aalst, W.: Process and deviation exploration with inductive visual miner. Presented at the (CEUR-WS.org) (2014)

Privacy-Preserving Continuous Event Data Publishing

Majid Rafiei(✉) ⓘ and Wil M. P. van der Aalst ⓘ

RWTH Aachen University, Aachen, Germany
majid.rafiei@pads.rwth-aachen.de

Abstract. Process mining enables organizations to discover and ana-lyze their actual processes using event data. Event data can be extracted from any information system supporting operational processes, e.g., SAP. Whereas the data inside such systems is protected using access control mechanisms, the extracted event data contain sensitive information that needs to be protected. This creates a new risk and a possible inhibitor for applying process mining. Therefore, privacy issues in process mining become increasingly important. Several privacy preservation techniques have been introduced to mitigate possible attacks against static event data published only once. However, to keep the process mining results up-to-date, event data need to be published continuously. For example, a new log is created at the end of each week. In this paper, we elaborate on the attacks which can be launched against continuously publishing anonymized event data by comparing different releases, so-called *corre-spondence attacks*. Particularly, we focus on group-based privacy preser-vation techniques and show that provided privacy requirements can be degraded exploiting correspondence attacks. We apply the continuous event data publishing scenario to existing real-life event logs and report the anonymity indicators before and after launching the attacks.

Keywords: Process mining · Privacy preservation · Correspondence attacks · Event data

1 Introduction

Process mining bridges the gap between *data science* and *process science* using event logs. Event logs are widely available in different types of information sys-tems [1]. Events are the smallest units of process execution which are character-ized by their attributes. Process mining requires that each event contains at least the following main attributes to enable the application of analysis techniques: *case id*, *activity*, and *timestamp*. The *case id* refers to the entity that the event(s) belongs to, and it is considered as a process instance. The *activity* refers to the activity associated with the event, and the *timestamp* is the exact time when the activity was executed for the case. Moreover, depending on the context of a process, the corresponding events may contain more attributes. Table 1 shows a part of an event log recorded by an information system in a hospital.

© Springer Nature Switzerland AG 2021
A. Polyvyanyy et al. (Eds.): BPM Forum 2021, LNBIP 427, pp. 178–194, 2021.
https://doi.org/10.1007/978-3-030-85440-9_11

Table 1. Sample event log (each row represents an event).

Case Id	Activity	Timestamp	Resource	Disease
1	Registration (RE)	01.01.2019-08:30:00	Employee1	Flu
1	Visit (VI)	01.01.2019-08:45:00	Doctor1	Flu
2	Registration (RE)	01.01.2019-08:46:00	Employee1	Corona
3	Registration (RE)	01.01.2019-08:50:00	Employee1	Cancer
...	...	...	...	...
1	Release (RL)	01.01.2019-08:58:00	Employee2	Flu
3	Visit (VI)	01.02.2019-10:15:00	Doctor3	Cancer
2	Release (RL)	01.02.2019-14:00:00	Employee2	Corona
3	Blood Test (BT)	01.02.2019-14:15:00	Employee5	Cancer
...	...	...	...	...

Table 2. A simple event log derived from Table 1 (each row represents a simple process instance).

Case Id	Trace	Disease
1	$\langle RE, VI, ..., RL \rangle$	Flu
2	$\langle RE, ..., RL \rangle$	Corona
3	$\langle RE, ..., VI, BT, ... \rangle$	Cancer
...	...	...

In Table 1, each row represents an event. A sequence of events, associated with a *case id* and ordered using the timestamps, is called a *trace*. Table 2 shows a simple trace representation of Table 1 where the *trace* attribute is a sequence of activities. Some of the event attributes may refer to individuals, e.g., the *case id* refers to the patient whose data is recorded, and the *resource* refers to the employees performing activities for the patients, e.g., surgeons. Also, some sensitive information may be included, e.g., the *disease* attribute in Table 1. When individuals' data are included in an event log, privacy issues emerge, and organizations are obliged to consider such issues according to regulations, e.g., the European General Data Protection Regulation (GDPR)[1].

The privacy/confidentiality issues in process mining are recently receiving more attention. Various techniques have been proposed covering different aspects, e.g., confidentiality frameworks [19], privacy guarantees [5,11,18], inter-organizational privacy issues [3], privacy quantification [16,20], etc. Each of these approaches considers a single event log shared at some point in time. This even log is published considering the privacy/confidentiality issues of a single log in isolation. However, event logs are recorded continuously and need to be published continuously to keep the results of process mining techniques updated.

Continuous event data publishing lets an adversary launch new types of attacks that are impossible when event data are published only once. In this paper, we analyze the so-called *correspondence attacks* [7] that an adversary can launch by comparing different releases of anonymized event logs when they are continuously published. Particularly, we focus on group-based Privacy Preservation Techniques (PPTs) and describe three main types of correspondence attacks including *forward attack*, *cross attack*, and *backward attack*. We analyze the

---

[1] http://data.europa.eu/eli/reg/2016/679/oj.

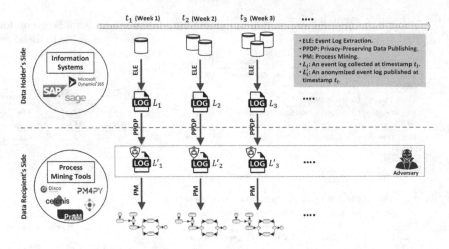

Fig. 1. The general data collection and publishing scenario.

privacy/anonymity losses imposed by these attacks and show how to detect such privacy losses efficiently. The explained anonymity analyses could be attached to different PPTs to empower them against the attacks or to change the data publishing approaches to bound such attacks. We applied different continuous event data publishing scenarios to several real-life event logs and report the anonymity indicators before and after launching the attacks for an example event log.

The remainder of the paper is organized as follows. In Sect. 2, we present the problem statement. In Sect. 3, the preliminaries are explained. Different types of correspondence attacks are analyzed in Sect. 4. In Sect. 5, we explain the attack detection techniques and privacy loss quantification. Section 6 presents the experiments. Section 7 discusses different aspects to extend the approach. Section 8 discusses related work, and Sect. 9 concludes the paper.

2   Problem Statement

Figure 1 shows our general data collection and publishing scenario. Information systems, e.g., SAP, provide operational support for organizations and continuously generate a lot of valuable event data. Such data are continuously collected and published, e.g., weekly, to be used by process mining tools, e.g., ProM, Disco, etc. On the analysis side, process mining techniques are applied to event logs to discover and analyze real processes supported by operational information systems. With respect to the types of data holder's models, introduced in [9], we consider a *trusted model* where the *data holder*, i.e., the business owner, is trustworthy, but the *data recipient*, i.e., a process miner, is not trustworthy. Therefore, PPTs are applied to event logs when they are published.

Continuous data publishing is generally classified into three main categories: *incremental*, *decremental*, and *dynamic* [8]. Continuous event data publishing is

Table 3. An anonymized event log published at timestamp t_1 (e.g., week 1), meeting 2-anonymity and 2-diversity when the assumed BK is a sequence of activities with the maximum length 3.

Case Id	Trace	Disease
1	$\langle a, b, c, d \rangle$	Corona
2	$\langle a, b, c, d \rangle$	Flu
3	$\langle a, e, d \rangle$	Fever
4	$\langle a, e, d \rangle$	Corona

Table 4. An anonymized event log published at timestamp t_2 (e.g., week 2), meeting 2-anonymity and 2-diversity when the assumed BK is a sequence of activities with the maximum length 3.

Case Id	Trace	Disease
10	$\langle a, b, c, d \rangle$	Corona
20	$\langle a, b, c, d \rangle$	Flu
30	$\langle a, b, c, d \rangle$	HIV
40	$\langle a, e, d \rangle$	Fever
50	$\langle a, e, d \rangle$	Corona

considered as *incremental*, i.e., the events generated by an information system are cumulatively collected, and they are not updated or deleted after the collection. Thus, the so-called *correspondence knowledge* is gained. If we assume that in a continuous event data publishing scenario, the event logs are collected and published weekly, the correspondence knowledge is as follows: (1) Every case started in the i-th week is in the i-th event log L_i, and must be in L_j, $i < j$, and (2) Every case started in the j-th week is in the j-th event log L_j, and cannot be in L_i, $i < j$. Although each single anonymized event log L' meets the privacy guarantees specified in the corresponding PPT, the adversary, who has access to the different releases of anonymized event logs, can exploit the *correspondence knowledge* to degrade the provided privacy guarantees.

Consider Table 3 and Table 4 as two anonymized event logs, L'_1 and L'_2, published at timestamps t_1 (week 1) and t_2 (week 2), respectively. Note that the case identifiers are dummy identifiers independently assigned to the cases of each release. If we assume that an adversary's Background Knowledge (BK) is a sequence of activities with maximum length 3, both published event logs have 2-anonymity and 2-diversity. Assume the situation where the adversary knows that $\langle a, b, c \rangle$ is a subsequence of activities performed for a victim case, and that the process of the case has been started in the second week, i.e., it should be included in Table 4. Based on the correspondence knowledge, the only matching case is 30. Note that by a simple comparison of L'_1 and L'_2 based on the *disease* attribute, it is obvious that cases 10 and 20 have to be started in the first week and cannot match the adversary's BK. This is called *backward attack* (*B*-attack) which is a specific type of the correspondence attacks.

The provided attack scenario shows that when event logs are collected and published continuously, the corresponding PPDP approaches need to be equipped with some techniques to detect the potential attacks that can be launched by an adversary who receives various anonymized event logs. In this paper, we focus on simple event logs and group-based PPTs, i.e., k-anonymity, l-diversity, t-closeness, etc. We first describe the approach based on two releases of event logs, then we explain the possible extensions for any number of releases,

3   Preliminaries

We first introduce some basic notations. For a given set A, A^* is the set of all finite sequences over A. A finite sequence over A of length n is a mapping $\sigma \in \{1, ..., n\} \to A$, represented as $\sigma = \langle a_1, a_2, ..., a_n \rangle$ where $a_i = \sigma(i)$ for any $1 \leq i \leq n$. $|\sigma|$ denotes the length of the sequence. For $\sigma_1, \sigma_2 \in A^*$, $\sigma_1 \sqsubseteq \sigma_2$ if σ_1 is a subsequence of σ_2, e.g., $\langle z, b, c, x \rangle \sqsubseteq \langle z, x, a, b, b, c, a, b, c, x \rangle$.0 For $\sigma = \langle a_1, a_2, ..., a_n \rangle$, $pref(\sigma) = \{\langle a_1, ..., a_k \rangle \mid 1 \leq k \leq n\}$, e.g., $\langle a, b, c, d \rangle \in pref(\langle a, b, c, d, e, f \rangle)$.

Definition 1 (LCS and SCS). *Let $\sigma_1 \in A^*$ and $\sigma_2 \in A^*$ be two sequences. $CSB(\sigma_1, \sigma_2) = \{\sigma \in A^* \mid \sigma \sqsubseteq \sigma_1 \wedge \sigma \sqsubseteq \sigma_2\}$ is the set of common subsequences, and $LCS(\sigma_1, \sigma_2) = \{\sigma \in CSB \mid \forall_{\sigma' \in CSB(\sigma_1, \sigma_2)} |\sigma'| \leq |\sigma|\}$ is the set of longest common subsequences. $LCS^{\sigma_1}_{\sigma_2}$ denotes the length of a longest common subsequence for σ_1 and σ_2. Also, $CSP(\sigma_1, \sigma_2) = \{\sigma \in A^* \mid \sigma_1 \sqsubseteq \sigma \wedge \sigma_2 \sqsubseteq \sigma\}$ is the set of common super-sequences, and $SCS(\sigma_1, \sigma_2) = \{\sigma \in CSB \mid \forall_{\sigma' \in CSP(\sigma_1, \sigma_2)} |\sigma'| \geq |\sigma|\}$ is the set of shortest common super-sequences. $SCS^{\sigma_1}_{\sigma_2}$ denotes the length of a shortest common super-sequence for σ_1 and σ_2.*

Definition 2 (Event, Event Log). *An event is a tuple $e = (c, a, t, r, d_1, ..., d_m)$, where $c \in C$ is the case id, $a \in A$ is the activity associated with the event, $t \in T$ is the event timestamp, $r \in R$ is the resource, who is performing the activity, and $d_1, ..., d_m$ is a list of additional attributes values, where for any $1 \leq i \leq m, d_i \in D_i$. We call $\xi = C \times A \times T \times R \times D_1 \times ... \times D_m$ the event universe. For $e = (c, a, t, r, d_1, ..., d_m)$, $\pi_c(e) = c$, $\pi_a(e) = a$, $\pi_t(e) = t$, $\pi_r(e) = r$, and $\pi_{d_i}(e) = d_i$, $1 \leq i \leq m$, are its projections. An **event log** is $L \subseteq \xi$ where events are unique.*

In continuous event data publishing, event logs are collected and published continuously at each timestamp t_i, $i \in \mathbb{N}_{\geq 1}$. L_i is the event log collected at the timestamp t_i, i.e., $L_i = \{e \in \xi \mid \pi_t(e) \leq t_i\}$. For L_i and L_j, s.t., $i < j$, L_j could contain new events for the cases already observed in L_i and new cases not observed in L_i. In the following, we define a simple version of event logs which will later be used for demonstrating the attacks and corresponding anonymity measures.

Definition 3 (Trace, Simple Trace). *A trace $\sigma = \langle e_1, e_2, ..., e_n \rangle \in \xi^*$ is a sequence of events, s.t., for each $e_i, e_j \in \sigma$: $\pi_c(e_i) = \pi_c(e_j)$, and $\pi_t(e_i) \leq \pi_t(e_j)$ if $i < j$. A simple trace is a trace where all the events are projected on the activity attribute, i.e., $\sigma \in A^*$.*

Definition 4 (Simple Process Instance). *We define $P = C \times A^* \times S$ as the universe of simple process instances, where $S \subseteq D_1 \cup ... \cup D_m$ is the domain of the sensitive attribute. Each simple process instance $(c, \sigma, s) \in P$ represents a **simple trace** $\sigma = \langle a_1, a_2, ..., a_n \rangle$, belonging to the case c with s as the sensitive attribute value. For $p = (c, \sigma, s) \in P$, $\pi_c(p) = c$, $\pi_\sigma(p) = \sigma$, and $\pi_s(p) = s$ are its projections.*

Definition 5 (Simple Event Log). *Let* $\mathcal{P} = \mathcal{C} \times \mathcal{A}^* \times \mathcal{S}$ *be the universe of simple process instances. A simple event log is* $L \subseteq \mathcal{P}$, *s.t., if* $(c_1, \sigma_1, s_1) \in L$, $(c_2, \sigma_2, s_2) \in L$, *and* $c_1 = c_2$, *then* $\sigma_1 = \sigma_2$ *and* $s_1 = s_2$.

4   Attack Analysis

We analyze the correspondence attacks by focusing on two anonymized releases obtained by applying group-based PPTs to simple event logs. In general, group-based PPTs provide desired privacy requirements utilizing *suppression* and/or *generalization* operations. Particularly, the group-based PPTs introduced for the event data protection are mainly based on the *suppression* operation [5,18], where some events are removed to provide the desired privacy requirements. Hence, apart from any specific privacy preservation algorithm, we define a general anonymization function that converts an event log to another one meeting desired privacy requirements assuming a bound for the maximum number of events that can be removed from each trace, so-called the *anonymization parameter*. Note that this assumption is based on the *minimality principle* in PPDP [21]. Similar attack analysis can be done for the generalization operation as well.

Definition 6 (Anonymization). *Let* $\mathcal{P}$ *be the universe of simple process instances and* $n \in \mathbb{N}_{\geq 1}$ *be the anonymization parameter. We define* $anon^n \in 2^{\mathcal{P}} \rightarrow 2^{\mathcal{P}}$ *as a function for anonymizing event logs. For all* $L, L' \subseteq \mathcal{P}$, $anon^n(L) = L'$ *if there exists a bijective function* $f \in L \rightarrow L'$, *s.t., for any* $p = (c, \sigma, s) \in L$ *and* $p' = (c', \sigma', s') \in L'$ *with* $f(p) = p'$: $\sigma' \sqsubseteq \sigma$, $|\sigma| - n \leq |\sigma'|$, *and* $s' = s$.

L_1

Cld	Trace	Disease
1	(a,b,d,c)	Corona
2	(a,b,d,c)	Corona
3	(a,b,d,c)	Corona
4	(a,b,d)	HIV
5	(a,b,d)	HIV

$anon^1(L_1) = L_1'$

L_1'

Cld	Trace	Disease
10	(a,b,d)	Corona
20	(a,b,d)	Corona
30	(a,b,d)	Corona
40	(a,b,d)	HIV
50	(a,b,d)	HIV

L_2

Cld	Trace	Disease
1	(a,b,d,c)	Corona
2	(a,b,d,c)	Corona
3	(a,b,d,c)	Corona
4	(a,b,d,e)	HIV
5	(a,b,d,e)	HIV
6	(a,b,f,c)	HIV
7	(a,b,d,c)	HIV
8	(a,b,d,e)	HIV
9	(a,b,f,e)	Corona
10	(a,b,f,e)	Corona

$anon^1(L_2) = L_2'$

L_2'

Cld	Trace	Disease
11	(a,b,e)	HIV
21	(a,b,e)	HIV
31	(a,b,e)	HIV
41	(a,b,e)	Corona
51	(a,b,e)	Corona
61	(a,b,c)	HIV
71	(a,b,c)	HIV
81	(a,b,c)	Corona
91	(a,b,c)	Corona
95	(a,b,c)	Corona

Fig. 2. L_1 and L_2 are two simple event logs collected at timestamps t_1 and t_2. L_1' and L_2' are the corresponding anonymized releases of event logs given $n = 1$ as the anonymization parameter. Both L_1' and L_2' have 5-anonymity and 2-diversity assuming a sequence of activities as the BK.

Note that we assume the anonymization function promises to preserve all the cases and not to produce new (fake) cases. Figure 2 shows two simple event logs that were published using the anonymization function given $n = 1$. *Specialization* is the reverse operation of the anonymization defined as follows.

Definition 7 (Specialization). *Let $\mathcal{P}$ be the universe of simple process instances and $n \in \mathbb{N}_{\geq 1}$ be the anonymization parameter. For $p = (c, \sigma, s) \in \mathcal{P}$ and $p' = (c', \sigma', s') \in \mathcal{P}$, we say p is a specialization for p' w.r.t. n, denoted by $p' \preceq_n p$ iff $\sigma' \sqsubseteq \sigma$, $|\sigma| \leq |\sigma'| + n$, and $s = s'$.*

Consider $p' = (81, \langle a, b, c \rangle, Corona)$ as a process instance from the anonymized event log L'_2 in Fig. 2. Given $n = 1$, the cases 1, 2, and 3 from L_2 could be a specialization for p' which are possible original process instances. We assume that the adversary's BK is a subsequence of activities performed for a victim case which can be considered as the strongest assumable knowledge w.r.t. the available information in simple event logs. Given an anonymized event log and the anonymization parameter, the adversary can distinguish a *matching set* in the anonymized release containing all the process instances having at least one specialization matching the adversary's knowledge. One of the process instances included in such a matching set belongs to the victim case.

Definition 8 (Matching Set, Group). *Let $n \in \mathbb{N}_{\geq 1}$ be the anonymization parameter and L' be an anonymized event log. $ms^{L',n} \in \mathcal{A}^* \to 2^{L'}$ retrieves a set of matching process instances from L'. For $bk \in \mathcal{A}^*$, $ms^{L',n}(bk) = \{p' \in L' \mid \exists_{p \in \mathcal{P}} p' \preceq_n p \wedge bk \sqsubseteq \pi_\sigma(p)\}$. A **group** g in a matching set is a set of process instances having the same value on the sensitive attribute.*

Consider $bk = \langle d, e \rangle$ as the adversary's knowledge and $n = 1$. For the anonymized event logs in Fig. 2, $ms^{L'_1,n}(bk) = L'_1$, and $ms^{L'_2,n}(bk) = \{(c', \sigma', s') \in L'_2 \mid c' \in \{11, 21, 31, 41, 51\}\}$. The elements of matching sets can be identified using the following theorem without searching the space of specializations.

Theorem 1 (Elements of matching sets). *Let $n \in \mathbb{N}_{\geq 1}$ be the anonymization parameter and L' be an anonymized event log. For $bk \in \mathcal{A}^*$ and $p' = (c', \sigma', s') \in L'$, $p' \in ms^{L',n}(bk)$ iff $n \geq |bk| - LCS^{bk}_{\sigma'}$.*

Proof. Theorem 1 follows because one needs to add at least $|bk| - LCS^{bk}_{\sigma'}$ activities to generate a super-sequence σ of σ', s.t., $bk \sqsubseteq \sigma$. σ can be considered as the trace of a process instance p which is a specialization for p'. Note that one can always assign a value for the sensitive attribute of p', s.t., $\pi_s(p) = \pi_s(p')$.

Consider a scenario where the data holder publishes L'_1 and L'_2 as two anonymized event logs at timestamps t_1 and t_2, respectively. An adversary, who is one of the data recipients, attempts to identify a victim case vc from L'_1 or L'_2. We assume that the adversary's knowledge is a subsequence of activities performed for the vc, i.e., $bk \in \mathcal{A}^*$, and the approximate time at which the process of the vc has been started, which is enough to know the release(s) where the vc should appear. For example, if event logs are published weekly, then the adversary knows that the process of the vc has been started in the second week. Thus, its data should appear in all the event logs published after the first week. The adversary has also the *correspondence knowledge* derived from the concept of continuous event data publishing, as described in Sect. 2. The following correspondence attacks can be launched by the adversary.

Forward Attack (F-Attack). The adversary knows that the process of the vc has been started at the approximate time t, s.t., $t \leq t_1$, and tries to identify the vc in L_1' exploiting L_2' and $bk \in \mathcal{A}^*$ as the BK. The vc due to its timestamp must have a process instance in L_1' and L_2'. If there exists a $p_1' \in L_1'$, s.t., $p_1' \in ms^{L_1',n}(bk)$ for an anonymization parameter n, there must be a $p_2' \in L_2'$ corresponding to p_1'. Otherwise, p_1' does not match the BK and can be excluded from $ms^{L_1',n}(bk)$.

Example 1. *Consider L_1' and L_2' in Fig. 2. Assume that the adversary's knowledge is $bk = \langle d, e \rangle$, and the anonymization parameter is $n = 1$. $ms^{L_1',n}(bk) = L_1'$ and $ms^{L_2',n}(bk) = \{(c', \sigma', s') \in L_2' \mid c' \in \{11, 21, 31, 41, 51\}\}$. Both matching sets meet 5-anonymity. However, by comparing L_1' and L_2', the adversary learns that one of the cases $10, 20, 30$ cannot have e after d. Otherwise, there must have been three cases with Corona in $ms^{L_2',n}(bk)$. Therefore, the adversary can exclude one of $10, 20, 30$. Note that the choice among $10, 20, 30$ does not matter as they are equal. Consequently, k is degraded from 5 to 4.*

Cross Attack (C-Attack). The adversary knows that the process of the vc has been started at the approximate time t, s.t., $t \leq t_1$, and attempts to identify the vc in L_2' exploiting L_1' and $bk \in \mathcal{A}^*$ as the BK. The vc because of its timestamp must have a process instance in L_1' and L_2'. If there exists a $p_2' \in L_2'$, s.t., $p_2' \in ms^{L_2',n}(bk)$ for an anonymization parameter n, there must be a $p_1' \in L_1'$ corresponding to p_2'. Otherwise, p_2' either is started at timestamp t, $t_1 < t \leq t_2$, or it does not match the BK and can be excluded from $ms^{L_2',n}(bk)$.

Example 2. *Consider L_1' and L_2' in Fig. 2. Assume that the adversary's knowledge is $bk = \langle d, e \rangle$, and the anonymization parameter is $n = 1$. $ms^{L_1',n}(bk) = L_1'$ and $ms^{L_2',n}(bk) = \{(c', \sigma', s') \in L_2' \mid c' \in \{11, 21, 31, 41, 51\}\}$. Both matching sets meet 5-anonymity. However, by comparing L_1' and L_2', the adversary learns that one of the cases $11, 21, 31$ must be started at timestamp t, s.t., $t_1 < t \leq t_2$. Otherwise, there must have been three cases with HIV in $ms^{L_1',n}(bk)$. Therefore, the adversary can exclude one of $11, 21, 31$. Again, the choice among $11, 21, 31$ does not matter as they are equal. Consequently, k is degraded from 5 to 4.*

Backward Attack (B-Attack). The adversary knows that the process of the vc has been started at the approximate time t, s.t., $t_1 < t \leq t_2$, and tries to identify the vc in L_2' exploiting L_1' and $bk \in \mathcal{A}^*$ as the BK. The vc has a process instance in L_2', but not in L_1'. Hence, if there exists $p_2' \in L_2'$, s.t., $p_2' \in ms^{L_2',n}(bk)$ for an anonymization parameter n, and p_2' has to be a corresponding process instance for some process instances in L_1', then p_2' must be started at timestamp t, s.t., $t \leq t_1$ and can be excluded from the matching set $ms^{L_2',n}(bk)$.

Example 3. *Consider L_1' and L_2' in Fig. 2. Assume that the adversary's knowledge is $bk = \langle d, c \rangle$, and the anonymization parameter is $n = 1$. $ms^{L_1',n}(bk) = L_1'$*

and $ms^{L'_2,n}(bk) = \{(c',\sigma',s') \in L'_2 \mid c' \in \{61,71,81,91,95\}\}$. *Both matching sets meet 5-anonymity. However, by comparing L'_1 and L'_2, the adversary learns that at least one of the cases $81,91,95$ must be started at timestamp t, $t \leq t_1$. Otherwise, one of the cases $10,20,30$ cannot have a corresponding process instance in L'_2. Thus, k is degraded from 5 to 4. Note that there are only two cases with Corona which are not in $ms^{L'_2,n}(bk)$ and could be corresponding for cases $10,20,30$. Hence, at least one of $81,91,95$ must be started at timestamp t, $t \leq t_1$.*

5   Attack Detection

The correspondence attacks mentioned in Sect. 4 are based on making some inferences about corresponding cases (process instances). However, there are many possible assignments of corresponding cases and each of those implies possibly different event logs, which are not necessarily the actual event logs collected by the data holder. In this section, we demonstrate the *attack detection* regardless of any particular choices. To this end, we first need to define a *linker* to specify all the valid assignments. Then, we provide formal definitions for different types of correspondence attacks and corresponding anonymity indicators.

Definition 9 (Linker, Buddy). *Let L'_1 and L'_2 be the anonymized event logs at timestamps t_1 and t_2, respectively, and $n \in \mathbb{N}_{\geq 1}$ be the anonymization parameter. $linker^n \in L'_1 \rightarrow L'_2$ is a total injective function that retrieves the corresponding process instances. For $p'_1 \in L'_1$ and $p'_2 \in L'_2$, $linker^n(p'_1) = p'_2$ iff there exist $p_1, p_2 \in \mathcal{P}$, s.t., $p'_1 \preceq_n p_1 \wedge p'_2 \preceq_n p_2 \wedge \pi_s(p_1) = \pi_s(p_2) \wedge \pi_\sigma(p_1) \in pref(\pi_\sigma(p_2))$. (p'_1, p'_2) is called a pair of **buddies** if there exists a linker, s.t., $linker^n(p'_1) = p'_2$.*

Definition 10 (F-attack). *Let L'_1 and L'_2 be two anonymized event logs released at timestamps t_1 and t_2, $n \in \mathbb{N}_{\geq 1}$ be the anonymization parameter, $t \leq t_1$ be the approximate time at which the process of the victim case has been started, and $bk \in \mathcal{A}^*$ be the BK. The F-attack attempts to identify x as the maximal excludable cases from $ms^{L'_1,n}(bk)$, s.t., for any linker, at least x cases from the matching set cannot match the BK. x is considered as crack size based on F-attack.*

Definition 11 (C-attack). *Let L'_1 and L'_2 be two anonymized event logs released at timestamps t_1 and t_2, $n \in \mathbb{N}_{\geq 1}$ be the anonymization parameter, $t \leq t_1$ be the approximate time at which the process of the victim case has been started, and $bk \in \mathcal{A}^*$ be the BK. The C-attack tries to identify x (crack size) as the maximal excludable cases from $ms^{L'_2,n}(bk)$, s.t., for any linker, at least x cases from the matching set cannot match the BK or the timestamp of the victim case.*

Definition 12 (B-attack). *Let L'_1 and L'_2 be two anonymized event logs released at timestamps t_1 and t_2, $n \in \mathbb{N}_{\geq 1}$ be the anonymization parameter, $t_1 < t \leq t_2$ be the approximate time at which the process of the victim case has been started, and $bk \in \mathcal{A}^*$ be the BK. The B-attack tries to identify x (crack* *size) as the maximal excludable cases from $ms^{L'_2,n}(bk)$, s.t., for any linker, at least x cases from the matching set cannot match the timestamp of the victim case.*

Based on the definitions for the correspondence attacks, the key for attack detection is the crack size. For calculating the crack sizes, we follow the similar approach introduced in [7] which is based on the concept of *comparability*. We define the comparability at the level of *sequences, process instances,* and *groups*. These definitions are later used to compute the crack sizes of attacks.

Definition 13 (Comparable Sequences). *Let $\sigma_1, \sigma_2 \in \mathcal{A}^*$ be two sequences of activities. We say σ_1 and σ_2 are comparable w.r.t. $n \in \mathbb{N}_{\geq 1}$, denoted by $\sigma_1 \overset{n}{\sim} \sigma_2$, if n is the minimum number of activities that needs to be added to σ_1 and/or σ_2 to generate a joint super-sequence, or if σ_1 can be a prefix of σ_2 by adding at least n activities to σ_2.*

Theorem 2 (Detecting comparable sequence). *Given $\sigma_1, \sigma_2 \in \mathcal{A}^*$ and*
$$n \in \mathbb{N}_{\geq 1}: \sigma_1 \overset{n}{\sim} \sigma_2 \iff \begin{cases} n \geq |\sigma_1| - LCS^{\sigma_1}_{\sigma_2} & \text{if } \exists_{\sigma \in LCS(\sigma_1,\sigma_2)} \sigma \in pref(\sigma_2) \\ n \geq SCS^{\sigma_1}_{\sigma_2} - min(|\sigma_1|, |\sigma_2|) & \text{otherwise} \end{cases}$$

Proof. If there exists a $\sigma \in LCS(\sigma_1, \sigma_2)$, s.t., $\sigma \in pref(\sigma_2)$, then $|\sigma_1| - LCS^{\sigma_1}_{\sigma_2}$ is the minimum number of activities that needs to be added to σ_2, s.t., $\sigma_1 \in pref(\sigma_2)$. Otherwise, since $SCS^{\sigma_1}_{\sigma_2}$ is the length of a shortest common super-sequence, one needs to add at least $SCS^{\sigma_1}_{\sigma_2} - min(|\sigma_1|, |\sigma_2|)$ activities to the shorter sequence to generate a joint super-sequence.

Definition 14 (Comparable Process Instances). *Let $p_1, p_2 \in \mathcal{P}$ be two process instances. We say p_1 and p_2 are comparable w.r.t. n, denoted by $p_1 \overset{n}{\sim} p_2$, iff $\pi_s(p_1) = \pi_s(p_2) \wedge \pi_\sigma(p_1) \overset{n}{\sim} \pi_\sigma(p_2)$.*

Definition 15 (Comparable Groups). *Let L'_1 and L'_2 be two anonymized event logs released at timestamps t_1 and t_2, $bk \in \mathcal{A}^*$ be the BK, and $n \in \mathbb{N}_{\geq 1}$ be the anonymization parameter. We say two groups $g'_1 \subseteq ms^{L'_1,n}(bk)$ and $g'_2 \subseteq ms^{L'_2,n}(bk)$ are comparable w.r.t. n, denoted by $g'_1 \overset{n}{\sim} g'_2$, iff $\forall_{p'_1 \in g'_1} \forall_{p'_2 \in g'_2} p'_1 \overset{n}{\sim} p'_2$.*

Lemma 1. *Let L'_1 and L'_2 be two anonymized event logs at timestamps t_1 and t_2, $bk \in \mathcal{A}^*$ be the BK, and $n \in \mathbb{N}_{\geq 1}$ be the anonymization parameter. Consider $g'_1 \subseteq ms^{L'_1,n}(bk)$ and $g'_2 \subseteq ms^{L'_2,n}(bk)$ as two groups, s.t., $g'_1 \overset{n}{\sim} g'_2$. If $p'_1 \in ms^{L'_1,n}(bk)$ and $p'_2 \in ms^{L'_2,n}(bk)$ are buddies for a linker, then $p'_1 \in g'_1$ iff $p'_2 \in g'_2$.*

Lemma 2. *Let L'_1 and L'_2 be two anonymized event logs released at timestamps t_1 and t_2, $bk \in \mathcal{A}^*$ be the BK, and $n \in \mathbb{N}_{\geq 1}$ be the anonymization parameter. Consider $g'_1 \subseteq ms^{L'_1,n}(bk)$ and $g'_2 \subseteq ms^{L'_2,n}(bk)$ as two groups, s.t., $g'_1 \overset{n}{\sim} g'_2$. Since the buddy relationship is injective, at most $min(|g'_1|, |g'_2|)$ process instances in g'_1 have a buddy in g'_2, and there are some linkers where exactly $min(|g'_1|, |g'_2|)$ process instances in g'_1 have a buddy in g'_2.*

Theorem 3 (Crack size based on F-attack). *Let $bk \in \mathcal{A}^*$ be the BK, $n \in \mathbb{N}_{\geq 1}$ be the anonymization parameter, and L_1' and L_2' be two anonymized event logs released at timestamps t_1 and t_2. Let $CG(ms^{L_1',n}(bk), ms^{L_2',n}(bk)) = \{(g_1', g_2') \mid g_1' \subseteq ms^{L_1',n}(bk) \wedge g_2' \subseteq ms^{L_2',n}(bk) \wedge g_1' \overset{n}{\sim} g_2'\}$ be the set of pair of comparable groups in the matching sets. For $(g_1', g_2') \in CG(ms^{L_1',n}(bk), ms^{L_2',n}(bk))$, g_1' has crack size $cs = |g_1'| - min(|g_1'|, |g_2'|)$. $F(ms^{L_1',n}(bk), ms^{L_2',n}(bk)) = \sum cs$ is the number of excludable cases from $ms^{L_1',n}(bk)$ exploiting the F-attack, where $\sum$ is over $(g_1', g_2') \in CG(ms^{L_1',n}(bk), ms^{L_2',n}(bk))$.*

Proof. Consider $(g_1', g_2') \in CG(ms^{L_1',n}(bk), ms^{L_2',n}(bk))$. Based on Lemma 2, if $|g_1'| > |g_2'|$, at least $|g_1'| - min(|g_1'|, |g_2'|)$ process instances in g_1' do not have a buddy in g_2' for any linker. Also, according to Lemma 1, these process instances cannot match the given BK. Otherwise, they must have had buddies in g_2'.

Example 4. *Consider L_1' and L_2' in Fig. 2, $n = 1$, and $bk = \langle d, e \rangle$. $|g_1'| = 3$ and $|g_2'| = 2$ for the Corona groups in $ms^{L_1',n}(bk)$ and $ms^{L_2',n}(bk)$, respectively. $cs = 3 - min(3, 2)$ is the crack size of $ms^{L_1',n}(bk)$ based on F-attack.*

Definition 16. (F-Anonymity). *Let L_1' and L_2' be two anonymized event logs at t_1 and t_2, and $n \in \mathbb{N}_{\geq 1}$ be the anonymization parameter. The F-anonymity of L_1' and L_2' is $FA^n(L_1', L_2') = \min_{bk \in \mathcal{A}^*} |ms^{L_1',n}(bk)| - F(ms^{L_1',n}(bk), ms^{L_2',n}(bk))$.*

Theorem 4. (Crack size based on C-attack). *Let $bk \in \mathcal{A}^*$ be the BK, $n \in \mathbb{N}_{\geq 1}$ be the anonymization parameter, and L_1' and L_2' be two anonymized event logs released at timestamps t_1 and t_2. Let $CG(ms^{L_1',n}(bk), ms^{L_2',n}(bk)) = \{(g_1', g_2') \mid g_1' \subseteq ms^{L_1',n}(bk) \wedge g_2' \subseteq ms^{L_2',n}(bk) \wedge g_1' \overset{n}{\sim} g_2'\}$ be the set of pair of comparable groups in the matching sets. For $(g_1', g_2') \in CG(ms^{L_1',n}(bk), ms^{L_2',n}(bk))$, g_2' has crack size $cs = |g_2'| - min(|g_1'|, |g_2'|)$. $C(ms^{L_1',n}(bk), ms^{L_2',n}(bk)) = \sum cs$ is the number of excludable cases from $ms^{L_1',n}(bk)$ exploiting the C-attack, where $\sum$ is over $(g_1', g_2') \in CG(ms^{L_1',n}(bk), ms^{L_2',n}(bk))$.*

Proof. Consider $(g_1', g_2') \in CG(ms^{L_1',n}(bk), ms^{L_2',n}(bk))$. Based on Lemma 2, if $|g_2'| > |g_1'|$, at least $|g_2'| - min(|g_1'|, |g_2'|)$ process instances in g_2' do not have a buddy in g_1' for any linker. Such process instances either cannot match the given BK, according to Lemma 1, or they have been started at timestamp t, $t_1 < t \leq t_2$.

Example 5. *Consider L_1' and L_2' in Fig. 2, $n = 1$, and $bk = \langle d, e \rangle$. $|g_1'| = 2$ and $|g_2'| = 3$ for the HIV groups in $ms^{L_1',n}(bk)$ and $ms^{L_2',n}(bk)$, respectively. $cs = 3 - min(2, 3)$ is the crack size of $ms^{L_2',n}(bk)$ based on C-attack.*

Definition 17 (C-Anonymity). *Let L_1' and L_2' be two anonymized event logs at t_1 and t_2, and $n \in \mathbb{N}_{\geq 1}$ be the anonymization parameter. The C-anonymity of L_1' and L_2' is $CA^n(L_1', L_2') = \min_{bk \in \mathcal{A}^*} |ms^{L_2',n}(bk)| - C(ms^{L_1',n}(bk), ms^{L_2',n}(bk))$.*

Lemma 3. *Let L_1' and L_2' be two anonymized event logs released at timestamps t_1 and t_2, $bk \in \mathcal{A}^*$ be the BK, and $n \in \mathbb{N}_{\geq 1}$ be the anonymization parameter. Consider $g_2' \subseteq ms^{L_2',n}(bk)$, $G_1' = \{p_1' \in L_1' \mid \exists_{p_2' \in g_2'} p_1' \overset{n}{\sim} p_2'\}$, and $G_2' = \{p_2' \in L_2' \mid$*

$\exists_{p'_1 \in G'_1} p'_1 \overset{n}{\sim} p'_2\}$. *Every process instance in G'_2 is comparable to all records in G'_1 and only those records in G'_1.*

Theorem 5 (Crack size based on B-attack). *Let $bk \in \mathcal{A}^*$ be the BK, $n \in \mathbb{N}_{\geq 1}$ be the anonymization parameter, and L'_1 and L'_2 be two anonymized event logs released at timestamps t_1 and t_2. Let $g'_2 \subseteq ms^{L'_2,n}(bk)$, $G'_1 = \{p'_1 \in L'_1 \mid \exists_{p'_2 \in g'_2} p'_1 \overset{n}{\sim} p'_2\}$, and $G'_2 = \{p'_2 \in L'_2 \mid \exists_{p'_1 \in G'_1} p'_1 \overset{n}{\sim} p'_2\}$. g'_2 has crack size $cs = max(0, |G'_1| - (|G'_2| - |g'_2|))$. $B(ms^{L'_2,n}(bk), L'_1, L'_2) = \sum_{g'_2 \in ms^{L'_2,n}(bk)} cs$ is the number of excludable cases from $ms^{L'_2,n}(bk)$ exploiting B-attack.*

Proof. According to Lemma 3, all process instances in G'_1 and only those process instances can have a buddy in G'_2. Therefore, each process instance in G'_1 has a buddy either in g'_2 or $G'_2 - g'_2$. If $|G'_1| > |G'_2| - |g'_2|$, then $|G'_1| - (|G'_2| - |g'_2|)$ process instances in g'_2 must be started at timestamp t, $t \leq t_1$.

Example 6. *Consider L'_1 and L'_2 in Fig. 2, $n = 1$, and $bk = \langle d, c \rangle$. $|g'_2| = 3$ for the Corona group in $ms^{L'_2,n}(bk)$, $G'_1 = \{p'_1 \in L'_1 \mid \pi_c(p'_1) \in \{10, 20, 30\}\}$, and $G'_2 = \{p'_2 \in L'_2 \mid \pi_c(p'_2) \in \{41, 51, 81, 91, 95\}\}$. $cs = max(0, 3 - (5 - 3))$ is the crack size of $ms^{L'_2,n}(bk)$ based on B-attack.*

Definition 18 (B-Anonymity). *Let L'_1 and L'_2 be two anonymized event logs at t_1 and t_2, and $n \in \mathbb{N}_{\geq 1}$ be the anonymization parameter. $BA^n(L'_1, L'_2) = \min_{bk \in \mathcal{A}^*} |ms^{L'_2,n}(bk)| - B(ms^{L'_2,n}(bk), L'_1, L'_2)$ is the B-anonymity of L'_1 and L'_2.*

Given $n \in \mathbb{N}_{\geq 1}$ as the anonymization parameter, $KA^n(L') = \min_{bk \in \mathcal{A}^*} |ms^{L',n}(bk)|$ is the k-anonymity of an anonymized event log L' w.r.t. n. Assuming L'_1 and L'_2 as two anonymized event logs at timestamps t_1 and t_2, we calculate *the proportion of the cracked cases* (PoCs) after launching the correspondence attacks as follows: $FC^n(L'_1, L'_2) = \frac{(KA^n(L'_1) - FA^n(L'_1, L'_2))}{KA^n(L'_1)}$, $CC^n(L'_1, L'_2) = \frac{(KA^n(L'_2) - CA^n(L'_1, L'_2))}{KA^n(L'_2)}$, and $BC^n(L'_1, L'_2) = \frac{(KA^n(L'_2) - BA^n(L'_1, L'_2))}{KA^n(L'_2)}$.

6 Experiments

In this section, we employ *Sepsis* [10] as a real-life event log and simulate different continuous event data publishing scenarios. We report privacy losses and anonymity values based on the correspondence attacks. Note that *Sepsis* is one of the most challenging event logs for PPTs [5,11,18]. We consider two main scenarios to cover various situations w.r.t. *event data volume* and *velocity of event data publishing*. In both scenarios, we consider two releases to be published.

In **Scenario I**, we consider the entire event log as the second collection of events $L_2(100)$. Keeping the second collection of events as $L_2(100)$, we generate four different variants for the first collection of events named $L_1(99)$, $L_1(95)$, $L_1(90)$, and $L_1(75)$, s.t., $L_1(x)$ contains $x\%$ of cases. Note that we ignore the decimal points for percentages, e.g., 90% could be 90.01% or 90.95%. In **Scenario II**, we filter 50% of cases as the first collection of events $L_1(50)$. Keeping the first collection of events as $L_1(50)$, we generate four different variants for the second collection of events named $L_2(51)$, $L_2(55)$, $L_2(60)$, and $L_2(75)$, s.t., $L_2(x)$ contains $x\%$ of cases. To filter the event logs, we use *time-frame filtering* where the start time is always the start time of the event log and the end time is changed to pick the desired percentage of cases.

In both scenarios, the gap between two collections varies, s.t., it contains at most 1%, 5%, 10%, or 25% new cases. We focus on the percentage of cases rather than a fixed time window, e.g., daily, weekly, etc., because a fixed time window could contain different amount of data in different slots. We employ the extended version of TLKC-privacy model [17] as the group-based PPT where one can adjust power and type of BK.[2] The model removes events from traces w.r.t. *utility loss* and *privacy gain* to provide the desired privacy requirements. We consider all the possible sequences of activities in the event log with the maximal length 5 as the candidates of BK, and $k = 20$ as the lower bound for k-anonymity, i.e., the privacy model guarantees that a single release of the event log meets at least 20-anonymity for all the candidates of BK. On the data recipient's side, in each scenario, four different pairs of anonymized releases are received. We developed a Python program to detect the attacks and report the anonymity values. The source code and other resources are available on GitHub.[3]

Figure 3 shows the anonymity values before and after launching the attacks in Scenario I. Note that when n is equal to the length of the BK, all cases already fall into the matching sets. Therefore, the maximal value for the anonymization parameter is 5 which is the maximal length assumed for the BK. Figure 3a shows that when the

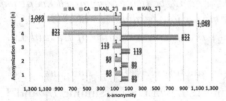

(a) The anonymity values when the gap between two releases is ≤1%, i.e., L_1' and L_2' were obtained from $L_1(99)$ and $L_2(100)$, respectively.

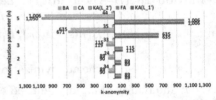

(b) The anonymity values when the gap between two releases is ≤5%, i.e., L_1' and L_2' were obtained from $L_1(95)$ and $L_2(100)$, respectively.

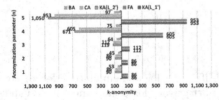

(c) The anonymity values when the gap between two releases is ≤10%, i.e., L_1' and L_2' were obtained from $L_1(90)$ and $L_2(100)$, respectively.

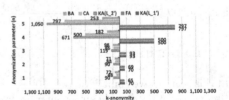

(d) The anonymity values when the gap between two releases is ≤25%, i.e., L_1' and L_2' were obtained from $L_1(75)$ and $L_2(100)$, respectively.

Fig. 3. The anonymity values for different variants of pairs of anonymized releases in Scenario I. $KA(L_1')$ is k-anonymity of L_1', $KA(L_2')$ is k-anonymity of L_2', FA is k-anonymity of L_1' after launching F-attack, CA is k-anonymity of L_2' after launching C-attack, and BA is k-anonymity of L_2' after launching B-attack.

---

[2] https://github.com/m4jidRafiei/TLKC-Privacy-Ext.
[3] https://github.com/m4jidRafiei/PP_CEDP.

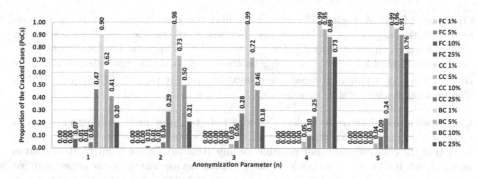

Fig. 4. Let x be the maximal gap between two anonymized releases. FC x%, CC x%, and BC x% show the PoCs exploiting F-attack, C-attack, and B-attack, respectively. For each anonymization parameter, the first, the second, and the third 4 bars show the results for F-attack, C-attack, and B-attack, respectively.

gap is at most 1% and $n = 1$, the anonymized release L_2' has 90-anonymity. However, after launching the B-attack, 81 cases are cracked, i.e., 90% of cases, and k-anonymity is degraded to 9, i.e., $BA^1(L_1', L_2') = 9$. For $n > 1$, the B-anonymity is 1, i.e., there exists a sequence of activities of the maximal length 5 that can be used to uniquely identify a case assuming that at most $n > 1$ activities have been removed by the PPT. Note that the second release includes only 1 new case when the gap is at most 1%.

Figure 4 shows how the PoCs are changed when we vary the anonymization parameter n in Scenario I. Each pair of the anonymized releases is indicated with the percentage of the gap, e.g., 1% in Scenario I indicates two releases obtained from $L_1(99)$ and $L_2(100)$. When the gap between two releases is small, the B-attack results in much higher values for the PoCs compared to the other attacks. However, when the gap becomes larger, the PoCs of the B-attack decreases. This happens because for the smaller L_1's, there exist fewer cases that can be excluded from the matching sets in L_2' because of their timestamps. The C-attack shows different behavior that is due to the assumed timestamp for the victim case, i.e., for the larger gaps, there exist more cases that their timestamps comply with the second release L_2' and cannot have a corresponding case in L_1'. The F-attack cracks fewer cases, which is expected because its target release is L_1', and it only exploits the BK mismatching. Note that greater values for the anonymization parameter mean that the adversary assumes higher data distortion which results in greater values for the anonymity. We had similar observations for Scenario II, and the results are available in our GitHub repository.

7   Extensions

The two releases scenario can be extended to the general scenario where more releases are involved. In the general scenario, we consider $m \in \mathbb{N}_{>2}$ collections of events $L_1, L_2, \ldots, L_m$ collected at timestamps $t_1, t_2, \ldots, t_m$ and published as $L_1', L_2', \ldots, L_m'$. The correspondence knowledge is also extended, s.t., every case in L_i' has a corresponding case in L_j', $i < j \le m$. Consider the introduced attacks based on two releases as *micro attacks*. Given more than two releases, the adversary can launch two other types of attacks, so-called *optimal micro attacks* and *composition of micro attacks* [7].

Optimal Micro Attacks: The idea is to find the best background release which results in the largest possible crack size. For instance, consider the F-attack on L_i'. The adversary can choose any L_j', $i < j \leq m$, as the background release. Let $bk \in \mathcal{A}^*$ be the background knowledge, $n \in \mathbb{N}_{\geq 1}$ be the anonymization parameter, and cs_{ij} be the crack size of a pair of comparable groups $(g_i', g_j') \in CG(ms^{L_i',n}(bk), ms^{L_j',n}(bk))$. The optimal crack size of g_i' is $\max_{i<j\leq m} cs_{ij}$.

Composition of Micro Attacks: The idea is to compose multiple micro attacks to increase the crack size of a group. The micro attacks are launched one after the other. Note that the composition is not possible for any arbitrary choice of micro attacks. It is possible only if all the micro attacks in the composition assume the same timestamp for the victim case, and the required correspondence knowledge holds for the next attack after the previous attack [7]. Hence, considering L_i', L_j', and L_l', as the anonymized releases, s.t., $i < j < l \leq m$, only two compositions are possible: (1) B-attack on L_i' and L_j' followed by F-attack on L_j' and L_l', and (2) B-attack on L_i' and L_j' followed by C-attack on L_j' and L_l'.

Here, we focused on k-anonymity which is the foundation for the group-based PPTs. The proposed approach can be extended to cover all the extensions of k-anonymity introduced to deal with *attribute linkage* attacks, e.g., l-diversity, (α, k)-anonymity, confidence bounding, etc. The measures of such PPTs can be modified to consider the cracked cases. Moreover, new group-based PPTs for process mining can be designed to consider $F/C/B$-anonymity. For example, a naive algorithm is to start with the maximal possible anonymity, i.e., having only one trace variant, e.g., the longest common subsequence, and then adding events w.r.t. their effect on data utility and privacy loss.

8   Related Work

Privacy/confidentiality in process mining is growing in importance. The work having been done covers different aspects of the topic including *the challenges* [2,4,13], *confidentiality frameworks* [19], *privacy by design* [12], *privacy guarantees* [5,6,11,18], *interorganizational privacy issues* [3], and *privacy quantification* [16,20]. Confidentiality is one of the important challenges of the bigger sub-discipline of process mining called *Responsible Process Mining* (RPM) [2]. In [13], the authors focus on data privacy and utility requirements for healthcare event data. A general framework for confidentiality in process mining is proposed in [19]. In [12], the goal is to propose a privacy-preserving system design for process mining. In [14], the authors introduce a privacy-preserving method for discovering roles from event logs. In [5], k-anonymity and t-closeness are adopted to preserve the privacy of *resources* in event logs. In [6,11], the notion of *differential privacy* is utilized to provide privacy guarantees. In [18], the TLKC-privacy is introduced to deal with high variability issues in event logs for applying group-based anonymization techniques. A secure multi-party computation solution is proposed in [3] for preserving privacy in an inter-organizational setting. In [20], the authors propose a measure to evaluate the re-identification risk of event logs. Also, in [16], a general privacy quantification framework, and some measures are introduced to evaluate the effectiveness of PPTs. In [15], the authors propose a privacy extension for the XES standard to manage privacy metadata.

9   Conclusion

In practice, event data need to be published continuously to keep the process mining results up-to-date. In this paper, for the first time, we focused on the attacks appearing when anonymized event data are published continuously. We formalized three different types of the so-called *correspondence attacks* in the context of process mining: F-attack, C-attack, and B-attack. We demonstrated the attack detection techniques to quantify the anonymity of event logs published continuously. We simulated the continuous event data publishing for real-life event logs using various scenarios. For an example event log, we showed that the provided privacy guarantees can be degraded exploiting the attacks. The attack analysis and detection techniques can be adjusted and attached to different group-based PPTs to enhance the privacy guarantees when event data are published continuously. In this paper, we mainly focused on *suppression* as the anonymization operation. In future, other anonymization operations such as *addition* or *swapping* could be analyzed. Similar attack analysis can be done for other types of PPTs, e.g., *differential privacy*, in the context of process mining to protect provided privacy guarantees. Moreover, one could evaluate the effect of continuous publishing scenarios on privatized process mining results.

Acknowledgment. Funded under the Excellence Strategy of the Federal Government and the Länder. We also thank the Alexander von Humboldt Stiftung for supporting our research.

References

1. van der Aalst, W.M.P.: Process Mining - Data Science in Action, 2nd edn. Springer, Heidelberg (2016). https://doi.org/10.1007/978-3-662-49851-4
2. Aalst, W.M.P.: Responsible data science: using event data in a "people friendly" manner. In: Hammoudi, S., Maciaszek, L.A., Missikoff, M.M., Camp, O., Cordeiro, J. (eds.) ICEIS 2016. LNBIP, vol. 291, pp. 3–28. Springer, Cham (2017). https://doi.org/10.1007/978-3-319-62386-3_1
3. Elkoumy, G., Fahrenkrog-Petersen, S.A., Dumas, M., Laud, P., Pankova, A., Weidlich, M.: Secure multi-party computation for inter-organizational process mining. In: Nurcan, S., Reinhartz-Berger, I., Soffer, P., Zdravkovic, J. (eds.) BPMDS/EMMSAD -2020. LNBIP, vol. 387, pp. 166–181. Springer, Cham (2020). https://doi.org/10.1007/978-3-030-49418-6_11
4. Elkoumy, G., et al.: Privacy and confidentiality in process mining - threats and research challenges. CoRR abs/2106.00388 (2021). https://arxiv.org/abs/2106.00388
5. Fahrenkrog-Petersen, S.A., van der Aa, H., Weidlich, M.: PRETSA: event log sanitization for privacy-aware process discovery. In: International Conference on Process Mining, ICPM 2019, Aachen, Germany (2019)
6. Fahrenkrog-Petersen, S.A., van der Aa, H., Weidlich, M.: PRIPEL: privacy-preserving event log publishing including contextual information. In: Fahland, D., Ghidini, C., Becker, J., Dumas, M. (eds.) BPM 2020. LNCS, vol. 12168, pp. 111–128. Springer, Cham (2020). https://doi.org/10.1007/978-3-030-58666-9_7
7. Fung, B.C.M., Wang, K., Fu, A.W., Pei, J.: Anonymity for continuous data publishing. In: 11th International Conference on Extending Database Technology. ACM International Conference Proceeding Series, vol. 261, pp. 264–275 (2008)

8. Fung, B.C., Wang, K., Fu, A.W.C., Philip, S.Y.: Introduction to Privacy-Preserving Data Publishing: Concepts and Techniques. Chapman and Hall/CRC, London (2010)
9. Gehrke, J.: Models and methods for privacy-preserving data analysis and publishing. In: Proceedings of the 22nd International Conference on Data Engineering, ICDE, p. 105. IEEE Computer Society (2006)
10. Mannhardt, F.: Sepsis Cases-Event Log. Eindhoven University of Technology (2016)
11. Mannhardt, F., Koschmider, A., Baracaldo, N., Weidlich, M., Michael, J.: Privacy-preserving process mining - differential privacy for event logs. Bus. Inf. Syst. Eng. **61**(5), 595–614 (2019)
12. Michael, J., Koschmide, A., Mannhardt, F., Baracaldo, N., Rumpe, B.: User-centered and privacy-driven process mining system design for IoT. In: Cappiello, C., Ruiz, M. (eds.) CAiSE 2019 CAiSE 2019. LNBIP, vol. 350, pp. 194–206. Springer, Cham (2019). https://doi.org/10.1007/978-3-030-21297-1_17
13. Pika, A., Wynn, M.T., Budiono, S., ter Hofstede, A.H., van der Aalst, W.M.P., Reijers, H.A.: Privacy-preserving process mining in healthcare. Int. J. Environ. Res. Public Health **17**(5), 1612 (2020)
14. Rafiei, M., van der Aalst, W.M.P.: Mining roles from event logs while preserving privacy. In: Di Francescomarino, C., Dijkman, R., Zdun, U. (eds.) BPM 2019. LNBIP, vol. 362, pp. 676–689. Springer, Cham (2019). https://doi.org/10.1007/978-3-030-37453-2_54
15. Rafiei, M., van der Aalst, W.M.P.: Privacy-preserving data publishing in process mining. In: Fahland, D., Ghidini, C., Becker, J., Dumas, M. (eds.) BPM 2020. LNBIP, vol. 392, pp. 122–138. Springer, Cham (2020). https://doi.org/10.1007/978-3-030-58638-6_8
16. Rafiei, M., van der Aalst, W.M.P.: Towards quantifying privacy in process mining. In: Leemans, S., Leopold, H. (eds.) ICPM 2020. LNBIP, vol. 406, pp. 385–397. Springer, Cham (2021). https://doi.org/10.1007/978-3-030-72693-5_29
17. Rafiei, M., van der Aalst, W.M.P.: Group-based privacy preservation techniques for process mining. Data Knowl. Eng. **134**, 101908 (2021). https://doi.org/10.1016/j.datak.2021.101908
18. Rafiei, M., Wagner, M., van der Aalst, W.M.P.: *TLKC*-privacy model for process mining. In: Dalpiaz, F., Zdravkovic, J., Loucopoulos, P. (eds.) RCIS 2020. LNBIP, vol. 385, pp. 398–416. Springer, Cham (2020). https://doi.org/10.1007/978-3-030-50316-1_24
19. Rafiei, M., von Waldthausen, L., van der Aalst, W.M.P.: Supporting confidentiality in process mining using abstraction and encryption. In: Ceravolo, P., van Keulen, M., Gómez-López, M.T. (eds.) SIMPDA 2018-2019. LNBIP, vol. 379, pp. 101–123. Springer, Cham (2020). https://doi.org/10.1007/978-3-030-46633-6_6
20. von Voigt, S.N., et al.: Quantifying the re-identification risk of event logs for process mining - empiricial evaluation paper. In: Advanced Information Systems Engineering, CAiSE (2020)
21. Wong, R.C.W., Fu, A.W.C., Wang, K., Pei, J.: Minimality attack in privacy preserving data publishing. In: Proceedings of the 33rd International Conference on Very Large Data Bases, pp. 543–554 (2007)

Expectations vs. Experiences – Process Mining in Small and Medium Sized Manufacturing Companies

Florian Stertz[1]([envelope]), Juergen Mangler[2], Beate Scheibel[1],
and Stefanie Rinderle-Ma[2]

[1] Faculty of Computer Science, University of Vienna, Vienna, Austria
{florian.stertz,beate.scheibel}@univie.ac.at
[2] Department of Informatics, Technical University of Munich, Garching, Germany
{juergen.mangler,stefanie.rinderle-ma}@tum.de

Abstract. While literature emphasizes the importance of process mining for pushing digital transformation in manufacturing, it remains unclear how process mining can be actually implemented and used by domain experts, especially in small and medium sized manufacturing companies (SMMC). This paper provides the findings of a focus group study, i.e., expectations on and experiences with the introduction of process mining in SMMC, including employees in different positions, e.g., process supervisors and shopfloor workers, and exposure to process mining. Transparency, for example, is an expected benefit for managers, facilitating the collaboration with business partners, error prevention, and legal protection. Shopfloor workers, in turn, perceive transparency as possible threat. The implementation of two process mining scenarios at one of the SMMC led to reduced documentation effort which helped to win over shopfloor workers. Altogether, the findings of this study can help to address concerns and challenges (e.g., with the infrastructure and data collection) early when introducing process mining at SMMC.

Keywords: Process mining · Manufacturing · Small and medium size companies · Focus group research

1 Introduction

Gartner reports a steep increase in process mining use cases for digital transformation and process automation [8]. A domain that poses particularly high demands on process transparency and digital transformation is manufacturing: it combines the physical world (e.g., sensors, machines), human work, and manufacturing systems. [16] presents best practice use cases and [5] emphasizes the

This work has been partially supported and funded by the Austrian Research Promotion Agency (FFG) via the "Austrian Competence Center for Digital Production" (CDP) under the contract number 881843. This work has been supported by the Pilot Factory Industry 4.0, Seestadtstrasse 27, Vienna, Austria.

(C) Springer Nature Switzerland AG 2021
A. Polyvyanyy et al. (Eds.): BPM Forum 2021, LNBIP 427, pp. 195–211, 2021.
https://doi.org/10.1007/978-3-030-85440-9_12

importance of process mining due to the data that is available in a manufacturing company. However, studies on process mining expectations and experiences in Small and Medium Sized Manufacturing Companies (SMMC), are missing although SMMC account for 55.4% of manufacturing companies in the EU[1] and for 44.4% of the employees in manufacturing in the US[2]. Moreover, these expectations and experiences have not been analyzed from the viewpoint of different organizational positions so far. It can be expected that due to the differences in daily work life as described below, expectations might vary which should be considered for a smooth introduction of process mining:

1. *Shopfloor workers* tend to perform their work in a process-oriented way due to the structure of manufacturing processes, since a certain set of tasks has to be applied in a logical order. Even though most machines nowadays have their own logging mechanism, there is often no software orchestrating resources as well as coordinating the cooperation with other departments.
2. *Supervising operatives* usually can observe specific steps in a process instance. If a workpiece or process subject is faulty due to an error, it is often unclear how and where in a process an error started occurring. Process mining can be vital for optimizing processes and detecting erroneous behavior.
3. For employees in *managing positions*, transparency is especially relevant. Transparency is a crucial aspect for companies nowadays, for legal protection as well as for cooperation with other companies. Process mining can increase the transparency by providing knowledge about business processes and their execution.

The following research questions aim at analyzing expectations on and experiences with process mining in SMMC from different viewpoints and with different exposure to process mining (before/after the introduction and application of process mining):

RQ1. What benefits and drawbacks are expected by SMMC when introducing process mining?
RQ2. What benefits and drawbacks are perceived by SMMC after the introduction of process mining?
RQ3. How can the implementation of process mining at SMMC be designed?

This work tackles *RQ1–RQ3* based on a focus group study following the guidelines stated in [10]. Focus groups have proven themselves as adequate means to assess the impact of process mining in practice [7]. The specific study design for addressing *RQ1–RQ3* is developed along a double layer approach enabling the distinction of the organizational position of participants and their exposure to process mining. The double layer approach is realized by two rounds of interviews with employees of two manufacturing companies covering organizational

---

[1] https://ec.europa.eu/eurostat/statistics-explained/pdfscache/10086.pdf.
[2] https://www.sba.gov/sites/default/files/advocacy/2018-Small-Business-Profiles-US.pdf.

positions ①, ②, and ③. Moreover, in one company, process mining has already been introduced and the other is planning the introduction of process mining in the near future. Two real-world cases for process mining in manufacturing, i.e., electroplating and electronics assembly, are described in detail.

The findings of this study show that the expectations involve increased transparency which is crucial for collaborations with business partners. In addition, it is expected that process mining can help to detect deviations in process executions at runtime. Main concerns regard employees feeling observed by the increased transparency and reluctance of them to share tacit knowledge. The introduction of process mining confirms that the expected benefits indeed occur. Moreover, the decreased documentation effort for employees, due to process mining, outweighs the fear of surveillance of employees.

The paper is structured as follows. Section 2 introduces fundamental terminology and discusses related work. Section 3 explains the detailed structure of the focus group study and the participants. Section 4 introduces the real-world scenarios for process mining application in manufacturing. Section 5 contains a summarized overview of the results of the focus group interviews. The findings that can be deducted from the interviews are discussed in Sect. 6 where also future implications based on these findings are discussed and the research question answered. The paper is concluded in Sect. 7.

2   Background and Related Work

Process mining aims at three analysis tasks: (i) process discovery detects a process model from a process execution log [2,3]. Several discovery algorithm exist, e.g., [11,21]. (ii) conformance checking compares a process execution log to a process model resulting in a fitness value [1]. (iii) process enhancement uses a process model and a process execution log to detect bottlenecks and helps improving the efficiency of a process.

Tasks (i)–(iii) use process execution logs (see e.g., [2,3]) as input. A process execution log consists of a set of traces where each trace stores the events that occurred when executing a process instance. Process execution logs reflect already finished process instances. If process mining techniques are applied on process execution logs, they are applied in an offline manner, i.e., ex post. If process mining is applied during runtime, process event streams are used instead of process execution logs [4,14,19,22]. An event stream consists of events of multiple process instances and is created and processed at the point in time an event is executed, with the typical stream features, i.e., it can only be processed once and in theory there might be an unlimited amount of events in a stream.

The advantage of online process mining is that domain experts can observe the results, as the process instances are being executed. This enables them to counteract undesired behaviour that could lead to errors, i.e., stopping a process instance that is not matching the behavior of the process model or discovering that the mined process model is not reflecting the planned logic at all. Plenty of tools and libraries are available to perform online and offline process mining on suitable data, i.e., the open source framework ProM [20] and PM4Py [3]. [13] provides an overview of process mining techniques, open source tools, and commercial tools in the context of the Business Process Intelligence Challenge.

But how are process mining techniques actually applied in practice? One aspect is the application of tools and systems. Here, [12] argues that commercial tools are often not user-friendly. Another aspect refers to challenges and solutions when introducing process mining independently of the tool. [7] conducted a focus group study looking at the challenges of introducing process mining from a managerial perspective. The usage of process mining in organizations and how to start an enterprise with process mining in mind, is explained in [16]. Here, several best practices are presented from projects in different organizations, like Siemens, BMW and Uber. A case study of how process mining can be used in the manufacturing domain is also represented in [9], where the usage of process mining is discussed for every category related to the Six Sigma quality management philosophy.

The study at hand aims at digging deeper into expectations and experiences with process mining in the manufacturing domain, especially for SMMC, considering different viewpoints and actual results of process mining projects.

3   Overview on Methodology and Study Design

This study employs focus groups [10] to assess the expectations on and experiences with process mining in SMMC.

The focus groups are organized according to the double-layer design depicted in Fig. 1. The first layer distinguishes the focus group participants by their organizational positions, i.e., shopfloor worker, supervising operative, and manager. This distinction aims to identify the impact of process mining from different work perspectives. The second layer distinguishes the participants by exposure to process mining in their current company, i.e., if process mining has already been used in the company or not. Doing so aims at comparing the general expectations on process mining to its actual results.

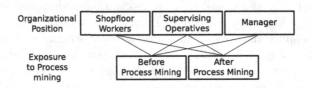

Fig. 1. Double layer focus group study. All participants are grouped along both layers.

Two rounds of focus group interviews were conducted. The first one consisted of three people who have not been using process mining in their work at the moment, but are planning to implement it in the near future. The second group consisted of four people, who are already using process mining, and plan to increase the usage of process mining.

As depicted in Fig. 1, participants of the focus group interviews can be distinguished along two layers.

The first layer focuses on the organizational position of a participant. In order to identify a set of participants for the focus group, we identified a representative set of roles and their responsibilities based on [6]. As both companies operate in a lean teamworking environment but are SMEs and thus not necessarily differentiate roles as much as big companies, we coordinated with them to narrow the set of roles down to a feasible number, that was then basis for organizing the actual focus group. ① reflects shopfloor workers who execute the tasks on the shopfloor. This task execution is then logged for applying process mining. Hence, the shopfloor workers can be seen as directly confronted with process mining and its results in their work life. ② reflects the supervising operatives of a company who are monitoring the shopfloor. Supervising operatives are interested in using process mining to discover rarely executed paths in a business process, use conformance checking to detect faulty process instances and tasks that caused a failure. ③ reflects the manager of a department or company. Process mining can be used to evaluate the general performance.

The second layer of this focus group study emphasizes the exposure of process mining in the company. The participants are therefore split into two groups. ① of the second layer, reflects employees in a company which has not used process mining yet. The second group, ② consists of employees who are using process mining already. The associated process scenarios are introduced in Sect. 4.

4   Applied Process Mining Scenario

The study design outlined in Sect. 3 demands that selected participants of the focus group have already been exposed to process mining which is an important part of the interviews and the findings. This section will thus introduce the scenarios in which participants of the focus group (Shopfloor Workers & Supervising Operatives) experienced the application of process mining.

4.1   Electroplating

Company E produces parts which have to be surface-treated. This is done by submerging these parts in a chemical bath, giving them certain desired properties. After the bath is used for a certain amount of parts, or if the bath has been inactive for a certain time, it has to be refilled. For refilling, certain (dangerous) chemicals have to be combined. Before introducing a BPMN process-based orchestration solution to support the process, workers were following guidelines, taking notes, and manually filling out reports. In cases where these guidelines were not followed, accidents have occurred. Avoiding these kinds of accidents was one of the main reasons to introduce an orchestration solution.

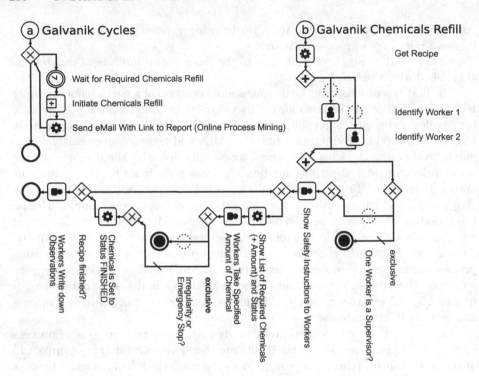

Fig. 2. Electroplating – a bath for surface treatment of parts has to be refilled after use or time

After introducing a process-based solution, the process was formalized as depicted in Fig. 2. The solution consists of two parts (CPEE [15] BPMN notation): Fig. 2 (a) depicts a control process that determines based on sensors and human input, when to start a refilling cycle. Figure 2 (b) depicts the actual refill process, carried out by two human workers. Figure 2 (b) starts with selecting a refill recipe. This can be either based on input from sensors in the bath or through human intervention from a supervising operative.

The recipe consists of a list of chemicals, and the required amount. Afterwards, the system waits for two workers to identify themselves through their NFC badges at the entrance of the chemicals storage locker. Only after their identity and role is established (one worker and one supervising operative are required), the locker can be opened. A screen shows which amount of which chemical has to be taken and added to the bath (in no particular order). Each chemical is in a container that is mounted on a digital weighting scale. Thus when the wrong amount of the chemical is taken, an emergency stop can be triggered. It is also possible to automatically track which chemicals have been used, as well as their exact amount. The workers are encouraged to write down their observations at a computer terminal after they are done (and the protective gear is removed).

Online process mining techniques, including mining for data elements, sensor data and time deviations, have been utilized to generate detailed reports about each instantiation of Fig. 2 (b). These reports are sent to all supervising operatives at the end of each cycle depicted in Fig. 2 (a).

4.2   Electronics Assembly

Company E manually assembles products which consist of different parts (> 100, including slight part variations). This leads to over 64, 000 possible variations that can be ordered by customers. Typical order sizes range from 2 to 500. The assembly involves soldering as well as intricate mechanical manipulation of parts that are less than 2 millimeters in size. This high variance, paired with the required intricate mechanical manipulation is a major hurdle for automatic assembly, thus the assembly is carried out by humans. The human workers have different skill levels. While some have the knowledge to assemble all variants from the back of their head, others need guidance which is provided by the experienced workers as well as through extensive technical documentation.

The problem is that many details involve tacit knowledge, i.e., knowledge that just exists in the minds of the workers. For quality assurance and product improvement it is not easy to determine which particular step during the assembly took how long, and which steps were most error prone.

In order to solve this problem, the assembly has been split into a number of sequential work packages, and for each work package a graphical worker assistance system has been designed. All logic for selecting individual steps and showing them on screen is implemented as a BPMN process-based solution. The worker assistance system automatically shows the correct set of steps for the work-piece in front of the worker (no variants have to be remembered), and also assumes a standard order of putting work-pieces together. Each step has to be acknowledged with a foot pedal. When a problem occurs, a worker can leave a (spoken, speech-to-text) note, and dismiss the work-piece for later fixing.

This setup forms a good basis for (online) process mining. It is possible to extract detailed information about durations and error rates, paired with information about the particular work-piece variation, used parts, and steps. Online process mining techniques are used to generate early warnings for supervising operators. Ex-post process mining is utilized for continuous process improvement. Though company E just started utilizing the system, early results have been deemed promising by workers, supervising operators, and management.

5   Results of Focus Group Interviews

The double layer design of the focus group study is depicted in Fig. 1 and explained in Sect. 3. The focus group features two interviews with employees from manufacturing companies CDP and E.

Manufacturing company CDP: The first focus group contained participants of two management levels. Three participants were interviewed, i.e., one supervising operative, and two general managers/CEOs. None of them was using process mining in their department at the time of the interview.

Manufacturing company E: The second focus group contained participants of three management levels. Company E is in the metal-processing domain and employs around 750 people. Four participants have been interviewed, i.e., two supervising operatives, a general manager and one shopfloor worker.

After an introduction into process mining, all participants revealed a good understanding of the basic principles of process mining and could identify scenarios in their company, where process models are already in place, i.e., in the electroplating department (cf. Sect. 4.1).

Table 1 provides a summary of the profile of the participants to identify theirs answers. In the following, the interview results are presented for each question.

Table 1. Focus group participants profile

Coding participants	Company	Position	Experience in company	Working with process mining
EA	E	Supervising operative	>10 years	Yes
EB	E	Supervising operative	2–4 years	Yes
EC	E	General manager	>10 years	Yes
ED	E	Shopfloor worker	>10 years	Yes
CA	CDP	Supervising operative	>3 years	No
CB	CDP	General manager	>2 years	No
CC	CDP	General manager	>4 years	No

What benefits do you see in a process-oriented view of your field?

ED thinks that one's workload is better structured using a process-oriented view, which increases the cooperation quality with other departments. The operative CA, sees benefits of process mining with respect to the transparency of their department and their company. Knowledge, in particular, domain specific knowledge is lost if an employee leaves, is a concern mentioned by CA. Workflows here are not explicitly available as formal models, but workers loosely follow learned rules/guidelines, hence it is difficult to detect the source of an error. Conformance checking and process model discovery are regarded as useful techniques to ease these problems. These benefits are confirmed by the operatives EA and EB. The correct execution of a process instance, supervised by process mining, allows them to detect and react to errors as soon as they happen. Moreover, the process models enable a good visual representation of the currently active tasks. EB mentions that, *"A huge advantage of a process-oriented view is the improved communication between employees from all levels"*.

The managers, CB and CC, share concerns regarding the usability of process mining in the daily routine of employees. The discovery of process models is seen as an important feature of process mining as it increases transparency, which is often required for cooperations with other companies. The correct process execution is crucial as well, to discover and fix problems. EC confirms the previously outlined benefits. In addition, the application of process enhancement is envisioned in the near future, through implementing lean management techniques and optimizing resource sharing between multiple departments.

How are processes and tasks executed and logged at the moment?

ED states, that their department uses work instructions as a basis for processes, obtained by interviewing workers. It was mentioned that this is useful for new employees, but yields some uncertainties (e.g., for rarely produced parts). CA explains that most of the activities are still logged manually in a rudimentary way without much information on the input/output of each task. The detection of faulty behavior in the process execution is crucial, but hard to track without a rich documentation. EA mentions, that unlike the electroplating unit, in his unit everything is currently only logged in an ERP-system. However, these event are only available at a high level and only for certain tasks, e.g., only measurements are logged, but not the production itself. These logs are used for making operational decisions, such as determining the delivery date. EA is aware that this leads to resource waste, as parallel processes are not properly synchronized, and departments sometimes have to wait on other departments, because they decided on a sub-optimal production order. EA also claims, that the work instructions mentioned by shopfloor workers, are often not followed, but instead slight variations learned from colleagues are used. CB emphasizes again, that identifying errors and increasing the efficiency is very important. Therefore, processes have been modeled showing the interaction between humans. These interactions are currently logged in an ERP system. Process mining techniques such as conformance checking or using a system to enact the correct tasks at the right time have not been used. EC is aware of the benefits of process mining in the implemented scenarios. Additionally EC mentioned the wish to implement process mining at the managerial level, i.e., mine and analyze management processes.

How is the correct execution of a process model currently ensured?

Process models are used and tasks are logged with a process execution engine in the application scenario of the electroplating unit as mentioned by ED. Currently active tasks are shown on a screen and are executed by interacting with the screen. CA, CB, and CC state that, as no process models are used, their correct execution is not ensured. EA explains that, correctness for the scenarios is enforced by a process engine, but for many other scenarios, the status quo has not changed. EB says, that additional process mining techniques to automatically notice errors is desirable, as currently root-cause analysis for errors is mostly done manually. EC is aware of the benefits of process mining in the implemented scenarios as decisions regarding high-level process changes become easier, and controlling is improved. EC again states that processes at managerial level should be formalized as well.

Which advantages do you see for your company with the support of process mining?

ED sees a reduced documentation effort due to automatic documentation. The instructions are well presented and help following the process model. CA emphasizes the importance of process enhancement as an important factor in the company, but is also keen on improving the efficiency using process mining techniques in general. EA sees a lot of potential, especially for protection against insurance claims if accidents happen or if products do not adhere to the quality standards. EB mentions that with increased process standardization they would be able to take on more risky projects. EA mentions an accident that happened in a sub-department where the cause could not be determined. To avoid such accidents in the future, it is essential to better structure the workflow, making it more transparent, provide support for the employees taking part in critical processes and log interactions with dangerous chemicals. CC sees advantages in understanding of processes for different positions in the organizational hierarchy. CB also thinks that processes can be communicated better between companies from different domains for a more efficient cooperation. With the help of process mining, especially process discovery and conformance checking, the perspectives of the shopfloor level and the management level should be more aligned. In the company, workflows rarely show deviations and more often follow a common path, which should allow for understandable process models. CC mentions explicitly that *"While a performance evaluation of a process can be done every three months and does not have to be online, a deviation of a process instances should be reported immediately"*. EC added, that there are additional benefits for planning and analysis that could be obtained by introducing process mining.

Which advantages do you see for your specific department with the support of process mining?

ED sees a big advantage, in the training of new employees with the use of process models and process mining. Process models provide a good visual representation of the workflow and allow for a better communication between departments. Online process mining can give immediate feedback about the current state of produced parts. CA points out the importance of identifying errors and the increased efficiency when communicating with other departments based on data produced by process mining. Both operatives, **EA** and **EB**, think that process transparency is increased due to the use of process models and a process execution engine. They mention automatic reports after each crucial step executed by shopfloor workers, which help to ensure the conformance of a process instance (regarding many aspects: process structure, timing, resource deviations, data deviations). **CA** emphasizes that not only the production should benefit from process mining techniques, but tasks involving only humans as well, such as creating reports, delivering a product, and communication between departments.

EC again emphasize that data obtained through process mining (e.g., duration & resource utilization for a multitude of product variations) are a huge benefit for planning and process optimization.

> **What problems do you anticipate for the introduction of process mining in your department?**

ED sees the benefits of process mining in one's department, but fears that long-term employees still might not see the purpose of process mining in other departments, because they are often not interested in changing their daily routine. However, **ED** states that if the benefits, i.e., less documentation effort, are clear to the employees, they can be convinced. CA voices concerns about the acceptance by the workers, since they tend to use their acquired knowledge to secure their position in the company. CA also fears high costs for heterogeneous workflows, since the discovery of the process model and its variants could imply a huge effort. The advantages of process mining are clear in CA's opinion. **EA** fears that the employees could feel observed. Hence, **EA** thinks it is important to encourage strong involvement of employees when implementing future scenarios. **CC** echos the concerns about employee acceptance. The increased process transparency is viewed as critical, as it paves the road towards cooperations with future customers and partners. CB voiced concerns, that the increased logging and data availability makes data leaks possible, which would harm the company. **EC** thinks that employee acceptance is a challenge, but in hindsight was easier to achieve than expected. **EC** thinks that the introduction for the whole company is too complex and that they will aim for implementing process mining in many small projects (as they want to focus on techniques that require heavy use of domain knowledge –analysis of process data, durations and resource usage). Lastly, *EC* raises the concern that the current IT infrastructure (networking and computational power– more sensors produce more data requires more analysis capabilities) and human resources are not sufficient. Currently, process mining has been successfully introduced in one department.

6   Discussion and Implications for Research and Practice

Based on the results of the focus group interviews as summarized in Sect. 5, we deduce the following findings. The findings can be categorized as follows:

- Requirements before process mining can be introduced.
- Expected results when introducing process mining.
- Actual improvements after process mining has been introduced.

The remainder of this section discusses these three categories in detail and answers the research questions set out in Sect. 1.

6.1   Requirements

The settings in both companies CDP and E distinguish themselves by the granularity of the logged tasks. The first focus group from CDP does not use any of the three fields of process mining at the moment, but is already working with the support of a process execution engine, which enables the creation of an event stream and the automatic documentation of each task in a process. In company E, by contrast, not every task is logged, but only certain checkpoints, i.e., a finished piece. This leads to inaccurate process execution logs, since it is not clear, how and when the different tasks have been executed. Company E is using a process execution engine only in a sub-department. In other departments of company E different approaches have been tried, i.e., a manually created handbook of business processes for new employees. Unfortunately, this handbook is rarely used and instead knowledge is transferred from senior employees to newer ones. This leads to undocumented steps, which renders retrieving fine granular results and therefore process mining on a more granular basis impossible.

The focus group interviews showed, that even though companies are putting effort in creating process models through intensive interviews with employees and are making these process models available, the documentation of tasks is often too time consuming. However, the introduction of process mining supported by a process execution engine showed, that employees are willing to log their tasks if enough support is available, like a monitor showing the current active task and an automated documentation. The supervising operatives and managers are benefiting from the generated reports about conformance of a process instance and general behavior through process mining.

6.2   Expected Results

Most of the participants share similar experiences concerning the process of creating process models i.e., through interviews, since employees often follow a process from tacit knowledge. Since it is important to be as transparent as possible for potential business partners as per the statements of the focus group participants, a better representation of the actual processes is desired. Another important factor concerns correct process execution as this increases transparency. The participants also emphasize the moment of time when a deviating process instance is detected. While the evaluation of a whole department can be calculated every few months, a process instance with a deviating conformance should be detected as early as possible. To check the conformance during execution, an event stream is required to apply process mining.

For the implementation, the participants raised concerns about the introduction of process mining in their departments. Employees could feel observed, since their daily routine could be analyzed from the process execution logs. Another problem is, that employees sometimes tend to gather knowledge and not share it, making themselves harder to be replaced. The participants agreed, that the employees should be involved in the process of introducing process mining. It was also mentioned that as soon as the benefits of the approach became very clear, acceptance was very high.

In addition, it was mentioned, that the IT infrastructure could be an issue for implementing process mining.

The findings discussed above summarize the expected benefits and drawbacks of process mining in companies and hence contribute to answer **RQ1**.

6.3 Improvements

The introduction of process mining in a department of company **E** results in the following improvements. The process of obliging two employees to perform several tasks, where one of them has to have a specific role, can be accurately logged with the support of a process execution engine. Conformance checking, taking the data perspective into account, can reveal deviations, if the criteria of the correct amount or the correct roles is not fulfilled. Another important aspect is the temporal perspective. Conformance checking allows to detect temporal deviations in the process, e.g., an extremely short duration for putting the protective gear on, leading to the assumption that the gear is not worn correctly.

When a deviation is detected at runtime, it is possible to provide the company with the information for which process instance the deviation occurred. With this information, it can be tried to explain the reason for this deviation through the information stored for a process instance by the process mining framework.

Based on the findings, **RQ2** concerning the actual benefits and drawbacks of process mining in SMMC can be answered. Creating automatic reports to detect undesired behavior in process instances and help to ensure the correct order of events is beneficial. Drawbacks such as the fear of surveillance can be avoided through outlining major benefits of process mining to shopfloor workers, including the automatic documentation of tasks.

RQ3 refers to how the implementation of process mining in SMMC can be designed. As pointed out in Sect. 5, a process model is often already available in the production, generated from the knowledge of the shopfloor workers and process supervisors. Based on the interviews, we conclude that correct process execution and its documentation are of utmost importance. This can be achieved by implementing and executing the existing process model through a process execution engine. The engine is used to orchestrate active process instances of process models and manages the documentation of tasks, i.e., timestamps of start and end events. To give shopfloor workers a better visualization of the process and the currently active task in a process instance, a screen can be used to provide additional information. Utilities, such as a hand scanner or a foot pedal, can be used to automatically complete the current task in a process instance which leads to the next task shown to the worker. A possible setup is the Electroplating process (cf. Sect. 4.1). To increase the knowledge of currently active process instances, wearable information systems can be connected to the process mining framework as well and display process instances not matching the expected behavior [18].

6.4   Discussion

When looking at the significance of the results, three groups can be established.

Not Surprising: Digitalization gaps exist and SMMC struggle to close them. All participants agree that explicit process orchestration from the business level to the shop-floor level will improve the quality of available event logs, and is a first step towards online process mining and process enhancement. It became clear that SMMC suffer from a lack of IT resources. However, they are aware that process mining and data analysis in general will help them with digitalization (i.e., new ways of interacting with their customers).

Expected, But Disappointing: Process discovery is not considered important. All participants agreed that process elicitation through explicit modeling leads to better results and understandability. This was not unexpected as SMMC often have flat hierarchies, hence involvement and knowledge of the processes is high. The participating companies (some of the participants also talked about previous employments) often utilize flexible manufacturing islands with unstructured manual labor instead of production lines. The effort for data collection there could very well be so high that focus group participants might be right.

Surprising: Shop-floor workers were expected to be critical of process mining supervising operatives and management alike. However, they were very easily convinced when demonstrating process mining results. Supervising operatives and management wish for the application of process mining on high-level processes, but can neither clearly express the expected results nor have a clear vision how to digitalize these processes. Conformance checking is well understood by the focus group participants. Mining of temporal deviations and performance indicators based on fine-grained sensor data are seen as an important short-term goal. Surprisingly, online process mining, i.e., making deviations visible and explainable at runtime, is considered more important than ex-post analysis.

6.5   Limitations and Threats to Validity

Focus group interviews bear certain threats to validity [10]. In particular, investigating expectations and experiences of process mining in SMMC is relatively complex. Hence, there is a threat of either made up answers, i.e., caused by insufficient experience of a participant or trying to avoid negative feedback by colleagues afterwards, or just trivial answers caused by too many participants. To minimize these threats, we opted for small focus groups, ensured a certain level of knowledge of processes in general, and developed the questioning route following the guidelines in [10]. Further limitations involve:

- *Transferability to Other Domains:* Manufacturing can be seen as "killer application". Hence it is promising to look at other domains such as medicine that also combine processes, physical world, and human work.
- *Generalizability:* SMMC struggle with specific problems, hence the generalizablity to bigger companies is questionable. Moreover, while a small focus group helps in getting meaningful results for complicated subjects, it can still

be argued that similar SMMC are not sharing the same experiences. More interviews with different SMMC could overcome this limitations.

Finally, the companies and participants of the focus group were all volunteers, that answered to an email to a list of companies that regularly participate in research projects. It is possible that (a) the results are not representative of SMMC, or (b) a John Henry effect (over-performance) [17] regarding process mining was observed.

7 Conclusion

This focus group study collected expectations on and experiences with process mining in SMMC, including two real-world process mining scenarios at one company's side. The main findings are:

Suitable Data Set Generation is a Main Challenge. The status quo in SMMC is that logging is part of the business logic and data-centric. Selected milestones in the production produce a data dump with a timestamp, while most process steps in the manufacturing domain just produce no events at all.

Transparency of Business Process Becomes Increasingly Important. Transparency is considered important for four key aspects: (a) legal protection against insurance claims, (b) protection against liability claims when dealing with bad parts, (c) reduction of erroneous parts before quality control, and (d) streamlining of processes when dealing with a huge number of product variants in combination with human resources.

Human Resources Should be Included into the Process. There is a high level of concern regarding transparency and human resources. Workers may feel observed and become reluctant to share their tacit knowledge. Successful communication and demonstration of the benefits of process mining, on the other hand led to high acceptance among workers.

Infrastructure Plays an Important Role for SMMC. The local IT infrastructure is a perceived bottleneck for the increasing data volume and velocity that comes with fine-grained logging of all steps involved manufacturing and production of goods.

Company E successfully introduced process mining in selected scenarios and regards the ability to detect deviations from the process structure, as well as temporal deviations at runtime as a major benefit. This actively helps to minimize the impact of errors, and allows for continuous process improvement to alleviate errors. The increase in transparency was expected and embraced by workers, as well as supervising operatives and management. Demonstrating the reduced documentation effort was the key to winning over workers.

For future work, process mining is to be introduced in company CDP. The solution will be implemented based on the findings of this study to meet the expectations of the company and avoid anticipated drawbacks.

References

1. Van der Aalst, W., Adriansyah, A., van Dongen, B.: Replaying history on process models for conformance checking and performance analysis. Data Mining Knowl. Discov. **2**(2), 182–192 (2012)
2. van der Aalst, W.M.P.: Process Mining: Discovery, Conformance and Enhancement of Business Processes. Springer, Heidelberg (2011). https://doi.org/10.1007/978-3-642-19345-3
3. Berti, A., van Zelst, S.J., van der Aalst, W.: Process mining for python (PM4PY): bridging the gap between process-and data science. arXiv preprint arXiv:1905.06169 (2019)
4. Burattin, A., Carmona, J.: A framework for online conformance checking. In: Teniente, E., Weidlich, M. (eds.) BPM 2017. LNBIP, vol. 308, pp. 165–177. Springer, Cham (2018). https://doi.org/10.1007/978-3-319-74030-0_12
5. Corallo, A., Lazoi, M., Striani, F.: Process mining and industrial applications: a systematic literature review. Knowl. Process Manage. **27**(3), 225–233 (2020)
6. Delbridge, R., Lowe, J., Oliver, N.: Shopfloor responsibilities under lean teamworking. Hum. Relat. **53**(11), 1459–1479 (2000)
7. Grisold, T., Mendling, J., Otto, M., vom Brocke, J.: Adoption, use and management of process mining in practice. Bus. Process Manage. J. **25**(6), 1291–1316 (2020)
8. Kerremans, M., Searle, S., Srivastava, T., Iijima, K.: Market guide for process mining (2020). www.gartner.com
9. Kregel, I., Stemann, D., Koch, J., Coners, A.: Process mining for six sigma: utilising digital traces. Comput. Ind. Eng. **153**, 107083 (2021). https://doi.org/10.1016/j.cie.2020.107083, https://www.sciencedirect.com/science/article/pii/S0360835220307531
10. Krueger, R.A.: Focus Groups: A Practical Guide for Applied Research. Sage Publications, Thousand Oaks (2014)
11. Leemans, S.J.J., Fahland, D., van der Aalst, W.M.P.: Discovering block-structured process models from event logs - a constructive approach. In: Colom, J.-M., Desel, J. (eds.) PETRI NETS 2013. LNCS, vol. 7927, pp. 311–329. Springer, Heidelberg (2013). https://doi.org/10.1007/978-3-642-38697-8_17
12. Leemans, S.J., Poppe, E., Wynn, M.T.: Directly follows-based process mining: exploration & a case study. In: Process Mining, pp. 25–32 (2019)
13. Lopes, I.F., Ferreira, D.R.: A survey of process mining competitions: the BPI challenges 2011–2018. In: Business Process Management Workshops, pp. 263–274 (2019)
14. Maggi, F.M., Burattin, A., Cimitile, M., Sperduti, A.: Online process discovery to detect concept drifts in LTL-based declarative process models. In: On the Move to Meaningful Internet Systems, pp. 94–111 (2013)
15. Mangler, J., Rinderle-Ma, S.: CPEE - cloud process execution engine. In: BPM Demos, p. 51 (2014)
16. Reinkemeyer, L.: Process Mining in Action - Principles, Use Cases and Outlook. Springer, Cham (2020)

17. Saretsky, G.: The OEO P.C. experiment and the John Henry effect. Phi Delta Kappan **53**, 579–581 (1972)
18. Schönig, S., Jablonski, S., Ermer, A., Aires, A.P.: Digital connected production: wearable manufacturing information systems. In: Debruyne, C., et al. (eds.) OTM 2017. LNCS, vol. 10697, pp. 56–65. Springer, Cham (2018). https://doi.org/10.1007/978-3-319-73805-5_6
19. Stertz, F., Mangler, J., Rinderle-Ma, S.: Data-driven improvement of online conformance checking. In: Enterprise Distributed Object Computing Conference, pp. 187–196 (2020)
20. van Dongen, B.F., de Medeiros, A.K.A., Verbeek, H.M.W., Weijters, A.J.M.M., van der Aalst, W.M.P.: The ProM framework: a new era in process mining tool support. In: Ciardo, G., Darondeau, P. (eds.) ICATPN 2005. LNCS, vol. 3536, pp. 444–454. Springer, Heidelberg (2005). https://doi.org/10.1007/11494744_25
21. Weijters, A., van Der Aalst, W.M., De Medeiros, A.A.: Process mining with the heuristics miner-algorithm. Technical report 166, TU Eindhoven (2006)
22. van Zelst, S.J., Bolt, A., Hassani, M., van Dongen, B.F., van der Aalst, W.M.: Online conformance checking: relating event streams to process models using prefix-alignments. Data Sci. Anal. **8**, 269–284 (2017)

Classifying and Detecting Task Executions and Routines in Processes Using Event Graphs

Eva L. Klijn$^{(\boxtimes)}$ ⓘ, Felix Mannhardt ⓘ, and Dirk Fahland ⓘ

Eindhoven University of Technology, Eindhoven, The Netherlands
{e.l.klijn,f.mannhardt,d.fahland}@tue.nl

Abstract. Business process management organizes work into several interrelated "units of work", fundamentally conceptualized as a task. The classical concept of a task as a single step executed by a single actor in a single case fails to capture more complex aspects of work that occur in real-life processes. For instance, actors working together or the processing of work in batches, where multiple actors and/or cases meet for a number of steps. Established process mining and modeling techniques lack concepts for dealing with these more complex manifestations of work. We leverage event graphs as a data structure to model behavior along the actor and the case perspective in an integrated model, revealing a variety of fundamentally different types of task executions. We contribute a novel taxonomy and interpretation of these task execution patterns as well as techniques for detecting these in event graphs, complementing recent research in identifying patterns of work and their changes in routine dynamics. Our evaluation on two real-life event logs shows that these non-classical task execution patterns not only exist, but make up for the larger share of events in a process and reveal changes in how actors do their work.

Keywords: Task execution patterns · Routines · Event graphs

1 Introduction

A central goal of Business Process Management (BPM) is organizing work into several interrelated "units of work" to achieve shared goals. The formal foundations of BPM, as used in process modeling and mining, conceptualize such a unit of work as a *task*. Tasks are planned, scheduled, distributed to suitable actors such that the overall work can be performed by a collaborating workforce. Most Process-aware Information Systems (PAIS) support this goal by assuming that work is performed in the context of a business process that is executed as a sequence of task executions called a *case*. Each task is executed by a specific actor and the BPM system is responsible that the correct tasks are performed in the correct order. Thereby the actual work happens outside the PAIS itself which only schedules tasks and checks completion [9].

© Springer Nature Switzerland AG 2021
A. Polyvyanyy et al. (Eds.): BPM Forum 2021, LNBIP 427, pp. 212–229, 2021.
https://doi.org/10.1007/978-3-030-85440-9_13

However, this concept of a task in process modeling and mining in BPM—a unit of work is a single step executed by a single actor in a single case—fails to capture many facets of work that occur in practice. In organizations research, a well-defined (atomic) step in a process is called an activity or *action* [2,20]. In contrast, a *task* is considered a slightly larger "unit of work" that has to be carried out to achieve an objective within the process, e.g., review CVs. Completing or *executing* a task often requires to perform multiple actions (e.g., download, open, take notes), not necessarily limited to a single case (e.g., all CVs received); these actions may be grouped differently depending on the actor(s) the task is assigned to.

This also has been acknowledged in the BPM field from several perspectives. Robotic Process Automation (RPA) uses *task mining* to identify how individual actors perform tasks by recording their desktop interactions revealing tasks spanning more than a single case, e.g., data entry from a spreadsheet to an information system [16]. Individual actors may batch actions in multiple cases, e.g., a manager reviewing and approving requests in different cases, which is still poorly supported by many PAIS [23]. Finally, actors often do not act independently from each other, multiple actors may perform work together even across multiple cases, e.g., the collaborative grading of student reports, and across multiple actions, e.g., delivering and installing a new washing machine. Despite this acknowledgment and many years of BPM research, there is no generally agreed definition of a task that captures such aspects of work in a process and that is compatible with the established process modeling and process mining concepts. In other words, the existing process mining and process modeling concepts are too simplistic.

In this paper, we investigate how to conceptualize task executions beyond the basic definition of an action performed by a single actor in isolated cases with the goal of capturing the various facets of tasks. Our approach combines event data analysis with conceptually modeling behavior in processes and actors as *two behavioral dimensions simultaneously* [10]: (1) the sequence of events recorded in a process case and (2) the sequence of events, across multiple process cases, in which an actor is involved. We use *event graphs* as introduced in [10] as data structure to model relations between events, cases, and actors as paths along cases and along actors over the same events; thereby escaping limitations of classical event logs (Sect. 3). In such a graph, a task execution emerges when a path along an actor meets a path along a case over one or more events.

We then perform a systematic, theoretical analysis of the types of task executions that can be expressed in an event graph depending on (1) how many paths along cases meet (2) how many paths along actors for (3) how many events (Sect. 4.1). From this theoretical analysis we derive a *taxonomy* of task execution types characterized by 5 different parameters (Sect. 4.2); the taxonomy describes 23 task execution types, several have not been described in literature before. We present methods for querying these task execution types in event graphs (Sect. 5) and evaluate the existence of these task execution types in the BPIC'17 and BPIC'14 event logs (Sect. 6). We specifically found that non-trivial task execution patterns over multiple steps, multiple cases, and even multiple actors frequently occur in two real-life event logs, as well as occurrences of several previously unknown patterns. We also observe changes in frequency of task execution patterns over time due to changes in the way actors do their work.

2   Related Work

Related research that also accounts for the more complex aspects of work beyond isolated cases has been conducted from several perspectives.

Process *modeling* literature studies actors performing work in terms of "resources" required for a task. Of the workflow resource patterns [24], only "Simultaneous Execution" and "Additional Resources" consider joint work by multiple actors. Only recently, actor behavior across multiple cases came into focus under *batching* across individual cases [23] and *instance-spanning constraints* [12]. Current BPM systems poorly support these phenomena and existing notations (e.g., BPMN) require extensions [13,23] to support them; but actor behavior is never modeled explicitly. Synchronous proclets [11] allow modeling individual actor behavior across individual cases in a network of Petri nets, each describing a process or an actor [6], that dynamically synchronize on single transition occurrences. The same synchronization principle has also been adopted for DCR graphs [4]. We contribute to this stream of modeling research by showing that actor-case interactions themselves form complex task execution patterns over multiple actions, cases, and actors, that should be supported in modeling.

In *process mining*, social network mining [27] analyzes actor interactions but excludes the control-flow perspective. Other approaches are mining of team composition and work assignment [25], resource skills, utilization, and productivity [22] and resource availability [17]; these works assume tasks to be single actions. Task executions by the same actor over multiple actions can be discovered as local process models [5]. Task mining analyzes behavior that may transcend multiple cases [16] by tapping into desktop interaction logs of actors. These works are limited to single actors in isolated cases due to the use of event logs. For analyzing instance spanning constraints [28], batch activities [18,19] and scheduled processes [26] process mining methods have been extended to consider inter-case relations; in these works actor behavior is described/modeled implicitly, whereas we analyze actor behavior explicitly.

Routines research [14,20,21] studies "work" in terms of a *narrative network* of actors interacting to achieve organizational goals. A narrative [20] is a *path* in the narrative network, i.e., a *"coherent, time-ordered sequence of actions or interactions [for] accomplishing an organizational task"* [14,21]. An action pattern that occurs repeatedly at an individual actor is called a *habit*; a recurrent action pattern involving multiple actors is called a *routine* [2]. Habits and routines capture how actors accomplish their tasks. A central question in routine dynamics research is to identify such patterns in the narrative network and how they change [14] and is approached through field studies.

We complement prior work by transforming an event log into an event graph which can be understood as data-based representation of a narrative network.

We use graph theory to detect patterns of task executions (i.e., habits and routines) and their changes over time. Our taxonomy of task executions extends and generalizes existing notions of tasks in BPM and process mining that are tailored towards either isolate cases, e.g., [5], or towards specific aspects of work behavior across cases, e.g., [12,13,16,18,19,23,26,28].

3   Preliminaries

We first discuss relevant concepts of the conventional, single-dimensional representation of event data. We then show how these concepts can be translated to a multi-dimensional representation using a general data model based on labeled property graphs [10], which we use as a foundation for our work.

Single-Dimensional Representation of Event Data. A PAIS can record an action execution as an *event* in an event log. Each event records at least the *action* that occurred, the *time* of occurrence, and an *entity identifier* indicating on which entity or *case* the action occurred. Often, the actor executing the action is recorded as *resource*. Table 1 shows an example event log containing 10 events occurring on the same day.

Process mining [1] analyzes event data by grouping events w.r.t. a chosen *case identifier* attribute, e.g., a loan application document or a patient in a hospital. Ordering all events of a case by time yields the *trace* as a sequence of events. Grouping the events in Table 1 by *Case* yields the traces $\langle e1, e2, e3, e4, e5 \rangle$ and $\langle e6, e7, e8, e9, e10 \rangle$. A set of such traces is a traditional *single-dimensional* event log along the case perspective [10].

Classically the *Resource* attribute in Table 1 is considered as event attribute describing the event further. However, the resource (the actor) is an entity in its own right and we can also study the sequence of events along each resource, defining a second behavioral dimension in the data. Choosing *Resource* as case

Table 1. Event table example

Event	Action	Time	Case	Resource
e1	A	12:02	3	1
e2	B	12:04	3	1
e3	E	14:38	3	5
e4	F	14:41	3	5
e5	C	16:21	3	29
e6	A	12:08	4	1
e7	B	12:09	4	1
e8	D	12:15	4	1
e9	E	14:54	4	5
e10	F	14:59	4	5

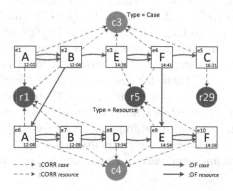

Fig. 1. Event graph containing the events and entities from Table 1

identifier yields a second event log with traces $\langle e1, e2, e6, e7, e8 \rangle$ (Resource 1), $\langle e3, e4, e9, e10 \rangle$ (R. 5), and $\langle e5 \rangle$ (R. 29).

Each event in Table 1 is related to 2 entity identifiers: a case identifier and resource identifier. Generally, an event can have multiple case identifiers and/or multiple resource identifiers [10]. The relation of events to multiple entities results in different behavioral dimensions between events that cannot be adequately represented or analyzed using a single-dimensional event log representation.

Multi-dimensional Representation of Event Data. We use a *labeled property graph* (LPG) to represent multiple behavioral dimensions together over a set of events.

Graph databases use LPGs [3, Chapter 2] for modeling various entities (as nodes) and various relationship (as edges) between them. An *event graph* [10] is a specific LPG, which can be obtained from an event table: each event and each entity (i.e., cases and resources) is represented by a node with label *Event* or *Entity*. Event and entity nodes are connected through directed binary *relationships*: a *CORR* relationship from e to n defines that event e is *correlated* to entity n. A *DF* relationship from e to e' defines that event e' *directly follows* e from the perspective of a specific entity n to which e and e' are correlated (i.e., e occurs before e' and there is no other event between them). Each node and relationship can hold a number of key-value pairs referred to as *properties*, e.g., whether an entity has *Type = Case* or *Type = Resource*. As short-hand notation we write $(e, e')^x$ for a *DF*-relationship in G from e to e' of type $x \in \{c, r\}$ (i.e., case or resource). See [10,15] for formal details.

The example in Fig. 1 shows the event graph derived from Table 1: each square (white) node is an event node; each circle is an entity node of the corresponding type (blue for *Case*, red for *Resource*). *CORR* relationships are shown as dashed edges, e.g., $e1, e2, e3, e4, e5$ are correlated to case $c3$ and $e1, e2, e6, e7, e8$ are correlated to resource $r1$. *DF* relationships are shown as solid edges. The DF-relationships between the events correlated to the same entity form a *DF-path* for that entity; the graph in Fig. 1 defines 2 DF-paths for case entities, e.g., $\sigma_{c3} = \langle (e1, e2)^c, (e2, e3)^c, (e3, e4)^c, (e4, e5)^c \rangle$ and 3 DF-paths for resource entities, e.g., $\sigma_{r1} = \langle (e1, e2)^r, (e2, e6)^r, (e6, e7)^r, (e7, e8)^r \rangle$.

In the graph in Fig. 1, we observe which resource executed which action in which case, e.g., $r1$ performed A in $c3$ (at event $e1$). However, we can also see that DF-paths for case and resource "flow in parallel" over multiple actions, e.g., σ_{c3} and σ_{r1} both contain $(e1, e2)^x$ meaning $r1$ performed A and B consecutively in $c3$ (events $e1$ and $e2$) forming a larger unit of work captured in Fig. 1 as the *connected subgraph* of events $\{e_1, e_2\}$ and the two DF-relationships between them. We can observe more such subgraphs of consecutive events along the same resource and case in Fig. 1, i.e., larger units of work.

4 Task Execution Patterns

We observed in Sect. 3 that event graphs reveal "units of work" that are not just individual events but are *connected subgraphs* where resources and case meet along several subsequent events. In this section, we conceptualize these connected subgraphs as *task executions* and explore in which forms they can manifest. We explain our approach in Sect. 4.1 and present a novel taxonomy of task execution patterns and their interpretation in Sect. 4.2. We thereby make use of standard graph theory concepts; see [15] for formal definitions.

4.1 Exploring Event Graphs for Forms of Task Executions

In the event graph in Fig. 1, we initially observe two ways in which a task execution manifests. (1) A resource follows a case over multiple events, e.g., $e6, e7, e8$; these event nodes form a subgraph induced by one DF-path σ_c of a case entity and one DF-path σ_r of a resource entity as follows: σ_c and σ_r *enter* the subgraph together (e.g., at $e6$) and *leave* the subgraph together (e.g., at $e8$) and are both *continuous* in this subgraph (all events of the DF-path are within the graph). (2) We also observe an execution of a classical task in the event graph in Fig. 1 consisting of only a single event, e.g., $e5$; the path of the resource and the path of the case synchronize for this step only, i.e., the subgraph is a single node.

We explored whether other subgraphs can be characterized by searching for different configurations of the following concepts in the subgraph: DF-path of a resource, DF-path of a case and their synchronization. We identified the following parameters and values:

1. The subgraphs in Fig. 1 contain at most *one* case DF-path. Are there (meaningful) execution patterns which have *multiple* case DF-paths?
2. If multiple case DF-paths are in the subgraph: are the case DF-paths disjoint (i.e., each event belongs to exactly one case) or can case DF-paths synchronize (i.e., have a shared event)?
3. The subgraphs in Fig. 1 contain at most *one* resource DF-path. Are there (meaningful) execution patterns which have *multiple* resource DF-paths?
4. If multiple resource DF-paths are in the subgraph: are the resource DF-paths disjoint (i.e., each event belongs to exactly one resource) or can resource DF-paths synchronize (i.e., have a shared event)?
5. In Fig. 1, all DF-paths are continuously in the subgraph (i.e., they only enter once and leave once). Are there (meaningful) execution patterns where a DF-path also temporarily leaves the subgraph and re-enters later?

4.2 Taxonomy of Task Execution Patterns

The above questions define a parameter space that allows for a set of different subgraph configurations that can be systematically described within the bounds of this space. We explored this parameter space by modeling abstract *task execution patterns* as subgraphs of event nodes of an event graph. We explain the patterns found, introduce a taxonomy to structure them systematically, and evaluate whether each pattern has real-world interpretation and whether it was already discussed in literature.

We considered subgraphs that emerge from multiple DF-paths synchronizing as some "unit of work". We identified the following necessary conditions for $n \geq 2$ DF-paths $\Sigma = \{\sigma_1, \ldots, \sigma_n\}$ to induce a subgraph G that describes a task execution: (**T1**) any two event nodes in G are connected via at least one DF-path $\sigma \in \Sigma$, (**T2**) for each event node e in G exists a case DF-path $\sigma_c \in \Sigma$ and a resource DF-path $\sigma_r \in \Sigma$ that contain e (i.e., G is traversed by at least one case and one resource DF-path), (**T3**) there is at least one DF-path $\sigma_1 \in \Sigma$ that is *continuously* in G (enters G once and leaves G once). We identified two stricter necessary conditions of task executions defining a spectrum:

- *Graph-structure based task execution*: in the strictest form of task executions the subgraph G is induced by $\Sigma = \{\sigma_1, \ldots, \sigma_n\}$ and satisfies (T1)–(T3) and additionally (**T2'**): each event node $e \in G$ is in *each* DF-path $\sigma \in \Sigma$ (i.e., all paths always synchronize in all events in G but some paths may leave in between). As a consequence, all paths *converge* at the first event of the continuous DF-path σ_1 in G and *diverge* at the last event of σ_1 in G, see (T3). All subgraphs in Fig. 2 have this property.
- *Domain-knowledge based task execution*: the paths in G do not converge and diverge at the same start and end events of G, yet are coherent. In addition to (T1)–(T3) the following condition holds: (**T3'**) all DF-paths are continuously in G. All subgraphs in Fig. 3 have this property. T3' requires domain-knowledge to decide whether DF-paths Σ form a valid subgraph G describing a task execution.

Next, we differentiate different types of subgraphs further by the following 4 parameters over a subgraph G (i) the number of case DF-paths, (ii) the number of resource DF-paths, and (iii) how often they enter and leave, and (iv) how they synchronize in G. We start with graph-structure based tasks executions.

Taxonomy of Graph-Structure-Based Task Execution Patterns. Figure 2 shows the graph-structure-based task execution patterns arranged according to the parameters identified in Sect. 4.1.

The taxonomy categorizes the patterns on the x-axis based on them containing a single DF-path from a single case (SC) or multiple DF-paths from multiple cases (MC). The patterns are categorized along the y-axis based on them containing a single DF-path from a single resource (SR) or multiple DF-paths from multiple resources (MR). Our taxonomy thus has four major quadrants: (SR,SC), (SR,MC), (MR,SC), (MR,MC).

Next, subgraphs within each of these quadrants are arranged based on the configuration of the paths they contain. A path is (1) *single step* (s) if it only contains a single event node within the subgraph, (2) *continuous* (c) if the path contains > 1 event node and is continuously within the subgraph, i.e., it only enters and leaves once, and (3) *interrupted* (i) if it contains > 1 event node and

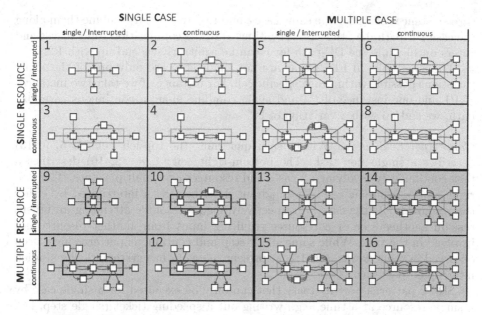

Fig. 2. Taxonomy of graph-structure-based task execution patterns

it leaves and enters the subgraph more than once. A single step path and an interrupted path are both *non-continuous*.

The set of resource DF-paths are configured separately from the set of case DF-paths. For each quadrant the subgraphs are arranged on the x-axis into columns for continuous and non-continuous case DF-paths and on the y-axis into rows for continuous and non-continuous resource DF-paths.

The bold letters in Fig. 2 indicate the short-hand notation we use in the following, e.g., MR_i, SC_c denotes pattern P10: Multiple Resource interrupted, Single Case continuous.

Structural Properties. A fundamental property of graph-structure-based patterns is that all entities (cases and resources) are involved in each step of the task execution.

A fundamental property of our taxonomy is that adding/removing resource or case DF-paths results in a corresponding pattern in another quadrant, e.g., adding more resource DF-paths to P3 returns P11 and adding both more resource and case DF-paths returns P15.

A second fundamental property of the taxonomy is that it distinguishes *elementary task execution patterns* that cannot be decomposed further into subgraphs fitting the parameter space (1, 4, 5, 8, 9, 12, 13, 16) and *non-elementary task execution patterns* that are compositions thereof (2, 3, 6, 7, 10, 11, 14, 15). By combining instances of elementary patterns along either a continuous resource DF-path or a continuous case DF-path, we end up with a non-elementary instance belonging to the same quadrant. For instance, if we take three instances of P1 for the same case c and resource r and combine them along the case DF-path, i.e., the case is continuous in the composition (only leaves and enters once) while the DF-path for r can be arbitrary, we end up with P2.

The subgraphs in Fig. 2 that are not single-step are only one of the many variations possible within each specific cell. For instance, if we take two instances of P1 and one instance of P4 and again combine along a continuous case DF-path, we end up with a variation of P2.

Conceptual Evaluation. Within each quadrant, the top-left cell (1, 5, 9, 13) describes a single-step task. The bottom-right cell (4, 8, 12, 16) describes a task continuously involving all cases and resources over multiple steps. The top-right and bottom-left cell of a quadrant describes tasks interrupted by either the resource(s) or the case(s), respectively, e.g., a resource attending an urgent task in another case or a resource requiring input from another resource not involved in the task. While some single step and continuous patterns have been observed in other works [5,6,18], at present, no work has systematically studied interrupted patterns.

SR,SC patterns portray tasks that can only be executed for a single case by a single resource at a time, e.g., writing out a speeding ticket (single step, i.e., P1), or finalizing a loan offer: ⟨call client about loan offer, create offer, send offer⟩ (multiple steps, i.e., P4). P2 describes an actor interrupting and returning to a larger unit of work in a case, e.g., compiling a report that is interrupted by other duties. P3 describes an actor continuously being concerned with the same case while other actors have to be involved as well, e.g., due checks based on a four-eyes principle. P1 has been extensively studied in traditional process analysis and P4 has been observed in [5].

SR,MC patterns portray tasks where a single resource handles *multiple cases together*, such as batch processing, e.g., lecturing a classroom of students (single step, i.e., P5) or analyzing a batch of blood samples, which involves transporting them to the lab, scanning them and analyzing them (multiple steps, i.e., P8). Only single step (P5) and multi-step batching (P8) have both been observed in [18].

Conversely, MR,SC patterns portray tasks where *multiple resources* work on a single case *together*. For instance in collaborative decision making, e.g., a master's defense (single step, i.e., P9), or due to practical or technical requirements, e.g., delivering, carrying, and installing a washing machine requires two people (multiple steps, i.e., P12). Only P9 has been observed in [6], where queues and conveyor belts synchronize as distinct resources for the same (single step) events.

Finally, MR,MC patterns portray tasks executed by multiple resources on multiple cases together. While theoretically possible, it is very unlikely multiple cases and resources synchronize that strongly in real-life processes especially over multiple steps. A very relaxed interpretation of such a task would be the co-chairing of a panel for a conference (single step, i.e., P13). We discuss more realistic manifestations of MR,MC task configurations when discussing domain-knowledge based patterns (shown in Fig. 3). At present, no work has systematically studied patterns involving both multiple cases and multiple resources.

Taxonomy of Domain-Knowledge-Based Task Execution Patterns. So far we discussed our taxonomy for the strictly synchronized graph-structure based patterns shown in Fig. 2. We now discuss our taxonomy for the domain-knowledge based patterns at the other end of the spectrum shown in Fig. 3. The domain-knowledge based task execution patterns allow that only some case/resource paths synchronize per event but require all paths to be uninterrupted; this yields "units of work" that are more distributed. While there is a considerable amount of other subgraphs that fit Fig. 3, we limit ourselves to discuss those that require only basic domain knowledge.

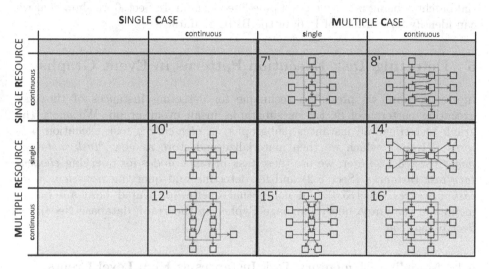

Fig. 3. Taxonomy of domain-knowledge-based task execution patterns

Structural Properties. We first observe that we can derive all the configurations in Fig. 3 by composing multiple of the same elementary pattern from Fig. 2. For instance, P7' and P10' are essentially multiple instances of P1 composed along the resource and case DF-path, respectively. P8' and P12' can be composed similarly using instances of P4. P14' can be composed of P5 instances along the case DF-path and P15' with P9 instances along the resource DF-path. In Fig. 3, P16' is composed of multiple instances of P1, both along the resource and case dimension. The pattern properties of this particular cell 16' allow for basically every combination of elementary patterns composed along both the resource and case dimension. In contrast to graph-structure-based non-elementary patterns, the conditions for composing the patterns in Fig. 3 require domain knowledge.

Conceptual evaluation. In Fig. 3, P7', P8', P15' portray different forms of sequential batching, i.e., the same step is executed for a sequence of cases one after the other, with a single resource (P7', SR_c, MC_s), with multiple resources

(P15', MR_c,MC_s) and with one resource executing multiple steps per case (P8', SR_c,MC_c). Sequential batching that involves a single resource (P7' and P8') has been observed in [18].

We also identify a subset of patterns in which multiple resources are separately involved, each performing a set of steps for a case after which it moves to the next resource for the next step(s) in a pipe-lined fashion (e.g., P10' and P12', $MR_{s,c},SC_c$), resembling a factory/production type of setting. Such a setting could also be realized for (simultaneous) batches of cases (P14', MR_s,MC_c). At present, no work has systematically studied these patterns.

P16' (MR_c,MC_c) is a combination of the former two types; it portrays sequential batching being performed in a pipe-lined fashion. In Sect. 6 we show that we can identify an instance of P16' in the BPIC'17 data.

5   Detecting Task Execution Patterns in Event Graphs

In this section, we present a technique for detecting instances of the task execution patterns of Sect. 4 as subgraphs in an event graph. We *query* the graph to retrieve all instances (subgraphs) of *elementary* task execution patterns (P1, P4), which we then materialize and store as new *"task instance"* nodes (Sect. 5.1). Later, we use these task instance nodes for querying *elementary task instances* (Sect. 5.2) and for detecting and querying *non-elementary task instances* (Sect. 5.3). All conceptual queries presented here are implemented in the graph query language Cypher on the graph database Neo4j; see Sect. 6 and [15].

5.1   Modeling Elementary Task Instances as High Level Events

We assume the data to be given in an event graph G (see Sect. 3). We describe how to detect in G subgraphs describing task instances (TIs) of elementary patterns P1 and P4 and how to materialize these as new nodes with label TI in the event graph. Finally, we lift the DF-edges from the $Event$ nodes in the task instance subgraph to the corresponding TI node. Figure 4 shows the result of constructing the TI nodes and all corresponding relationships for the event graph from Fig. 1.

We first search the graph for all pairs of events (e_i, e_{i+1}) that have both a case DF-edge $(e_i, e_{i+1})^c$ and a resource DF-edge $(e_i, e_{i+1})^r$ and create a new *"joint"* DF-edge $(e_i, e_{i+1})^j$. We then detect any task instance of elementary P4 as a maximal sequence of events $ti = \langle e_m, ..., e_n \rangle$ where for each $e_i, e_{i+1} \in ti$ there exists $(e_i, e_{i+1})^j$ and there exists no joint DF-edges $(e', e_m)^j$ or $(e_n, e')^j$. An instance of P1 is $ti = e$ without $(e', e)^j, (e, e')^j$. We materialize ti as a new node h_{ti} with label TI and a *contains* relationship from h_{ti} to each $e \in ti$. We treat h_{ti} as a "high-level" event and set properties $h_{ti}.time_{start} = e_m.time$ and $h_{ti}.time_{end} = e_n.time$ and correlate h_{ti} to each entity n to which $e_m, ..., e_n$ are correlated by adding $CORR$ relationships. Finally, we sort all TI nodes $h_1, ..., h_k$ correlated to the same entity n of type x by $time_{end}$ and introduce

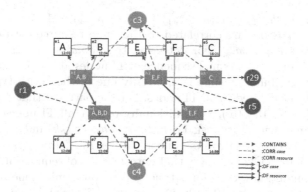

Fig. 4. Event graph containing the h_{ti} nodes constructed from the events from Fig. 1

corresponding DF-edges $(h_i, h_{i+1})^x$ of type x, which lifts DF-paths from events to task instances. See [15] for the Cypher query. For example, we detect in Fig. 1 $ti_1 = e_1, e_2$ and $ti_4 = e_6, e_7, e_8$ resulting in nodes $h1$ and $h4$ and $(h1, h4)^r$ in Fig. 4. Instances of the other elementary patterns (5, 8, 9, 12, 13, 16) can be found by checking for multiple $(e_i, e_{i+1})^c$ and/or $(e_i, e_{i+1})^r$ relationships over all events in ti.

The *elementary task execution* T described by an elementary task instance $ti = e_m, ..., e_n$ is its sequence of action names $T = e_m.action, ..., e_n.action$; we set $ti.task = T$ for easier querying.

5.2   Querying Elementary Task Instances

Having materialized all elementary task instances into TI nodes, we can query the graph of TI nodes and DF-relationships between them for insights. This allows for the following kinds of queries: (1a) Retrieve a *subset* of TIs based on a specific property, e.g., all TIs correlated to $r1$ ($h1$ and $h4$ in Fig. 4), or (1b) the subset of TIs of the most frequently executed tasks ($h2$ and $h5$ in Fig. 4). (2) Query for DF-paths between TI nodes, for instance the DF-path of TI nodes correlated to a specific case ($\langle h4, h5 \rangle$ for $c1$ in Fig. 4) or to a specific resource ($\langle h3 \rangle$ for $r29$ in Fig. 4). (3) Querying the DF-path of TIs of a specific resource on a specific day could give insight into habits [2] followed by this resource. Next, we query DF-paths between TI nodes along cases and resources to detect larger, non-elementary task execution patterns.

5.3   Querying Non-elementary Task Instances

We materialized elementary task instances as TI nodes connected through DF-edges in Sect. 5.1. We now show how to detect instances of non-elementary task execution patterns (NTI for short) as shown in Figs. 2 and 3 as compositions of TIs by querying for paths of TI nodes along DF-edges.

We detect any *interrupted* NTI (Fig. 2) involving resources $r_1, ..., r_l$ and cases $c_1, ..., c_m$ by querying for a maximal sequence of TI nodes $h_1, ..., h_k$ with

$(h_i, h_{i+1})^{r_1}, ..., (h_i, h_{i+1})^{r_l}$ or $(h_i, h_{i+1})^{c_1}, ..., (h_i, h_{i+1})^{c_m}, 1 \le i < k$ so that all underlying *Event* nodes are correlated to the same resource entities $n_{r_1}, ..., n_{r_l}$ and case entities $n_{c_1}, ..., n_{c_m}$. For detecting the *domain-knowledge-based* NTIs (Fig. 3), we also query a maximal sequence of TI nodes along either the resource-path or case-path, but this time require only one of the entity types (cases or resources) to be correlated to all TI nodes. For the patterns that describe batching behavior (7', 8', 15', 16'), we additionally require all TI nodes $h_1, ..., h_k$ to describe the same elementary task, i.e. $h_i.task = h_{i+1}.task$, and a maximum time difference Δt_{batch} between two subsequent TIs, i.e. $h_{i+1}.time_{start} - h_i.time_{end} < \Delta t_{batch}$; see [15] for a Cypher query that detects NTIs of sequential batching P8'. Using such domain knowledge for a time gap is commonly done in batch identification [18]. For patterns 10', 12', 14' and 16' additional domain-knowledge is required to determine if multiple TIs along the case-path form a task execution. Examples of NTIs of P2, P3, P7' and P8' are shown in Fig. 5.

6   Evaluation

We performed an exploratory analysis to investigate the occurrence of task execution patterns in two real-life event logs BPIC'14 [7] and BPIC'17 [8]. We realized the approach of Sect. 5 in Cypher queries invoked via Python scripts on the Graph DB Neo4j; available at https://github.com/multi-dimensional-process-mining/event-graph-task-pattern-detection. Creating all TI constructs (Sect. 5.1) took 44.57s for the BPIC'14 log and 68.81s for the BPIC'17 log on an Intel i7 CPU @ 2.2 GHz machine with 32 GB RAM.

We applied queries for detecting all patterns that did not require specific domain knowledge, i.e., all patterns except 10', 12', 14' and 16', in the event graphs of the BPIC'14 and BPIC'17 data. We found TIs of patterns 1, 2, 3, 4, 7' and 8'; TIs involving multiple resources and/or multiple cases per event simply do not occur in the data.

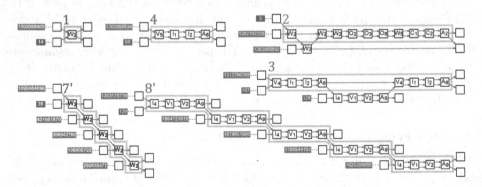

Fig. 5. Instances of task execution patterns 1, 2, 3, 4, 7' and 8' found in the BPIC'17 data

Table 2. General task execution pattern measurements for BPIC'17 and BPIC'14 with <30 m between all TIs in NTI or >30 m between at least one TI in NTI

log	pat.	# of TIs	# of events	% of events	length avg.	length st.dev	duration (min) avg.	duration (min) st.dev	# of TIs(1,4) in the NTIs avg.	# of TIs(1,4) in the NTIs st.dev
BPIC'17	1	11 995	11 995	1.4	1.0	0.0	0.0	0.0		
without	4	125 472	703 000	81.8	5.6	2.8	2.9	61.5		
User_1	$2^{>30}$	1 174	10 640	1.2	9.1	3.0	140.0	104.0	2.0	0.1
	$3^{>30}$	45	354	0.0	7.9	2.4	121.6	92.9	2.0	0.0
	$2^{<30}$	431	3 755	0.4	8.7	3.7	19.9	10.5	2.0	0.3
	$3^{<30}$	55	419	0.0	7.6	3.4	11.8	12.8	2.0	0.1
	$7'^{<30}$	269	1 297	0.2	4.8	1.1	23.8	16.1	4.8	1.1
	$8'^{<30}$	2 385	64 974	7.6	27.2	16.4	43.8	38.8	6.2	3.7
BPIC'17	*1*	*27*	*27*	*0.0*	*1.0*	*0.0*	*0.0*	*0.0*		
only	*4*	*33 706*	*144 683*	*16.8*	*4.3*	*1.6*	*0.2*	*0.4*		
User_1	$2^{<30}$	*1 788*	*10 687*	*1.2*	*6.0*	*0.3*	*0.8*	*0.8*	*2.0*	*0.1*
	$3^{<30}$	*255*	*1 530*	*0.2*	*6.0*	*0.0*	*0.7*	*0.5*	*2.0*	*0.0*
	$8'^{<30}$	*1 350*	*43 641*	*5.1*	*32.3*	*29.2*	*24.2*	*33.1*	*9.0*	*14.3*
BPIC'14	1	107 069	107 069	22.9	1.0	0.0	0.0	0.0		
	4	138 002	359 668	77.1	2.6	0.9	21.6	580.9		
	$2^{>30}$	16 489	80 585	17.3	4.9	2.0	116.1	102.5	2.4	0.8
	$3^{>30}$	1 631	7 364	1.6	4.5	2.0	103.3	87.5	2.1	0.3
	$2^{<30}$	16 963	70 965	15.2	4.2	1.5	10.7	14.9	2.2	0.4
	$3^{<30}$	11 085	40 029	8.6	3.6	1.4	6.5	18.0	2.0	0.1
	$7'^{<30}$	3 274	18 320	3.9	5.6	2.6	8.9	12.6	5.6	2.6
	$8'^{<30}$	228	1 988	0.4	8.7	1.5	10.4	12.4	4.3	0.7

Figure 5 shows for the BPIC'17 data for each detected pattern type a task instance annotated with resource and case identifiers. The P1 instance in Fig. 5 shows actor $r14$ executing a single step in a case before moving to a different case and the P4 instance shows $r95$ executing four actions in a case before moving to the next. The P2 instance shows $r3$ executing ten actions in a case with an interruption after the first step W_2, executing the same action W_2 also in another case before completing the task in the former case. The P3 instance shows $r107$ continuously working on a case, performing the same task execution ($\langle V_4, I_1, I_2, A_6 \rangle$) twice while $r128$ performs other actions in between. The P7' and P8' instances show $r35$ and $r126$ performing the same actions W_2 and $\langle I_4, V_1, V_2, A_9 \rangle$, respectively, for the same five cases in a sequential batch. We observe a min/avg/max time difference of 0/12/613 min and 0/4.8/512 min between any two subsequent steps in a batch for BPIC'17 and BPIC'14, respectively.

Table 2 shows the occurrence and other statistics of patterns 1, 2, 3, 4, 7' and 8' in the BPIC'14 and BPIC'17 data. We observe that P4 (multiple actions by same actor) makes up for the largest share of events in both logs (77.1% and 98.6% for BPIC'14 and BPIC'17, respectively) and has an average duration of 21.6 and 2.9 min and an average waiting time of 16.5 and 22.6 min between every pair of successive P4 instances for BPIC'14 and BPIC'17, respectively. It is therefore likely that these instances are composed of a single task execution as opposed to multiple tasks executions, rejecting the general assumption that a task execution is a single step executed by a single actor in a single case. We see P3 (actors interrupt a task execution and switch to another case) more often in BPIC'14 (1.6% + 8.6%) than in BPIC'17 (0.2%), showing that actors work differently in different processes. We observe that almost half of the interruptions P2 in BPIC'14 last more than 30 min, indicating that actors often switch context for long periods at a time. Task executions interrupted by waiting for another actor (P3) make up 10.2% of the BPIC'14 data, with a minor part lasting longer than 30 min, indicating either very long breaks or tasks in another process context not recorded in the data. Of these P3 interruptions, 60% lasted less than 10 s. TIs of P2 and P3 contain on average 2 other elementary TIs of P1 or P4 (last column). Executions of batch patterns P7' and P8' comprise 0.2+7.6% of the BPIC'17 data; although multi-step batches (P8') have > 5 times as many steps as single-step batches (P7') they only take twice as long in duration; indicating large deviations in executions of batching tasks in the BPIC'17 data. We observe a mean duration of 21.6 m for analyzing problems in IT components (BPIC'14) and 2.9 m for handling loan applications (BPIC'17) for elementary TIs, confirming our intuition that a task execution is short.

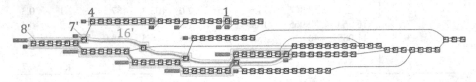

Fig. 6. Event graph of loan applications 1111458873, 1372864243, 206394826, 1877008365 and 1992048266 in BPIC'17 revealing five different task execution patterns

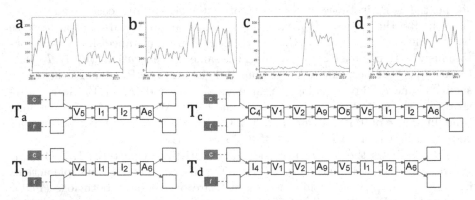

Fig. 7. Trends and subgraphs of four elem. task executions T in BPIC'17 showing concept drift

To investigate the manifestation of different task execution patterns on a case level, we visualized the events of five process executions in Fig. 6, revealing instances of five different task execution patterns P1, P4, P7', P8', and notably the most complex P16'. In Fig. 6, we observe six instances of P1 (one separately and five as part of P7'). All other task instances are of type P4, meaning that most actors perform tasks over multiple steps in the same case before handing the case over to the next actor. Existing process discovery techniques lack the resource perspective necessary to actually structure a trace into a sequence of P4 (and P1) instances, required to reveal these handovers of work. We observe $r1$ executing $\langle A_4, A_8, H_1, H_3, W_1, A_3 \rangle$ in a batch for five cases in row (P8') and $r19$ executes W_2 for the same fives cases in a batch (P7') directly afterwards. The instances of P8' and P7' together form an instance of P16' along the cases. While domain knowledge is required to verify whether this instance of P16' is intentional, we show that structured task executions involving multiple resources and cases exist in the data. This particular type of structured collaboration over multiple steps suggests a routine; confirming this requires further investigation.

We finally explored whether we find evidence for task executions changing over time, as stipulated in [14]. We queried the frequency of all task executions in BPIC'17 over time; Fig. 7 shows 4 selected task executions T_a–T_d and their frequency. T_a changes into T_b in July 2016 by changing only the first action from V_5 (lifecycle complete) to V_4 (lifecycle abort), suggesting a minor change in directive but not a change in the way people work. We see similar lifecycle changes in other task executions of the BPIC'17 data (not shown here). Around the same time, T_c and T_d emerge, which both contain T_a at the end suggesting that also the way people worked changed. In total we found 6 more task executions with this characteristic that also show this change.

7 Conclusion

In this paper, we considered event data along both the case and actor dimension. Doing this in event graphs revealed different ways in which non-trivial tasks manifest as patterns in the data and uncovered dynamics that have not been described before in established process mining and modeling; these range from interruptions and batching to the more complex production-type settings.

This lays the foundation for a fundamentally different way of conceptualizing processes as the interplay of cases and actors engaging in recurrent patterns of work, i.e., routines and habits as studied in routines research [2]. We found evidence in existing real-life event logs that such patterns make up the larger share of events. We believe the taxonomy of task execution patterns aids in task mining and many other process analysis problems where actor and case perspectives meet. For example, the relation between certain actor behavior and process performance or process outcomes, the adherence to queuing policies [26] as well as questions related to the study of complete systems of processes, resources and queues together [6].

Our approach is limited in that our taxonomy does not cover the entire spectrum of possible task patterns; we currently do not account for graph-structure-based patterns with a less strict synchronization of paths, while real-life manifestations thereof do exist. This includes other possible patterns or aspects that may have been overlooked. Some patterns of the taxonomy involving multiple actors and cases were not found in the data as such data was not available. However, such patterns do exist, e.g., delivering and installing a washing machine by two actors does happen. A next step is finding and exploring other data for the existence of these patterns. Important to note is that our work does not identify a task itself but only the patterns of actions used to achieve a task. Finding out what these patterns mean and what real-life tasks they portray is future work.

References

1. van der Aalst, W.M.P.: Process Mining: Data Science in Action. Springer, Heidelberg (2016). https://doi.org/10.1007/978-3-662-49851-4_1
2. Becker, M.C.: Organizational routines: a review of the literature. Ind. Corp. Change **13**(4), 643–678 (2004)
3. Bonifati, A., Fletcher, G.H.L., Voigt, H., Yakovets, N.: Querying Graphs, Synthesis Lectures on Data Management. Morgan & Claypool Publishers, San Rafael (2018)
4. Debois, S., López, H.A., Slaats, T., Andaloussi, A.A., Hildebrandt, T.T.: Chain of events: modular process models for the law. In: Dongol, B., Troubitsyna, E. (eds.) IFM 2020. LNCS, vol. 12546, pp. 368–386. Springer, Cham (2020). https://doi.org/10.1007/978-3-030-63461-2_20
5. Delcoucq, L., Lecron, F., Fortemps, P., van der Aalst, W.M.P.: Resource-centric process mining: clustering using local process models. In: SAC, pp. 45–52. ACM (2020)
6. Denisov, V., Fahland, D., van der Aalst, W.M.P.: Repairing event logs with missing events to support performance analysis of systems with shared resources. In: Janicki, R., Sidorova, N., Chatain, T. (eds.) PETRI NETS 2020. LNCS, vol. 12152, pp. 239–259. Springer, Cham (2020). https://doi.org/10.1007/978-3-030-51831-8_12
7. van Dongen, B.F.: BPI Challenge 2014. Dataset (2014). https://doi.org/10.4121/uuid:c3e5d162-0cfd-4bb0-bd82-af5268819c35
8. van Dongen, B.F.: BPI Challenge 2017. Dataset (2017). https://doi.org/10.4121/12705737.v2
9. Dumas, M., La Rosa, M., Mendling, J., Reijers, H.A.: Process monitoring. In: Fundamentals of Business Process Management, pp. 413–473. Springer, Heidelberg (2018). https://doi.org/10.1007/978-3-662-56509-4_11
10. Esser, S., Fahland, D.: Multi-dimensional event data in graph databases. J. Data Semant. **10**, 109–141 (2021)
11. Fahland, D.: Describing behavior of processes with many-to-many interactions. In: Donatelli, S., Haar, S. (eds.) PETRI NETS 2019. LNCS, vol. 11522, pp. 3–24. Springer, Cham (2019). https://doi.org/10.1007/978-3-030-21571-2_1
12. Fdhila, W., Gall, M., Rinderle-Ma, S., Mangler, J., Indiono, C.: Classification and formalization of instance-spanning constraints in process-driven applications. In: La Rosa, M., Loos, P., Pastor, O. (eds.) BPM 2016. LNCS, vol. 9850, pp. 348–364. Springer, Cham (2016). https://doi.org/10.1007/978-3-319-45348-4_20

13. Gall, M., Rinderle-Ma, S.: Visual modeling of instance-spanning constraints in process-aware information systems. In: Dubois, E., Pohl, K. (eds.) CAiSE 2017. LNCS, vol. 10253, pp. 597–611. Springer, Cham (2017). https://doi.org/10.1007/978-3-319-59536-8_37
14. Goh, K., Pentland, B.: From actions to paths to patterning: toward a dynamic theory of patterning in routines. Acad. Manage. J. **62**, 1901–1929 (2019)
15. Klijn, E.L., Mannhardt, F., Fahland, D.: Classifying and detecting task executions and routines in processes using event graphs. Extended version of conference article, Zenodo (2021). https://doi.org/10.5281/zenodo.5091611
16. Leno, V., Polyvyanyy, A., Dumas, M., La Rosa, M., Maggi, F.M.: Robotic process mining: vision and challenges. BISE **63**(3), 301–314 (2020)
17. Martin, N., Depaire, B., Caris, A., Schepers, D.: Retrieving the resource availability calendars of a process from an event log. Inf. Syst. **88**, 101463 (2020)
18. Martin, N., Pufahl, L., Mannhardt, F.: Detection of batch activities from event logs. Inf. Syst. **95**, 101642 (2021)
19. Martin, N., Swennen, M., Depaire, B., Jans, M., Caris, A., Vanhoof, K.: Retrieving batch organisation of work insights from event logs. Decis. Support Syst. **100**, 119–128 (2017)
20. Pentland, B., Feldman, M.: Narrative networks: patterns of technology and organization. Organ. Sci. **18**, 781–795 (2007)
21. Pentland, B., Feldman, M., Becker, M., Liu, P.: Dynamics of organizational routines: a generative model. J. Manage. Stud. **49**, 1484–1508 (2012)
22. Pika, A., Leyer, M., Wynn, M.T., Fidge, C.J., ter Hofstede, A.H.M., van der Aalst, W.M.P.: Mining resource profiles from event logs. ACM Trans. Manag. Inf. Syst. **8**(1), 1–30 (2017)
23. Pufahl, L., Weske, M.: Batch activity: enhancing business process modeling and enactment with batch processing. Computing **101**(12), 1909–1933 (2019)
24. Russell, N., van der Aalst, W.M.P., ter Hofstede, A.H.M., Edmond, D.: Workflow resource patterns: identification, representation and tool support. In: Pastor, O., Falcão e Cunha, J. (eds.) CAiSE 2005. LNCS, vol. 3520, pp. 216–232. Springer, Heidelberg (2005). https://doi.org/10.1007/11431855_16
25. Schönig, S., Cabanillas, C., Ciccio, C.D., Jablonski, S., Mendling, J.: Mining resource assignments and teamwork compositions from process logs. Softwaretechnik-Trends **36**(4), 1–6 (2016)
26. Senderovich, A., et al.: Data-driven performance analysis of scheduled processes. In: Motahari-Nezhad, H.R., Recker, J., Weidlich, M. (eds.) BPM 2015. LNCS, vol. 9253, pp. 35–52. Springer, Cham (2015). https://doi.org/10.1007/978-3-319-23063-4_3
27. Song, M., van der Aalst, W.M.P.: Towards comprehensive support for organizational mining. Decis. Support Syst. **46**(1), 300–317 (2008)
28. Winter, K., Stertz, F., Rinderle-Ma, S.: Discovering instance and process spanning constraints from process execution logs. Inf. Syst. **89**, 101484 (2020)

Looking Beyond Activity Labels: Mining Context-Aware Resource Profiles Using Activity Instance Archetypes

Gerhardus van Hulzen[1][✉][ID], Niels Martin[1,2][ID], and Benoît Depaire[1][ID]

[1] Hasselt University, Research Group Business Informatics, 3500 Hasselt, Belgium
{gerard.vanhulzen,niels.martin,benoit.depaire}@uhasselt.be
[2] Research Foundation Flanders (FWO), 1000 Brussels, Belgium

Abstract. Efficient resource management is a critical success factor for all businesses. Correct insights into actual *resource profiles*, i.e. groups of resources performing similar activity instances, is important for successful knowledge and (human) resource management. To this end, organisational mining, a subfield of Process Mining, focuses on techniques to extract such resource profiles from event logs. However, existing techniques ignore contextual factors that impact how and by whom an activity is performed. This paper introduces the novel method *ResProMin* to discover *context-aware resource profiles* from event logs. In contrast to the state-of-the-art, this method builds upon the notion of activity instance archetypes, which incorporates the activity instance's context. An evaluation of the method on real-life event logs demonstrates its feasibility and potential to uncover valuable business insights.

Keywords: Process mining · Organisational mining · Resource profiles · Context-aware process mining

1 Introduction

Efficient resource management is a key success factors for all businesses. A comprehensive understanding of the complex relation between resources and activities enables efficient resource allocation and potential cost reductions [5,15]. To this end, process owners first need an objective insight into the *context-aware resource profiles*, i.e. *who* does *what* in *which context*?

Organisational mining – a subfield of Process Mining – focuses on discovering organisational structures and social networks within organisations from event logs [17] and addresses this need. Several research efforts focused on discovering resource profiles from event logs [1,2,9,17,20]. However, existing algorithms ignore context, i.e. the circumstances in which the activity was executed, and rely solely on activity labels to mine resource profiles. In real-life settings, this limiting assumption can hide important nuances. For instance, two nurses can perform the same set of activities, but the patient's health condition might dictate the preference of one nurse over the other. While both nurses are equal

A. Polyvyanyy et al. (Eds.): BPM Forum 2021, LNBIP 427, pp. 230–245, 2021.
https://doi.org/10.1007/978-3-030-85440-9_14

based on activity labels, the context reveals that both nurses have a different profile. Consequently, there is a need for mining context-aware resource profiles from an event log.

This paper introduces the method *ResProMin* to generate context-aware resource profiles from event logs. Firstly, the method discovers *activity instance archetypes* reflecting the activity instance's context, i.e. the circumstances under which the activity instance was executed, such as case attributes and variables capturing the system state. Secondly, it assigns resources to these activity instance archetypes in a probabilistic manner, from which it discovers context-aware resource profiles. Not only do these profiles reveal *who* does *what* in *which context*, but it also allows the distinction between specialists and generalists.

The contribution of this work is twofold:

- The design of a novel method for discovering context-aware resource profiles is presented and discussed.
- A demonstration of the method on real-life datasets is presented to evaluate the method's feasibility and the ability to uncover valuable business insights.

An overview of the related work on this topic is provided in Sect. 2. Section 3 introduces the design of the ResProMin method. Next, the feasibility and value of ResProMin are evaluated in Sect. 4. Finally, the conclusion and opportunities for future research are discussed in Sect. 5.

2   Related Work

While the field of Process Mining traditionally focused on discovering the control-flow of processes from event logs, the sub-field *organisational mining* is receiving more and more attention [20]. Song and van der Aalst [17] were among the first to explore resource-related topics within a Process Mining context. They focused on discovering organisational structures and social networks from event logs leveraging task-based metrics based on joint activities [17]. These ideas are still used today, for instance, by Camargo *et al.* [4] to discover resource groups that perform similar tasks in their tool *Simod*.

Various resource-related topics have been investigated in Process Mining literature. To describe resource behaviour, Pika *et al.* [14] provide a framework to extract metrics on skills, productivity, utilisation, and collaboration patterns from event logs. Similarly, Nakatumba and van der Aalst [13] describe resource behaviour but specifically focus on the effect of workload on resource performance. Other researchers focused on rule mining to assign resources to tasks. Cabanillas *et al.* [3] developed *RALph Miner*, which is a tool to discover graphical resource-aware process models in which various task assignment rules are incorporated. Schönig *et al.* [16] also focused on finding assignment rules, but from a team perspective.

The most closely related research stream focuses on the discovery of groups of similar resources. In this respect, Jin *et al.* [9] propose an approach to mine resource roles, which are groups of resources that have performed the same tasks in similar volumes. This creates an abstraction layer between the individual resources and activities. A similar approach is proposed by Burattin et al. [2], who look at roles from the perspective of the handover of activities. However, they assume that a specific activity cannot belong to multiple groups at the same time. This assumption does often not hold in reality, where employees who possess several skills are not necessarily bound to one group [20].

To the best of our knowledge, there have been only two research efforts on detecting groups of resources that allow such overlapping group membership. Firstly, Appice [1] analysed the progress of communities over time in dynamic social networks while allowing communities to overlap. These communities represent a company's organisational units, and each resource has a certain degree to which it belongs to a particular unit. The second related research effort was conducted by Yang et al. [20]. They propose a Model-based Overlapping Clustering (MOC) model. The output of the MOC model is a boolean-valued membership vector, which indicates whether a particular resource belongs to a group or not.

All of the aforementioned papers which discover groups of similar resources rely on the *performer-by-activity matrix* as an input, except for Appice [1], who used a modified Louvain algorithm, and Burattin et al. [2], who relied on the notion of the handover of roles. The performer-by-activity matrix counts for each resource – i.e. the "performer" – how often (s)he executed each activity [17]. Although this is an effective and easy way to derive resource profiles, it is limited to only two dimensions: *who* did *what*. Therefore, information such as *when* or *under which circumstances* gets lost. Our paper anticipates upon this limitation by proposing a method to mine context-aware resource profiles.

3   Method

This paper introduces the novel method ResProMin to discover context-aware resource profiles from event logs, which consists of three steps (cfr. Fig. 1). Firstly, we enrich the event log by adding relevant contextual variables. Secondly, we cluster the enriched event log from the first step to find *activity instance archetypes* using probabilistic model-based clustering and profile these clusters to get an overview of the different archetypes. Finally, we discover resource profiles by calculating, for each resource, the conditional probability that (s)he performs each activity instance archetype. Moreover, we determine whether a resource specialises in his/her work.

Step 1: Context Enrichment. ResProMin assumes the presence of an event log that minimally describes each event by a case identifier, a timestamp or other attribute that allows temporal ordering of events, an activity label, and a resource identifier. Additionally, it also assumes that each activity instance corresponds to a single event in the event log, which is common for most real-life event logs.

The first step adds computed and derived attributes to obtain an enriched event log. This allows us to describe *when* and *under which circumstances* an

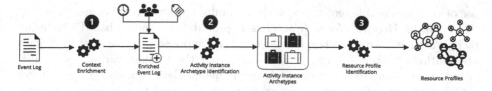

Fig. 1. The three steps of ResProMin: (1) context enrichment, (2) activity instance archetype identification, and (3) resource profile identification.

activity was executed: e.g., weekday, morning or evening shift, case type, activity duration, workload within parts of the process, and many more. The richer the event log, the more interesting patterns can be uncovered. An example of such an enriched event log is shown in Table 1, where each row represents an activity instance with various contextual attributes.

The number and which attributes can be added is different for each event log and mainly depends on the availability of information. However, it is important to consider that Step 2 will apply clustering directly to the enriched event log. Therefore, it is essential to include only attributes which are meaningful in a cluster analysis, e.g. it is best to omit the raw timestamp and use a more aggregated attribute, such as weekday, instead.

Table 1. Example of an enriched event log.

Activity	Resource	Case Procedure	Weekday	Active cases	...
Create purchase requisition	Anna	Comprehensive	Wednesday	15	...
Amend request for quotation	Mike	Regular	Monday	22	...
Send invoice	Jane	Regular	Thursday	12	...
Confirm purchase order	Anna	Comprehensive	Friday	6	...
Create purchase requisition	John	Regular	Friday	14	...
Pay invoice	Jane	Regular	Tuesday	18	...
...	...	...	...	...	...

Step 2: Activity Instance Archetype Identification. Next, we cluster the enriched event log to find *activity instance archetypes*. Each activity instance archetype comprises a set of activity instances that exhibit a high homogeneity with instances of the same archetype and high heterogeneity with instances in other archetypes. To identify activity instance archetypes, we propose to use Finite Mixture Models, which has the inherent advantage of using probabilities, providing statistical criteria to choose the number of clusters, and allowing the

use of variables of different types, such as nominal, discrete, and continuous [19].

A *Finite Mixture Model (FMM)* is a probabilistic model-based clustering technique that allows overlapping clusters [11]. Suppose we have a set of N data observations $\mathbf{Y} = (\mathbf{y}_1, \ldots, \mathbf{y}_N)$ and assume that the random variable $\mathbf{y}_n$ is distributed according to a mixture of K components. Each component – or cluster – represents an activity instance archetype, is assumed to follow a parametric distribution, and has an assigned weight, i.e. the prior probability of observing cluster k, with $k = 1, \ldots, K$. The mixture density function h is given by Eq. 1.

$$h(\mathbf{y}_n \mid \vartheta) = \sum_{k=1}^{K} \pi_k f_k(\mathbf{y}_n \mid \theta_k), \tag{1}$$

where $f_k(\mathbf{y}_n \mid \theta_k)$ is the kth component density function with parameter vector θ_k, $\vartheta = (\pi_1, \ldots, \pi_K, \theta_1, \ldots, \theta_K)$ is the vector of all model parameters, and π_k is the prior probability, or mixture proportion, which must satisfy $\sum_{k=1}^{K} \pi_k = 1$, where $\forall k : \pi_k > 0$. The parameters of this model (ϑ) can be fitted using the *Expectation-Maximisation (EM)* algorithm, which tries to maximise the log-likelihood [11].

Gaussian distributions are often used in FMMs, which is then called a Gaussian Mixture Model (GMM). GMMs are used in many applications, including biology, physics, medicine, marketing, and economics [6]. However, because variables such as the activity label and resource identifier are nominal, we cannot use Gaussian distributions. Instead, we use multinomial distributions for these variables.

To determine the number of components – i.e. K – we use the *Bayesian Information Criterion (BIC)*, which tries to balance the goodness-of-fit with the model complexity, i.e. it penalises more components harder. One should choose the number of components resulting in the lowest BIC [6], or the point where adding additional components barely improves the BIC [10].

Once the appropriate number of clusters (K) is determined, the intra-cluster distributions are used to profile each activity instance archetype using a label and a brief description. This makes it easier to refer to a particular archetype and enhances its recognisability by domain experts.

Step 3: Resource Profile Identification. Context-aware resource profiles are groups of resources that perform similar activity instances, taking into account contextual information, and, hence, move beyond hierarchical functions or resource groups solely defined using activity label information. To identify these profiles, we first need to calculate the probability that a resource belongs to a particular activity instance archetype based on the intra-cluster resource distribution fitted by the FMM. To this end, we apply Bayes' Theorem:

$$P(Cluster = c \mid Resource = r) \propto$$
$$P(Resource = r \mid Cluster = c)P(Cluster = c), \tag{2}$$

where $P(Resource = r \mid Cluster = c)$ is the probability of observing resource r in cluster c, and $P(Cluster = c)$ is the mixture proportion (also denoted by π_c).

After calculating these probabilities, we discover the resource profiles and determine whether a resource specialises in his/her work. We do this by first constructing a distance matrix using the Euclidean distance between the probabilities derived from Eq. 2. Resources with a smaller "distance" are more closely related than resources with a larger "distance". Next, we cluster this matrix using *Agglomerative Hierarchical Clustering (AHC)* and choose the number of clusters where the *Total Within Sum of Square (WSS)* plot shows an "elbow" pattern [8]. These clusters form our final *resource profiles*.

Additionally, we can also find groups of resources with a similar degree of specialism. First, we transform the table derived using Eq. 2, so that the probabilities of belonging to a particular cluster are ordered from left to right, i.e. the first column contains the cluster with the highest probability for a particular resource and the last column the cluster with the lowest probability. Next, we use the same clustering technique used to find the resource profiles. In this way, we can discern "specialists" – i.e. resources which mainly focus on a selective set of activity instance archetypes – from "generalists" – i.e. resources who divide their time over more archetypes [5].

4   Demonstration

In this demonstration, we will validate whether the application of ResProMin is feasible on real-life data and capable of finding valuable business insights. To this end, we used the publicly available event logs of the 2015 BPI Challenge, which describe the process of building permit applications of five Dutch municipalities [18]. These five logs contain information about the performed activities with the associated resource, as well as other case-related attributes.

Section 4.1 highlights how the three steps in our method are applied. Section 4.2 will discuss the results for municipality 1. Due to space restrictions, the other municipalities' results, along with the code used to fit the FMMs, can be consulted in an online appendix[1]. Section 4.3 will discuss the findings across municipalities and compare whether the same process is organised differently.

4.1   Setup

Step 1: Context Enrichment. In Step 1, the event log is enriched with contextual factors. Table 2 shows an overview of the attributes used in the cluster model. Some attributes were already present in the event log; others have been derived from existing attributes. For instance, the weekday is derived from the event's timestamp.

The activity attribute contains many distinct activity labels (on average, each log contains over 280 different labels). To obtain interpretable results, and in the

---

[1] https://doi.org/10.5281/zenodo.4606757.

absence of domain knowledge to compose meaningful groups of activity labels, we opted to use the "phase" as the activity label. To determine the phase, the code of an activity instance is used, e.g. "01_HOOFD_xxx" refers to an activity in the first phase [18]. It should be stressed that we did not remove any events while abstracting the activity label, e.g. when five different activities of phase 0 were executed, we referred to each of these activities as "phase 0".

Table 2. BPIC'15 attributes with description. Attributes with an asterisk (*) have been derived from existing attributes.

Attribute	Description
Phase*	The phase within the process. Derived from the "concept.name" attribute, where the first digit of the last part expresses a phase within the process. A total of nine phases are present: Phase 0–8
Resource	The unique identifier of the resource who executed this activity instance, e.g. "560462"
Case procedure	Either blank (no value), "Regulier" (regular), or "Uitgebreid" (comprehensive)
Case status	Either "G" or "O". We filtered out "T", because this only applied to two cases across all logs
Weekday*	Number indicating the day of the week, starting with "1" for Monday. Derived from the timestamp indicating when the activity was completed
Case parts*	The category/ies the application relates to. Derived from the "(case) parts" attribute and transformed into dummy variables. An activity instance applies to at least one category, but multiple categories could be applicable. Some categories were aggregated to limit the number of variables, e.g. everything related to environment was bundled into one dummy "Environment"

Step 2: Activity Instance Archetype Identification. To determine the appropriate number of clusters of the FMM, we decided to fit two to ten components on each log as considering even more components would hamper the interpretability. Each model was repeated five times to limit the risk of finding a local optimum. The stability of the results across repetitions confirmed that five runs per component were sufficient. This resulted in a total of 45 models per municipality: nine potential numbers of clusters, each with five repetitions. We fitted the mixture models using the R-package *flexmix* (version 2.3-17) [7] (R version 3.6.1). It took, on average, 3.7 min for a model to converge to a solution.

To decide for each municipality which of the 45 models to select, we applied three rules: (1) per number of components, we selected the repetition with the highest log-likelihood, (2) we looked where the BIC-curve showed an "elbow" pattern: adding more clusters would make the model more complex, harder to interpret, and barely improves the model, and (3) no cluster should become smaller than 5% of all observations. This resulted in 7, 8, 7, 6, and 9 clusters for municipality 1–5, respectively. For example, Fig. 2 shows the evolution of the BIC when adding more clusters to the model of municipality 1. An "elbow" pattern can be spotted at seven clusters. The BIC could be slightly improved by adding one additional cluster. However, this would make the second cluster smaller than 5%, violating our third rule.

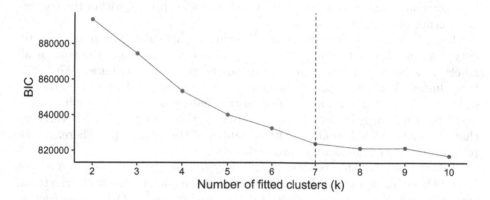

Fig. 2. BIC evolution when adding more clusters to the model of municipality 1.

Step 3: Resource Profile Identification. In the final step, we apply Agglomerative Hierarchical Clustering to discover the context-aware resource profiles and find groups of resources with similar degrees of specialism.

4.2 Intra-municipality Results for Municipality 1

The results of the fitted parameters of the FMM (Step 2) for municipality 1 are shown in Table 3. In Table 3a we see the intra-cluster phase distribution. For instance, cluster 3 mainly (88.27%) contains activities from phase 0, while cluster 4 mainly focuses on phase 4 and 5. If we add up each probability from largest to smallest until we reach a threshold of 70% for each cluster, we could identify the most dominant phases for each activity instance archetype, e.g. in cluster 4 this would be phase 4 and 5.

If we look at the case procedures in Table 3b, we notice that all clusters describe activity instance groups with a "blank" case procedure, except for the first cluster, which is more likely to contain activity instances that required a comprehensive procedure.

Regarding case status in Table 3c, clusters 1, 2, and 7 mainly contain activities with case status "G", whereas cluster 6 is more likely to have an "O" status. The case status in clusters 3, 4, and 5 is evenly spread among "G" and "O".

The probabilities of observing an event on a particular part of the week for each cluster is given in Table 3d. We aggregated the probabilities of Monday, Thursday, and Friday to "Beginning/end of week"; Tuesday and Wednesday to "Midweek"; and Saturday and Sunday to "Weekend". This makes the relation between the cluster and weekday more distinct. We notice that clusters 1, 2, and 3 are mainly performed during the beginning/end of the week, whereas the others are more spread out over the working week. In addition, it is improbable to observe an event during weekends, which is not surprising within the context of a permit application process.

Table 4 shows the probability of observing a particular case part (or category). As multiple labels might apply to an activity instance, the sum of all labels does not equal 100%, in contrast to the previous attributes. We notice that clusters 3, 4, and 5 predominantly concerns an application related to construction. Cluster 2 is always related to tree felling, 1 always to environment, and 7 predominantly to demolition. In cluster 6, there is not really one category that is mainly related to all activity instances of this archetype. Therefore, we refer to this archetype as a residual archetype.

Table 5 describes the six identified activity instance archetypes based on the insights from Table 3 and Table 4, together with the relative size of the cluster to the entire log. For instance, activity instance archetype 5 ("Other construction cases") is the largest cluster which applies to around a third (34.19%) of all events recorded for municipality 1.

The *input* columns of Table 6 show the result of applying Bayes' Theorem in the third step, i.e. the conditional probability of executing an activity instance from a particular activity instance archetype, given a specific resource. We can look at these probabilities from two different angles. Firstly, we could look for resources that work on the same activity instance archetypes, i.e. resource profiles. We cluster the input columns of Table 6 using AHC into seven clusters as the Total Within Sum of Square plot in Fig. 3a shows the typical "elbow" pattern there. Figure 3b shows the resulting resource profiles, which are also labelled in the *output* column in Table 6. For instance, resources "4936828", "560462", and "560950" mainly perform activity instances from activity instance archetype 1. Therefore, we refer to this profile as resources that work on "environmental cases". "Tree felling" (cluster 2) is mainly executed by "560872" and "5726485". However, as tree felling is a relatively small archetype (only 7.83% of the complete event log), these resources likely have to fill their remaining time with other work, such as construction-related activity instances.

Table 3. Intra-cluster distributions for phase, case procedure and status, and weekday variables for municipality 1 (in %).

(a) Intra-cluster phase distribution for municipality 1.

Phase	Clust1	Clust2	Clust3	Clust4	Clust5	Clust6	Clust7
Phase 0	50.89	31.43	88.27	18.89	35.47	28.19	35.56
Phase 1	12.64	11.87	11.35	2.95	19.50	11.62	18.91
Phase 2	4.23	6.03	<0.01	1.62	11.61	7.65	10.66
Phase 3	4.12	7.00	<0.01	1.44	13.04	8.86	9.20
Phase 4	13.83	17.22	<0.01	25.73	18.97	25.59	14.83
Phase 5	7.72	15.19	0.02	46.04	1.19	16.28	10.23
Phase 6	0.79	<0.01	<0.01	0.05	0.05	0.08	<0.01
Phase 7	1.82	3.45	0.11	0.93	0.08	0.40	0.52
Phase 8	3.95	7.81	0.25	2.34	0.09	1.33	0.09

(b) Intra-cluster case procedure distribution for municipality 1.

Procedure	Clust1	Clust2	Clust3	Clust4	Clust5	Clust6	Clust7
blank	35.98	100.00	93.62	89.41	96.65	91.85	94.32
Regular	<0.01	<0.01	1.55	3.44	1.50	0.88	2.26
Comprehensive	64.02	<0.01	4.84	7.15	1.85	7.27	3.42

(c) Intra-cluster case status distribution for municipality 1.

Status	Clust1	Clust2	Clust3	Clust4	Clust5	Clust6	Clust7
G	81.21	89.13	47.62	48.29	50.68	26.86	85.43
O	18.79	10.87	52.38	51.71	49.32	73.14	14.57

(d) Intra-cluster part of week distribution for municipality 1. The individual probabilities for each weekday can be consulted in the online appendix.

Part of week	Clust1	Clust2	Clust3	Clust4	Clust5	Clust6	Clust7
Beginning/end of week	79.79	89.76	86.34	43.30	59.13	51.58	48.45
Midweek	20.13	10.21	13.20	56.67	40.83	48.42	51.54
Weekend	0.08	0.02	0.46	0.03	0.04	<0.01	0.02

Secondly, we could focus on whether a resource is a "specialist" or "generalist". We transformed the input columns of Table 6 so that the probabilities of belonging to a particular cluster are ordered from left to right, i.e. the first column contains the cluster with the highest probability and the last column the cluster with the lowest probability. We use the same clustering technique used for discovering the resource profiles to find six degrees of specialism. For instance, resource "4936828" always works on activity instances from archetype 1, whereas "560999" always works on archetype 6. We could say that they are both specialised in their work, but they do not do the same things. In contrast, resource "560464" more evenly spreads his/her time among clusters 3, 4, 5, and 7. This resource clearly does not specialise in a particular activity instance archetype.

Table 4. Intra-cluster case part distribution for municipality 1 (in %). Note that unlike the variables in the Table 3, we assume that the values of case part are independent, i.e. an observation may have multiple case parts. Therefore, the summation over case parts does not add up to 100%.

Case part	Clust1	Clust2	Clust3	Clust4	Clust5	Clust6	Clust7
Installation	<0.01	1.65	5.60	0.39	0.50	28.96	<0.01
Construction	21.24	<0.01	83.70	100.00	100.00	17.49	16.38
Fireproof	0.74	<0.01	2.96	2.12	0.40	13.12	<0.01
Flora & Fauna	<0.01	<0.01	<0.01	<0.01	<0.01	<0.01	<0.01
Area protection	4.81	<0.01	<0.01	<0.01	<0.01	<0.01	<0.01
Acting in violation of SPR	5.40	<0.01	15.43	8.43	7.81	45.98	0.49
Tree felling	0.24	100.00	1.17	1.24	0.47	3.72	3.18
Entrance/exit	<0.01	<0.01	1.54	0.77	0.76	4.95	<0.01
Environment	100.00	<0.01	6.04	5.76	6.38	0.84	<0.01
Monument	<0.01	<0.01	4.41	9.17	3.91	3.97	6.99
Advertisement	<0.01	<0.01	1.77	1.10	0.85	6.57	<0.01
Demolition	0.30	<0.01	4.16	4.39	3.04	0.01	98.42

SPR = Spatial Planning Rules

Table 5. Activity instance archetypes with descriptions for municipality 1.

Cluster	Label	Description	Size (%)
1	Environmental cases	Mainly occur at the beginning/end of the week, more likely require a comprehensive procedure, with typically a "G" case status	8.97
2	Tree felling cases	Mainly occur at the beginning/end of the week, always have a "blank" procedure, with typically status "G"	7.83
7	Demolition cases	Occur evenly across the week, typically have a "blank" procedure with status "G"	5.20
3	Construction cases in phase 0	Mainly occur at the beginning/end of the week, typically have a "blank" procedure, and are evenly split between status "G" and "O"	17.95
4	Construction cases in phase 4 and 5	Occur evenly across the week, typically have a "blank" procedure, and are evenly split between status "G" and "O"	17.77
5	Other construction cases	Occur evenly across the week, typically have a "blank" procedure, and are evenly split between status "G" and "O"	34.19
6	Other cases	Occur evenly across the week, typically have a "blank" procedure with status "O"	8.09

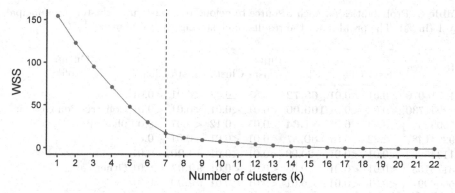

(a) Total Within Sum of Square (WSS) plot to determine the number of clusters. In this case, we choose seven clusters.

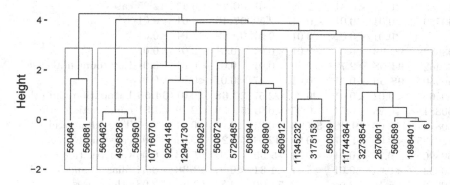

(b) Cluster dendrogram of the resource profiles. From left to right: demolition and other construction cases; environmental cases; construction cases in phase 0; tree felling and construction cases; construction cases in phase 4 and 5, and other cases; other cases; and other construction cases.

Fig. 3. Resources working on the same activity instance archetypes in municipality 1.

Table 7 tabulates the number of resources for each profile-specialism combination. The degree of specialism is ordered from left – "pure specialist" – to right – "pure generalist". For instance, we notice that environmental cases are only performed by resources with the highest specialisation degree.

Table 6. Probabilities for each resource to belong to a particular cluster in municipality 1 (in %). The profiles are the results of clustering the table using AHC.

Resource	Clust1	Clust2	Clust3	Clust4	Clust5	Clust6	Clust7	Output Profile
10716070	<0.01	<0.01	**63.72**	35.85	0.42	<0.01	<0.01	
12941730	<0.01	<0.01	**100.00**	<0.01	<0.01	<0.01	<0.01	Construction cases in
560925	3.93	6.26	**81.64**	0.05	0.12	<0.01	8.00	phase 0
9264148	2.22	16.91	**80.87**	<0.01	<0.01	<0.01	<0.01	
11345232	<0.01	<0.01	20.00	<0.01	<0.01	**80.00**	<0.01	
3175153	<0.01	<0.01	0.03	<0.01	<0.01	**99.97**	<0.01	Other cases
560999	<0.01	<0.01	<0.01	<0.01	<0.01	**99.99**	<0.01	
11744364	<0.01	<0.01	<0.01	<0.01	**59.59**	40.41	<0.01	
1898401	<0.01	<0.01	0.03	<0.01	**99.97**	<0.01	<0.01	
2670601	0.10	0.33	0.09	0.03	**85.21**	13.02	1.22	Other construction
3273854	<0.01	<0.01	2.08	0.01	**80.24**	5.43	12.25	cases
560589	<0.01	<0.01	<0.01	2.59	**97.40**	<0.01	<0.01	
6	<0.01	<0.01	0.01	<0.01	**99.99**	<0.01	<0.01	
4936828	**99.99**	<0.01	0.01	<0.01	<0.01	<0.01	<0.01	
560462	**94.98**	2.72	2.30	<0.01	<0.01	<0.01	<0.01	Environmental cases
560950	**98.53**	<0.01	<0.01	1.47	<0.01	<0.01	<0.01	
560464	<0.01	<0.01	20.20	22.57	**22.68**	<0.01	**34.56**	Demolition and other
560881	0.29	0.54	0.37	<0.01	**53.19**	2.29	**43.31**	construction cases
560872	18.03	**29.06**	**50.86**	<0.01	<0.01	<0.01	2.05	Tree felling and
5726485	<0.01	**34.17**	<0.01	12.54	**53.29**	<0.01	<0.01	construction cases
560890	0.17	<0.01	<0.01	**75.95**	<0.01	**17.83**	6.06	Construction cases in
560894	<0.01	<0.01	4.77	**44.31**	<0.01	**42.38**	8.54	phase 4 and 5, and
560912	5.16	2.94	18.62	**54.00**	4.71	**12.50**	2.08	other cases

4.3   Inter-municipality Results

In the previous subsection, we discussed the finding of applying ResProMin in municipality 1. We found similar patterns in the other municipalities, e.g. all municipalities have an archetype for environmental cases. The construction

Table 7. Number of resources per profile-specialism combination in municipality 1.

Profile	Specialism group					
	1	2	3	4	5	6
Construction cases in phase 0	3	1	0	0	0	0
Other cases	3	0	0	0	0	0
Other construction cases	5	1	0	0	0	0
Environmental cases	3	0	0	0	0	0
Demolition and other construction cases	0	1	0	0	0	1
Tree felling and construction cases	0	0	2	0	0	0
Construction cases in phase 4 and 5, and other cases	1	0	0	1	1	0

Table 8. Number and proportion of specialists in each municipality.

Municipality	1	2	3	4	5
Specialised resources	18	5	8	7	12
Total resources	23	11	14	10	21
Proportion specialised	78%	45%	57%	70%	57%

cases were present as well, but not always with a focus on the same phases. In addition, each municipality has several specialists and generalists.

However, we also found some differences between the municipalities. Firstly, only municipality 1 exhibited the pattern where some activity instance archetypes were mainly performed during either the end or the beginning of the week. Instead, a frequently observed pattern in the other municipalities was a much lower conditional probability to observe a particular activity instance archetype on Friday. In other words, Fridays seemed to be quieter than other weekdays. In municipality 1, Wednesday was often the quieter day. Secondly, the more resources a municipality has – most likely bigger municipalities – the larger the proportion of resources seems to specialise in particular archetypes, as shown in Table 8. This offers face validity to our method as it seems reasonable that when there are more resources to divide the work among, there is more room to specialise. However, an interesting exception is that the smallest municipality (i.e. 4) has the second-highest specialist rate of all municipalities. This might indicate that municipality 4 uses a different way of handling the permit application process. Thirdly, activity instance archetypes requiring a comprehensive procedure, typically related to environment (such as cluster 1 in municipality 1, as described in Table 5) are more likely to have specialised resources involved. Finally, activity instance archetypes that involve predominantly construction-related activity instances are also more likely to have specialised resources involved, albeit less clearly than the comprehensive environment archetype.

5 Conclusion

In this paper, we extend the existing work on organisational mining by introducing our method, *ResProMin*. In contrast to the state-of-the-art, ResProMin is capable of finding context-aware resource profiles based on the notion of activity instance archetypes. Instead of solely considering activity labels to group resources, ResProMin accommodates contextual information such as case attributes and variables capturing the system state. In addition, our method allows activities to belong to multiple profiles simultaneously and is capable of discerning specialists from generalists. Our demonstration confirms the feasibility of our method to discover context-aware resource profiles from real-life event logs. This provides rich insights to process owners, which can help them manage their resources better by uncovering, e.g. (potentially implicit) task division patterns.

Besides these contributions, we also acknowledge some limitations of our method. Firstly, estimating a Finite Mixture Model's parameters is a computationally demanding process and suffers from *the curse of dimensionality*. However, this study's focus was on demonstrating whether our method is capable of uncovering meaningful resource-related insights that are valuable in a business context and not on optimising its execution. Moreover, this kind of analysis is typically not performed in real-time, supporting that runtime optimisation will not be the primary goal as long as execution times remain practically feasible. Secondly, we had no access to domain experts in the municipalities to validate and elaborate more on our findings. Nevertheless, our demonstration shows that ResProMin is capable of finding interesting and valuable insights into the prevailing resource profiles.

We identify several directions for future work. Firstly, heuristics could be developed to improve our method's computational efficiency while still obtaining near-optimal solutions. For instance, a quasi-Newton approach could be adopted to accelerate the convergence of the EM algorithm [12]. Secondly, instruments to facilitate the enrichment of an event log with context-related information can be developed. Thirdly, it could be investigated whether different resource-related organisations between municipalities are associated with process performance differences. Finally, we could determine how the insights of ResProMin can be leveraged by models which require fine-grained resource allocation information, such as Business Process Simulation models.

Acknowledgements. This study was supported by the Special Research Fund (BOF) of Hasselt University under Grant No. BOF19OWB20.

The resources and services used in this work were provided by the VSC (Flemish Supercomputer Center), funded by the Research Foundation - Flanders (FWO) and the Flemish Government.

References

1. Appice, A.: Towards mining the organizational structure of a dynamic event scenario. J. Intell. Inf. Syst. **50**(1), 165–193 (2018). https://doi.org/10.1007/s10844-017-0451-x
2. Burattin, A., Sperduti, A., Veluscek, M.: Business models enhancement through discovery of roles. In: Proceedings of the 2013 IEEE Symposium on Computational Intelligence and Data Mining, CIDM 2013, pp. 103–110 (2013). https://doi.org/10.1109/CIDM.2013.6597224
3. Cabanillas, C., Ackermann, L., Schönig, S., Sturm, C., Mendling, J.: The RALph miner for automated discovery and verification of resource-aware process models. Softw Syst. Model. **19**, 1415–1441 (2020). https://doi.org/10.1007/s10270-020-00820-7
4. Camargo, M., Dumas, M., González-Rojas, O.: Automated discovery of business process simulation models from event logs. Decis. Support Syst. **134**, 113284 (2020). https://doi.org/10.1016/j.dss.2020.113284
5. Dumas, M., La Rosa, M., Mendling, J., Reijers, H.A.: Fundamentals of Business Process Management, 2nd edn. Springer, Heidelberg (2018). https://doi.org/10.1007/978-3-662-56509-4

6. Frühwirth-Schnatter, S.: Finite Mixture and Markov Switching Models. Springer Series in Statistics, vol. 692, Springer, New York (2006). https://doi.org/10.1007/978-0-387-35768-3

7. Grün, B., Leisch, F.: FlexMix version 2: finite mixtures with concomitant variables and varying and constant parameters. J. Stat. Softw. **28**(1), 1–35 (2008). https://doi.org/10.18637/jss.v028.i04

8. Hair, J.F., Black, W.C., Babin, B.J., Anderson, R.E.: Multivariate Data Analysis: A Global Perspective. USA, 7th edn, Pearson Education, Upper Saddle River (2010)

9. Jin, T., Wang, J., Wen, L.: Organizational modeling from event logs. In: Proceedings of the 6th International Conference on Grid and Cooperative Computing, GCC 2007, pp. 670–675 (2007). https://doi.org/10.1109/GCC.2007.93

10. Masyn, K.E.: Latent class analysis and finite mixture modeling. In: The Oxford Handbook of Quantitative Methods in Psychology. Statistical Analysis, vol. 2, pp. 551–611. Oxford University Press, New York (2013). https://doi.org/10.1093/oxfordhb/9780199934898.001.0001

11. McLachlan, G.J.: Model-based clustering. In: Comprehensive Chemometrics, vol. 2, pp. 655–681. Elsevier, Oxford (2009). https://doi.org/10.1016/B978-044452701-1.00068-5

12. McLachlan, G.J., Krishnan, T.: The EM Algorithm and Extensions, 2nd edn. Wiley Series in Probability and Statistics, vol. 1345. Wiley, Hoboken (2007). https://doi.org/10.1002/9780470191613

13. Nakatumba, J., van der Aalst, W.M.P.: Analyzing resource behavior using process mining. In: Rinderle-Ma, S., Sadiq, S., Leymann, F. (eds.) BPM 2009. LNBIP, vol. 43, pp. 69–80. Springer, Heidelberg (2010). https://doi.org/10.1007/978-3-642-12186-9_8

14. Pika, A., Leyer, M., Wynn, M.T., Fidge, C.J., ter Hofstede, A.H.M., van der Aalst, W.M.P.: Mining resource profiles from event logs. ACM Trans. Manage. Inf. Syst. **8**(1), 1–30 (2017). https://doi.org/10.1145/3041218

15. Reijers, H.A., Liman Mansar, S.: Best Practices in business process redesign: an overview and qualitative evaluation of successful redesign heuristics. Omega **33**(4), 283–306 (2005). https://doi.org/10.1016/j.omega.2004.04.012

16. Schönig, S., Cabanillas, C., Di Ciccio, C., Jablonski, S., Mendling, J.: Mining team compositions for collaborative work in business processes. Softw. Syst. Model. **17**(2), 675–693 (2018). https://doi.org/10.1007/s10270-016-0567-4

17. Song, M., van der Aalst, W.M.P.: Towards comprehensive support for organizational mining. Decis. Support Syst. **46**(1), 300–317 (2008). https://doi.org/10.1016/j.dss.2008.07.002

18. van Dongen, B.F.: BPI Challenge 2015. 4TU.ResearchData (2015). https://doi.org/10.4121/uuid:31a308ef-c844-48da-948c-305d167a0ec1

19. Vermunt, J.K., Magidson, J.: Latent class cluster analysis. In: Applied Latent Class Analysis, pp. 89–106. Cambridge University Press, Cambridge (2002). https://doi.org/10.1017/CBO9780511499531.004

20. Yang, J., Ouyang, C., Pan, M., Yu, Y., ter Hofstede, A.H.M.: Finding the "Liberos": discover organizational models with overlaps. In: Weske, M., Montali, M., Weber, I., vom Brocke, J. (eds.) BPM 2018. LNCS, vol. 11080, pp. 339–355. Springer, Cham (2018). https://doi.org/10.1007/978-3-319-98648-7_20

Decision Support for Knowledge Intensive Processes Using RL Based Recommendations

Asjad Khan[✉], Aditya Ghose, and Hoa Dam

Decision Systems Lab, University of Wollongong, Northfields Avenue, Wollongong, NSW 2522, Australia
maak458@uowmail.edu.au, {aditya,hoa}@uow.edu.au

Abstract. Supporting knowledge workers involved in the execution of unstructured Knowledge-Intensive Processes by providing context-specific recommendations remains an interesting challenge. Case data that represents expert decisions recorded in the past can be exploited for building a decision support tool for knowledge workers that can recommend which tasks to execute next. Reinforcement learning (RL) provides a framework for learning from interaction with the environment in order to achieve a certain process goal. RL has widely been used to model sequential decision problems and has shown great promise in solving large scale complex problems with long time horizons, partial observability, and high dimensionality of observation and action spaces [5]. In this paper, we propose a novel framework based on RL aimed at supporting knowledge workers by recommending the optimal course of action to the knowledge worker.

Keywords: Knowledge intensive processes · Prescriptive analytics · Decision support

1 Introduction

There has been a growing emphasis within the BPM research community in recent years on supporting decision making in Knowledge-Intensive Processes (KIPs) [7], in part as a consequence of knowledge workers being regarded as the most valuable organizational assets [9]. Knowledge work is characterised by unstructured processes which can be hard to specify at design-time but which must be customized to the current context and optimized to meet desired KPIs. Supporting knowledge workers with appropriate recommendations in such settings remains a largely open problem [6,15,20].

Data-centric AI approaches hold the promise of providing a solution [7]. Reinforcement Learning (RL) [31] provides a framework for learning from interaction with the environment to achieve a certain goal (implicitly defined by the reward function). RL has widely been used to model sequential decision problems and has shown great promise in solving large scale complex problems with long time

© Springer Nature Switzerland AG 2021
A. Polyvyanyy et al. (Eds.): BPM Forum 2021, LNBIP 427, pp. 246–262, 2021.
https://doi.org/10.1007/978-3-030-85440-9_15

horizons, partial observability, and high dimensionality of observation and action spaces [5]. In our work, we explore the application of RL in the settings discussed above. We present a novel framework for recommending the next best action (or sequence of actions) taking into account asset characteristics and process context. For example, our approach can recommend clinical interventions at the right time, based on similar past cases which had a good outcome.

In KIPs, case progression is dependent on a combination of decision making, operational context and availability of the right information. The specific research question we address is: *For a given case state in a KIP, can we leverage past case data to recommend the next best steps to execute?*. Our specific contributions are as follows:

1. We propose a framework based on RL that recommends the best sequence of next steps given a partially completed case. In particular, our framework supports: (1) Flexible process execution; (2) Maintaining and improving process performance by learning optimal policies from past case execution data in addition to leveraging contextual data from various heterogeneous data sources; (3) Deep reinforcement learning along with off-policy evaluation methods to tackle large scale case modeling problems involving high dimensionality in both action and observation space, making it highly applicable in real-world settings.
2. We demonstrate the effectiveness of our proposed framework by conducting a large scale experiment on a real-world sepsis critical-care dataset. We show that our proposed framework is capable of learning best practices and giving recommendations to clinicians, that are individualised based on the dynamic condition of the patient at a particular time.

2   Background and Related Work

Knowledge Intensive Processes: KIPs are processes that require very specific expert tacit knowledge, involvement of knowledge workers, and consist of activities that do not have the same level of repeatability as the traditional structured processes [7]. Instead of assuming a rigid process structure, KIPs are goal-oriented, characterised by activities that are complex, unstructured and hard to anticipate or model in advance. It is hard to predict the event flow of KIPs in advance and there is significant variation in every instance of the process, making activities hard to plan apriori [6]. KIPs represent a shift from the traditional process management view (where processes are characterized by repeated tasks captured in a process model), to a model where task execution depends on decisions made by knowledge workers and requires flexibility at design and run-time [7].

Adaptive Case Management: Adaptive Case Management (ACM) is aimed at supporting knowledge workers involved in the execution of dynamic, unstructured knowledge-intensive processes(KIPs) where the course of action for the fulfilment of process goals is highly uncertain [15,20]. ACM offers a way to manage the entire life-cycle of a "case" by following the 'planning-by-doing' principle, where work is done by considering the context and is continually adapted based on the changing characteristics of the environment [20]. In the case management paradigm, the focus is on the case and it is hard to pre-define the sequence of process activities. For example, Case is the 'Product' being manufactured or a 'patient' being treated and the primary driver of case progress is the case data and information that emerges as the case evolves. There however can exist template or patterns that represent the structured aspects of the process. Here process could be seen as a recipe for handling cases of specific type [2]. A Case template is created by the knowledge worker, allowing a high degree of flexibility on how to go about executing a particular case. It can be used to instantiate case instances and represents the middle ground between a completely specified structured process and an unstructured process. Case templates incorporate knowledge from experts and try to capture the best practices of knowledge work that has happened in the past. Case execution allows us to gather feedback and adapt the templates to be reused in a particular context [19].

Even though ACM has been gaining significant interest for handling unpredictable situations in processes, Hauder et al. [15] point out that ACM still lacks a proper theory and model. Furthermore, in [20] the authors reviewed the research challenges associated with ACM and have highlighted the need for flexible solutions that support knowledge workers in a 'worker-driven holistic manner'. Similarly, in [7] the authors highlighted the lack of a holistic system for supporting process adaptation and inadequate support for knowledge workers involved in modeling and runtime planning.

Prescriptive Analytics for Unstructured Processes: Prescriptive Analytics aims at providing intelligent assistance to process users by offering concrete recommendations in various process-related decisions like resource allocation decisions or action recommendations. Such type of assistance can improve the process performance for running process instances and help avoid the risk of failure [13,28]. Process-aware Recommender Systems have been proposed to assist knowledge workers, in context-aware adaptable fashion by recommending best practices for executing a particular process/task, enhance resource allocation policies and so on [28]. Such systems leverage technologies like machine learning to build recommender systems that monitor process instances, predict future states and recommend appropriate actions. Groger et al. [13] introduce the concept of recommendation-based business process optimization for data-driven process optimization. Their data-mining driven solution supports adaptive processes and recommends next action steps to take for a given process instance.

The specific problem of recommending next steps in a case management system based on the knowledge of past similar cases(which is the focus of this work) has been addressed by Schonenberg et al. [28] and Motahari-Nezhad et al. [21]. Schonenberg et al. attempt it by first finding similar cases based on abstraction, then using support and Trace Weights to consider the relative importance of a log trace. Similarly, Motahari-Nezhad et al. [21] have looked at the problem of decision support for guiding case resolution based on how similar cases were resolved in the past.

Decision Modeling with Offline Reinforcement Learning: Reinforcement Learning (RL) assumes that there is an agent operating in the real world. At each step t the agent, Executes action A_t, Receives an observation O_t and Receives scalar reward R_t. The Problem can be formulated as a Markov Decision Process [31] defined by $(\mathcal{S}, \mathcal{A}, T, R)$ tuples where $\mathcal{S}$ and $\mathcal{A}$ refer to the state and action spaces; $T : \mathcal{S} \times \mathcal{A} \to \mathcal{S}$, is the state transition function and $R : \mathcal{S} \times \mathcal{A} \to \mathbb{R}$ represents the reward function. The goal of the agent is to estimate an optimal policy $\pi : \mathcal{S} \to \mathcal{A}$ or an optimal action value function $q_\pi(s, a) = \mathbb{E}_\pi [G_t \mid S_t = s, A_t = a]$ which maximizes the expected return $\mathbb{E} \left[\sum_{t=1}^{L} \gamma^t R_t \mid \pi \right]$ over a given MDP [31].

A lot of RL success so far has been in academic environments where access to a simulator is assumed and experiments are performed on simulated benchmark environments [8]. Offline Reinforcement learning (also referred to as safe or batch reinforcement learning) is a promising sub-field of RL which provides us with a mechanism for solving real-world sequential decision making problems where access to a simulator is not available. Offline Reinforcement learning allows us to learn a policy that optimizes for long-term reward in a sequential setting, from fixed dataset of trajectories, where further interaction with the environment is infeasible [18]. Agarwal et al. have [3] shown that offline RL algorithms when trained on sufficiently large and diverse offline datasets can produce close to optimal policies and have the ability to generalize beyond training data. Moreover, offline reinforcement learning has been applied successfully for solving real-world large scale problems and it has been shown that it can outperform supervised learning approaches or heuristic-based policies for solving real-world decision-making problems [10].

3   Approach

Knowledge workers are highly trained individuals with specialized expertise in performing complex tasks autonomously. They typically rely on their experience and domain expertise to accomplish business goals. Their work is less characterised by explicit procedures and more by creative thinking which usually cannot be planned apriori. Therefore, in knowledge-intensive scenarios, decisions are made based on the expertise of knowledge workers along with the availability of contextual information as the specific case scenario unfolds. The problem of generating recommendations for knowledge workers is challenging due to several reasons: a) first we must identify similar cases in logged data, that have been resolved in the past and can form the basis for the current recommendation b) secondly, we must consider the contextual information available from various heterogeneous data sources c) Lastly, we have to rank the proposed recommendations based on the current context (from the universe of possible valid recommendations). In addition to these challenges, Ciccio et al. [7] have provided a set of requirements for processes oriented systems aimed at supporting Knowledge-Intensive Processes. Keeping these requirements and challenges in mind we propose a data-driven reinforcement learning based recommender system for supporting knowledge workers that considers the past execution data in addition to characteristics of the objects involved (e.g. product or user). In this section, we show how Markov Decision Processes can be used to model decision-driven process structure, where data inputs are contextual and dynamic, responsible for driving decision making and process flow. Here for each process instance, we consider the sequence of interactions (actions taken along with state changes) with the environment, as observed in the case logs along with performance outcomes. A decision process specifies how states S_t, actions A_t, and rewards R_t are distributed: $p(S_0, \ldots, S_T, A_0, \ldots, A_T, R_0, \ldots, R_T)$. Using case logs, we are interested in modeling the effects of actions A_t on future rewards. We do so by training Deep Reinforcement learning models, which take historic data in order to learn the optimal policy, which gives us next step recommendations that can lead to desired outcomes [18]. We cast the sequential decision problem of step recommendations as a Markov Decision Process [31].

Definition 1 (Markov Decision Process). Markov Decision Process are defined as:

$(\mathcal{S}, \mathcal{A}, P, R, \rho_0,)$ where
  $\mathcal{S}$: state space describing the possible case states;
  - $\mathcal{A}$: a discrete action space, consisting of step available for recommendation;
  - $P : \mathcal{S} \times \mathcal{A} \times \mathcal{S} \to \mathbb{R}$ is the state transition probability;
  - $R : \mathcal{S} \times \mathcal{A} \to \mathbb{R}$ is the reward function, where $r(s, a)$ is the immediate reward obtained by performing action a at given state s ;
  - ρ_0 is the initial state distribution;

Training Data: Case handling systems can generate huge amounts of data representing knowledge objects, case patterns and events recorded in case histories [7]. Case handling system logs typically records events like execution of tasks. e.g. $\langle \tau_1, \tau_2, \ldots, \tau_i, \ldots, \tau_n \rangle$ along with every state change in the case life-cycle [14]. We assume the availability of the effect log which records observed changes in the states of objects impacted by a process. Our framework exploits such data sources, in particular the good performing instances, for learning optimal behaviour. This dataset however is rarely directly generated in this format and needs to be extracted from a Case Handling System log. A behaviour policy is a policy enacted by the knowledge worker (or the decision maker) in the past and is represented by this historical data and forms the input for our proposed machinery.

Definition 2 (Case Event Log). *A case log is generated by behaviour policy π_b where each case instance is a tuple defined as $\varphi := \{c_{id}, c_a, c_{time}, c_{cxt}, c_{eff}\}$ where, c_{id} is the case identifier, c_a, $(a_i \mid a_i \in A \wedge f_{executed}(a_i) = true)$, set of activities that were executed, c_{cxt}, is a set of attribute-value pairs of the process context, c_{time} is the timestamp, c_{eff} is the effect assertion in the underlying state description language.*

Action Space: Cases are handled by execution of activities which are logical units of work (with ACID properties) [1]. Less formally, we can view them as steps in a process that must be performed by a knowledge worker in order to complete a task. During process design-time phase, business analysts specify the rules and tasks as part of the case model. We describe knowledge actions as context-dependent activities represented by their post-conditions.

Definition 3 (Knowledge Actions). *Let A be a set of finite activities where each $a \in \mathcal{A}$ is a set triple of form $a := \langle ID, pre\_condition(a), post\_condition(a) \rangle$ action ID along with set of associated pre-conditions contained in knowledgebase $(\mathcal{KB})$ and set of context-independent post condition $\mathcal{E} = \{e_1, \ldots e_n\}$.*

This set is typically constrained by feasible capabilities (i.e., the set of conditions that a knowledge worker is capable of bringing about), business rules and constraints on how to operate in a given business environment. Additionally, in high-risk environments (where executing a bad policy could cause harm) limiting the action space to known options is a sensible choice to increase the safety of the policy. Therefore, each action $a \in A$ applicable in state is $s \in S$ dependent on precondition function $S \times A \rightarrow \{true\}$. This means that only if a *condition* (or pre-condition) holds in a given state, then the corresponding action can be executed in that state [27].

State Representation: We represent case history in a compact way, such that it retains sufficient information for estimation of the expected value of an optimal policy. This helps effectively predict the course of the process and recommend next steps to take. Here we must take into account features or factors that might causally affect both process decisions and the process outcome. We divide the information obtained from observations into two types, namely, exogenous information and endogenous information. Endogenous is information describing the structured characteristics of the process (which can be pre-defined) and Exogenous is information that can provide useful context for decision making based on the current state of the environment. We can construct an aggregated feature set by combining temporal features (if applicable) representing exogenous information along with static features(representing endogenous information) most relevant to the decisions. For example, in case of patient treatment, our feature set would consist of the concatenation of patient's static information with the raw physiological data over several timesteps (so that it incorporates all available temporal information).

To obtain a sequence of states (or partial states) from an event log, we accumulate effects using a state update operator in a manner similar to the approach adopted in [35]. Note that there exists a predecessor-successor relationship between temporally adjacent sets of states. i.e. a state in the posterior set can be arrived at only from some (but possibly not all) of the states in the prior set. We will therefore first extract from an event log a state set sequence consisting of pairs of states, where the first element is the predecessor and the second element is the successor as follows [27]. Given an event log $\langle e_1, e_2 \ldots, e_n \rangle$, we compute a state set sequence $\langle\, StateSet_1, StateSet_2, \ldots, StateSet_n\rangle$, where each $StateSet_i$ is of the form $\{\, StatePair_1, StatePair_2, \ldots, StatePair_k\}$ and each $StatePair_i$ is of the form $\langle\, state_{\mathrm{pred}}, state_{\mathrm{succ}}\rangle$ (i.e., these are predecessor-successor pairs) as follows:

- $StateSet_1 = \{\langle\emptyset, \epsilon_1\rangle\}$ (where $\langle\epsilon_1, \tau_1\rangle$ is the first entry in the temporally ordered event log).
- $StateSet_2 = \{\langle\epsilon_1, s\rangle \mid s \in \epsilon_1 \oplus e_2\}$
- For $i = 3 \ldots n$, $StateSet_i = \{\langle s_{i-1}, s_i\rangle \mid s_{i-1} \in \mathrm{StateSet}_{i-1}$ and $s_i \in s_{i-1} \oplus e_i\}$

Contextual-Information: Context is defined as body of exogenous knowledge potentially relevant to the execution of the task that is available at the start of the execution of the task, and that is not impacted/modified via the execution of the task [29]. Context-Aware processes will perform better than their counterparts because they offer flexibility and consider environmental influences. in addition to traditional data sources (like case log) our framework leverages Process execution data can come from all available data sources like case logs, event logs, provisioning logs, decision logs. Such sources contains rich information about the current task and can potentially provide useful contextual information for effective decision making [15].

Definition 4 (Case Context). *Given a state description S, and a context C of a case $s' = S \ominus C = s \cup c$ and s' describes the same state of the system with S. each contextual dimension c, can be defined by a set of* q *attribute-value pairs* $\{c_1, \ldots c_q\}$.

Here $\ominus$ operator enriches S with the information in context C, which consists of a set of assertions. Our state represents the compact history retained function of history having markov property: $S_t = f(H_t)$ where $H_t = \langle\tau_1, o_1, \tau_2, o_2, \ldots, \tau_m, o_m\rangle$ representing semantic execution trace of case.

Our input is formed by historical log $\mathcal{D}$ representing the behaviour policy π_b is defined as a bag of trajectories $\mathcal{D} = \{\tau_1, \ldots, \tau_N\}$, where trajectory τ_i is the tuple $\tau = ((s_1, a_1), \ldots, (s_T, End)$. where state s is constructed from definition 4, using a temporally ordered event log.

State Transitions. State transition are caused by external event (environmental triggers) that cause changes to the state of the running process. They are sometimes recorded as by altering of data values in the information model. Alternatively can estimate the transition matrix T(s',s,a) from an event log by counting the number of times each transition is observed (e.g. $\langle\tau_1, o_1, \tau_2, o_2, \ldots, \tau_m, o_m\rangle$) and converting the transition counts to a stochastic matrix. Note that this is an approximatation of 'true' transition probabilities.

Reward Function: In reinforcement learning, the reward function provides us with mechanism for representing one or more process goals. Here we take the goal orchestration view of process modeling [27]. We assume the process goals are known apriori and predefined. We can define our reward function based on metrics that we care about maximizing or minimizing (e.g. time required to complete a case). This approach fits well with the Adaptive Case Management view, which encourages management by objective where we optimise for specific results. We construct the reward function from the set of case outcomes $R_o = (r_o^1, \ldots r_o^j)$ observed at the last time step of each case instance Here reward in a state is described as $\mathcal{R}_s = \mathbb{E}[R_{t+1} \mid S_t = s, A_t = a]$ [31].

It is often challenging to capture the process goals in one global reward function. We can easily misspecify the reward function which can lead to undesired behaviour. Therefore, in such scenarios where reward function is complex, instead of specifying a reward directly, we can extract the underlying reward function directly from the observational data using inverse reinforcement learning (IRL) [22]. IRL allows us to infer the objective by observing the expert human behaviour which can later be used for training an RL agent. Several IRL Methods have been proposed including Maximum Entropy IRL, Apprenticeship Learning and Bayesian IRL [4].

Another challenge that arises when defining a global reward function is the balance of multiple sub-goals where multi-dimensional costs need be minimized simultaneously. e.g. we want to minimizing the execution cost and flow time of a process case at the same time. To solve this we utilize the Hybrid Reward Architecture proposed by Seijen et al. [33] where we compute a value function by first decomposing the reward function into n sub-functions $R_{env}(s, a, s') = \sum_{k=1}^{n} R_k(s, a, s')$, for all s, a, s' and then aggregate the individual values to get an estimate of action-values of the current state.

Decision Model for Generating Recommendations: An RL policy defines the behaviour of an agent in a given environment. Formally it is defined as the distribution over actions given states [31]. $\pi(a \mid s) = \mathbb{P}[A_t = a \mid S_t = s]$ where S is the observed state, represented by a feature vector; A is the set of action recommended during the execution of a partially completed process case (within an enabled work item). The associated value function is given by $v^\pi(s) := \mathbb{E}[\sum_{t=1}^{\infty} \gamma^{t-1} R_t \mid \pi, S_1 = s]$ [31].

We argue that an RL policy is an effective proxy for capturing the behaviour model of a case and can facilitate decision making by generating individualized action recommendations that help meet desired process goals. An RL Policy gives us the flexibility to start from any particular state and guides us on how to act optimally from that state onwards, making it naturally a good fit for sequential decision making in case management [31]. Similar to case templates, Policies in essence capture the best practices of knowledge work that can be reused in a particular context, giving knowledge workers effective recommendations on how to tackle similar problems from their best performing colleagues. Compared to the rigid process structures, modeling behaviour with policies provides several benefits. e.g. Policies can capture the uncertainty of the environment and provide mechanisms for recovery. Furthermore, Policies allow us the flexibility to go back and forth (revisiting old states) providing an excellent support for following the case management philosophy and addressing its shortcomings. Similar to planning in traditional AI, RL policy allows us to recommend appropriate actions (interventions) for each given input state such that, if executed will lead to high value states (as defined by the reward function) in the near future and the desired goal state eventually. The difference here is that the requirements for executing the activities are less rigid. i.e. knowledge workers are not being forced to execute activities in a pre-defined manner rather the optimal learned policy guides the action based on the current process state.

Definition 5 (Case Decision Model). *A Case decision model learned using historical $\mathcal{D}$ is represented by the value function $v^\pi(s)$ and associated policy $\pi : S \rightarrow A$ that computes the optimal step recommendation, given the current case state represented as $s_a = (a_i \mid a_i \in A \wedge f_{executed}(a_i) = true)$, and set of tasks $\langle \tau_1, \tau_2, \ldots, \tau_i \rangle$ that have been executed thus far.*

Learned value functions (and policies) are functions of the environment state. Here we rely on deep learning for learning the right representations (that characterizes how the features will be treated into higher levels of abstraction), thus allowing us to effectively approximate the value function. High-capacity function approximators like Deep Neural Networks allow us to model large state spaces (common in real world settings) and find a compact representation that generalizes across state. Additionally, it allows us to abstract and extract high-level features directly from input data. In our work we consider a number of Deep Learning based methods that takes as input the state feature vector and learn the approximate value function for each of the actions $\hat{q}(s, a_1, w) \cdots \hat{q}(s, a_m, w)$ that can be taken in that particular state.

4   Dynamic Treatment Regime for Managing Sepsis in ICU

A good example of knowledge work is patient case management which is highly case specific and requires a knowledge-driven approach. Clinical decision making in patient case management, depends on highly specific medical domain knowledge and evidence that emerges from patient's test results and real-time sensors. Clinicians face complicated decision problems during the patient treatment process. On a high level medical diagnosis process consists of gathering data, classifying and diagnosing a specific problem and suggesting specific course of treatment. When we dig into the details of such medical processes it becomes complex really quickly. i.e. requiring 10s of 1000s of rules which don't form a neat decision tree. It is partly because new knowledge is being discovered constantly, diagnostic heuristics are changing and new treatment strategies are being suggested constantly, making it hard to maintain an up-to-date knowledge bases of rules [20].

We pick the example of sepsis treatment to showcase the entire spectrum of process management (which ranges from fully structured to fully un-structured activities). Sepsis is a dangerous condition and costs the healthcare system, billions of dollars in treatment costs each year. Management of this disease is quite challenging for the clinicians and consists of giving patients intravenous fluids and vasopressors which can greatly influence the outcome.

In healthcare, Clinical pathways are care plans that attempt to standardise clinical or medical treatment processes. Such processes are highly knowledge driven and consist of predictable and unpredictable elements. As the Process evolves the knowledge workers (team of doctors) makes decisions based on the clinical observations and patient data that is being constantly updated. Decision making in this context requires a team of experts to come up with goals and plans of action that drives the progress of process (as opposed to control-flow where progress is dependent on completion of activities). Coming up with decision-making strategies that improve treatment policies and dynamically suggest optimal treatment for patients remains a key challenge for building next generation of data driven clinical decision support systems [11].

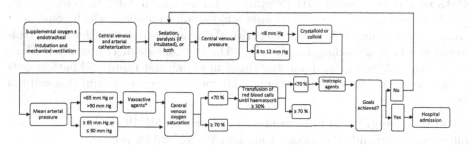

Fig. 1. Protocol for early goal directed therapy- figure adapted from [26]

Here instead of standardisation we customise the process to individual needs and consider the history of patient when making treatment decisions. Complete process of managing the disease and associated decision making policy is fairly complicated where treatment can include administration of antibiotics, source-control, intravenous fluid therapy and organ system support with vasopressor drugs, mechanical ventilation, and renal replacement therapy as required [18,19]. The overall treatment and can be broken down into detailed sub-processes (e.g. see Fig. 1 for handling patients in the state of septic shock). To simplify We consider decisions in a restricted sepsis management setting, where we focus on a subset of five interventions including mechanical ventilation administration, vasopressor administration, adenosine administration, dobutamine administration and dopamine administration.

5   Evaluation

We show that our proposed framework is useful for modeling sequential decisions problems involving decision support in the complicated setting of clinical care. Specifically, our evaluation seeks to answer the following question:

Given a particular patient's characteristics and physiological information at each time step as input, can our proposed framework learn an optimal treatment policy that can prescribe the right intervention (e.g. use of ventilator) to the patient at each stage of the treatment process, in order to improve the final outcome (e.g. patient mortality)?

We argue that a data-driven approach for discovering an effective sepsis treatment strategy is a good representative for evaluating our proposed RL based decision-making framework.

Markov Decision Process (MDP) Formulation: We will now formalize the sepsis management problem into our proposed Deep Reinforcement Learning framework. We start by explaining the details of the dataset and pre-processing and move on to define three key components of the Markov decision Process: a state space, an action space, and a reward function.

Patient Cohort: MIMIC-III ('Medical Information Mart for Intensive Care') [17] is a large open-access anonymized single-center database which consists of comprehensive clinical data of 61,532 critical care admissions from 2001–2012 collected at a Boston teaching hospital. The Dataset consists of 47 features (including demographics, vitals,administration of fluids,lab test result and patient outcome) on a cohort of sepsis patients who meet the sepsis-3 definition criteria [30].

Pre-processing: In our implementation, we rely on MIMIC-Extract [34] which offers guidelines and establishes a community standard for pre-preprocessing the MIMIC dataset for various machine learning tasks. We have included patients with age >15, whose ICU stay is between 12 h and 10 d resulting in 34,472 patients representing a diverse cohort. Further we excluded entries containing outliers and missing values. Lastly for every patient time-stamped physiological measurements are aggregated (e.g. hourly heart rate, arterial blood pressure, or respiratory rate) into one hour windows, with the mean or sum being recorded when several data points were present in one window.

State Representation: Our feature set consists of relevant covariates representing a patient's physiological state at a given point in time. Specifically, it consists of four static features (like gender, ethnicity, age etc.) concatenated with six time varying patient vitals (e.g., heart rate, blood pressure, respiratory rate, oxygen saturation level) representing information most relevant to the decisions. After feature encoding, our final MDP state is the relevant patient covariates represented by a feature vector of size 21×1 updated at each time step.

Actions Space: The pre-processed dataset includes hourly indicators of various device and drug treatments provided to the patient overtime. These treatments are available to the clinician in ICU and impact patient mortality. To manage the complexity we make some simplifying assumptions. i.e. we don't consider the exact dosage of each intervention and only focus on selected interventions like: mechanical ventilation administration, vasopressor administration, adenosine administration, dobutamine administration and dopamine administration.

Our action (or treatment) space consists of five discrete actions, combination of them represents various interventions when patient has been admitted in ICU.

Reward Function: In Reinforcement learning, the decision-making agent's goal is to learn a policy which maximizes the total reward collected over time. We define our reward function by 'in-hospital mortality' indicator (which is the final outcome of interest) as our reward function. The RL agent optimizes for longer-term outcomes as it receives no immediate rewards but only receives a final positive reward at the end if the patient survives and a negative reward if the patient dies.

Model Implementation: We define an optimal policy as a mapping from the patient's history H (History of their measurements and treatments to date) to the next treatment decision in a way that it leads to optimal outcomes in the long run. We consider the data-driven formulation of RL where RL agent doesn't have access to the environment for additional data collection, rather relies on already collected static dataset. Several Offline (or Batch RL) algorithms have been proposed in the literature. In our experiments we focus on popular state-of-the-art algorithms such as Deep Q Learning(DQN), Double Deep Q Learning (DDQN), Mixed Monte Carlo(MMC) and Persistent Advantage Learning (PAL) [18]. Using these methods we train an RL agent to find the optimal policy that corresponds to optimum treatment path for a given patient state. In our experiments, we divide the data with a 70%–30% ratio for train and evaluate set respectively. We our DeepRL models learn a treatment policy and we use Off-Policy Evaluation methods on testset to estimate the value of this learned policy.

Off-Policy Evaluation: In real world settings we rarely have to access to a simulator to safely test our models, and direct deployment of our learned policy could be risky and dangerous. Therefore, in our implementation, we rely on various well known off-policy and counterfactual policy evaluation (CPE/OPE) metrics that leverage historical data, to give us an expected performance of the newly trained RL model without having to deploy it [24]. Historical data represents Behaviour policy, and is the probability of a clinician deciding on the chosen medical intervention, given the patient's physiological state.

The OPE problem as is defined as follows [32]: Given an evaluation policy, π_e, historical logged data, D, and an approximate model (determined by deep RL), the goal is to produce an estimator, $\hat{v}(D)$, of $v(\pi_e)$ that has low mean squared error (MSE): $\text{MSE}(\hat{v}(D), v(\pi_e)) := \mathbf{E}\left[(\hat{v}(D) - v(\pi_e))^2\right]$ [25]. The OPE problem is challenging because of the distribution mismatch between current policy and the behaviour policy (used to collect the data). i.e. we don't know the actual reward of a new action (learned by the model policy) that wasn't taken by the logged policy. Several OPE methods have been developed over the years and in our experiments we rely on Weighted Importance Sampling and Inverse Propensity Score estimator [16,32]. Weighted importance sampling (WIS) is a modern estimator method and is trusted to represent realistic estimates of the policies values in full RL settings [12]. It can however sometimes provides biased estimates as it aims to trade increased bias for reduced variance. We aim to get a more balanced realistic value estimate by considering both weighted and unweighted estimators [12].

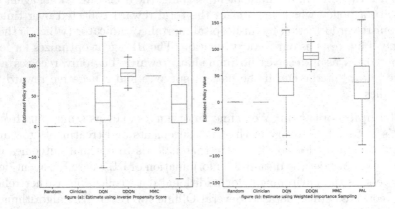

Fig. 2. Comparison of policy value estimates using IPS and WIS estimators to evaluate treatment policies learned by the Deep Reinforcement Learning models.

Results: In our experimental evaluation, we are interested in evaluating the potential improvement a new policy can bring in terms of reduction in patient mortality. We profile various deep RL methods (such as DQN, DDQN, Monte-Carlo etc.) and compare the policy value estimates for the values of three different policies: RL policy, clinician policy and random intervention policy (which takes actions uniformly at random). In real world settings like healthcare the true value of behaviour policy is unknown and is often estimated from the historical data [12]. Therefore we estimate the clinician policy (also known as the behaviour policy) from the patient trajectories in our dataset using monte-carlo returns to get an on-policy estimate.

Figure 2 shows a Box Plot comparison of estimates for the values of five different policies, with each sub-figure representing the performance measured by one of the modern off-policy evaluation (OPE) methods. Both Estimators (Inverse Propensity Score) and Weighted Importance Sampling) show that DDQN, MMC models yield a much higher expected value than the clinician policy outperforming both baselines. Further we observe that except for Mixed Monte Carlo (MMC), all methods have quite significant variance. While variance of DDQN and MMC is small compared to DQN and PAL, it might be optimistically biased.

MMC has also shown good performance on various RL bechmarks in literature as it learns action values not only by bootstrapping the current action value prediction, it mixes in the total discounted return as well [23]. Therefore we conclude that we can put more confidence in the Mixed Monte Carlo method when picking a final model.

Discussion: In real world settings accurate OPE estimation is challenging due to several reasons. Firstly, in healthcare settings we have problem of observing sparse rewards. i.e. decisions made now have an impact several time steps later measured by the impact on outcome. Having sparse outcomes makes it challenging to asses newly learned policies and the effect an individual decision by a physician can have on the patient. Secondly, the statistical tools for evaluation like Importance Sampling estimators have limitations and can be unreliable in scenarios where data is limited. We should note that to learn an optimal policy, even if we have large amounts of data available, we require it to be sufficiently diverse as the number of sequences that match the evaluation policy decays exponentially leaving only a tiny fraction of trajectories (after being assigned non-zero weight) that match the treatments that our policy recommends [3,11]. This results in high-variance estimates of evaluation policy. Lastly, behaviour policies are not known and model terms are hard to estimate [25]. We should also note that each of the estimator comes with a tradeoffs between bias and variance in off-policy evaluation, so we can't rely on a single estimator for evaluation in the sepsis management problem [12]. Due to all these challenging aspects, we have to take special care in evaluating the newly proposed policies.

Even though here has been a lot of excitement around using RL for adaptive decision making, we remain cautious in being overly optimistic and making the claim that our proposed RL system can fundamentally discover new treatments. We should rather stick to picking policies that don't significantly differ from those present in the given historical dataset [12]. Our treatment recommender system can suggest small changes to refine existing clinician policies. Fundamentally, we see our framework playing the role of providing decision support and recommending actions leading to good outcomes (as measured by patient mortality). We recommend consulting the domain expert at each stage, for setting up the RL problem in the right way, picking the right the reward scheme and expert evaluation of the final learned policy.

Having said all of that, RL still remains a powerful tool for optimizing sequential decisions which can provide us with mechanism to improve upon and refine existing expert policies. Overall, in our experiment we show that given a sufficiently rich dataset generated by a behaviour policy, Offline Reinforcement learning can learn optimal policies that can recommend sensible actions to the knowledge worker involved in the clinical car process.

6   Conclusion

Supporting knowledge work when rigid definitions of process models are not available or cannot be designed apriori (with structured or unstructured data) remains an interesting challenge for the BPM community to tackle. Retrospective data that represents expert decisions in the past offers an opportunity that can be exploited for building a decision support solution for knowledge workers. In this work, based on recent advances in deep reinforcement learning we proposed an RL based decision framework, that can provide recommendations to knowledge workers given a case state. We demonstrated the efficacy of our approach by conducting an experiment on a real world sepsis treatment ICU dataset. We show our proposed framework is useful in coming up with policies that can offer treatment recommendations and suggest small improvements over existing expert policies, leading to good outcomes(as measured by patient mortality). We further show that our proposed framework is adaptable enough to balance between the structured and unstructured aspects of the knowledge Intensive Processes by providing support for repetitive tasks yet be flexible enough to facilitate creative aspects of problem solving during execution at run-time.

References

1. Van der Aalst, W.M., Berens, P.: Beyond workflow management: product-driven case handling. In: Proceedings of the 2001 International ACM SIGGROUP Conference on Supporting Group Work, pp. 42–51 (2001)
2. Van der Aalst, W.M., Stoffele, M., Wamelink, J.: Case handling in construction. Autom. Constr. **12**(3), 303–320 (2003)
3. Agarwal, R., Schuurmans, D., Norouzi, M.: An optimistic perspective on offline reinforcement learning (2020)
4. Arora, S., Doshi, P.: A survey of inverse reinforcement learning: challenges, methods and progress. Artif. Intell. **297**, 103500 (2021)
5. Berner, C., et al.: Dota 2 with large scale deep reinforcement learning. arXiv preprint arXiv:1912.06680 (2019)
6. Di Ciccio, C., Marrella, A., Russo, A.: Knowledge-intensive processes: an overview of contemporary approaches. In: KiBP@ KR, pp. 33–47 (2012)
7. Di Ciccio, C., Marrella, A., Russo, A.: Knowledge-intensive processes: characteristics, requirements and analysis of contemporary approaches. J. Data Semant. **4**, 29–57 (03 2015). https://doi.org/10.1007/s13740-014-0038-4
8. Dulac-Arnold, G., Mankowitz, D., Hester, T.: Challenges of real-world reinforcement learning. arXiv preprint arXiv:1904.12901 (2019)
9. Fischer, L.: How Knowledge Workers Get Things Done: Real-World Adaptive Case Management. Future Strategies Inc. (2012)
10. Gauci, J., et al.: Horizon: Facebook's open source applied reinforcement learning platform. arXiv preprint arXiv:1811.00260 (2018)
11. Gottesman, O., et al.: Guidelines for reinforcement learning in healthcare. Nat. Med. **25**(1), 16–18 (2019)
12. Gottesman, O., et al.: Evaluating reinforcement learning algorithms in observational health settings. arXiv preprint arXiv:1805.12298 (2018)
13. Gröger, C., Schwarz, H., Mitschang, B.: Prescriptive analytics for recommendation-based business process optimization. In: Abramowicz, W., Kokkinaki, A. (eds.) BIS 2014. LNBIP, vol. 176, pp. 25–37. Springer, Cham (2014). https://doi.org/10.1007/978-3-319-06695-0_3
14. Günther, C.W., Van der Aalst, W.M.: Process mining in case handling systems. In: Proceeding of Multikonferenz Wirtschaftsinformatik (2006)
15. Hauder, M., Pigat, S., Matthes, F.: Research challenges in adaptive case management: a literature review. In: 2014 IEEE 18th International Enterprise Distributed Object Computing Conference Workshops and Demonstrations, pp. 98–107. IEEE (2014)

16. Horvitz, D.G., Thompson, D.J.: A generalization of sampling without replacement from a finite universe. J. Am. Stat. Assoc. **47**(260), 663–685 (1952)
17. Johnson, A.E., et al.: MIMIC-III, a freely accessible critical care database. Sci. Data **3**(1), 1–9 (2016)
18. Levine, S., Kumar, A., Tucker, G., Fu, J.: Offline reinforcement learning: tutorial, review, and perspectives on open problems. arXiv preprint arXiv:2005.01643 (2020)
19. Marin, M.A., Hauder, M., Matthes, F.: Case management: an evaluation of existing approaches for knowledge-intensive processes. In: Reichert, M., Reijers, H.A. (eds.) BPM 2015. LNBIP, vol. 256, pp. 5–16. Springer, Cham (2016). https://doi.org/10.1007/978-3-319-42887-1_1
20. Motahari-Nezhad, H.R., Swenson, K.D.: Adaptive case management: overview and research challenges. In: 2013 IEEE 15th Conference on Business Informatics, pp. 264–269. IEEE (2013)
21. Motahari-Nezhad, H.R., Bartolini, C.: Next best step and expert recommendation for collaborative processes in IT service management. In: Rinderle-Ma, S., Toumani, F., Wolf, K. (eds.) BPM 2011. LNCS, vol. 6896, pp. 50–61. Springer, Heidelberg (2011). https://doi.org/10.1007/978-3-642-23059-2_7
22. Ng, A.Y., Russell, S.J., et al.: Algorithms for inverse reinforcement learning. In: ICML, vol. 1, p. 2 (2000)
23. Ostrovski, G., Bellemare, M.G., Oord, A., Munos, R.: Count-based exploration with neural density models. In: International Conference on Machine Learning, pp. 2721–2730. PMLR (2017)
24. Precup, D., Sutton, R.S., Singh, S.P.: Eligibility traces for off-policy policy evaluation. In: Proceedings of the 17th International Conference on Machine Learning, ICML 2000, pp. 759–766. Morgan Kaufmann Publishers Inc., San Francisco (2000)
25. Raghu, A., et al.: Behaviour policy estimation in off-policy policy evaluation: calibration matters. arXiv preprint arXiv:1807.01066 (2018)
26. Rivers, E., et al.: Early goal-directed therapy in the treatment of severe sepsis and septic shock. N. Engl. J. Med. **345**(19), 1368–1377 (2001)
27. Santipuri, M., Ghose, A., Dam, H.K., Roy, S.: Goal orchestrations: modelling and mining flexible business processes. In: Mayr, H.C., Guizzardi, G., Ma, H., Pastor, O. (eds.) ER 2017. LNCS, vol. 10650, pp. 373–387. Springer, Cham (2017). https://doi.org/10.1007/978-3-319-69904-2_29
28. Schonenberg, H., Weber, B., van Dongen, B., van der Aalst, W.: Supporting flexible processes through recommendations based on history. In: Dumas, M., Reichert, M., Shan, M.-C. (eds.) BPM 2008. LNCS, vol. 5240, pp. 51–66. Springer, Heidelberg (2008). https://doi.org/10.1007/978-3-540-85758-7_7
29. Sindhgatta Rajan, R.: Data-driven and context-aware process provisioning. Ph.D. thesis, School of Computing and IT, University of Wollongong (2018)
30. Singer, M., et al.: The third international consensus definitions for sepsis and septic shock (Sepsis-3). J. Am. Med. Assoc. **315**(8), 801–810 (2016)
31. Sutton, R., Barto, A.: Reinforcement Learning: An Introduction. MIT Press (2018)
32. Thomas, P., Brunskill, E.: Data-efficient off-policy policy evaluation for reinforcement learning. In: International Conference on Machine Learning, pp. 2139–2148. PMLR (2016)
33. Van Seijen, H., Fatemi, M., Romoff, J., Laroche, R., Barnes, T., Tsang, J.: Hybrid reward architecture for reinforcement learning. In: Proceedings of the 31st International Conference on Neural Information Processing Systems, NIPS 2017, pp. 5398–5408. Curran Associates Inc., Red Hook (2017)

34. Wang, S., McDermott, M.B., Chauhan, G., Ghassemi, M., Hughes, M.C., Naumann, T.: Mimic-extract: a data extraction, preprocessing, and representation pipeline for MIMIC-III. In: Proceedings of the ACM Conference on Health, Inference, and Learning, pp. 222–235 (2020)
35. Weber, I., Hoffmann, J., Mendling, J.: Beyond soundness: on the verification of semantic business process models. Distrib. Parallel Databases **27**(3), 271–343 (2010)

Generating High Quality Samples of Process Cases in Internal Audit

Yaguang Sun[1]($\boxtimes$), Lyth AI-Khazrage[2], and Ömer Özümerzifon[3]

[1] KPMG AG Wirtschaftsprüfungsgesellschaft, Stuttgart, Germany
yaguangsun@kpmg.com
[2] Karlsruhe University of Applied Sciences, Karlsruhe, Germany
lyth.al-khazrage@hs-karlsruhe.de
[3] University of Mannheim, Mannheim, Germany
oezuemerzifon@bwl.uni-mannheim.de

Abstract. Business Process Mining (BPM) has become an essential tool in internal audit (IA), which helps auditors analyze potential risks in clients' core business processes. After finishing the risk analysis task for the target business process with BPM, auditors need to sample a small set of representative process cases from event log, based on which clients will verify the analysis results and analyze the triggers for the risks in the target business process. This process case sampling (PCS) step is important because it is difficult to check each single case from a large event log. Therefore, the quality of the set of case samples (SCS) from PCS is regarded as one of the success factors in IA project. Manual PCS and simple random PCS are two basic methods for executing PCS. However, both methods cannot assure the quality of the generated SCS. In this paper, we propose an advanced PCS method. It first defines the risk of process cases as well as the factors that affect the quality of SCS, before dynamically optimizing the quality of SCS during PCS. Our experimental evaluation highlights that our approach yields higher quality SCS than manual PCS and simple random PCS.

Keywords: Business process mining · Business process management · Process case sampling · Process risk management · Internal auditing

1 Introduction

In IA project, one of the main tasks for an internal auditor is to discover and analyze the potential risks that appear in company's major business processes such as purchase to pay (P2P) and order to cash (O2C) process. These underlying risks might give rise to violations of laws and company regulations, as well as loss of profitability and efficiency [1]. For instance, maverick-buying (purchase without involving procurement department) is regarded as a potential risk in P2P process which can result in the purchase of goods with higher price [2].

Figure 1 illustrates the basic steps for implementing BPM in IA. In the step of preparation (step 1), auditors select the target business process in clients'

© Springer Nature Switzerland AG 2021
A. Polyvyanyy et al. (Eds.): BPM Forum 2021, LNBIP 427, pp. 263–279, 2021.
https://doi.org/10.1007/978-3-030-85440-9_16

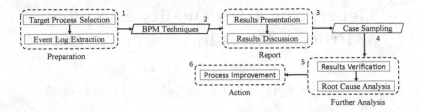

Fig. 1. Illustration of basic procedures for executing process mining in internal audit.

company and extract the event log from the corresponding information systems. Afterwards, risk analysis (step 2) on the event log is carried out with BPM techniques of which the analysis results are then presented to and discussed with clients (step 3). Moreover, the auditors sample a small set of representative process cases of high risk (step 4). By referencing the selected case samples, the clients together with auditors will verify the analysis results, analyze the root causes which trigger the risks in the target process (step 5) and improve the process by tackling the discovered root causes in the step of action (step 6).

The step of process case sampling (PCS) is regarded as one of the success factors for an IA project as clients take actions (improve process) by referencing the case samples from PCS, considering that there are usually a large number of cases in real-life event logs and it is hard for clients to check each single case. Hence, the quality of case samples from PCS is of great importance. According to our experiences gathered from a number of IA projects, a high quality set of case samples (SCS) should:

- consist of high-risk cases (*risk-level*).
- cover as multiple process risks as possible (*risk-diversity*).
- contain cases with dissimilar combinations of risk types (*risk-dissimilarity*).
- include cases pertaining to the most common process variants (*universality*).

Manual PCS (M-PCS) and simple random PCS (S-PCS) are two basic methods to implement PCS. M-PCS inherits the idea of judgment sampling (non-probability sampling approach) [3], in which auditors manually select cases according to their judgment on the goodness of the candidates. S-PCS pertains to probability sampling approach which assumes that each case from the event log has the same possibility of being selected [3]. M-PCS is very time consuming and only applicable for sampling a small number (less than 50) of cases. Moreover, both M-PCS and S-PCS cannot assure the quality of the potential SCS.

Against this background, we therefore put forward an advanced PCS approach named A-PCS in this paper. It considers the four quality factors (i.e. *risk-level*, *risk-diversity*, *risk-dissimilarity* and *universality*) of the resulting set of case samples from PCS. More specifically, it first defines *risk-level*, *risk-diversity*, *risk-dissimilarity* and *universality* in a formal way, before dynamically optimizing the four factors for the underlying SCS during PCS.

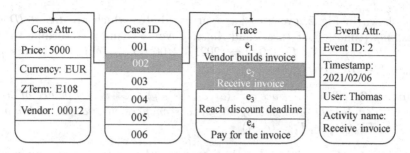

Fig. 2. An example event log of P2P process

In the remainder of this paper, we first recall the concepts and exemplify the issues of applying M-PCS and S-PCS (Sect. 2). We then elaborate on the details of the proposed A-PCS technique (Sect. 3). To test the efficiency of our method, we implement a comprehensive evaluation with two real-world event logs (Sect. 4). As part of that, we also compared A-PCS with M-PCS and S-PCS. Finally, we review related work (Sect. 5) and conclude (Sect. 6).

2   Issues of M-PCS and S-PCS

In this section, we first introduce the preliminary concepts such as event log, case and trace. Afterwards, the four concepts: *risk-level*, *risk-diversity*, *risk-dissimilarity* and *universality* which determine the quality of a SCS are defined. Using these concepts, we exemplify the issues of M-PCS and S-PCS.

2.1   Preliminaries

Event Log. A business process depicts a set of activities executed in a certain order. During the execution of the business process in information systems, historical data is recorded in event log. Figure 2 shows an example event log of P2P process that consists of activities such as "Receive invoice" and "Pay for the invoice". Each event log is a set of cases, each standing for a process instance and uniquely identified by case ID. We define an event log as follows [4,5]:

Definition 1. *(Universes) Let $\mathcal{A}$ denote the universe of unique activities of a business process. $\mathcal{E}$ denotes the event universe, i.e. the set of all possible event identifiers. $\mathcal{C}$ denotes the universe of cases, i.e. the set of all possible case identifiers. $\mathcal{N}_e$ and $\mathcal{N}_c$ denote the set of all possible attribute names for event and case respectively. $\mathcal{V}_e$ and $\mathcal{V}_c$ denote the universes of attribute values for event and case respectively.*

Definition 2. *(Event, Attribute) Each event $e \in \mathcal{E}$ denotes the execution of an instance of a particular activity $a \in \mathcal{A}$. For each attribute name $n \in \mathcal{N}_e$, the function $\Gamma_n(e)$ returns the value of attribute n of event e, i.e. $\Gamma_n(e) \in \mathcal{V}_e$*

As shown in Fig. 2, event e_2 has four attributes which are *Event ID* (id), *Timestamp* (time), *User* (user) and *Activity Name* (name). According to Definition 2, $\Gamma_{id}(e_2) = $ "2", $\Gamma_{time}(e_2) = $ "2021/02/06", $\Gamma_{user}(e_2) = $ "*Thomas*" and $\Gamma_{name}(e_2) = $ "*Receive invoice*".

Definition 3. *(Trace) A trace $\sigma = \langle e_1, e_2, \cdots, e_k \rangle \in \mathcal{E}^*$ is a sequence of events, where $\mathcal{E}^*$ denotes the universe of all finite sequences over $\mathcal{E}$. In addition, for $1 \leq i < k$, $\Gamma_{time}(e_i) \leq \Gamma_{time}(e_{i+1})$.*

Definition 4. *(Case, Attribute) Each case $c \in \mathcal{C}$ denotes the execution of an instance of a particular process. For each attribute name $n \in \mathcal{N}_c$, the function $\Lambda_n(c)$ returns the value of attribute n of case c, i.e. $\Lambda_n(c) \in \mathcal{V}_c$.*

Definition 5. *(Event Log) An event log $L = \{c_1, \cdots, c_{|L|}\}$ is a set of cases, i.e. $L \subseteq \mathcal{C}$.*

The example P2P event log (Fig. 2) contains six cases. The case with ID *002* (c_{002}) has four attributes: *Price, Currency, ZTerm* and *Vendor*. According to Definition 4, $\Lambda_{Price}(c_{002}) = 5000$, $\Lambda_{Currency}(c_{002}) = $ "*EUR*", $\Lambda_{ZTerm}(c_{002}) = $ "*E108*" and $\Lambda_{Vendor}(c_{002}) = $ "00012". Furthermore, case c_{002} has a special attribute *trace*, i.e. $\Lambda_{trace}(c_{002}) = \langle e_1, e_2, e_3, e_4 \rangle$.

Jaccard Similarity. Let I be a set of items (we will later consider names of case attributes as items), $S(I)$ be the universe of all finite set of unique items over I. A set $s^I \in S(I)$ of length m is denoted $\{it_1, it_2, \cdots, it_m\}$, where each element it_k is an item from I. For two sets $X = \{x_1, x_2, \cdots, x_j\}$ and $Y = \{y_1, y_2, \cdots, y_q\}$ from $S(I)$, the *Jaccard Similarity* [6] between X and Y is defined as:

$$J(X, Y) = \frac{|X \cap Y|}{|X \cup Y|} \tag{1}$$

2.2 Risk-Level, Risk-Diversity, Risk-Dissimilarity and Universality

Risk-level, risk-diversity, risk-dissimilarity and universality are four major factors that determine the quality of a SCS from PCS. Here, we give the formal definitions of the four notions.

Risk of Case. With $\mathcal{R}$ as set of all possible risks for the target business process, we define a risk for a particular case as follows:

Definition 6. *(Risk of Case) A risk $r \in \mathcal{R}$ for a case $c \in \mathcal{C}$ is an attribute of c, where $\mathcal{R} \subset \mathcal{N}_c$. Function $\Pi : \mathcal{C}, \mathcal{R} \rightarrow \{0, 1\}$ assigns a risk with a certain value to case c, where $\{0, 1\} \subset \mathcal{V}_c$. $\Lambda_r(c) = 1$ indicates presence of r in case c while $\Lambda_r(c) = 0$ indicates absence of r in case c.*

Due to lack of event of activity "Build purchase order" in the trace, case c_{002} from the example P2P event log (Fig. 2) is judged as a maverick-buying case. As introduced, maverick-buying is an underlying risk for P2P process which might lead to the purchase with higher cost. Thence, auditor can assign value of 1 to risk maverick-buying for c_{002}, i.e. $\Pi(c_{002}, "maverick - buying"):=1$. Another risk (loose-discount) can be discovered from the trace of c_{002}, where the event of activity "Reach discount deadline" happens before the event of activity "Pay for the invoice". This means that the invoice is payed too late to get a discount from vendor, which increases the purchase cost. Similarly, auditor can assign value of 1 to risk loose-discount for c_{002}, i.e. $\Pi(c_{002}, "loose - discount"):=1$.

Risk-Level. *Risk-level* is employed to estimate the risk degree of one case or a SCS. Let L denote an event log, $R_L \subseteq \mathcal{R}$ denote the set of risks for L, $c \in L$ denote a case. We define *risk-level* of case $RLC(c)$ as a measure to quantify the risk degree of case c:

$$RLC(c, L) = \frac{ARLC(c)}{\Psi(L)} \tag{2}$$

$$ARLC(c) = \sum_{r \in R_L} \Lambda_r(c) \tag{3}$$

where $ARLC(c)$ represents the absolute *risk-level* of c, which is in the range of $[0, |R_L|]$. For the example P2P event log (Fig. 2), presume that case c_{002} has two risks with value 1, i.e. $\Lambda_{maverick-buying}(c_{002}) = 1$ and $\Lambda_{loose-discount}(c_{002}) = 1$, all the other risks have value 0. The absolute *risk-level* of c_{002} is $ARLC(c_{002}) = 2$. $\Psi(L) = max(ARLC(c_1), ARLC(c_2), \cdots, ARLC(c_{|L|}))$ is a function with an input of event log and an output of maximal ARLC value that can be found by considering all the cases in L. The RLC of a case c equals the quotient of $ARLC(c)$ and $\Psi(L)$ which is in the range of $[0, 1]$.

Let $l \subseteq L$ denote a non-empty SCS generated by PCS over log L. The *risk-level* of SCS RL is defined as a measure to quantify the risk degree of l:

$$RL(l, L) = \frac{\sum_{c \in l} RLC(c, L)}{|l|} \tag{4}$$

where $0 \leq RL(l, L) \leq 1$. Let L_{e1} denote the example P2P event log as shown in Fig. 2. Assume that $l_{e1} = \{c_{002}, c_{004}, c_{006}\}$ is a SCS generated by PCS over L_{e1}, $ARLC(c_{002}) = 2$, $ARLC(c_{004}) = 3$, $ARLC(c_{006}) = 1$ and $\Psi(L_{e1}) = 10$. According to Eq. 4, the *risk-level* of l_{e1} is $RL(l_{e1}, L_{e1}) = 0.2$.

Risk-Dissimilarity. A high quality SCS should cover cases that contain dissimilar combination of risks, so that the mechanism for the co-appearance of different kinds of risks can be analyzed. Let $\Delta: \mathcal{C}, \mathcal{R} \rightarrow \mathcal{R}$ be a function which extracts the set of all risks with value 1 for a certain case. For log L_{e1}, let $R_{L_{e1}}$ denote the set of risks for L_{e1}, "maverick−buying" and "loose−discount" are two risks from $R_{L_{e1}}$, presume that case c_{002} from L_{e1} only has risks *"maverick−buying"* and *"loose−discount"* with value 1. Then we have $\Delta(c_{002}, R_{L_{e1}}) = \{$ *"maverick-buying"*, *"loose-discount"* $\}$.

Given a SCS l for log L, $CP = \{(c_1, c_2) \mid c_1 \in l \wedge c_2 \in l \wedge \Lambda_{ID}(c_1) < \Lambda_{ID}(c_2)\}$ denotes the set of all possible pairs of cases from l, where $\Lambda_{ID}(c_k)$ stands for the value of case ID for case $c_k \in L$, we define the *risk-dissimilarity* of SCS *RD* as a measure which quantifies the average dissimilarity of risk types of all possible pairs of cases from l:

$$RD(l, L) = \frac{\sum_{(c_1, c_2) \in CP} RDP(c_1, c_2, L)}{|CP|} \tag{5}$$

$$RDP(c_1, c_2, L) = 1 - J(\Delta(c_1, R_L), \Delta(c_2, R_L)) \tag{6}$$

where $RDP(c_1, c_2, L)$ stands for the *risk-dissimilarity* of a particular pair of cases, which is expressed by the difference between 1 and the *Jaccard Similarity* of the risk types of the two cases and in the range of $[0, 1]$. As shown in Eq. 5, the *risk-dissimilarity* of a SCS is expressed by the mean of dissimilarity of risk types of all possible pairs of cases from the SCS.

Risk-Diversity. *Risk-diversity*, which reflects the richness of risk types in a SCS, is determined by both RL and RD of the SCS. A SCS tends to contain higher number of different types of risk if the values of both RL and RD are higher. For instance, for a SCS l, if $RD(l, L)$ has a very high value and $RL(l, L)$ has a very low value, the *risk-diversity* of l can still be very low because the cardinal number of risks for l is too low.

Universality. In IA, the event logs in hand usually stem from business processes implemented in highly flexible systems such as SAP and often contain a large number of process variants [4]. The risks of cases that belong to the process variants with higher frequency of occurrence are more interesting because these variants usually have greater business impact.

Let T denote the universe of process variants, function $\Upsilon: T, C \to \mathbb{Z}^+$ calculates the frequency of occurrence for an input process variant in a certain log. For instance, let $T_L \subset T$ be the set of all process variants from log L, $vt \in T_L$ be a process variant, $\Upsilon(vt, L) = 100$ implies that there are totally 100 cases that adhere to vt in L. $\Omega: C \to T$ denotes a function which outputs the corresponding variant for a give case. Let l be a SCS for log L, we define the *universality* of SCS *UNI* as follows:

$$UNI(l, L) = \frac{\sum_{c \in l} UNIC(c, L)}{|l|} \tag{7}$$

$$UNIC(c, L) = \frac{\Upsilon(\Omega(c), L)}{\Theta(T_L)} \tag{8}$$

Table 1. Evaluation results on M-PCS and S-PCS by using event log LO2C.

PCS method	Risk-level	Risk-dissimilarity	Risk-diversity	Universality
M-PCS	0.53	0.72	56	0.02
S-PCS	0.49	0.63	36	0.11

where $\Theta(T_L) = max(\Upsilon(vt_1, L), \cdots, \Upsilon(vt_{|T_L|}, L))$ is a function that returns the maximal frequency of occurrence that can be found by considering all process variants in T_L. As shown in Eq. 8, the *universality* of a case (UNIC) equals the quotient of the frequency of occurrence of the variant for this case and the maximal variant occurrence frequency, which is therefore in the range of $(0, 1]$. The *universality* of a SCS is measured through the average occurrence frequency of the variants for the cases in the SCS (Eq. 7).

2.3 Research Issues

In M-PCS, auditors intuitively judge whether a candidate case from event log can benefit the quality of the underlying SCS. As real-life event log often contains a large number of cases, auditors are not capable of checking every case. As a result, M-PCS usually generates a local optimal SCS with low quality. S-PCS presumes that every case from the event log has equal chance to be selected. However, in the scenario of PCS, the cases which tend to improve the quality of the potential SCS should be assigned a higher possibility of selection. Thus, S-PCS can also generate low quality SCS.

We illustrate the issue with experimental insights obtained for a real-life O2C event log (LO2C) extracted from SAP. By analyzing LO2C with BPM techniques, 69 types of process risk are discovered and assigned as case attributes to the cases from LO2C. Using M-PCS (by our auditor) and S-PCS, setting the sampling size to 50, yields the evaluation results shown in Table 1.

The results illustrate that both PCS methods perform poorly on one or more quality factors. For instance, the SCS generated by M-PCS has relatively high *risk-level*, *risk-dissimilarity* and covers 56 types of risk which accounts for 81% (56/69) of the entire risk types. However, this SCS has very low *universality* of which the value is only 0.02. The SCS generated by S-PCS has relatively low *risk-level* and *risk-dissimilarity*. Particularly, it has a very low *risk-diversity* which only covers 36 types of risk.

The above results exemplify that both M-PCS and S-PCS cannot assure the quality of the output SCS. In the remainder, we will therefore present an advanced PCS technique (A-PCS) that helps generate high quality SCS.

3 Approach Design

This section presents a novel PCS technique named A-PCS. An overview of our approach is given in Fig. 3. In essence, we proceed in three stages. In the first

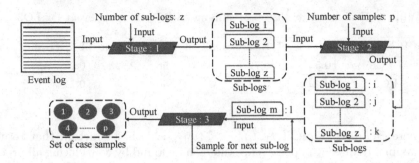

Fig. 3. Outline of the basic idea for the proposed PCS technique A-PCS

stage, the input event log with risk information is clustered into sub-logs. The cases with similar risk types are put in the same sub-log. In the second stage, a sampling size is assigned to each sub-log according to its quality reflected by *risk-level*, *risk-diversity*, *risk-dissimilarity* and *universality*. The sub-log with higher quality will be assigned a higher sampling size. In Fig. 3, the sampling sizes for sub-log 1, sub-log 2 and sub-log z are set to i, j and k respectively. The sum of sampling sizes for all sub-logs equals the entire sampling size p, i.e. $i + j + \cdots + k = p$. In stage 3, our novel case sampling method is executed on each sub-log, which then outputs a SCS with optimal quality.

3.1 Stage 1: Case Clustering

From the perspective of distribution of risk types, the original event log is usually comprised of several homogeneous groups of cases. Stratified random sampling that adheres to probability sampling approach is designed to deal with such a situation [3]. It first divides the members of the population into homogeneous subgroups. Then, for each subgroup, it samples a certain number of members. For the first stage of our approach, we inherit the idea of stratified random sampling through clustering the cases with similar risk types into the same sub-log. In this way, the case samples selected from different sub-logs tend to have dissimilar risk types. Thus, the *risk-diversity* and *risk-dissimilarity* of the generated SCS can be improved to a certain extent. A number of clustering algorithms from academia, e.g. K-Means and K-Modes [7], can be employed to implement the case clustering task.

3.2 Stage 2: Sampling Size Assignment

In the second stage, each sub-log generated in stage 1 will be assigned a sampling size based on the assessment of its quality. A sub-log with higher quality will receive a larger sampling size. Let L denote an event log with risk information, SL denote the set of sub-logs from the first stage, $sl_i \in SL$ denote a sub-log of L, the quality of a sub-log QS is defined as:

$$QS(sl_i, L, w_l, w_d, w_u) = \frac{3 \times RL(sl_i, L)^{w_l} \times RD(sl_i, L)^{w_d} \times UNI(sl_i, L)^{w_u}}{RL(sl_i, L)^{w_l} + RD(sl_i, L)^{w_d} + UNI(sl_i, L)^{w_u}} \quad (9)$$

where the value of QS is in the range of $[0, 1]$. According to Eq. 9, the quality of a sub-log considers *risk-level*, *risk-dissimilarity* and *universality* at the same time[1]. QS reaches the maximum value of 1 as RL, RD and UNI all achieve the maximum value of 1. The three exponents $w_l \in \mathbb{Z}_0^+$, $w_d \in \mathbb{Z}_0^+$ and $w_u \in \mathbb{Z}_0^+$ can be deemed as weights that are used to compensate for the scale gap between RL, RD and UNI. For instance, the QS will be sensitive to RL if the value of RL is often much smaller than the value of RD and UNI. To deal with this issue, we need to increase the weights of RD and UNI.

Let p denote the entire case sampling size for L, the sampling size of a sub-log *SSL*, which is proportional to the quality of the sub-log, is defined as:

$$SSL(sl_i, SL, L, w_l, w_d, w_u, p) = \frac{QS(sl_i, L, w_l, w_d, w_u)}{\sum_{sl \in SL} QS(sl, L, w_l, w_d, w_u)} \times p \quad (10)$$

Let $SL_{e2} = \{sl_1, sl_2, sl_3\}$ be a set of sub-logs generated in the first stage for an example log L_{e2}, where $|sl_1| = 4$, $|sl_2| = 15$ and $|sl_3| = 20$. Let $p_{e2} = 20$ denote the entire sampling size for L_{e2}. Presume that sl_1, sl_2 and sl_3 have QS values of 0.8, 0.5 and 0.7 respectively. Based on Eq. 10, the sampling size for sl_1 equals $(0.8/(0.8 + 0.5 + 0.7)) \times 20 = 8$. Similarly, the sampling size for sl_2 is 5 and 7 for sl_3.

Sub-log Sampling Size Assignment (SSA). Using the above notions, Algorithm 1 describes our sub-log sampling size assignment method. The example log L_{e2}, set of sub-logs SL_{e2} and entire sampling size p_{e2} are employed for interpreting each step of Algorithm 1. The SSL of sl_1 (SSL_{sl_1}) is first calculated based on Eq. 10 which gets a value of 8 (step 3). Due to the size of sl_1 ($|sl_1| = 4$) is smaller than SSL_{sl_1} (step 6), the value of SSL_{sl_1} is then replaced by $|sl_1|$ and appended in set S^o (i.e. $S^o = \{4\}$), meanwhile, the value of p_{e2} is updated by subtracting the value of SSL_{sl_1} (i.e. $p_{e2} = 16$) in step 7. The same process iterates over sub-log sl_2 and sl_3 in which set SL^t and S^t are updated (i.e. $SL^t = \{sl_2, sl_3\}$ and $S^t = \{5, 7\}$). Afterwards, it is checked if there exists any sub-log which gets a SSL that is larger than its size (i.e. $|S^o| > 0$) in step 10. In our example, sl_1 meets this condition which then triggers a second-level execution of SSA with SL^t and p_{e2} as inputs (step 11). In the second-level execution, the SSLs for both sl_2 and sl_3 are calculated again (steps 2–3). This time sl_2 gets a SSL with value of $(0.5/(0.5 + 0.7)) \times 16 \approx 7$ and the SSL of sl_3 acquires a vale of $(0.7/(0.5 + 0.7)) \times 16 \approx 9$. Both SSL values are smaller than the sizes of the corresponding sub-logs and therefore appended in set S^t (steps 4–5). As no sub-log gets a SSL that is lager than its size (step 12), set S^o is updated by

---

[1] As introduced in Sect. 2, *risk-diversity* is affected by both *risk-level* and *risk-dissimilarity*. Therefore, QS indirectly takes *risk-diversity* into account.

Algorithm 1. Sub-log sampling size assignment: SSA

Input: log L with risk information, set of sub-logs SL for L, the entire sampling size p, weights w_l for RL, w_d for RD and w_u for UNI.

　　Let S^t and S^o be two sets of sampling sizes, SL^t be a set of sub-logs.
1: $S^t \leftarrow \emptyset$, $S^o \leftarrow \emptyset$, $SL^t \leftarrow \emptyset$
2: **for** each sub-log $sl \in SL$ **do**
3: 　　$ssl \leftarrow SSL(sl, SL, L, w_l, w_d, w_u, p)$　　# calculate sampling size for sl
4: 　　**if** $ssl \leq |sl|$ **then**
5: 　　　　$SL^t \leftarrow SL^t \cup \{sl\}$, $S^t \leftarrow S^t \cup \{ssl\}$
6: 　　**else**
7: 　　　　$ssl \leftarrow |sl|$, $S^o \leftarrow S^o \cup \{ssl\}$, $p \leftarrow p - ssl$
8: 　　**end if**
9: **end for**
10: **if** $|S^o| > 0$ **then**
11: 　　$S^o \leftarrow S^o \cup SSA(L, SL^t, p, w_l, w_d, w_u)$
12: **else**
13: 　　$S^o \leftarrow S^o \cup S^t$
14: **end if**
Output: a set of sampling size for the input sub-logs S^o.

---

combining the elements from S^t (i.e. $S^o = \{7, 9\}$) in step 13 and returned to the first-level execution of SSA. Afterwards, set S^o in the first-level execution is updated by combining the elements from the returned set (step 11). Finally, set $S^o = \{4, 7, 9\}$ is output by SSA, where 4, 7 and 9 stand for the sampling sizes assigned to sl_1, sl_2 and sl_3 respectively.

3.3 Stage 3: Case Sampling

In the third stage, case sampling is carried out on each sub-log. As introduced in Sect. 2.3, a case that can help improve the quality of the underlying SCS ought to obtain a higher sampling possibility. In the remainder, we first define the sampling possibility of a case, before elaborating on a novel possibility-based case sampling method designed for A-PCS.

Let L denote an event log, R_L be the set of risks for L, $SL = \{sl_1, sl_2, \cdots, sl_k\}$ denote the set of sub-logs generated for L in stage 1, $S^o = \{ssl_1, ssl_2, \cdots, ssl_k\}$ denote the set of sampling sizes generated for the sub-logs in SL in the second stage. Presume that sl_i $(1 \leq i \leq k)$ denotes a sub-log on which the PCS is being executed, $SL_s = \{sl_1, \cdots, sl_{i-1}\}$ denotes a set that contains the sub-logs from SL on which the PCS has been finished, $l = l_s \cup l_i$ denotes a SCS, where l_s contains the cases sampled from the sub-logs in SL_s and l_i $(|l_i| < ssl_i)$ contains the cases sampled from sl_i. Let $c_u \notin l_i$ be a case from sl_i, we first define the average dissimilarity (AD) of c_u to all the cases from l:

$$AD(c_u, l) = \begin{cases} \frac{\sum_{c \in l} 1 - J(\Delta(c_u, R_L), \Delta(c, R_L))}{|l|}, & |l| > 0 \\ 1, & |l| = 0 \end{cases} \tag{11}$$

Algorithm 2. Possibility-based case sampling: PBCS

Input: log L, set of sub-logs SL for L, set of sampling sizes S^o for the sub-logs in SL,
weights w'_l for RL, w'_d for AD and w'_u for UNI, sampling frequency f.
    Let l be a SCS, S_c be a set of cases, S_{sp} be a set of sampling possibilities.
1: $l \leftarrow \emptyset$, $S_c \leftarrow \emptyset$, $S_{sp} \leftarrow \emptyset$
2: **for** $sl_i \in SL$, $ssl_i \in S^o$ **do**
3:    **for** $m \leftarrow 1$ *to* ssl_i **do**
4:      **for each** case $c_j \in sl_i$ **do**
5:        $S_{sp} \leftarrow S_{sp} \cup \{SP(c_j, l, L, w'_l, w'_d, w'_u)\}$
6:      **end for**
7:      **for** $v \leftarrow 1$ *to* f **do**
8:        $S_c \leftarrow S_c \cup \{\Xi(sl_i, S_{sp})\}$
9:      **end for**
10:     $l \leftarrow l \cup \{\Sigma(S_c)\}$, $sl_i \leftarrow sl_i \backslash \{\Sigma(S_c)\}$, $S_{sp} \leftarrow \emptyset$, $S_c \leftarrow \emptyset$
11:    **end for**
12: **end for**
Output: a SCS l.

The sampling possibility (SP) for case c_u is defined as:

$$SP(c_u, l, L, w'_l, w'_d, w'_u) = \frac{3 \times RL(c_u, L)^{w'_l} \times AD(c_u, l)^{w'_d} \times UNI(c_u, L)^{w'_u}}{RL(c_u, L)^{w'_l} + AD(c_u, l)^{w'_d} + UNI(c_u, L)^{w'_u}} \quad (12)$$

where the value of SP is in the range of $[0, 1]$. As shown in Eq. 12, the calculation of SP for case c_u considers both the *risk-level* and *universality* of c_u. Besides, the average dissimilarity of c_u to the already sampled cases in l is also taken into account. A case with higher *risk-level*, *universality* and AD to the cases that have been selected will acquire a higher SP. Similarly to Eq. 9, weights $w'_l \in \mathbb{Z}_0^+$, $w'_d \in \mathbb{Z}_0^+$ and $w'_u \in \mathbb{Z}_0^+$ are employed to compensate for the scale gap between RL, AD and UNI.

Possibility-Based Case Sampling (PBCS). With the notions defined above, Algorithm 2 describes the case sampling approach designed for the third stage of A-PCS. Before diving into Algorithm 2, we first introduce two instrumental functions. For an input sub-log $sl = \{c_1, \cdots, c_k\}$ and the set of SP $S_{sp} = \{sp_1, \cdots, sp_k\}$ for the cases in sl, function $\Xi(sl, S_{sp})$ returns a randomly sampled case $c_q \in sl$ by considering the SP of each case in sl. A case with higher possibility will get a higher chance to be selected by Ξ. Let S_c denote a set of cases, function $\Sigma(S_c) = c_g$ can be used to find one case (c_g) from S_c which has the highest frequency of occurrence. For instance, $\Sigma(\{c'_1, c'_2, c'_1, c'_3\}) = c'_1$ because the occurrence frequency of case c'_1 is 2 which is larger than the occurrence frequency of both c'_2 and c'_3.

In Algorithm 2, for each sub-log sl_i (with sampling size ssl_i) from the input set of sub-logs SL (steps 2–12), ssl_i cases will be sampled (steps 3–11). The SP of each case c_j from sl_i will first be calculated based on Eq. 12 and appended

---

Algorithm 3. Advanced process case sampling: A-PCS

Input: log L, number of sub-logs z, entire sampling size p, weights w_l, w_d, w_u, w_l', w_d'
   and w_u', sampling frequency f.
   Let SL be a set of sub-logs, S^o be a set of sampling sizes, l be a SCS.
1: $SL \leftarrow \emptyset$, $S^o \leftarrow \emptyset$, $l \leftarrow \emptyset$
   Stage 1: *case clustering*
2: $SL \leftarrow K\text{-}Modes(L, z)$
   Stage 2: *sub-log sampling size assignment*
3: $S^o \leftarrow SSA(L, SL, p, w_l, w_d, w_u)$
   Stage 3: *case sampling*
4: $l \leftarrow PBCS(L, SL, S^o, w_l', w_d', w_u', f)$
Output: a SCS l.

---

to the set of sampling possibilities S_{sp} (steps 4–6). Afterwards, function Ξ will
be executed f times on sl_i and the generated f cases will be appended in set
S_c (steps 7–9). Finally, function Σ is employed to find the case with highest
occurrence frequency from S_c which is then appended in SCS l and removed from
sub-log sl_i (step 10). The same procedure iterates until ssl_i cases are sampled
from sl_i. The approach PBCS is characterized by two advantages. On the one
hand, it repeatedly updates the SP of the remaining cases in the sub-log sl_i
based on the already sampled cases in SCS l (steps 4–6) so that the quality of
l can be continuously optimized. On the other hand, PBCS can be applied to
both possibility and non-possibility case sampling tasks. If the input sampling
frequency f is set to 1, PBCS serves as a possibility sampling approach which
can be used for the task for generating a SCS that reflects the entire quality of
log L. If a larger value is assigned to f, PBCS then mimics M-PCS.

3.4   The Advanced Process Case Sampling (A-PCS) Algorithm

Putting the above techniques together, the complete approach of advanced process case sampling is formalized in Algorithm 3. In stage 1, the cases from input
log are clustered into z sub-logs (step 2). In our approach, the K-Modes algorithm [7] is used for case clustering. In stage 2, the sampling size for each sub-log
generated in stage 1 is calculated by algorithm SSA (step 3). In stage 3, case
sampling is executed on each sub-log by using PBCS which then outputs the
SCS for the input log.

4   Evaluation

This section presents an experimental evaluation of the proposed method A-PCS.
We first introduce the used event logs and experimental setup, before turning to
a discussion of the obtained results.

Table 2. Basic Information of the evaluated event logs.

Event log	# Cases	# Risk types	# Variants
LP2P	82245	43	1325
LO2C	138665	69	1907

Datasets. We tested the effectiveness of A-PCS on two real-life event logs: an event log of a P2P process (LP2P) and a log of an O2C process (LO2C), which are extracted from the SAP system of a manufacturing enterprise for a case study in the data science lecture in Karlsruhe University of Applied Sciences. Descriptive statistics of these event logs are given in Table 2.

Experimental Setup. In our experiments, we further use the MinHash LSH [8] for approximately calculating the *Jaccard Similarity* between any two cases in A-PCS because MinHash LSH can achieve a sublinear cost of calculation which greatly speeds up the execution of A-PCS.

When executing A-PCS, the number of clusters z for K-Modes is set to 10 for both LP2P and LO2C. For log LP2P, the sampling size p is set to 38 which is consistent with the number of cases sampled by our auditor for LP2P, the weights w_l, w_d, w_u, w'_l, w'_d and w'_u are set to 5, 2, 1, 8, 10 and 1 respectively. For log LO2C, the sampling size p is set to 50 (i.e. 50 cases are manually sampled from LO2C by auditor), the weights w_l, w_d, w_u, w'_l, w'_d and w'_u are set to 8, 2, 1, 10, 20 and 1 respectively. When the sampling frequency f is set to 1 for A-PCS, we rename A-PCS to A-PCS-R which can be used to generate a SCS that reflects the quality of the original event log. A-PCS is renamed to A-PCS-M when f is set to 400, which mimics M-PCS.

Results. A first overview of the evaluation results is shown in Table 3. For each measure and log, Table 3 gives the obtained value for the SCS generated by A-PCS-M and A-PCS-R. For instance, the *risk-level* of the SCS (RL) generated by A-PCS-M for log LP2P is 0.56, the *risk-dissimilarity* of the SCS (RD) is 0.72 and the *universality* of the SCS (UNI) is 0.18. Furthermore, this SCS contains 35 risk types which accounts for 81% of the entire risks in LP2P. The entire running time (T-ALL) of A-PCS-M on LP2P is 9.7 min, where the execution time of K-Modes in the first stage (T-Stage 1) is 6.1 min which accounts for 63% of the total execution time of A-PCS-M. According to Table 3, for both logs, A-PCS-M is able to generate relatively high quality SCS. For log LO2C, A-PCS-R doesn't perform well because the SCS generated only covers 45 risk types which only accounts for 65% of the total types of risk. The main reason is that A-PCS-R is designed to tackle the task for generating a SCS that is capable of reflecting the actual quality of the original log, which doesn't pursue a SCS with 100% optimized quality.

We also made a comparison between A-PCS-M, A-PCS-R, M-PCS and S-PCS based on LP2P and LO2C. Table 4 shows the comparison results. For each

Table 3. Evaluation results for the SCS generated by A-PCS.

Event log	Method	RL	RD	UNI	# Risk type	T-Stage 1	T-All
LP2P	A-PCS-M	0.56	0.72	0.18	35	6.1 min	9.7 min
	A-PCS-R	0.54	0.71	0.16	36	6.1 min	9.6 min
LO2C	A-PCS-M	0.55	0.68	0.31	52	21 min	28 min
	A-PCS-R	0.55	0.67	0.24	45	21 min	28 min

log, A-PCS-M and A-PCS-R share the same stage 1 (case clustering) and stage 2 (sampling size assignment). Moreover, the stage 3 (case sampling) of each of A-PCS-M and A-PCS-R is executed five times on each log. In this way, both A-PCS-M and A-PCS-R generate five SCSs for LP2P and five SCSs for LO2C respectively. Afterwards, for each method, the mean of the quality factors of the five SCSs for each log is calculated. For instance, for log LP2P, the average *risk-level* of the five SCSs (AVG. RL) output by A-PCS-M is 0.56, the average *risk-dissimilarity* (AVG. RD) is 0.72, the average *universality* (AVG. UNI) is 0.18 and the average number of risk types (AVG. #Risk Type) is 35.2. Similarly, S-PCS is also executed five times on each log and the mean of the quality factors is calculated.

For log LP2P, as shown in Table 4, A-PCS-M and A-PCS-R have the best performance. The *risk-level* of the SCSs generated by M-PCS and S-PCS are much lower than the *risk-level* of the SCSs from A-PCS-M and A-PCS-R. In addition, the *universality* of the SCSs from M-PCS has a very low value which is only 0.09 while the SCSs from S-PCS only cover 65% of the entire risk types on average.

For log LO2C, A-PCS-M has the best average performance. Considering *risk-level*, *risk-dissimilarity* and number of risk types covered, M-PCS performs best. Nevertheless, the *universality* of the SCS from M-PCS is too low which only has a value of 0.02. This implies that the cases selected by M-PCS have very low business impact.

The experimental results are also examined by our auditor who confirms that the SCSs generated by A-PCS have much better quality. Hence, we conclude that under a comprehensive assessment, our PCS method A-PCS improves beyond the fundamental PCS methods (i.e. M-PCS and S-PCS) in the context of IA.

5   Related Work

In the literature, sampling techniques have been widely used for improving the performance of process model discovery and conformance checking techniques. In [9], the authors put forward an algorithm for mining Petri-net from an event log. It first searches for all the Parikh vectors in the traces of the log. Afterwards, the obtained Parikh vectors are converted to polyhedra by joining which a polyhedron is constructed. Finally, invariants are extracted from the polyhedron based on which a Petri-net can be formed. To speed up the joining

Table 4. Comparison of the quality of the sets of case samples output by A-PCS-M, A-PCS-R, M-PCS and S-PCS.

Event log	Method	Avg. RL	Avg. RD	Avg. UNI	Avg. # Risk type
LP2P	A-PCS-M	**0.56**	**0.72**	**0.18**	**35.2**
	A-PCS-R	0.55	0.71	0.17	**35.2**
	M-PCS	0.44	0.7	0.09	31
	S-PCS	0.43	0.69	0.15	28.6
LO2C	A-PCS-M	**0.56**	0.68	**0.29**	52
	A-PCS-R	**0.56**	0.67	0.27	49.2
	M-PCS	0.53	**0.72**	0.02	**56**
	S-PCS	0.45	0.66	0.14	35.8

operation on polyhedra, a sampling algorithm for Parikh vector is then developed which reduces the number of polyhedra. In [10], the authors proposed a trace sampling algorithm based on statistical sampling so that the performance of Heuristics Miner can be improved for dealing with big event logs. In [11], for helping process model discovery algorithms to reduce the run time and memory footprint, the authors developed a method which is able to sample a suitable number of traces from an input log by predicting whether the remaining traces in the log can bring new workflow information. In [12,13], the authors proposed four biased trace sampling strategies to help existing process model discovery techniques to handle large event logs: frequency-based sampling, length-based sampling, similarity-based sampling and structure-based sampling. In addition, based on these strategies, the authors presented the hybrid sampling approach which is capable of combining two or more sampling strategies. The authors in [14] pointed out that the state-of-the-art conformance checking techniques scale exponentially in the size of the input event log. To reduce the size of the event log and speed up the conformance checking procedure, the authors utilized the similar trace sampling algorithm as in [11] which randomly selects traces from event log until no further workflow information can be offered by the remaining traces.

However, most of the sampling methods proposed in the area of BPM are based on traces which cannot be employed to solve the case-level sampling task in IA. Therefore, we proposed the case sampling technique A-PCS for generating high quality SCS for the later root cause analysis.

6   Conclusions

In this paper, we proposed a new process case sampling technique named A-PCS to generate SCS with high quality that is reflected by *risk-level*, *risk-dissimilarity*, *risk-diversity* and *universality*. In a first stage, it clusters the cases with similar risk types into the same sub-log. In a second stage, for each sub-log, the sampling size is calculated. In a third stage, a possibility-based case sampling algorithm is executed on each sub-log. Our experimental results demonstrated the effectiveness of our technique, also in comparison to two fundamental sampling methods M-PCS and S-PCS in IA.

In future work, we will focus on combining other type of case attributes (except for risk) into our case sampling framework, as it is an interesting topic to understand different triggers for the same process risk in IA. Also, techniques that help to explore the parameter spaces in the configuration of our technique (such as the number of sub-logs for case clustering or the weights for RL, RD and UNI) will be explored. Moreover, we plan to conduct further evaluation studies, validating our methods in additional IA projects.

References

1. Chuprunov, M.: Auditing and GRC Automation in SAP. Springer, Berlin (2013). https://doi.org/10.1007/978-3-642-35302-4
2. Seeliger, A., Nolle, T., Mühlhäuser, M.: Process explorer: an interactive visual recommendation system for process mining. In: KDD Workshop on Interactive Data Exploration and Analytics (2018)
3. Fricker, R.D.: Sampling methods for web and e-mail surveys. In: Fielding, N., Lee, R.M., Blank G. (eds.) The Sage Handbook of Online Research Methods, pp. 195–216. Los Angeles, CA: Sage (2008)
4. van der Aalst, W.M.P.: Process Mining: Data Science in Action. Springer, Berlin (2016). https://doi.org/10.1007/978-3-662-49851-4
5. Lu, X., Tabatabaei, S.A., Hoogendoorn, M., Reijers, H.A.: Trace clustering on very large event data in healthcare using frequent sequence patterns. In: Hildebrandt, T., van Dongen, B.F., Röglinger, M., Mendling, J. (eds.) BPM 2019. LNCS, vol. 11675, pp. 198–215. Springer, Cham (2019). https://doi.org/10.1007/978-3-030-26619-6_14
6. Niwattanakul, S., Singthongchai, J., Naenudorn, E., Wanapu, S.: Using of Jaccard coefficient for keywords similarity. In: Proceedings of the International Multiconference of Engineers and Computer Scientists, vol. 1. pp. 1–5 (2013)
7. Han, J., Kamber, M.: Data Mining: Concepts and Techniques. Morgan Kaufmann, Amsterdam (August 2000)
8. Rajaraman, A., Ullman, J.: Mining of Massive Data Sets. Cambridge University Press, Cambridge (2011)
9. Carmona, J., Cortadella, J.: Process mining meets abstract interpretation. In: Balcázar, J.L., Bonchi, F., Gionis, A., Sebag, M. (eds.) ECML PKDD 2010. LNCS (LNAI), vol. 6321, pp. 184–199. Springer, Heidelberg (2010). https://doi.org/10.1007/978-3-642-15880-3_18
10. Berti, A.: Statistical sampling in process mining discovery. In: The 9th International Conference on Information, Process, and Knowledge Management, pp 41–43 (2017)
11. Bauer, M., Senderovich, A., Gal, A., Grunske, L., Weidlich, M.: How much event data is enough? a statistical framework for process discovery. In: CAiSE, pp. 239–256 (2018)
12. Fani Sani, F., van Zelst, S.J., van der Aalst, W.M.P.: Improving the performance of process discovery algorithms by instance selection. Comput. Sci. Inf. Syst. **17**(3), 927–958 (2020)

13. Fani Sani, F., van Zelst, S.J., van der Aalst, W.M.P.: The impact of biased sampling of event logs on the performance of process discovery. In: Computing (2021)
14. Bauer, M., van der Aa, H., Weidlich, M.: Estimating process conformance by trace sampling and result approximation. In: Hildebrandt, T., van Dongen, B.F., Röglinger, M., Mendling, J. (eds.) BPM 2019. LNCS, vol. 11675, pp. 179–197. Springer, Cham (2019). https://doi.org/10.1007/978-3-030-26619-6_13

Author Index

AI-Khazrage, Lyth 263
Augusto, Adriano 73

Bano, Dorina 162

Cecconi, Alessio 73
Corea, Carl 3, 37

Dam, Hoa 246
Delfmann, Patrick 3, 37
Depaire, Benoît 230
Di Ciccio, Claudio 73
Dumas, Marlon 92

Eshuis, Rik 54

Fahland, Dirk 212

Gall, Manuel 126
Ghose, Aditya 54, 246
Goldstein, Maayan 20
González-Álvarez, Cecilia 20
Grohé, Carl-Christian 37

Khan, Asjad 246
Klijn, Eva L. 212

López-Pintado, Orlenys 92

Maggi, Fabrizio Maria 92
Mangler, Juergen 195
Mannhardt, Felix 212
Martin, Niels 230
Mendling, Jan 3

Nagel, Sabine 3
Nikaj, Adriatik 162

Özümerzifon, Ömer 263

Rafiei, Majid 178
Rehse, Jana-Rebecca 109
Rennemeier, Jonas 109
Rinderle-Ma, Stefanie 126, 195

Scheibel, Beate 195
Soffer, Pnina 145
Stertz, Florian 195
Sun, Yaguang 263

van der Aalst, Wil M. P. 178
van Hulzen, Gerhardus 230

Weber, Barbara 145
Weske, Mathias 162

Yerokhin, Maksym 92

Zandkarimi, Fareed 109
Zerbato, Francesca 145

Printed in the United States
by Baker & Taylor Publisher Services